*Blasphemy and Apostasy in Islam*

Based at the Aga Khan Centre in London, the Aga Khan University Institute for the Study of Muslim Civilisations is a higher education institution with a focus on research, publications, graduate studies and outreach. It promotes scholarship that opens up new perspectives on Muslim heritage, modernity, religion, culture and society. The Institute aims to create opportunities for interaction among academics and other professionals in an effort to deepen the understanding of pressing issues affecting Muslim societies today.

In Translation: Modern Muslim Thinkers

*Series Editor:* Abdou Filali-Ansary

This series aims to broaden current debates about Muslim realities which often overlook seminal works produced in languages other than English. By identifying and translating critical and innovative thinking that has engendered important debates within its own settings, the series seeks to introduce new perspectives to the discussions about Muslim civilisations taking place on the world stage.

Available titles:

*Islam: Between Message and History*
Abdelmadjid Charfi
Translated by David Bond

*Islam and the Foundations of Political Power*
Ali Abdel Razek
Translated by Maryam Loutfi

*The Sorrowful Muslim's Guide*
Hussein Ahmad Amin
Translated by Yasmin Amin and Nesrin Amin

*Secularism in the Arab World: Contexts, Ideas and Consequences*
Aziz al-Azmeh
Translated by David Bond

*Human Rights and Reformist Islam*
Mohsen Kadivar
Translated by Niki Akhavan

*Blasphemy and Apostasy in Islam: Debates in Shi'a Jurisprudence*
Mohsen Kadivar
Translated by Hamid Mavani

edinburghuniversitypress.com/series/tmmt

# Blasphemy and Apostasy in Islam

## Debates in Shiʿa Jurisprudence

MOHSEN KADIVAR

*Translated by*
Hamid Mavani

EDINBURGH
University Press
IN ASSOCIATION WITH

THE AGA KHAN UNIVERSITY
INSTITUTE FOR THE STUDY OF MUSLIM CIVILISATIONS

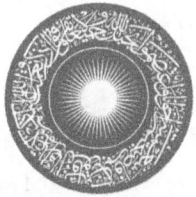

The opinions expressed in this volume are those of the authors and do not necessarily reflect those of the Aga Khan University Institute for the Study of Muslim Civilisations.

Edinburgh University Press is one of the leading university presses in the UK. We publish academic books and journals in our selected subject areas across the humanities and social sciences, combining cutting-edge scholarship with high editorial and production values to produce academic works of lasting importance. For more information visit our website: edinburghuniversitypress.com



Edinburgh University Press Ltd
The Tun – Holyrood Road
12 (2f) Jackson's Entry
Edinburgh EH8 8PJ

First published in hardback by Edinburgh University Press 2021

Typeset in 10.5/13 Adobe Garamond by
IDSUK (DataConnection) Ltd

A CIP record for this book is available from the British Library

ISBN 978 1 4744 5757 6 (hardback)
ISBN 978 1 4744 5757 6 (paperback)
ISBN 978 1 4744 5759 0 (webready PDF)
ISBN 978 1 4744 5760 6 (epub)

# *Contents*

*Acknowledgements* vii
*Foreword by Gianluca P. Parolin* ix

Introduction 1
1 Literature Review of Religious Freedom and Apostasy in Contemporary Sunni Islam 1
2 Literature Review of Religious Freedom and Apostasy in Contemporary Shiʿi Islam 25
3 The Genealogy of the Book's Ideas and its Merits 69

**Part I Blasphemy and Apostasy**

1 The Background of the Treatise 105
1 Legal Rulings (*Fatāwā*) on Assassination and Statement of Delight at its Implementation 105
2 Objections to the *Fatwa* of Assassination – by Kadivar 109
3 Response to Doubts Surrounding Apostasy – by Lankarānī Jr 116

2 Treatise on Refuting the Punishment for Blasphemy and Apostasy – by Kadivar 146
I Issuing a Ruling on the Death Penalty by a Process that Falls Outside the Sphere of a Competent Court . . . will Engender Lawlessness and Anarchy 154
II Claiming the Validity of the Death Penalty for Blasphemy and Apostasy is Based on One Deficient "Isolated Report" (*khabar al-wāḥid*). 166
III Refuting the Claim that Most of the Hadiths on Apostasy are "*Mutawātir* in Meaning or in their General Tenor" 175
IV Refuting the Claim of Consensus (*ijmāʿ*) and the Necessity to Implement the Death Penalty for Blasphemy and Apostasy 182
V No One, during the Time of the Prophet, Imam Ali and the other Imams, was Sentenced to Death Solely for Apostasy 186

VI The Absolute Cessation of the *Ḥudūd* Punishments or those that Necessitate the Death Penalty and Injury, and Suspension during the Time of the Imam's Occultation 194

VII "Isolated Reports" (*khabar al-wāḥid*) are Non-probative (non-*ḥujjiyya*) in Matters of Critical Importance 207

VIII Issuing *fatwa*s on Killing an Apostate or a Blasphemer Weakens and Impairs (*wahn*) Islam 214

IX Alteration of the Subject (*mawḍū'*) of Apostasy and Objecting to the Perpetual Applicability of the Death Penalty for Blasphemy and Apostasy 225

X The Incompatibility of Executing a Blasphemer or an Apostate with Explicit Qur'anic Verses 238

Appendix 1 A Further Clarification of Lankarānī Jr's Position 273

Appendix 2 Rāfiq Taqī in his Own Words and in the Words of his Defenders 283

**Part II Freedom of Expression and Hate Speech – by Kadivar**

1 Islam: Between the Freedom of Expression and the Prohibition of Hate Speech 321

2 Letter of Censure to the Jurists who Issued the Latest Judgement on Apostasy 325

3 Insulting the Prophet is a Form of Hate Speech 335

4 Request for Clarification from the Jurists who Defend "Suffocating the Religionists" 342

Appendix 3: Imam [Ali]: Political Leader or Exemplary Role Model – by 'Alī Aṣghar Gharavī 363

*Bibliography* 371

*Glossary* 385

*Index* 402

# *Acknowledgements*

It is a pleasure to record my gratitude to a number of scholars from whom I benefited in enhancing the quality of the Persian text of this translated work (Part I, chapter 4: "Treatise on Refuting the Punishment for Blasphemy and Apostasy" of original Persian book), released February 2012: Abolghasem (Ali) Fanaei (Mofid University, Qom); Mohsen Ārmīn, Ali Paya (Islamic College, London), Hossein Hooshmand and Mohammad Mehdī Mojāhedī (Āzād University, Tehran); and Ḥasan Yousefī Eshkavarī. Others provided me with important pointers on certain aspects of the discourse of the same chapter: Shirin Ebadi (2003 Nobel Peace Prize), Abdolali Bazargan, Abdolkarim Lahiji, Hassan Fereshtiyān, Hossein Kamālī (Hartford Seminary), and Arash Naraghi (Moravian College).

The first draft of my "Treatise on Refuting the Punishment for Blasphemy and Apostasy" was meticulously reviewed by Hossein Modarressi (Princeton University), from which I benefited greatly. Kiyān Pourkermānī (scholar of law), brought to my attention certain matters dealing with law in the same chapter. I extend my profound appreciation to each and every one of them. It goes without saying that any shortcomings remaining in the Persian treatise are mine alone.

I benefited from consultation with Ebrahim Moosa (University of Notre Dame) and Hossein Modarressi (Princeton University) on Section 1 of the Introduction, and Abdolkarim Soroush on Section 2 of the Introduction. I wrote the Introduction at the beginning of my fellowship at the National Humanities Center (NHC) at Research Triangle Park, North Carolina. Providing the many sources for the Introduction would have been impossible without the help of the librarians at NHC. I would like to express my deep gratitude to all of them.

We (author and the translator) are indebted to Ms Jennifer Bryson for obtaining a generous grant from Templeton Religion Trust to undertake the translation of this work into English and thank the Trust for their generosity. In addition, she prepared the book prospectus that was submitted to Edinburgh University Press (EUP) for internal and peer review.

We also received a great deal of support and cooperation from Adela Rauchova (Commissioning Editor) and Kirsty Woods (Assistant Commissioning Editor) at EUP, Charlotte Whiting (Manager, Publications Department) at AKU-ISMC and Lyn Flight (our copy-editor). We are grateful for their patience and advice and polishing up the text to give greater clarity to the concepts and issues. Also, we thank the two blind reviewers for their insightful remarks and useful critique, which we have tried to incorporate to the best of our abilities. However, it goes without saying that, ultimately, we are solely responsible for any flaws and errors.

*Transliteration*: we have followed the *IJMES* transliteration guide for the most part.

*Qur'an Translation*: M. A. S. Abdel Haleem's translation of the Qur'an has been used for the Introduction, and the translator has also used this in conjunction with A. J. Arberry and M. Pickthall.

*Note*: the upper case 'I' in the word 'Imam' is used when referencing one of the Imams in Twelver Shiʿism, whereas the lower case 'i' is employed in its lexical meaning of a leader (imam) in some minor or major capacity. Finally, all the dates are given in the Common Era (CE).

# *Foreword*

*Gianluca P. Parolin*

On 23 November 2011, Rafīq Tağı mysteriously died while recovering from surgery in a hospital in Baku, Azerbaijan. The surgery was precipitated by seven stab wounds received a few days earlier, on 19 November 2011. After the initial treatment for his wounds and the removal of his spleen, Rafīq Tağı declared from his hospital bed that he had been attacked by two individuals who did not utter a single word while knifing him. The sixty-one-year-old Azerbaijani journalist and literary critic was optimistic about his recovery and speculated that the attack had been a response to an article he had just published against Iran. His unexpected death prompted the family to voice their concerns both over the state's inability to apprehend the assailants and for what they saw as a case of medical negligence on the part of the chief physician of the hospital where he had been treated.

A few days later, Moḥammad Javād Fāżel Lankarānī (Lankarānī Jr) publicly saluted the implementation of his late father's opinion that it was incumbent upon anyone having access to Rafīq Tağı to kill him on several counts of apostasy from Islam. Lankarānī's father (Lankarānī Sr) had deduced Tağı's apostasy from Islam from a series of critical pieces that the latter had penned and published in a local, low-distribution newspaper, *Ṣanʿat*. One of these articles, titled "Europe and Us", had also landed Rafīq Tağı in jail on a count of breaching Article 283, paragraph 1, of the Criminal Code of Azerbaijan. The court had concluded that Rafīq Tağı's piece could be construed as hate speech for which Article 283 of the Criminal Code, in a section on crimes against the state, provides for sentencing with a fine and imprisonment of between two and four years.

The chain of causation between Lankarānī Sr's opinion on the obligation to kill Rafīq Tağı, and Rafīq Tağı's actual death more than five years later looks rather hard to establish, yet Lankarānī Jr's jubilation at the "execution" of Rafīq Tağı prompted the reaction of a former classmate of his in the revered seminaries of Qom: Mohsen Kadivar (Muḥsin Kadīvar). At the time a visiting professor at Duke University, Kadivar addressed to his former classmate a list of "objections to the fatwá of assassination", which is at the origin of this volume, translated into English by Hamid Mavani. A couple of rounds of responses provide an illuminating insight both into the dynamics of the debate between two legal scholars on opposite sides of the spectrum, but also into the articulation of Kadivar's argument against the current handling of cases of blasphemy and apostasy. The lengthy and rich Introduction offers a further delve into the working of the author's mind in relation to his sources, both within and without the classical reference works of Qom legal scholars.

Born in Iran's southwest Fārs Province in 1959, Mohsen Kadivar was an engineering student in the provincial capital (Shirāz) when the 1979 Revolution broke out. After the revolutionary triumph, Kadivar first left the faculty of engineering for that of religious studies, but then left the university altogether to be trained in formal religious education in Qom's ḥawzas (*ḥawza ʿilmiyya* or seminaries for the education of the Imami Shiʿi clergy). Not only did Kadivar pursue higher studies (*khārij*) in Islamic jurisprudence in the Iranian holy city, but, in 1997 he also received one of the few written permissions to practise *ijtihād* from one of the country's most revered scholars: Grand Ayatollah Montazeri (Ḥussayn-ʿAlī Muntaẓarī, 1922–2009). Kadivar has been an extremely prolific writer in political theology, engaging with some of the most fundamental yet divisive doctrines of Imami Shiʿi theories of government. His bold and reformist views have often generated frictions with the country's political and religious establishment, have landed him in jail, and eventually forced him into self-exile. Even if he resides overseas and his writings are banned in the country, Kadivar has become a reference point for reformists in Iran. Yasuyuki Matsunaga, one of Kadivar's closest observers in the international academic community, argues that Kadivar's thinking and arguments are best appreciated if their author's position on the Iranian intellectual horizon are taken into account.[1] After defining the various trends within modern Iranian religious thinkers, Matsunaga classifies Kadivar as a "post-revivalist new-thinker of religion" not only on the basis of Kadivar's positionality, but also on his drawing from modernist, revivalist and post-revivalist tendencies. Matsunaga's classification also comes in handy to situate Kadivar's opponent in the debate featured in this volume: Lankarānī Jr. Besides a significantly lower intellectual profile than Kadivar's, Lankarānī Jr also comes from a very different background, and in a way epitomises a certain tradition of the conservative religious establishment in the country, without the aura of the previous generation (like his father's, Lankarānī Sr, whose fatwá Lankarānī Jr simply celebrates and poorly defends in the debate in this volume).

It is quite meritorious that the editors of the series "In Translation" and its publisher have decided to offer to readers unable to access the original text in Farsi the opportunity to get a closer look at this volume, which lends itself to multiple levels of analysis. On a first, macro level the volume allows the reader to plunge into the unfolding of a real-life, unstaged debate between two important constituencies of the Iranian religious landscape. On a micro level, the reader is given the opportunity to observe both the fine details of two different takes on the regulations of blasphemy and apostasy in Jaʿfarī jurisprudence but also the way in which these details are articulated in forms that easily escalate into confrontations and dead-ends. On a broader level, this volume in a way captures some of the tensions that animate discussions on blasphemy and apostasy in Muslim contexts beyond the Iranian setting that this volume so eloquently captures. In what follows, I will try and provide a few elements that may aid readers in situating the volume's content and peculiar style within these broader contexts in the hope that the comparative dimension will allow them to fully appreciate the richness of the present volume.

Blasphemy and apostasy, with their inescapable death sentences in premodern confessional law, have persuaded many reformists to re-engage with the primary sources and sift through the scholarly works of premodern jurists with a view to establishing whether these death sentences are as inescapable as modern and contemporary conservative scholars contend. It is thus unsurprising that most of the literature on blasphemy and apostasy comes from the reformist camp, while conservatives rarely feel the need to engage. Conservatives do engage, however, against the perceived laxity of the state response to blasphemy and apostasy. In other words, reformists challenge the grounding and nature of the punishment for blasphemy and apostasy in confessional law, while conservatives challenge the inadequate provisions of state law on blasphemy and apostasy, taking for granted the premodern position. As a consequence, scholarship on blasphemy and apostasy is rarely structured as a debate across camps (unlike the classical practice of scholarly debates on matters legal, known as *jadal*); it is therefore rather uncommon to come across a dialogical engagement like the one included in the present volume: Kadivar and Lankarānī Jr laying out their arguments and responding to each other's objections. The debate ends with Lankarānī Jr's sudden retrenchment, but until then readers are offered a precious insight into the distance between the two readings and the margins of rapprochement between the two sides.

A rare, yet interesting, parallel to the debate compiled in the present volume is a compilation published more than half a century earlier in Egypt: *al-Ḥurriyya al-dīniyya fī 'l-islām* (*Religious Freedom in Islam*, 1956). In 'Abd al-Mit'āl al-Ṣa'īdī's compilation, the debate is between himself (1894–1966), Azhari professor and member of the Majma' al-Lugha al-'Arabiyya (the Arabic Language Academy), and 'Īsá Manūn (1889–1956), Azhari professor and member of the Jamā'at Kibār al-'Ulamā' (the Body of Senior Scholars, the antecedent of the current Hay'at Kibār al-'Ulamā'). In their case, the controversy was generated by a piece, "Ijtihād jadīd fī āya$^{t}$: 'Wa-'alá 'l-lādhīn$^{a}$ yuṭīqūnah$^{u}$, fidya$^{tun}$'" ("New Interpretation of the Verse: 'And Upon Those Who Are Able, a Ransom'" (Q. 2:184)), in which 'Abd al-Mit'āl al-Ṣa'īdī engaged with an opinion that had just cost another Azhari scholar, 'Abd al-Ḥamīd Bakhīt, his post. The matter was the permissibility, under certain conditions, not to observe the standard fasting practices during Ramadan. With a bit of a flashback technique, 'Abd al-Mit'āl al-Ṣa'īdī opens with 'Īsá Manūn's response to 'Abd al-Ḥamīd Bakhīt: "Matá yajūz al-ijtihād wa-matá lā yajūz?" ("When is Interpretation Allowed, and When is It Not?"), published in the *al-Azhar* magazine. In it, 'Īsá Manūn briefly defines the domain of *ijtihād* against the conventional definition of provisions that cannot be revisited: provisions that are certain (*aḥkām yaqīniyya qaṭ'iyya*) and have been transmitted by multiple sources since the time of the Prophet Muhammad, and are also known to scholars and non-scholars alike. As an example, he lists fasting during Ramadan, which 'Abd al-Ḥamīd Bakhīt had partly allowed non-observance under certain conditions. 'Īsá Manūn thus quickly underlines that by denying or rejecting any of these provisions, the Muslim becomes an unbeliever and an apostate from Islam – and promptly reminds the reader that apostasy entails death, and the killing of the apostate is in itself one of the "provisions that are certain". 'Īsá Manūn's warning – or threat – to 'Abd al-Ḥamīd Bakhīt is certainly more subtle than Lankarānī Sr's opinion on the obligation to kill Rafīq Tağı, but it is no less serious or stern.

In defence of 'Abd al-Ḥamīd Bakhīt, 'Abd al-Mit'āl al-Ṣa'īdī published a brief commentary on new *ijtihād*, taking the verse on exceptions to fasting (Q. 2:184) as a case study; the *cause célèbre* of 'Abd al-Ḥamīd Bakhīt was offering 'Abd al-Mit'āl al-Ṣa'īdī an opportunity to frame the controversy within the broader context of religious renewal (*tajdīd*), which he strongly advocated – especially at al-Azhar – throughout his career. 'Īsá Manūn took offence at 'Abd al-Mit'āl al-Ṣa'īdī's "Ijtihād jadīd fī āya$^{t}$: 'Wa-'alá 'l-lādhīn$^{a}$ yuṭīqūnah$^{u}$, fidya$^{tun}$'" and penned an inflammatory response in the same official magazine of his previous piece under the definitive title "'Ḥukm al-murtadd fī 'l-sharī'a al-islāmiyya" ("The Rule on Apostasy in Islamic Law") (*al-Azhar*, March 1956). 'Abd al-Mit'āl al-Ṣa'īdī's response would not in turn be published in the same magazine, so he resorted to compiling all the texts in the volume *al-Ḥurriyya al-dīniyya fī 'l-islām*, along with two further scripts connected to the theme ("Al-Ḥurriyya al-dīniyya lil-kitābī wa-ghayrih" ("Religious Freedom for Adherents of a Revealed Religion and Not"), and "Ibṭāl ikrāh al-murtadd 'alá al-islām" ("Stopping Forcing Islam on Apostates")). Just as in the case of the debate between Kadivar and Lankarānī Jr in this volume, the dispute between 'Abd al-Mit'āl al-Ṣa'īdī and 'Īsá Manūn comes to a sudden halt with the retrenchment of the latter.

Mohsen Kadivar, reflecting on the parallels between the present volume and that of 'Abd al-Mit'āl al-Ṣa'īdī, emphasises how the story behind both publications shows that the first struggle facing reformists – across decades and across jurisdictions – is to make their ideas known and available to the wider public. I would also add that, in both cases, by discussing matters of blasphemy and apostasy reformists and conservatives engage with much weightier matters of renewal and convention, *ijtihād* and *taqlīd*, and the role of the religious establishment as ultimate gatekeepers of religious knowledge. The similarities are all the more remarkable and striking if one considers how different the two contexts are, in terms of structure of the religious establishment across Sunni/Shi'a divides, in terms of the ideological moments in which they unfold between the bold 1950s and the timid 2010s, but also in terms of the institutional governance spectrum from early Nasserism to the resilient Islamic Republic.

Largely confined to the margins of premodern jurisprudential debates, discussions on blasphemy and apostasy moved from the fringes to centre stage with the emergence of modern nation-states and the rising challenges facing them. As most scholars admit, matters of blasphemy and apostasy have rarely ever been treated by jurists as purely religious matters, their provisions generally betraying broad considerations of their political dimensions. But things changed dramatically with the emergence of modern nation-states. Reconfiguring political units away from strict bonds of confessional affiliation created the impression that matters of apostasy no longer carried political significance, and blasphemous acts remained relevant only insofar as they represented instances of hate speech. Yet the provisions that modern scholars could find in premodern law had not shed those political dimensions. Modern and contemporary discussions on the merits of the premodern provisions on blasphemy and apostasy hardly ever succeed in maintaining the two domains of confessional and state law separate. Readers should thus not be surprised to find, in the midst of extremely technical disquisitions between Kadivar and Lankarānī Jr over fine points of Jaʿfarī jurisprudence, references to structures and functions of modern states, namely, the Islamic Republic of Iran.

Due process is particularly dear to Mohsen Kadivar, ever since his first reflections on matters of blasphemy and apostasy in the late 1990s, and it has remained one of his top concerns all the way down to this volume. In time, Kadivar grounded his insistence on due process in his own appreciation of how Islam's texts and traditions should be read in line with human rights (his celebrated work titled *Ḥaqq al-nās: Islām va-ḥuqūq-i bashar* (*Right of People: Islam and Human Rights*, 2008) has been translated into English and is published in this series alongside the present translation). Throughout his work, due process features generally among the first points on all his lists of priorities. This is where an apparent alignment with the conservative camp seems to emerge: deciding on matters of blasphemy and apostasy should be incumbent upon the political authority – the state – through its "competent courts", not upon individual scholars such as Lankarānī Sr. Crucially, one needs to realise that Kadivar intends to challenge the very "jurisdiction" of individual religious scholars on matters of blasphemy and apostasy so as to avoid pronouncements like Lankarānī Sr's. On the other hand, the likes of Lankarānī Jr intend to challenge the inactivity of state courts on matters of blasphemy and apostasy which prompts ordinary citizens to take justice into their own hands and seek the opinion of religious scholars like his father; in their eyes, modern states and their courts should be more active in stamping out the social evil of blasphemy and apostasy.

In order to deconstruct this apparent alignment of reformists and conservatives, one needs to delve deeper into the intricate and elaborate functioning of formal and informal law. I will take as an example Azerbaijan, where the incident that precipitated the dispute between Kadivar and Lankarānī Jr took place. As far as formal law is concerned, Azerbaijan's criminal law – like most Muslim-majority legal systems – does not provide for the execution of an apostate or blasphemer. Azerbaijan's criminal law nonetheless contains provisions that can be construed as including blasphemous utterances and writings: the very Article 283 of the Criminal Code that a court in Baku invoked to find Rafīq Tağı guilty and mete out to him and his publisher time in prison. Strong in its jurisprudential grounding in legal positivism, the legal system of Azerbaijan ignores the existence of any law other than the one it produces and its courts find applicable within the country's internationally recognised borders: the formal law. This leaves the provisions of confessional law on blasphemy and apostasy in the domain of informal law: that is, law that state courts will refuse to apply. These provisions would thus be completely ineffective unless they had other channels of application: extra-judicial killings are one of the most extreme examples of other such channels. These are assumed to be the circumstances of Rafīq Tağı's murder in Baku, years after his release from prison. Extra-judicial killings are treated as murders by formal law and its court system, but state courts find themselves caught between multiple fires when adjudicating on them. At times, they hear "expert witnesses" who claim that the court should consider circumstances of exclusion or at least mitigating factors because the murder complied with a religious duty (probably the most well-known instance of this was Muḥammad al-Ghazālī's statement during Faraj Fawda's murder trial in Egypt in the 1990s). At times, they come under pressure from other state authorities concerned with the maintenance of public order because of popular support for the murderer (probably here the most well-known instance was the extreme security measures taken by state authorities for the trial, sentence and execution of the murderer of Salmān Tā̠sīr in Pakistan in the mid-2010s).

Before proceeding on to the issue of popular support for severe punishments for blasphemy and apostasy, I believe it is imperative to mention that the jurisdiction of state courts and due process do not seem to be a very effective strategy for reformists. Two of the most well-known cases that Kadivar cites, that of Mahmud Muhammad Taha in Sudan and Naṣr Ḥāmid Abū Zayd in Egypt, were both decided by state courts. In the mid-1980s, a Sudanese court sentenced Mahmud Muhammad Taha to death on a count of apostasy, and in the mid-1990s an Egyptian court terminated Naṣr Ḥāmid Abū Zayd's marriage on grounds of the latter's apostasy from

Islam. Crucially, both Taha and Abū Zayd objected to the state court's jurisdiction over what they believed to be their individual matters of belief. Naṣr Ḥāmid Abū Zayd's case illuminates also the legal consequences of someone's alleged apostasy, beyond capital punishment. His case precipitated a legislative reform in 1996 that channelled the *actio popularis* (*ḥisba*) through the public prosecutor's office. Yet a case was filed a few years later, in the early 2000s, for the termination of the marriage of another prominent Egyptian intellectual, Nawāl al-Saʿdāwī, on grounds of her alleged apostasy from Islam. The personal status court dismissed the case on procedural grounds (the public prosecutor had not authorised the filing of the case as the 1996 reform required), but the harassment of Egyptian intellectuals for challenging mainstream religious views did not end there, and went as far as filing cases in the administrative court system to strip them of their citizenship on grounds of apostasy, as Nawāl al-Saʿdāwī had to endure a decade later in the early 2010s.

Besides due process (and jurisdiction), Kadivar and like-minded reformists expend much effort into unsettling the common belief that blasphemy and apostasy deserve severe punishments, including death. The reformists' uphill battle seems to lie in what statistical surveys describe as a self-evident and unquestioned truth among the wider population on the propriety of severe punishment for blasphemy and apostasy. By leveraging this widespread belief to maintain public support for questionable political manoeuvres, accusations of blasphemy and apostasy have become an expedient and effective means to discredit and harm opponents. Over the years, various forms of takfirism have targeted individuals and groups, and have also been used to justify acts of terrorism. In response, a number of political and religious authorities devised responses geared at denying the claims of blasphemy and apostasy, leaving the legal consequences of blasphemy and apostasy that underpin takfirism unchallenged. For instance, the Amman Message, drafted in 2004 and signed by a large number of political and religious authorities, focuses on offering a broad definition of who the Muslim is, so as to shield those who fall under the specification of the first of the three points of the Message from accusations of apostasy. The operation of reformists like Kadivar runs at a deeper level, in that they challenge the very foundation of the danger of *takfīr*: the belief that apostasy (and blasphemy) must entail death. Without this foundation, accusations of apostasy or blasphemy would no longer have either edge or consequence.

By addressing seemingly technical points of sheer jurisprudential relevance, Kadivar and like-minded reformists bring back into the domain of what can be discussed matters of law that – as Bourdieu would have probably put it – had already moved from the scholars' orthodoxy to the public's doxa. The highly sophisticated jurisprudential discussions are thus intended to challenge the orthodoxy underpinning the doxa, even if the temptation is to dismiss them as an exercise in hair-splitting and sophistry. Discussing the matter sets the stage for bringing the common belief that blasphemy and apostasy deserve severe punishments into the universe of discourse, of what can be discussed, contested, and requires explanation or justification. Kadivar's ability to prompt Lankarānī Jr's response is therefore already quite an accomplishment for reformists, just as 'Abd al-Mit'āl al-Ṣa'īdī's was in the 1950s. Lankarānī Jr's boastful response proved a phyrric victory, just like 'Īsá Manūn's with 'Abd al-Mit'āl al-Ṣa'īdī. When both Kadivar and al-Ṣa'īdī challenge the soundness of the jurisprudential foundations of the orthodoxy of the conservative position, Lankarānī Jr and Manūn both seem to realise the dangers of simply discussing the matter and retrench. The "definitiveness" of Lankarānī Jr and Manūn's tone is a strenuous attempt to reaffirm both the doxic belief and the solidity of the jurisprudential orthodoxy, but they have already let the genie out of the bottle. Conservatives quickly realised that disputing with reformists is risky, not only because reformists challenge the weak and shaky jurisprudential foundations of their position on blasphemy and apostasy, but also because disputing the matter has two immediate important ramifications, regardless of the outcome. A first, sociological, ramification is that the matter is brought to public attention as a matter on which different opinions are held; the question of the consequences of blasphemy and apostasy is thus brought back into the "universe of discourse". A second, jurisprudential, ramification is that the mere existence of a dispute over the matter makes a dent in the conservatives' chief claim that there is consensus on the punishment to be applied to apostates and blasphemers. In his first response to Kadivar, Lankarānī Jr postulates the existence of consensus (*ijmā'*) over the matter, which, in the conservative view, would in and of itself end the discussion. But Lankarānī Jr then confidently compiles evidence from primary sources in support of the consensus opinion. In doing so, the self-confidence of conservatives unveils the questionable foundations of their consensus. The outstanding contribution of Kadivar – and other reformists – rests not only on his ability to rekindle a discussion over matters of blasphemy and apostasy, and the solidity of his arguments, but also on his talent in prompting Lankarānī Jr – just as other like-minded conservatives – to disclose and lay bare the strength and firmness of the evidence underpinning their consensus.

## *Note*

1. Yasuyuki Matsunaga, "Mohsen Kadivar, an Advocate of Postrevivalist Islam in Iran", *British Journal of Middle Eastern Studies* 34(3) (2007): 317–329. Further biographical details can be found in Matsunaga's article.

# *Introduction*

This Introduction seeks to elaborate on the following issues under the rubric of blasphemy and apostasy: what is the situation of religious freedom in contemporary Islam? What are the positions of conservative and reformist Muslims on blasphemy, apostasy and heresy? Are there any substantive differences between Sunnis and Shi'is on the main points of this subject? What is this book's original contribution to scholarship?

Although the focus of this book is the critical analysis of religious freedom and the penalty sanctioned for the commission of blasphemy and apostasy from a Shi'i perspective, this inquiry would be incomplete without a review of the general outline of Sunni Muslim positions on the same subjects. Thus, Section 1 of this Introduction explores the literature review on religious freedom, blasphemy and apostasy in contemporary Sunni Islam. Section 2, which is more detailed, engages in a similar literature review, but from the perspective of contemporary Shi'i Islam. These two sections allow a comparative study of Islam's two major denominations, their exchanges, influences and effects.

In this book, "contemporary Islam" refers to the time period from the early twentieth century and onwards. I did not find any relevant material before that period. In these two literature reviews, "apostasy" is used in its expansive meaning, which includes blasphemy. My literature reviews contain major turning points in the history of religious freedom and apostasy among Sunni and Shi'i Muslims, respectively. I briefly point out these two denominations' most important figures and their ideas on this subject. Section 3 describes the story of how this book unfolded, analyses the genealogy of my ideas in detail, introduces novel ideas applied by other Sunni and Shi'i thinkers, and highlights the original contribution made by this book.

## *1 Literature Review of Religious Freedom and Apostasy in Contemporary Sunni Islam*

"Religious freedom" is a recent phenomenon in human history. Free-thinking, political liberalism and its philosophy were the products of eighteenth-century

Europe and were introduced to Muslims during the colonial period. According to the research of Muhammad al-Ṭāhir Ibn ʿĀshūr (d. 1973), the term *hurriyya* in its recent meaning of freedom or liberty entered Arabic after books on the 1789 French Revolution were translated. We do not know of any word in Arabic that indicated this new meaning; rather, combinations of several words were used to express it.[1] But it was not only the term, for even the concept and, more than that, the reality of the phenomenon of freedom that were new and innovative. But this coin had another side: "In fact, what was claimed was not the right to think freely, but the right not to believe [in any religion]. So, the concept of religious liberty unhappily became the synonym of secularism, agnosticism and atheism. Consequently, a stubborn fight was carried on against it as such."[2] Add the pressure of European countries in their colonies as well as the weak Ottoman response to Christian missionary activities to this context. Almost all members of the *ʿulamāʾ* (traditional experts of Islamic law or *fiqh*) class emphasised the Abrahamic traditions' premodern aspects: denying religious freedom after voluntary conversion and continuing to criminalise blasphemy and apostasy. The vast majority of the *ʿulamāʾ* – now called "conservative Muslims" or "traditionalists" – are no different. We can say that the mainstream twentieth- and twenty-first-century Sunni scholars still do not believe in the full meaning of religious freedom and strongly advocate capital punishment for blasphemy and apostasy. But this does not represent the consensus view, for there is a growing minority, composed of both *ʿulamāʾ* and non-*ʿulamāʾ*, who are a majority among educated Muslims known as "Muslim reformists". In the spectrum of reformists, we can observe positions ranging from a strong tendency towards religious freedom to its full acceptance, on the one hand, and from denying the death penalty for some types of apostates to the decriminalisation of all types of apostasy, on the other hand. I describe briefly the approaches of conservatives, moderate reformists and progressive reformists, respectively, in this section.

## The Conservative Approach

This subsection has two parts: the traditional context and contemporary rulings. I start with a succinct summary of the four Sunni schools' legal rulings taken from the report of Wahba al-Zuḥaylī (1932–2015), the Syrian professor of Islamic law and legal philosophy. The decree on apostasy is more complex than that on unbelief (*kufr*), because the former represents a return to *kufr* by displaying it through one's intentions, actions or statements (e.g., mocking Islam, expressing animosity towards it or rejecting its doctrines).

Apostasy is defined as denying God's existence, rejecting or denying even one of the prophets, considering an item unlawful (*ḥarām*) when consensus (*ijmāʿ*) has ruled it lawful (*ḥalāl*) and vice versa, rejecting an obligation upon which consensus has been reached, belief that something is mandatory when consensus says that it is not so, and remaining steadfast or being indecisive in unbelief (*kufr*). A *zindīq* is one who outwardly represents him- or herself to be Muslim but inwardly is an unbeliever. Such a person is also considered deserving of execution if he does not repent.

The four Sunni legal schools have reached consensus that a Muslim man who insults a prophet or one of the angels (*malāʾika*) is to be executed. The Mālikī school, based upon a widespread opinion, says that repenting is not an option.

Sunni jurists are united on the issue that a male apostate must be executed. The Ḥanafī school has ruled that a female apostate must be imprisoned indefinitely and released only if she returns to Islam or dies. Every three days she should receive a bodily punishment. The person who kills her cannot be held liable for anything.

The Ḥanafī school also considers it recommended to present Islam to the male apostate for each of the three days so that he might repent and return to the fold. If he does not, he is to be executed on the fourth day. Sunni jurists belonging to the other schools view it as mandatory (*wājib*) that Islam be presented three times prior to execution or exile in order to clear up any possible ambiguity or confusion in the male or female apostate's mind and lead him or her towards repentance.

Only the ruler or his deputy can carry out the punishment. Thus, anyone who kills an apostate without his permission is to be subjected to a discretionary punishment (*taʿzīr*), however, that person cannot be held liable for murder.

Male or female apostates who do not recant forfeit their entire estate. According to Abū Ḥanīfa (d. 767), Abū Yūsuf (d. 798) and Mālik (d. 795), if either spouse apostatises their marriage is automatically annulled (*faskh*) and there is no need to proclaim the divorce formula. The Shāfiʿī and Ḥanbalī schools suspend the annulment until the wife's *ʿidda* (the waiting period or three menstrual cycles) ends. If the apostate repents before that, the marriage remains valid.[3]

I selected three well-known and the most distinguished *'ulamā'* who could be said to represent clearly the contemporary Muslim traditionalist community: Muhammad al-Tāhir Ibn 'Āshūr (1879–1973), the Shaykh al-Islām of Tunis; and two Egyptian al-Azhar graduates, Muḥammad al-Ghazālī (1917–1996), chairman of the Academic Council of the International Institute of Islamic Thought in Egypt; and Yūsuf al-Qaradāwī (b. 1926), chairman of the International Union of Muslim Scholars in Doha, Qatar.[4] I narrate their ideas below in chronological order.

A. In 1963, Moḥammed al-Ghazālī chose the title *Freedom of Apostasy* instead of *Freedom of Religion* for his book. He strongly rejected the former phrase and classified conversion away from Islam as either to disbelief (atheism) or to other (Abrahamic) religions. He viewed it as not merely a personal issue and a matter that is yielded to the heart. Instead, according to him, apostasy is usually the cover for rebelling against divinely mandated worship, the *shari'a* and Islamic rulings, and, more than this, against the foundation of the state and forging alliances with its foreign enemies. Therefore, as apostasy is commonly perceived as the synonym of "the crime of high treason", resistance against it is a divine obligation. The survival of this "rare evil" in an Islamic system, with its public order and influential authority, is unthinkable. Thus, any acceptance of it is absolutely impossible.[5]

This extremely negative perspective, which is not exclusive to al-Ghazālī, was the understanding of mainstream of conservative Islam in the twentieth century. The Egyptian writer Faraj Fawda was assassinated in 1992 by a young extremist who implemented a conservative jurist's *fatwa* that accused him of apostasy. Al-Ghazālī, one of the *shari'a* experts invited to testify at his trial, said that killing an apostate is the religious duty of all Muslims if governments do not fulfil their duty and there is no punishment for a non-governmental killer![6]

B. Nine years later, in 1972, Ibn 'Āshūr wrote:

> If a Muslim completely abandons Islam, he or she breaks the covenantal relationship that he or she had entered upon becoming Muslim. The apostate is asked to repent (*istitāba*) during a period of three days. If he does not repent, then he will be killed to cleanse the vein of society from the lethal drug. The reason (*ḥikma*) for this punishment could be explained in this way: when a person

> converts to Islam, agrees to obey [its rules] and become a part of all [member of the community], his entrance into Islam is a covenant that he is required to fulfil. When he or she breaks it, it becomes a type of evil. The community must cleanse itself from his existence so that (1) the society's solidarity will not be broken because of his separation; (2) converts do not disdain it by testing it as an experience: if it fits their desires they remain within it, and if it does not they leave it; (3) weak-minded people are not given a false or misleading impression that the apostate tested Islam and did not enjoy it; and (4) it would prevent the presence of those who would spy on the community by fraudulently converting to Islam.[7]

I think that Ibn ʿĀshūr reported conservative Islam's perspective on apostasy clearly and correctly. We can elaborate on the restricted dimension of its conservative mentality on religious freedom.

C. Yūsuf al-Qaradāwī justified apostasy's harsh punishment in 1993 in this way: the Islamic community is based on belief and faith. Belief is the foundation of its identity, the axis of its life, the spirit of its existence. Therefore, no one can be allowed to get this foundation or touch this identity. Because of this, declared apostasy (*ridda muʿlana*) or unhidden apostasy is among the highest-ranking crimes in Islam, as it endangers society's personality and spiritual entity and is the first of the five necessities, namely, religion, life, progeny, mind and property. The believer sacrifices his life, country and property for his religion. He prescribed social isolation and ostracism – the deprivation of friendship, love and assistance, which is more severe than physical execution.[8]

In 1996, Qaradāwī compared apostasy with innovation (*bidʿa*) and classified it as thick and light, on the one hand, and as preacher (*dāʿiya*) and non-preacher, on the other hand. If the apostasy is "thick" – such as that of Salman Rushdie – and the apostate is preaching his innovation via his tongue and pen, he recommended the thickened punishment (execution, termination of the marital contract without divorce, and nullification of ownership of his or her estate, which is to be distributed to his or her heirs before execution). He added that if this punishment is not accepted, then it is possible to follow al-Nakha'i and like-minded *ʿulamāʾ* (i.e., the continuous request of repentance means stopping the execution). The first type of person is not only an apostate and an unbeliever, but also a belligerent fighter (*muhārib*, the subject of Q. 5:33) against God and His community. The second type of person (who hides his apostasy and does not preach it to anyone) is punished according to the appropriate *ta'zīr* (discretionary punishment determined by the ruler or the judge). He emphasised the first type of apostasy as the crime of high treason.[9]

In his latest book, al-Qaradāwī decriminalised the first type of apostasy, but stated that it remains a sin that will be punished in the other world,[10] while emphasising that the second type constitutes the crime of high treason.[11]

As we will see, a Muslim who hides his or her conversion to another religion or to atheism is not the subject of our discussion. The challenging subject here is whether his or her "public" expression of this conversion is a crime that calls for punishment and even execution. The clear response of the three individuals being discussed in this section is that this crime must be punished by execution. Therefore, they are considered conservative Muslims. We should keep in mind that they are familiar with and even responded to the Muslim reformers' arguments, and that although they were aware of the reformist framework of religious freedom, they still called for the criminalisation of apostasy, execution of apostates and denial of religious freedom.[12]

## Concluding Remarks

In sum, the key points of the conservative approach to apostasy are: (1) abandoning Islam, if not hidden and declared publicly, is a crime punishable, at least for men, by execution; (2) doing so is essentially evil and identical to rebellion against God. Its evilness is self-evident and requires no further explanation; and (3) religious freedom is not absolute, but is exclusive to the true religion, namely, Islam.

A few products of this approach are the 1985 execution of Mahmud Muhammad Taha, the Sudanese thinker, reformist and political activist; the 1989 *fatwa* against Salman Rushdie; the 1992 assassination of the Egyptian dissident writer Farag Fawda; and the 1995 condemnation of Naṣr Ḥāmid Abū Zayd, the well-known Qur'anic researcher, by an Egyptian court.

## The Moderate Reformer Approach

Moderate reformers accept religious freedom as an essential principle of Islamic thought; highlight the lack of any worldly punishment prescribed for apostasy in the Qur'an; find no punishment for it during the time of Prophet; understand the so-called wars against apostasy (*hurūb al-ridda*) after the Prophet's death as the first caliph's political decision as opposed to being a permanent religious ruling; and strongly criticise the hadith and consensus arguments made to support such executions in the framework of traditional jurisprudence (*fiqh*). The pioneer reformer was Muhammad 'Abduh. There are at least nine distinguished twentieth-century scholars, both *'ulamā'* and non-*'ulamā'*, who strongly criticised the conservative approach and elaborated innovative ideas and arguments in an attempt to build bridges to reach an absolutely new framework of religious freedom.

A. Muhammad 'Abduh (1849–1905), the student of Jamal al-Din al-Afghani (1838–1897), was a key founding figure of Islamic modernism and the Grand Mufti of Egypt (1899–1905). His student Muhammad Rashid Rida (1865–1935) published his innovative ideas in their Qur'anic exegesis by the name of *Tafsīr al-Manār*. Elaborating on Q. 4:90 "If they withdraw and do not fight you and offer you peace, then God gives you no way against them",[13] was written for the first time ever in this context in *Tafsīr al-Manār*: the apostates are not killed if they are peaceful and do not commit war. No Qur'anic verse abrogates this verse. Mentioning the hadith that supports killing the apostate, he explicitly stated that hadith cannot abrogate the Qur'an. Abū Bakr's decision to make war against those who refused to pay the *zakāt* at the beginning of his caliphate was his opinion (*ijtihād*). An individual (in place of a group) who refuses to pay *zakāt* is not killed, even in traditional Islam.[14]

At the end of the ninth surah, *Tawba* (Repentance), Rida wrote: three principles on religious freedom and how to treat hypocrites.

Principle one: the freedom of belief and conscience should be taken care of. There is neither governmental control nor cultural control by the teachers and guides, because the job of the latter is to train and educate. Therefore, no one is allowed to accuse a human being of harbouring hidden disbelief, of intending to commit treason against his religion or country, of wishing evil upon his nation or community, of punishing a person either physically or financially for this reason, or of depriving the person of those rights that all other members of community enjoy.

Principle two: the person who hides disbelief in God or the Prophet cannot be allowed to spread sedition among the people, preach and call people to his disbelief, challenge their beliefs, express or practice something against public beliefs, even if no call or challenge is involved. If he does [one or more of] these actions and yet claims to be following Islam, he is condemned as an apostate if what he has expressed frankly, definitely and unanimously cannot be interpreted as anything other than disbelief. If he refuses the demand to repent, he will be punished according to the *shari'a*, namely, the prevention of inheritance between him and his Muslim heirs, the annulment of his marriage with Muslim wives, the denial of a religious funeral, the related prayers and burial in a Muslim cemetery. This is because the freedom of belief for one person depends on the freedom of the others, especially respecting the beliefs, rituals and worship of the religion under which he lives, that is, the light of its own *shari'a*.

The reader should know that many jurists have been prodigious in their chapters on apostasy, in the issues that sentenced such persons to disbelief, in the sense of their exclusion from Islam. Many of them based a lot of remote or probable correlations on this sentence for close interpretations. The characteristics of the hypocrites in this surah (*Tawba*) are arguments against them. One is required to accept the words of a person who self-identifies as Muslim and does not explicitly say anything contrary to a potentially acceptable interpretation. All scientific discussions that are in conflict with the apparent meaning of the religious texts (*ẓawāhir al-nuṣūṣ*) according to the principles of *uṣūl al-fiqh* should be accepted [and their adherents must not be accused of apostasy].

Principle three: discussed the duty of the ruler when confronted with practical hypocrisy.[15]

There are several innovative points in *al-Manār*'s exegesis or 'Abduh's ideas, as seen in the report of Rashid Rida: first, the apostate is not executed for apostasy, but for fighting against Islam (*muhārib*). Second, because neither governments nor religious authorities can control religious freedom, no one can be punished or deprived of his or her social rights after being accused of hidden disbelief. Third, a Muslim who expresses his or her conversion explicitly has to be punished, as mentioned in the *shari'a*, but not executed. 'Abduh condemned the conservative jurists' discussions on expanding such punishments and he clearly removed apostates from the list of apostasy-related punishments. This was a courageous and an important *fatwa* to issue during the late 1890s or early 1900s.

B. Muhammad Tawfiq Sidqī (1881–1920), a young Egyptian physician wrote: "executing the apostate for converting and changing the faith is against the clear Qur'anic principle on religious freedom, and any hadith that contradicts the Qur'an is invalid".[16] Both of these points were correlated in 'Abduh's discussions, but not stated explicitly. Sidqī highlighted them clearly for the first time in the 1900s.

C. In 1935, the Egyptian historian Hassan Ibrāhim Hassan (1892–1968) concluded, based on his research on the so-called wars of apostasy during Abū Bakr's caliphate, that: "The death penalty for apostates was the requirement of a state's politics more than taking care of their Islam." According to his research there was no apostasy because those who did not pay *zakāt* to the caliphate had not abandoned Islam and the other fighters were hypocrites.[17] Hassan expanded and elaborated upon what 'Abduh had started. 'Abduh described these wars as Abū Bakr's personal *ijtihād*, by which he meant that it was a political issue but not a permanent Islamic ruling. Hassan went one step further and described the death penalty for apostates as a "political" decision of the caliph and the state at that time, as opposed to an element of Islamic jurisprudence.

D. 'Abdul'Azīz Jāwīsh (1876–1929), an Egyptian reformist and politician, wrote in his book that the Qur'an contains no verse on executing the apostate. In early Islam, apostasy meant not only abandoning Islam, but also attaching oneself to its enemies and fighting against Muslims. The subject of the hadiths was these belligerent apostates. Therefore, those who did not rebel against Islam, attach themselves to its enemies and betray it at all, but, rather, were misled by some suspicions and doubts that they could not resolve with arguments and proofs, are not considered apostates until the religious authorities dispel their doubts and guide them to the path of Islam. When the people are plagued by such fossilised (*jāmidin*) *'ulamā'*, and the misgivings and doubts are rampant in the hearts of simple-minded Muslims, how can those who leave Islam be punished? It sounds as if he was close to Nakha'i's approach (continuous request for repentance and not killing the apostate who does not rebel against Islam or the state).[18]

Jāwīsh's family published his book posthumously, two decades after his death. In it, he highlighted and explicitly stated what 'Abduh had mentioned only implicitly: removing execution for an individual who had abandoned Islam but did not rebel against it. His innovative point was the decriminalisation of pure apostasy. His removal of all types of punishments for such people, not only execution, is another step forward based on the teachings of Muhammad 'Abduh.

E. 'Abd al-Mit'āl al-Ṣa'idī (1894–1966), faculty of Arabic language at al-Azhar University, and a member of the Egyptian Arabic language department, was a pioneer member of the second generation of Egyptian reformists. Along with others, he participated in a debate on religious freedom and the punishment of apostates with his collogue 'Isā Manūn (1889–1957) of the faculty of Shari'a at al-Azhar and a former member of the Egyptian Supreme Academy of 'Ulamā'. After publishing Manūn's article,[19] the *al-Azhar Journal* did not publish Ṣa'idi's response! And so he compiled the debates in *Al-Hurriyya al-Diniyya fil-Islam* and published it in 1955.[20] This is the first book in the Islamic world to deal specifically with this topic, especially by an al-Azhar scholar.

Whereas the conservative Manūn supported the death penalty for apostates and denied religious freedom, al-Ṣa'idi believed that "The apostate is not compelled to Islam through execution or imprisonment. We call him to Islam with wisdom and good admonition, and dispute with him in the better way. If he returns to Islam, he will be delivered from God's punishment in the world to come, and if he does not return, there will be no salvation." He concluded that his approach is closer to Islam's leniency than that of Manūn. Al-Ṣa'idi justified his approach with Nakha'i's *fatwa* on continually requesting the accused apostate to repent, which, according to him, means not killing that person.[21]

Ṣa'idi followed 'Abduh and expanded his approach by citing more Qur'anic verses and practical traditions of the Prophet, on the one hand, and by criticising the verbal traditions or hadiths that support executing apostates in detail, and concluding that such hadiths were exclusively about those apostates who fought against Islam, as opposed to those who just abandoned it. He was the revivalist of the religious freedom trend started by 'Abduh. Fifty years after 'Abduh's death the mainstream of al-Azhar and Sunni Islam had not changed their minds and thus they were still conservatives. Therefore, al-Ṣa'idi's brave position was essential for continuing the line of those who were advocating religious freedom in the 1950s.

F. Mahmoud Shaltūt (1893–1963), the Grand Imam of al-Azhar (1958–1963), the most prominent jurist and theologian after 'Abduh and member of the same school of thought, advocated strongly for religious freedom and added an innovative point to it. In his famous *Al-Islam, 'Aqida wa Shari'a*, written in the late 1950s, he divided the worldly punishments into textual or fixed punishment (*ḥudūd*) for specific crimes, and those that the ruler had discretionary authority to impose (*taʿzīrāt*). The first fixed and prescribed punishment is the one related to violating the religion by committing apostasy. After defining apostasy, he explained that the advocates of punishment for the apostates argue that Q. 2:217 only includes the punishment meted out in the next world, as the worldly punishment for this crime is execution. The jurists based their ruling upon a hadith narrated on the authority of Ibn ʿAbbās that Prophet had said: "Kill anyone who changes his religion!" There are at least four scholarly discussions about the indication and meaning of this hadith. "But the viewpoint of the issue changes if we know that many *ʿulamāʾ* believe that *ḥudūd* punishment cannot be proven by an isolated hadith and that disbelief in and of itself does not permit execution. What does permit it is the apostate's fighting against Muslims, displaying enmity toward them, and attempting to lead them astray. The appearance of many verses of the Qur'an refrain compulsion of religion."[22]

In his exegesis of the Qur'an, Shaltut explained two important principles: (1) the sanctity of human life is a certain and unequivocal principle; and (2) this sanctity can be removed only if the cause for doing so is both certain and definite. In other words, a cause that is uncertain cannot break this sanctity, and the causes in equivocal texts, even if the *ʿulamāʾ* permitted them, cannot remove this sanctity and allow someone to be executed. The *shariʿa* provides only three certain causes for execution: aggression against life (*qiṣāṣ*, Q. 2:178); against the social order (*muḥāraba*, Q. 5:133); and against the Muslim community (*difāʿ*, Q. 3:91).[23] Clearly, apostasy is not on this list.

Shaltut's writings contain several innovative points. First, they prove that applying a *ḥudūd* punishment requires certain evidence, such as a Qur'anic verse or a *mutāwatir* hadith. An isolated hadith is unacceptable. According to this *uṣūlī* principle, there is no evidence for executing an apostate. This argument is also acceptable in the framework of traditional *fiqh*. Second, the criterion for execution is neither original disbelief (*kufr aṣlī*) nor abandoning Islam (*al-kufr baʿd al-Islām*); rather, it is the former Muslim joining an offensive attack upon them and displaying enmity towards them. Third, the sanctity of human life can be removed by the abovementioned three unequivocal causes; apostasy or abandoning Islam is not one of them.

Shaltut's three innovative points are formidable and valid. There is only one interjection here. He said "many *ʿulamāʾ* believe that the *ḥudūd* punishment is not proven by an isolated hadith". Who are these "many *ʿulamāʾ*"? In fact, only one jurist, Abu al-Hassan al-Karkhī (d. 951), rejected the validity of such an isolated hadith report on the grounds that it would be vulnerable to fabrication, oversight and error. These probabilities are considered as obscure, vague and suspicious (*shubahāt*), and thus one should resort to the famous prophetic principle of "abandon the *ḥudūd* punishments in obscure cases". Abu 'Adullah al-Basri (d. 1068) followed Karkhi for a while and then changed his mind.

G. In 1966, Abdul-Hamid Mutawalli (1900–1978), professor of law at Egypt's University of Alexandria, summarised the positions of both sides objectively and fairly, and made five important points:

First, rebelling against Islam (*al-khurūj 'alā-l-Islām*) and exiting from Islam (*al-khurūj 'ani-l-Islām*) are completely different subjects. The former – that it was not an individual act, but mostly a collective one – was a political crime against the state as well as a religious crime against the rulings of Islam, whereas the latter – the very recent ruling that it is an individual event – leaving Islam does not threaten the Islamic sociopolitical system or entity. If it is criminalised, then the punishment should be imprisonment or financial, as Abū Zuhrā prescribed.

Second, forbidding (*taḥrīm*) is not identical to criminalisation (*tajrīm*). Islam has made many things forbidden (*ḥarām*), but has prescribed no worldly punishments for engaging in them. Apostasy could be one of these forbidden acts, but the disputed point is criminalising it, and especially executing the person.

Third, the proponents of execution have not categorised it as a fixed punishment (*ḥudūd*), but rather as an unfixed and discretionary punishment (*ta'zīrāt*). Thus, the ruler is responsible for choosing the appropriate punishment, namely, one that does not prescribe execution.

Fourth, the Qur'an explains all types of execution and the Sunna details them; however, none of them deal with apostasy. But the fact that the Qur'an determined the lighter punishments, such as lashing for a few *ḥudūd* crimes, means that it forbade execution for apostasy.

Fifth, all the evidence found in the hadith for important issues such as execution should be of the category that is transmitted recurrently (*mutawātir*) or at least be contained within well-known (*mashhūr*) hadiths. However, the hadiths that support execution are isolated hadiths (*khabar al-wāḥid*) and provide nothing but conjecture or presumption (*ẓann*), whereas certainty (*qat'*) is required when proving what is religiously required and prohibited (*al-wājibāt wa al-muḥarramāt*). Even in these hadiths the Prophet, in his capacity as a prophet and not as a ruler, decreed no eternally valid punishment for apostates. Mutawalli therefore concluded that executing an apostate was a political punishment and not a permanent religious one.[24]

Although almost all of these points could be found implicitly in the ideas of previous thinkers, his approach of highlighting and focusing on each one of them as a separate point in a legal formula is innovative. Both execution and all punishments, as well as religiously required and prohibited issues, require the definitive evidence that isolated hadiths cannot provide. Mutawalli discussed this established and uncontested important point once again, and for the first time, in the twentieth century. His remarkable points affected almost all the scholars who came after him. In other words, they have shaped Sunni Islam's scholarship on the discussions of apostasy since the 1960s.[25]

H. Muhammad Fathi ʻUthmān (1928–2010), an Egyptian thinker, mentioned during the 1960s that the punishment of apostasy needs revisiting and revision. If we criminalise converting from Islam, then we should tell them clearly at the outset that they will literally lose their heads if they leave it after accepting it. (Will they consciously and out of free volition become Muslim at this point?!) We should distinguish between before and after legal puberty (*bulūgh*), for in the former the minor's status in religion is dependent upon his or her father, whereas in the latter he or she can choose consciously their religion. (A post-pubescent Muslim child who chooses another religion (or no religion) is not an apostate because he was never truly and consciously a Muslim.)[26]

According to ʻUthmān, the "Islam" in "*abandoning Islam*" means the Islam that was chosen consciously after puberty, and that potential converts should be clearly informed about the harsh punishment meted out to apostates beforehand. On the basis of this profound point, almost all cases of apostasy become invalid and the accused are not really apostates.[27]

K. In 2006, the Sudanese political and religious figure Sadiq al-Mahdi noted that the punishment for apostasy is against Muslims' welfare and best interests (*maṣlaḥa*). First, it contradicts the *shariʻa*'s goals, which are based on freedom of belief. Second, due to practical reasons, converts to Islam number several times more than those who abandon Islam. Third, one-third of Muslims reside as minorities in other societies, and thus non-Muslims may punish them harshly based on the principle of reciprocity (*muqābala bi-l-mithl*). The *shariʻa*'s goals and the interests of Islam require that we recognise the freedoms of thought, consciousness and belief.[28] This in itself is a practical and pragmatic justification for ending the execution of apostates and is reasonable even for conservative jurists. The theory of reciprocity could be regarded as another new and fresh point advanced in his discussion.[29]

## Concluding Remarks

The figures of this approach can be classified into three categories: (1) members of the *'ulamā'*, including Muhammad 'Abduh and Mahmoud Shaltut, whom the conservatives have deemed liberal! (2) Azhari scholars, but not scholars of the *sharī'a*. Although they were educated in a conservative seminary, they are not considered to belong to the class of *'ulamā'*. Among them are 'Abdul'Azīz Jāwīsh and 'Abd al-Mit'āl al-Ṣa'idī. (3) Non-*'ulamā'* scholars like Muhammad Tawfīq Sidqī (physician), Hassan Ibrāhim Hassan (historian), Abdul-Hamid Mutawalli (professor of law), Muhammad Fathi 'Uthmān (scholar of Islamic studies) and Sadiq al-Mahdi (political activist).

All of the moderate reform scholars were Egyptian except for the last one, who is Sudanese but published his book in Cairo. We can therefore say that Egypt has been – and remains – the global capital of moderate reform for Sunni Islam. Moderate reform was started in the late nineteenth century and continues to this day. Although this approach is supported by a large majority of educated Muslims, within the academy where the number of its adherents have been growing rapidly, it remains an absolute minority in comparison with the conservative approach.

The approach's key points could be outlined in this way: first, two separate subjects that were amalgamated and, as a result, engendered confusion need to be separated: abandoning Islam or joining another religion; and combating Islam or exhibiting belligerency against it. The subject matter of apostasy is the former, whereas the latter is something else. The core point here is that apostasy should gradually be decriminalised so that neither execution nor any other worldly punishment can be applied.

Second, as "religious freedom" is one of Islam's principles, any such criminalisation, especially execution, explicitly and clearly contradicts this immutable and uncontested principle.

Third, the Qur'an not only supports religious freedom absolutely, but restricts the punishment for apostasy to God in the next world. However, as God determined and lays out the punishments for lighter sins, this means that, according to the Qur'an, apostasy is a sin that has no worldly punishment.

Fourth, criminalising the abandonment of Islam in *fiqh* is based on some isolated hadiths. According to the principles of *uṣūl al-fiqh*, execution, the *ḥudūd* punishments, and even what is religiously required and prohibited (*al-wājibāt wa-l-muḥarramāt*) cannot be proven by such hadiths even if they have an authentic chain of transmission, because proof requires definitive evidence, such as hadiths that are *mutawātir*. Thus, consensus on the issue of criminalising apostasy is not authoritative and is non-probative.

Fifth, there is no authoritative evidence for criminalising the abandonment of Islam, and especially punishing such a person with execution, in either the Qur'an or the Sunna (including the hadith and consensus).

Sixth, say that an individual changes his or her religion, publicises his or her decision, preaches his or her new religion or atheism, and states his or her will to destroy Islam culturally and peacefully. It seems that such actions would be enough to prove that the individual intends to launch an offensive attack on Islam, and that the punishment for such a serious crime would be execution. This approach does not deny criminalisation, punishment and execution in this particular case.

## The Progressive Reformist Approach

Since the 1980s, a new brand of Muslim thinkers have published their elaborations and vigorous discourses on apostasy. They have expanded the moderate reformers' criticism, critically analysed the conceptual evolution in the signification of an apostate and removed any worldly punishment for apostasy (including leaving Islam and attacking it culturally and peacefully). Religious freedom has been promoted to the essential principle of Islamic thought. I have selected six figures and describe their ideas in chronological order.

**A.** Gamal al-Banna[30] (1920–2013), an Egyptian author, liberal scholar and trade unionist who published eight books directly related to apostasy and religious freedom.[31] In his first book, in 1977, al-Banna wrote that "It is essential to consider faith as an outcome of a personal will. God wants difference and diversity. Therefore, all forms of force and compulsion, even intervention in the circle of religious belief, must be abandoned and this issue must be dealt with within the 'call and dialogue' framework practised by the messenger of God. This ruling applies all human beings, without differentiating between Muslims and non-Muslims."[32] Al-Banna, the vanguard of this approach and its most prolific and popular figure, considers religious freedom as one of the principles of Islamic theology.

B. Muhammad Sa'id al-'Ashmawi (1930–2013), Egypt's Supreme Court Justice and specialist in comparative and Islamic law at Cairo University, was one of the most influential contemporary liberal Muslim thinkers. He wrote in 1980 that the foundation of the medieval state conflicts with that of the modern state. In the former, the theory of state was not clear and identified in terms of its essence. Religion was its foundation because religiosity was nationality or, in modern terms, citizenship. In the Middle East Islam was the state, and in Europe Christianity was the state. A Muslim was a citizen of any Muslim community and a member of all Muslim groups, just as was the case with a Christian in any Christian community and group. The religious minorities in each society were under the protection of the majority.

In this conceptualisation, leaving a religion approximates committing high treason because adopting his former enemy's religion meant becoming a citizen of his former enemy's state as well. This is the context of those prophetic hadith about executing those who leave Islam. There is no evidence that the Prophet punished anyone who had been charged with apostasy. The Qur'an recognises the individual's freedom to choose his or her religion and condemns any compulsion in this matter. Negating compulsion right at the beginning supports negating compulsion in perpetuity. There is no advantage or benefit in a person who remains Muslim out of fear and compulsion. Those who freely choose to join another religion would not be held culpable on behalf of their former religion. Religion loses nothing due to such a person's departure, for the real loss would be if he or she were forced to continue to live as a disbeliever in his or her heart, feigning to have faith in Islam that he or she, in actuality, does not really have.

The Qur'anic concept of religious freedom became one of the essential human rights recognised in national covenants and constitutions. Perhaps what helps the concept of free thought in the modern era – in addition to its being one of the natural human rights – is that the modern state is not based on religion, but rather on belonging to a homeland, a nation-state and a history. Religion is one element that should be considered in the state's political, economic and/or cultural system, for it can no longer function as the state's sole basis or foundation, as it did during the medieval era, for those foundations and bases no longer exist.[33] After releasing his book, 'Ashmawi was accused of apostasy and sentenced to *mahdūr al-damm* (one whose blood may be shed with impunity). He narrated this tragic story in his other book.[34]

Contextualising the hadiths and *fatwa*s on apostasy by pointing out that religion occupied the place of the nation in the premodern era and that membership in a tradition had been stronger than citizenship in comparison with our own age, that of the nation-state age, were two of 'Ashmawi's innovative points. The texts derived from a socio-historical context that no longer existed and could not be understood in the modern context. Therefore, he contended, we need a new understanding or, in other words, a new discourse for apostasy and religious issues.

C. Mohamed Talbi (1921–2017), a Tunisian historian, professor and prolific author, published his important article "Religious Liberty: A Muslim Perspective" in 1985. We can find "*a new discourse*" in it, as it includes several original points:

First: "The problem of religious liberty, as a common human concern and international preoccupation, is relatively new." There are a lot of similarities between traditional Islamic theology and Jewish theology on apostasy: "The Jew who is converted to another religion ceases *ipso facto* to belong to his State-Community. So, his conversion is felt as a betrayal and, as such, it warrants the penalty of death." He describes the foundation of such theologies as: "Power and Religion conserved more or less their old relations or resumed them. They needed each other so much. The intolerance of the dominant social group asserted itself everywhere in the world with internal and external wars, and many forms of more or less tough discrimination."[35] The penalty for apostasy, especially execution in the hadith, Qur'anic exegesis and *fiqh*, is the effect of Jewish tradition and not the Prophet's sayings or actions. It is not a divine fact, but rather a historical issue. This historical and comparative discussion is the best starting point.

Second, Talbi discovers the context of the first confrontation between Muslims and religious freedom: "The concept of religious liberty unhappily became the synonym of secularism, agnosticism and atheism. Consequently, a stubborn fight was carried on against it as such. To deal with the subject honestly and calmly, we have to free ourselves of this false notion."[36] Unfortunately, almost all conservative Muslims do not consider this core point, which explains the pessimistic confrontation of most Muslims with religious freedom.

Third, Talbi introduces his new discourse: "Each man has the right to be different. In this new world, there is no longer room for exclusiveness. We have to accept one another as we are. Diversity is the law of our time. Today, because of mass media, which are becoming increasingly sophisticated and pervasive, everyone is truly the neighbour of everyone else."[37] This is another key point. Conservative theology and jurisprudence are exclusivist and anti-diversity. The harsh punishment for apostasy is a direct product of this narrow-minded ideology.

Fourth, another new dimension of this new discourse is the acknowledgement of disbelief's existence as an undeniable reality. "It is only recently that we have begun to be confronted with secularism. It is now our turn to experience from the inside the growth of agnosticism and atheism. We have to be conscious of this overwhelming change in our societies, and accordingly we have to exercise our theological thinking in this new and unprecedented context."[38] He continued: "We never underline enough that religious liberty is not an act of charity, or a tolerant concession towards misguided persons. It is a fundamental right for everybody. To claim it for myself implies *ipso facto* that I am disposed to claim it for my neighbour too."[39] This is a progressive standpoint: equal rights to believe and disbelieve. It is another contextualisation of apostasy. In the modern context, monotheism has many rivals such as subjective secularism, agnosticism and atheism. This is completely different from the premodern context, in which religion was dominant. Premodern texts cannot be the criteria in the modern context. We are sure that the conservative jurists ignored this essential contextual shift, and thus their discussions are problematic.

Fifth, Talbi defined religious freedom and clarified its core points: "Religious liberty is basically the right to decide for oneself, without any kind of pressure, fear or anxiety, the right to believe or not to believe, the right to assume with full consciousness one's destiny, the right of course to get rid of all kinds of faith as superstitions inherited from the dark ages, but the right also to espouse the faith of one's choice, to worship and to bear witness freely . . . The cornerstone of all human rights is religious liberty."[40] This definition is the product of a paradigm shift: every person has the essential right to choose any religion or to leave his or her religion. Religious freedom does not mean the right to choose the religion that we think is correct. This is not the fundamental right only at the time of choosing one's religion, but it continues until the end of one's life.

Sixth, after interpreting Q. 2:256, Talbi stated: "To the best of my knowledge, among all the other revealed texts only the Qur'an stresses religious liberty in such an accurate and unambiguous way. The reason why is that faith, to be true and reliable faith, needs absolutely to be a free and voluntary act."[41] This is an honour for Muslims. However, he added: "Muslim traditional theology developed in a way, that, for historical reasons in my opinion, does not always fit in with the spirit of the Qur'an."[42] He continued:

> This theology abridged seriously the liberty of choice of one's religion. According to this theology, though conversion to Islam must be and is in fact without coercion, it is practically impossible, once inside Islam, to leave it. Conversion to another religion from Islam is considered as treason and the apostate is liable to the penalty of death. The traditional theologians, in their elaboration, rely, on the one hand, on the precedent of the first caliph of Islam, Abu Bakr (632–634), who energetically fought the tribes who rejected his authority after the Prophet's death and refused to pay him the alms taxes, likening their rebellion to apostasy. On the other hand, they mainly put forward the authority of this hadith: "Anyone who changes his religion must be put to death."

He highlighted that "the hadith, upon which essentially the penalty of death relies, is always more or less mixed, in traditional writings, with rebellion and highway robbery".[43] Talbi fairly distinguished between the wonderful religious freedom in the Qur'an and the narrow-mindedness of Islamic theology, jurisprudence, hadith and Qur'anic exegesis. The penalty for apostasy is the fruit of the latter, not the former. Islamic teachings need structural reform in order to expand the Qur'anic outline of religious freedom.

Seventh, following the moderate reformers, Talbi proclaimed that "this hadith is not *mutawatir*, and, consequently, according to the traditional system of hadith, it is not binding". His conclusion is brave and solid: "In my opinion we have many good reasons to consider it as undoubtedly forged. It may have been forged under the influence of Leviticus (24:16) and Deuteronomy (13:2–19) – where it is ordered to stone the apostate to death – if not directly, then perhaps indirectly through the Jews and Christians converted to Islam."[44] The moderate reformers concluded that no isolated hadith, even one with an authentic chain of transmission, could justify punishment or execution, let alone any prohibition or requirement. However, the innovative point of the progressive approach goes beyond this by raising the possibility that such hadiths were fabricated and forged under the influence of specific Jewish literature. We have no reliable evidence in Islam for supporting any worldly punishment for apostasy.

Eighth, Talbi's final point is removing any worldly punishment for apostasy absolutely:

> How to treat those who try to draw them into their camp or to manipulate them? . . . We say that there is no specified *hadd* in this matter. On the contrary, Muslims are advised to forgive and overlook till God accomplishes His purpose . . . The debate is between God and the apostate's conscience and it is not our role to interfere in it . . . Muslims are only authorised to take up arms in one case, the case of self-defence, when they are attacked, and their faith seriously jeopardised. Muslims are urged not to yield, when their conscience is at stake and to take up arms against "those who will not cease fighting you until they turn you back from your faith, if they can". (2:217)[45]

He concluded: "To respect man's freedom is to respect God's Plan. To be a true 'Muslim' is to submit to this Plan."[46]

As leaving Islam and becoming a disbeliever is not a crime, there is no punishment for doing so; neither execution nor imprisonment, neither *ḥadd* nor *taʿzīr*, neither religious nor governmental or political punishment. This means the absolute decriminalisation of apostasy. But more than this, to be or to become a non-Muslim, or to chose a path that others may consider to be wrong, is the right of everyone. From the Islamic viewpoint, there is a linkage between an apostate or a non-believer and God that will appear in the other world, and no one is allowed to intervene in this relationship. The importance of Talbi's discourse is not only his progressive approach to religious freedom and apostasy, but also the strong textual evidence and argumentation that he provides to support his audacious and innovative approach.

D. Hmida Ennaifer is a Tunisian professor of Shariʿa.[47] His 1987 article[48] opens with a comparison between historical Islam or the lived experince of Muslims, on the one hand, and some definite Qur'anic verses and a few Islamic principles, on the other hand. The former supports force and pressure, whereas the latter advocates freedom, tolerance and justice. These are two opposing understandings of one religion, resulting in a contradition. Ennaifer classified two major streams of thought among modern Muslim thinkers. The key point of the first, estublished by Muhammad 'Abduh and continued by Mohamed Talbi, is that the faith is based on the freedom of belief. Despite the many discussants in this line of thinking, their influence in the Muslim community was limited in comparison with the second stream of thought. Established in India by Abul A'la Maududi (d. 1979) and transferred to the Arab world, that line asserted that re-establishing the caliphate is the essential condition to authentically implement faith and religion in its totality. Maududi discussed the subject in 1933, Sayyid Qutb (d. 1966) based his theory of the "ignorant society" (*jāhiliyya*) on Maududi's, and Muslim fundamentalist groups inherited them.

The Muslim modernist's key question is "Why?": why does a Muslim convert? The problem is located in contemporary faith. The prevailing faith in the Islamic Arabic space is the product of socio-political factors that shaped Muslim life during the early centuries, the age of conquests and victories of the Umayyad, 'Abbasid and Ottoman empires. The rulings made on apostates by all legal schools (Sunni and Shi'i) were made in the framework of a faith designed by the jursits on the assumption of victorius authority and a triumphant army.

He categorises three approaches to apostasy in our age: (1) anyone who abandons Islam should be executed; (2) the apostate is not executed, but he is asked to repent before he dies – religious freedom can be seen in this approach; and (3) the call to establish a new faith is made. The realities of the modern age demand a new approach in understanding the belief system because the archaic interpretations are not compatible or intelligible in the modern era. The representatives of this approach are Gamal al-Banna and Mohamed Talbi.

These two scholars qualitatively evolved the issue of apostasy in contemporary Islamic thought and got rid of the internal viewpoint that was restricted to the Muslim state being surrounded by enemies and spies, which originally engendered the *fatwa* of executing apostates. Their approach is dynamic and internal–external. It is internal because they understood the historical context in which such *fatwa*s were promulgated, although they did not confirm it for the modern era and instead established a new approach based on religious freedom.

This approach is also external because it understands the deep change that the Islamic world needs to undergo and stated that a new faith must be established in the new (i.e., modern) world that does not treat apostasy from a legal viewpoint, but from the viewpoint of awareness and understanding. This faith allows the dialogue between God and the apostate and does not permit anyone to intervene in it.

Ennaifer's article is one of the most comprehensive works of this approach. He continued and deepened Talbi's discourse. His first innovative point is to differentiate between 'Abduh and Maududi's lines or, respectively, the lines of religious freedom and of religious restriction. His second innovative point is classifying Islamic approaches into three groups. Although some of his choices about which group a few figures belong to are problematic, Islamic scholarship has accepted the logic of this classification, albeit with some reservations. Another interesting point is highlighting the question of *why*: why does a Muslim convert? It then advances to the level of a legal question: how to punish an apostate? In this new discourse, epistemologic, historical and hermenetical studies are far more determinative than legal or traditional theological and juridical studies. And this accounts for their success in terms of designing new discourse.

E. Abdelmadjid Charafi[49] (b. 1942), a Tunisian professor and scholar of thought and civilisation, wrote in 1989:

> The issue of apostasy has preoccupied Muslims since the time of the first caliphate, when some Arab tribes refused to pay *zakāt*. The Companions hesitated to fight them in the beginning because they neither denied Islam nor disbelieved after having embraced the faith. However, Abū Bakr emphasized fighting them and thereby opened the door of legitimacy of fighting opponents [of the ruler's understanding of Islam] as an official interpretation of Islam. [This official interpretation of Islam] did not limit the ruling of apostasy to those Muslims who chose to convert from Islam to another religion – regardless of whether they inherited it or chose it voluntarily – but imposed it upon any dissidents accused of *zandaqa* (heresy) under the 'Abbasids and even upon the opponents of official Sunni ideology.

He narrated the incidents of 1017 from Ibn al-Jawzī's *al-Muntazam* that "The 'Abbasids ordered the execution of Mu'tazilis, Rejectionists (Rāfiḍa), Isma'ilis,

Qarmatians, Jahmiyya, and Mushabbiha and to crucify, imprison and exile them; that they be cursed from the pulpits of the Muslims; and that all types of heretics (*ahl al-bidaʿ*) be removed and driven out of their homelands, all of which became a tradition (*sunna*) in Islam."[50] Charafi also categorised the approach of contemporary Muslims to apostasy into three groups,[51] resembling Ennaifer's classification. The importance of Charafi's work is historical. He held Abū Bakr to be the first Companion to play the initial primary role in shaping the penalty for apostasy; second, the role of the ʿAbbasid caliphs in attempting to subsume all types of dissidents as guilty of heresy (*zindaqa*) from official Sunni Islam. This restricted understanding of Islam became the Sunna (Tradition) – the tragic reality of apostasy that we should always keep in mind.

F. Farag Fawda (b. 1945), an Egyptian dissident, was sentenced to *mahdūr al-damm* (a person whose blood may be shed with impunity) as an apostate because of his writings based on a conservative jurist's *fatwa*. He was assassinated in 1992 by a young fundamentalist who took it upon himself to implement the *fatwa*. In 1993, his colleague Ahmad Subhi Mansour, an Egyptian historian who had studied and taught at al-Azhar, wrote *Ḥadd al-ridda*[52] to criticise the prevailing penalty for apostasy. According to his research, this penalty is the result of the dictatorial Umayyad and ʿAbbasid dynasties to provide cover to advance their political aims under a religious facade. Bridging the gap between the Qur'an's teachings and the Prophet's practised Tradition, on the one hand, and the caliphs' attitudes, on the other hand, was done by fabricating the death penalty for an apostate in a few hadiths attributed to the Prophet. He detailed the absolute fabrication of two hadiths, that of ʿIkrima and of al-Awzāʿī, how their chains of transmissions were fabricated, and how they were inserted into the authentic hadith compilations.[53]

Mansour continued Charafi's work and focused on how those two dynasties shaped Islamic theology and jurisprudence, especially the death penalty for apostasy. His book is important because it provides a great deal of detailed evidence on the fabrication of those hadiths that support the execution of so-called apostates or political dissidents.

## Concluding Remarks

A. Three of these major figures are Egyptian, and the other three are Tunisian. Due to the significance of Mohamed Talbi, Hmida Ennaifer and Abdelmadjid

Charafi's ideas, we can designate Tunisia as the heart of the progressive reformist approach in contemporary Sunni Islam. Egypt has been the heart of both conservative and moderate reformer approaches in Sunni Islam.[54]

B. Although none of them are members of the *'ulamā'*, all of them, except the trade unionist Gamal al-Banna, were professors. Mansour was the former professor of Islamic history at al-Azhar; Muhammad Sa'id al-'Ashmawi, comparative and Islamic law; Mohamed Talbi, historian; Hmida Ennaifer, *shari'a*; and Abdelmadjid Charafi, thought and civilisation. The amount of academic scholarship underlying this approach represents yet another paradigm shift, one that is moving away from the traditional seminary and towards the modern university. Most of these scholars are also historians.

C. The approach's key points could be outlined in the following way: first, religious freedom is the essential principle of Islam. It has never been abrogated, particularised (*takhsīs*) or restricted (*taqyīd*). On the other hand, any conjectural (*ẓannī*) evidence (including isolated hadiths and conjectural indications and significations of the Qur'anic verses or even *mutāwatir* hadith) that contradicts this principle is invalid and unreliable. Thus, this principle is among the strongest principles of Islamic thought.

Second, religious freedom offers equal rights to every human being in terms of voluntarily choosing to join any religion; believing (or not believing) in any teaching and implementing (or not implementing) any of its rulings; preaching his or her religion publicly; criticising other religions and being criticised by them in turn; changing his or her religion and announcing this fact publicly; being or becoming an agnostic or an atheist, and preaching either of them. As none of these can be considered a crime, there can be no punishment for them. In other words, given that religious belief is a personal affair and a private issue between the individual and God, apostasy must be totally decriminalised. No one, including the government and the religious establishment, is allowed to interfere in this relationship.

Third, religion's role in the premodern context differs completely from its role in the modern context. In the former, religion was the core element of identity and therefore leaving it meant changing one's identity and joining the enemy. In the latter, religion has been replaced with the nation-state and citizenship. Whereas apostasy used to be considered high treason, today it is the individual's basic right to leave Islam. Disregarding this paradigm shift has caused a great deal of confusion and misunderstanding.

Fourth, this is a new discourse based on epistemology, philosophy, hermeneutics and history, which means that theology, jurisprudence and law are secondary. The key question is not *how* to punish the apostate, but *why*, why does a Muslim abandon Islam? The answer to this question cannot be found in theology or jurisprudence.

Fifth, among all the other revealed texts, only the Qur'an stresses religious liberty in such a precise, unconditional and unambiguous way. But Islamic theology, jurisprudence, Qur'anic exegesis and hadith compilations went astray at the very beginning. Islamic studies were influenced by Jewish teachings and scholarship, as opposed to those of the Qur'an, on apostasy.

Sixth, those hadiths attributed to the Prophet that support a penalty for apostasy, especially execution, are not only conjectural isolated hadiths that directly contradict the Qur'an, but were also fabricated and forged under the influence of a particular Jewish literature during the Umayyad and 'Abbasid dynasties. Classifying those who dissented from the official Sunni denomination as apostates guilty of *zandaqa* (heresy) has been the Islamic world's official policy since the eleventh century.

## *2 Literature Review of Religious Freedom and Apostasy in Contemporary Shi'i Islam*

The evidence for penalising apostasy in Shi'i Islam is more than that in Sunni Islam, for several hadiths were narrated by the Imams over a period of more than two centuries. Because some of these hadiths are acknowledged as authentic, mainstream Shi'i jurisprudence accepted the penalty consensually. There are differences over a few details, but none over the penalty itself. The change among the Shi'i *'ulamā'* and scholars has been slower and more restricted than among their Sunni counterparts. The Shi'i approaches to this issue can be classified into three categories: conservative, semi-reformer and reformist. Conservative jurists have been in a strong majority, whereas the semi-reformer jurists are in the minority but growing. The reformists are fewer than even the semi-reformers, but they are also growing. This section is longer than the previous one, and most of its data and information is new not only in English but also in Arabic and Persian.

## The Conservative Approach

Modernity has not affected conservativism, even in a minor way. Its jurists understand the subject of and rulings on apostasy as did their pre-twentieth-century predecessors. Thus, their opinion on the penalty for apostasy is absolutely the same as the one held by jurists since the tenth century. I have selected two main texts and two supplementary short texts to analyse in this section.[55]

A. The first main source, the legal rulings in Khomeini's legal manual, presents the typical contemporary Shi'i juridical and official opinion. Ruhollah Mousawī Khomeini (1902–1989) was a Shi'i authority (*marja' taqlīd*), as well as the founder and leader of the Islamic Republic of Iran (1979–1989). Analysed here is a section of his *Taḥrīr al-wasīla*, the most important of his *fatwa* books,[56] which continues to function as the foundation of the *shari'a* rulings and law, including the penal code, in Iran.

An apostate, defined as a Muslim who leaves Islam for unbelief or another religion, is considered either a *fiṭrī* or a *millī* apostate. The first one signifies that he had one Muslim parent at the time of his conception, expressed his belief in Islam after attaining maturity or reaching puberty (*bulūgh*), and renounced Islam later on. The second one signifies one whose parents were unbelievers at the time of his conception, had expressed his own unbelief (*kufr*) after having attained maturity, but at some point became Muslim and, later on, returned to unbelief.

A male *fiṭrī* apostate is sentenced to three punishments: (1) execution; (2) annulment of his marriage without any need to recite the divorce formula; however, his wife must complete the regular term of *'idda* (waiting period) prescribed for a new widow (four months and ten days); and (3) instant forfeiture of his property. After his debts are paid off, the rest of his estate is divided among his heirs (based on the Islamic formula of inheritance). Apparently, these punishments are carried out even if he repents and sincerely professes Islam.

A male *millī* apostate: (1) should be given an opportunity to repent and if he refuses to do so, then he may be killed. However, before carrying out that punishment and based on caution (*iḥtiyāt*), he should be given three days of grace and encouraged to repent and recant. If he persists in his apostasy, then he should be killed on the fourth day. (2) His marriage is automatically annulled immediately if the marriage was not consummated or the wife is in menopause;

otherwise, it would be annulled if he fails to repent during his wife's *'idda*. (3) His property is distributed to his inheritors but only after his death.

A female *fiṭrī* or *millī* apostate: (1) is sentenced to life imprisonment; (2) should be whipped during the five daily prayers and receive only meagre amounts of food and water, as well as insufficient clothes, to induce her to repent and recant. If she does so, she will be freed; and (3) if she did not consummate her marriage, it is dissolved immediately without any need for her to observe *'idda*. If she did, her marriage remains valid if she repents during the regular *'idda* period (three months and ten days). She retains ownership of her property, and it is not distributed until after her death.

A *fiṭrī* or *millī* apostate's prepubescent children are considered Muslim; however, if they choose unbelief after maturity, then they are given a chance to repent. If they refuse to do so, then they should be killed. This also applies to a Muslim's children who reject Islam after having attained maturity but prior to having professed it.

One who hears a person abuse and/or slander the Prophet is obliged to kill him or her without waiting to receive authorisation or consent from the infallible Imam or his general deputy, provided that there is no fear or danger to his and to other believers' life and honour. This obligation is lifted if he fears that doing so will cost him or another Muslim considerable property loss. This same legal ruling applies to one who abuses any of the twelve infallible Imams. With regard to the Prophet's daughter Fāṭima, it depends upon whether insulting her leads to denigrating the Prophet. If it does, then that person must be killed as well.

Any Muslim who hears someone claiming to be a prophet is obliged to kill him or her immediately, except in cases of fear and other extenuating circumstances, as mentioned above. One who professes Islam outwardly but simultaneously says that he does not know if Muhammad was a prophet should also be killed.[57]

B. The second main source of this approach is the long and detailed article on *Irtidād* (apostasy) in *Mawsū'a al-fiqh al-Islāmi tibqan li madhab Ahl al-Bayt*.[58] I will outline this concise article here:

1. Conceptual Discussions
1.1. Apostasy in Islamic studies means disbelief after Islam in either word or deed, regardless of whether Islam preceded disbelief or not. Apostasy is forbidden (*ḥarām*), the greatest sin,

the most heinous rebellion against God, the obscenest type of disbelief, and the harshest in terms of sentence and punishment in this world and the next.[59]

1.2. Jurists have agreed that disbelief after Islam is necessarily apostasy. The criterion of disbelief is denying God or His definitive attributes, the Prophet's prophethood or mission, some of what he brought [in the revelation]; or the religious essentials (*ḍarūriyyat*) such as prayer (*ṣalāt*), fasting, *zakāt*, prohibition of alcoholic drinks, and so on. These essentials require no argumentation and/or demonstration because they are clearly self-evident and accepted by all Muslims.[60]

1.3. Does denying the *madhhab*'s essentials, such as the leadership of one of the Imams, cause apostasy? There are two approaches: (1) Yes for a Shi'i, in contrast to the denial by a Sunni, which does not cause apostasy, and (2) this only causes one to exit the *madhhab*, not Islam.[61]

1.4. The jurists consider that denying the essential proves the denier's apostasy because belief in them is part of the religion. If any denier of an essential does not know that it is as such, then he cannot be considered an apostate.[62]

1.5. The jurists agree that denying an essential causes apostasy. The point of contention here is whether it is an independent cause of apostasy devotionally (*ta'abbudī*) or only if it causes one to deny the Prophet or his prophethood. If such a denier claims to be confused (*shubha*) and his ignorance is probable, then his claim is accepted and the *ḥadd* punishment is suspended.[63]

1.6. The jurists have reached a consensus that blasphemy (*sabb Allāh*, *sabb al-Rasūl* or *sabb* of one of the Imams) is apostasy and the person is considered *mahdūr al-dam* (a guilty person whose blood may be shed with impunity). Blaspheming Fāṭima [the Prophet's daughter] and other prophets is attached to apostasy. Blasphemy and apostasy are not the same, even though sometimes they do occur together; executing a blasphemer does not require the ruler's permission.[64]

1.7. The use of certain phrases found in the works of some jurists indicates that internal disbelief on its own, meaning the lack of any words, deeds, and so on, cannot prove apostasy, for clear expression is required. Proof via words constitutes the explicit indication of denial (*jaḥd*) of a religious essential or belief in a prohibited essential religious belief (e.g., negation of the Creator or prophets and denial of the Prophet or the resurrection). Proof via deed constitutes any action that explicitly indicates one's mockery and hatred of religion, such as writing a book or an article or not implementing the religious essentials in the belief that such actions are permitted.[65]

2. Apostasy's Affirmation

2.1. Apostasy is proved by the confession or testimony of two male witnesses. The testimony of women is absolutely not accepted, regardless of whether it is independent or accompanies the man's testimony, because penalising apostasy is the right of God (*ḥaqq Allāh*) [and there is absolutely no role for women testimony in a case that involves the rights of God]. The testimony should include the circumstances of why one has been accused. As having reached puberty, of sound mind, and free choice are general conditions for the penalty to be applied, minors, the insane and those who are under compulsion cannot be punished.[66]

2.2. As apostasy is chosen deliberately, one who is inattentive (*ghāfil*), asleep, heedless (*sāhī*) or unconscious (*mughmā 'laih*) cannot be punished for it. Whatever one says while in a state of anger that has surged beyond his or her control is excused and excluded. If the person claims that he did not intend to say such things, forgot that its meaning or indication requires disbelief, did not pay attention to it, or narrated it from someone else then his claim is accepted without oath, provided that he is not a known liar.[67]

3. Apostasy's Typology

3.1. The well-known (*mashhūr*) of jurists have classified apostasy as either *fiṭrī* or *millī*. The Islam of the former is not preceded by disbelief, whereas that of the latter is. The former is sentenced to immediate execution and his repentance, if any, is rejected. The minority of jurists did not accept this classification and thus petitions all apostates to repent. The male apostate is executed if he refuses to do so.

3.2. A *fiṭrī* apostate is one who was born into Islam. In the first interpretation, which had become the majority opinion up to the fourteenth century, was that at least one of his parents was Muslim at the time of his birth. In the second interpretation, which has been the majority opinion since the fourteenth century, the relevant criterion is the time of sexual intercourse. However, the jurists disagree over whether it is essential for a *fiṭrī* apostate to be a Muslim after puberty in addition to being born into Islam. Some of them thought that both conditions, or judicial Islam (*al-Islām al-ḥukmī*), were sufficient and that Islam after puberty or true Islam (*al-Islām al-ḥaqīqī*) plays no role in defining apostasy. But Islam after puberty or true Islam is absolutely essential in the other approach, which is stronger because (1) there is no evidence for the sufficiency of judicial Islam, (2) the primary principle is disproving *fitrī* apostasy, (3) the principle of canceling the punishment due to uncertainty (*dar' al-hudūd bi al-shubuhāt*), and (4) the principle of caution when it comes to human life (*al-ihtiyāt fi al-dam*).[68]

3.3. A *millī* apostate is one whose parents were disbelievers at the time of sexual intercourse, and the child converted to Islam and later on left it. All apostates are considered *millīs*, except if certain evidence for classifying them as *fitrīs* is available.[69]

4. Penalties of Apostasy

4.1. The rulings on apostates: these differ whether the [accused] is a *fitrī* or a *millī* and male or female. The penalty of a *fitrī* male apostate is immediate execution without *istitāba* (given a chance to repent). The minority approach supports no classifications at this point and negates the stated punishment of immediate execution without a chance to repent. Evidence for the first approach consists of a few hadiths of the Imams; however, they are contested in terms of their signification and chain of transmission.[70]

4.2. A *millī* male apostate: if he is asked to repent, does so, and returns to Islam, then there is no punishment. If not, his execution is consensual. A female *fitrī* or *millī* apostate is asked to repent. If she refuses, she is imprisoned, pressured, whipped during the prayer times, and subjected to severe punishments until she repents or dies. The evidence for this process is contained in hadiths of the Imams and is not disputed.[71]

4.3. Challenges in repentance of male *fitrī* apostate: (1) absolutely rejecting the option of repentance, both in appearance and internally, leaves all of the rulings intact, even what is between him and his Lord; (2) absolutely accepting the repentance, both in appearance and internally, removes all of the punishments, including execution; (3) accepting his repentance internally but not in appearance. This means that the textual penal codes (i.e., execution, automatic separation from his spouse, and the division of his property among his heirs) are not waived as a result of his repentance, whereas other rulings are; (4) accepting the repentance internally (in what is attached to himself), but not in appearance (in what is related to the others); and (5) accepting the repentance in denial of the essentials (*darūriyyāt*) and not accepting it in denial of the creedal confessions of God's unity and Muhammad's prophethood (*shahādatayn*).[72]

4.4. Ruling of *istitābah*: is asking the female and *millī* male apostate to repent recommended or required? It is described as required. There are three approaches to its duration (in the case of *millī* male apostate): (1) three days, (2) to be continued as long as possible in the hope that he will return to Islam, and (3) not restricted at all. A female apostate absolutely has a grace period of three days, after which, if she continues to refuse to repent, she will be imprisoned.[73]

4.5. Who is responsible or allowed to kill the apostate? There are two approaches: (1) the Imam or his special deputy and, in the absence of both, the general deputy. If a Muslim killed the apostate without first securing the necessary permission to do so, he has committed a sin but is subjected to neither retaliation (*qisās*) nor blood-money (*dīya*), because the deceased apostate's blood was not inviolable (*hadar*); and (2) an apostate can be killed by anyone, a position that relies on a hadith that some jurists have challenged. In the case of blasphemy, the execution does not have to be approved by the Imam or his deputies consensually.[74]

4.6. Some jurists have classified the penalty for apostasy as *ta'zīr* (discretionary punishment) and not as *hadd* (a fixed punishment); however, the majority view it as *hadd.* There are many differences between these two, such as canceling the punishment due to uncertainty (*dar' al-hudd bi al-shubha*); the lack of any oath, guarantee, or intercession in *hadd*; and the Imam can forgive the *hadd* if it was the result of confession instead of testimony.[75]

4.7. If a *millī* apostate repeats his apostasy, there are at least two approaches: (1) he will be executed after the fourth time. There is no specific evidence for execution, and one cannot be executed based on general evidence.[76]

4.8. The second punishment is dividing the apostate's property among his heirs. In the case of a *fitrī* male apostate, his property is seized and divided regardless if he is executed or allowed to live, was attached to the territory of war (*dār al-harb*), or his execution is held up for some reason pending advice from the Imam. The core issue here is his property, before his apostasy. The jurists disagree about the new property he acquires after his apostasy. The female apostate absolutely retains ownership of her property, and it is divided only after her death. This is also the case with a *millī* male apostate.[77]

4.9. The third punishment is annulling the marriage. In the case of a *fitrī* male apostate, his marriage is annulled, he is separated from his wife immediately, and his wife should begin the waiting period of death (*'idda al-wafāt*) even while he is still alive, because apostasy is like death. In the case of a *millī* male apostate, if apostasy occurs before sexual intercourse then the marriage is annulled immediately; if after, then its annulment is suspended up to the end of waiting period. If he returns to Islam during this period, his marriage continues; if not, they are separated. In the case of a female apostate (*fitrī* or *millī*), if the apostasy occurs before sexual intercourse, the marriage is annulled immediately and no waiting period has to be observed. If it occurs after sexual intercourse, then its annulment is suspended up to the end of waiting period for divorce.

If she does not return to Islam during this period, then it is annulled and the spouses are separated.[78]

4.10. General rulings on all types of apostates: (1) an apostate's impurity (*nijāsa*) based on the disbelievers' impurity. There are two approaches here: (a) the impurity of non-Muslims and (b) the impurity of only disbelievers (atheists and polytheists). The apostate will be purified (*tāhir*) after repentance; (2) if the apostate dies (or is executed) without having repented, he or she cannot receive a traditional Islamic burial, including *ghusl* (a mandatory full-body post-death ritual purification), a shroud, the death prayer (*salāt al-mayyit*), and burial in any Muslim cemetery; (3) the former apostate must make up his or her missed prayers after repenting; (4) the apostate cannot be captured and enslaved; and (5) the apostate's guardianship of his children is severed. In addition, (6) the apostate is forbidden to inherit anything from a Muslim. The disbeliever does not inherit from the apostate if the latter has some Muslim heirs. If he does not, then there are two approaches: (a) his inheritance belongs to the Imam and his disbeliever heirs inherit nothing from him, and (b) they inherit from him, but the Imam does not; (7) meat of ritually slaughtered or hunted [animals] by an apostate is prohibited for Muslims; (8) if a Muslim kills an apostate, there is no retaliation (*qisās*) except for paying the blood-money; however, if he had converted to Judaism or Christianity, there are two approaches: (a) no retaliation because his blood was not inviolable; however, the killer committed a sin because he did not have the Imam's permission, and (b) blood-money is required; (9) the apostate's testimony is rejected in cases involving a Muslim or a person like himself due to his ungodliness and evildoing.[79]

4.11.1. Collective apostasy: it was said that there were two types of apostates after the Prophet's death: (1) those who left Islam and became disbelievers, such as Musaylama and his companions, and (2) those tribes that remained Muslim but did not pay *zakāt*. We regard the collective apostates as comprising only the first group.[80]

> 4.11.2. There are two kinds of collective apostasy: (1) leaving Islam, denying it and accepting a new religion (Judaism, Christianity, Zoroastrianism or other religions). The ruling here is the same as the ruling of personal apostasy; and (2) deviating (*intihāl*) from Islam via innovation (*bid'ah*), as seen in the cases of the Exaggerators (*Ghulāt*), anthropomorphists (*Mujasima*), and the Khawarij and Nawāṣib (those who hated the Prophet's Household). The rulings for this kind of apostasy differ from the first kind: 1. If they are in a castle (*mun'a*), they must be fought before fighting the people of war (belligerent disbelievers). 2. Their repentance is absolutely accepted, even if they are *fitrī*. 3. They do not have to make up the prayers they missed during their apostasy.[81]

Two more points that should be added here.

C. Aḥmad Khwānsārī[82] (1887–1985), a distinguished Iranian jurist who was well-known for his caution in issuing *fatwas*, as well as a contemporary Shi'i authority (*marja' taqlīd*), did not discuss apostasy in his *Jāmi'al-madārik fi sharh al-mukhtasar al-nāfi'*. However, following al-Muhaqqiq al-Hillī Ja'far Ibn al-Hassan (1205–1277), he did mention an important criterion in the chapter on *hadd* punishments in the last volume of his book (1981), one that could be applied as penalties for apostasy as well. It deals with restricting the domain of the authoritativeness (*ḥujjiyya*) accorded to "isolated hadiths" (*khabar al-wāḥid*):

> The credibility of an "isolated hadith" (*thiqa* or *'adl*) hadith based on authorization (*tawthīq*) or validating narrators (*ta'dīl*) of the scholars of *Rijāl* (science of transmitters of hadith) is because of the rationale of reasonable people (*binā' al-'uqalā'*) or some hadiths [as the evidence of solitary hadith] is problematic in the case of human life (blood/*dam*), in addition to intensive care in the case of human life (blood). Don't you realize that reasonable people (*'uqalā*) do not confine themselves to solitary authentic (*thiqa*) hadith in critical and vital (*khatīra*) issues, although they confine themselves with "isolated" authentic hadith in other issues?
>
> Al-Muhaqqiq al-Ardabilī Ahmad ibn Muhammad (1500–1585) wrote in his book *Majma' al-fā'ida wa al-burhān fi sharh irshād al-adhān*:

> "Keep in mind! Execution is a great issue, because of the Lawmaker's special concern with protecting human life (*nafs*). As that is the orbit of religious duties and happiness (*madār al-takālif wa al-sa'ādāt*), its protection is mandatory. This principle cannot be abandoned even in the case of a preemptive strike to preserve one's own life. Although human reason may provide some support for this, the preservation of life deserves all possible precautions and considerations."[83]

Khwānsārī applied this principle on several occasions in his book, whereas other jurists issued *fatwas* of execution based on "isolated hadiths" (*khabar al-wāḥid*), and condemned the person to execution except in the case of blasphemy which he neglected to apply.[84] Although Khwānsārī's valuable principle was neglected by both conservative and semi-reformer jurists, it was adhered to strongly by the reformists, as I will show later.

D. Mohammad Rezā Mousawi Golpāyegāni (d. 1993), another contemporary Shi'i authority (*marja' taqlīd*) and well-known conservative jurist, mentioned a very important point in his discussions on Islamic penal codes: "proving apostasy in our age is problematic, because it has been increasing and [becoming] widespread. They make fun of religion and mock the rulings of the *Shari'a* as soon as they see something from the jurists and the clergy or the Muslim government that does not fit their pre-set assumptions. They may say that we [have] abandoned Islam or religion, left the prayer or otherwise."[85]

This conservative jurist was not among those who believed in suspending the penal codes (*hudūd*) during the period of occultation, but rather one who saw the specific implementation of penal code of apostasy in modern times as problematic. Those who could be classified as apostates at this point in time are many, and it would be mistaken to sentence all of them to death. So, he suspended issuing such *fatwas*.

## Concluding Remarks

The key points of this approach could be outlined in this way: first, the main Shi'i sources on penalties for apostates are hadiths of the Imams, most of which are neither Qur'anic verses nor found within the Prophet's Sunna. These hadiths are more in number and more detailed than their

Sunni counterparts and clearer in terms of executing an apostate on the grounds that he has changed his religion. In other words, they were focused on leaving Islam and not necessarily rebelling against it. As some of these hadiths have authentic chains of transmission, the evidence for executing apostates in conservative Shi'i Islam is stronger than it is for its conservative Sunni Islam.

Second, there is big difference between conservative Shi'is and conservative Sunnis. For example, the majority of Shi'is have divided apostates into *fitrī* and *millī*; however, the majority of Sunnis do not categorise apostates in this way. According to the majority of Shi'i jurists, the male *fitrī* apostate should be executed immediately and given no chance to repent. According to the *fatwas* of some Shi'i jurists, such an apostate's repentance is rejected both in appearance and internally (i.e., in this world and the next). Sunni Islam always gives apostates a chance to repent. Shi'i *fiqh* does not allow a female apostate to be executed, as is the case with Hanafi *fiqh*, in contrast to other Sunni legal schools.

Third, one of the most controversial elements of apostasy is denying the religious essentials. In Shi'i *fiqh*, this clearly occurs if, and only if, the apostate himself acknowledges the essentials and then denies them or denies God's unity. Therefore, the focus is on something's essentiality but if the apostate does not think so, then it is incorrect to accuse him of apostasy. This point is not clear in conservative Sunni *fiqh*.

Fourth, a few conservative Shi'i jurists make two astute points: (1) the non-authoritative nature of an "isolated hadith" (*khabar al-wāḥid*) applied to crucial and vital issues, such as execution. This is very close to the idea held by the moderate reformer Sunni jurist Mahmoud Shaltut three decades ago; and (2) the penalty of apostasy is suspended whenever disbelief becomes dominant and the public denial of Islam's essential principles becomes widespread.

Fifth, the Shi'i conservative jurists have paid no attention to the paradigm shift and the profoundly different context of apostasy in the premodern and modern era. We can say that all of these *fatwas*, except the last one, were issued in isolation from the present time and context.

Sixth, although by the early twentieth century the Shi'i jurists were Persian and Arab, the Shi'i authorities and jurists in two main seminaries of Najaf (Iraq), Qom (Iran) and elsewhere since early twentieth century have been Iranian (majority) and Iraqi (minority).

## The Semi-reformers' Approach

This approach is conservative in methodology (i.e., *usūl al-fiqh*), but semi-reformist in terms of *ijtihād* and practice. These jurists seek to restrict the domain of apostasy (conceptual restrictions), harden its approval (approval restrictions) and minimise the number of apostates as much as possible (practical restrictions). Their understanding of modernity, especially of religious freedom, is limited, but they do understand that the issue of apostasy in the modern era injures Islam's credibility. They are also on a spectrum, ranging from semi-conservative to semi-reformist. The criteria of semi-reformers are two: (1) denial of at least one dimension of the conservative approach; and (2) reverting from Islam and engaging in public preaching and non-violent activity against Islam merits execution. Although this approach meaningfully restricts the punishment of apostasy, it does not completely close the door on execution. The threat or abuse of execution remains intact under the trumped-up accusation of "heresy" or instigating "mischief and corruption" on Earth. I chose fourteen figures from this approach and analyse them chronologically.

A. Muhammad al-Khālisī (1888–1963) was an Iranian jurist who lived in Iraq.[86] In 1953, he issued a *fatwa* that a *fitrī* apostate would be asked to repent, the same as a *millī* apostate.[87] Although the execution of a male *fitrī* apostate immediately without accepting his repentance has been the ruling of mainstream Shi'i jurisprudence since the beginning, it never attained consensus. In fact, a few jurists such as Ibn al-Junayd al-Iskāfī Muhammad ibn Ahmad, one of the eleventh-century's first eminent Shi'i jurists, is one of the dissenters. Although his books have not survived, his ideas have been narrated in Shi'i juristic books. Al-Shahīd al-Thānī Zayn al-Dīn al-Juba'i al'Āmilī (Shahīd II) (1506–1558), who narrated Ibn al-Junayd's idea, sounds like he tended to accept his position.[88]

This approach still exists among contemporary Shi'is semi-reformers not only by al-Khālisī, but also by a few jurists whose names I will mention while analysing their ideas.[89] This solution is helpful practically, for it prevents the immediate killing of apostates, especially out of court and without a trial. The other benefit of allowing them to repent removes the classifications of *fitrī* and *millī*, which represents a step forward to decreasing the executions of those accused of apostasy; however, it is not considered a fundamental solution.

B. Muhammad al-Husseinī al-Shirāzī (d. 2001), a prolific Iranian jurist and Shi'i authority (*marja' taqlīd*), wrote: "The proofs of apostasy in hadiths are exclusively applied to individual apostasy. 'Ali ibn Abī Tālib did not accuse any of his opponents in the young community's three civil wars of apostasy. The *ridda* wars (wars of apostasy) after the Prophet's death were purely political in nature."[90] Shirāzī is the second contemporary Shi'i jurist who agreed that a male *fitrī* apostate should be allowed the opportunity to repent.[91]

Al-Shirāzī, basing himself on two proofs, excluded collective apostasy and restricted *fiqhi* discussions to individual apostasy: (1) the wars of apostasy that broke out immediately after the Prophet's death were purely political (the caliph's temporal decision based on his own *ijtihād*); and (2) Ali did not accuse his opponents of apostasy. As it is clear that one's political position or the outbreak of war does not mean abandoning Islam, Shi'i *fiqhī* discussions focus on individual apostasy. This is a helpful point for restricting the penalty of apostasy to religious transgressions only; not for political concerns. I talked about the second point earlier.

C. Mahmoud Ayoub, a Lebanese scholar,[92] emeritus professor of religious and inter-faith studies, and former director of Islamic Studies at Philadelphia's Temple University, analysed both Sunni and Shi'i approaches to this vital issue in his article "Religious Freedom and the Law of Apostasy in Islam".[93] As this is the first such article from a Shi'i perspective, I will outline it in more detail.

This article can be divided to two parts. The first part is Ayoub's reading of general Islamic teachings on apostasy. He wrote from a comparative perspective: "The social and religious problems of apostasy are not unique to Islam and the Muslim community. Rather, the negative attitudes towards apostates and the harsh laws dealing with them have much in common in the three Abrahamic traditions. For all three, apostasy is a public act of religious and social dissent which cuts its perpetrator off from the community socially and spiritually, if not physically."[94]

He continued: "A careful study of the early sources of Islamic tradition reveals an increasingly hardening attitude towards apostasy. This attitude is reflected in the harsh laws which grew harsher as the political, economic and religious interrelations among the three communities of the book worsened."[95] After examining all first-hand evidence, he concluded that "there is no real basis for the *riddah* law in either the Qur'an or Prophetic tradition. Furthermore, the few traditions that exist appear to be late and confused."[96]

He justified the reality of *fiqh* on apostasy in this way: "For Islamic law, this means that apostasy is not only a crime against God, but also potentially it is an act of treachery against the Islamic state and society. Because apostasy is considered as dangerous to social order and security as murder, fornication and highway robbery, like them it is punishable by death."[97] Ayoub's points in this general part are comparable with that of Mohamed Talbī and other figures of the Sunni progressive reformists' approach.

According to him, "Apostasy was never a problem for the Muslim community. It remained a theoretical issue because the people executed for apostasy until the end of the 'Abbasid caliphate in the thirteenth century were very few. Apostasy became a political issue with the rise of Western colonialism and consequent intensification of Western Christian missionary activities in Muslim areas."[98] This claim needs evidence.

His innovative ideas can be found in the second part of the article, which focused on Shi'i hadiths and the *fiqh* of apostasy. Ayoub correctly mentioned that: "Shi'i hadith tradition provides a more extensive treatment of the subject, but this is no doubt due to the fact that Shi'i hadith and legal tradition has had a longer formative period than its Sunni counterpart."[99] On the other hand: "Significantly, Shi'i traditions on apostasy contain neither Prophetic hadiths nor any reference to the actions and opinions of the Prophet's immediate companions. Instead, reports of Ali's treatment of apostates during his short caliphate are used as material sources for the *riddah* law."[100] This point is acceptable if we keep in mind that the hadiths of other Imams are, in total, not less than Imam Ali's, on the one hand, and that it is unclear that Imam Ali's hadiths are necessarily the sources of all hadiths of the other Imams on apostasy.

Ayoub highlighted his third point: "The Imams, from 'Ali to the eleventh Imam Hasan al-'Askari, had to be continuously on their guard against internal extremist religio-political movements. Many non-Arab converts (*mawali*) claimed divinity not only for the Imams, but [also] for themselves as well. Such claims, of course, constituted the worst form of apostasy. Thus, Shi'i tradition provides an interesting context for the account of 'Ali's burning of apostates."[101] It seems that Ayoub accepted the validity of these reports and justified them. This is problematic, for while it is correct that the Imams clearly condemned all such exaggerations, it is also very difficult to find even one authentic hadith that supports executing the Exaggerators, especially by burning. I will return to this point at the end of this section.

The most important point in Ayoub's article is his fourth point: "The Imams after 'Ali, who exercised no civil authority, gave legal pronouncements to hypothetical questions posed by their followers. This fact, as well as the ever present spectre of Shi'i extremism, rendered the Imams' rulings on apostasy both theoretically systematic and unusually severe. These pronouncements, although numerically greater than those of Sunni tradition, are limited to a few Imams."[102]

He expanded on this in his concluding remarks, which show that it is his core point:

> Islamic jurisprudence makes a fundamental distinction between theoretical formulations of law and its practical applications. Thus, while legal judgments may be harsh and uncompromising, they remain somewhat tentative and widely divergent. This is especially true with regard to maximum or ultimate penalties (*hudud*), such as those of adultery, theft, murder and apostasy. This distinction is based on the important cautionary hadith: "Guard against (*idra'ū*) maximum penalties (*hudud*) by means of uncertainties (*shubuhāt*)". Most of the arguments in favor of repentance are meant to remove any doubt regarding an act of apostasy that may be based on ignorance, mental or psychological defect or even imprudence.[103]

This is his innovative, but problematic, point. First, if we assume that this argumentation is correct, then it is exclusive to the teachings of all the Imams except Imam Ali. But this does not work with the first Imam's hadiths that, according to Ayoub, were "used as material sources for the *riddah* law". Second, an apostate can be assassinated secretly, and not executed publicly, as it was mentioned in some weak hadiths attributed to the Imams. Third, Ayoub accepts the harshness of the penalty, but it is only a theoretical formulation for some reason, such as preventing its occurrence, although he claimed that its practical applications were so few. The problem is its theoretical formulation, not its practical application, which means that Ayoub clearly acknowledged the problem and found no solution for it.[104]

D. Muhammad Hassan Mar'ashī Shoushtarī (1937–2008), an Iranian jurist and member of the Iranian Supreme Judiciary Council during the 1980s, wrote in the first book chapter on apostasy in contemporary Shi'i Islam in 1994:

> [the] righteousness of Islam shines, but sometimes [the] human being is afflicted with heart blindness and because of it goes astray . . . It is necessary to guide such a person and return him to Islam. This should be done through the logic of argumentation and demonstration, not the logic of the sword and force. If, after guidance and completing the comprehensive advice, he or she does not accept Islam intentionally and, based on stubbornness, continues in disbelief and apostasy and becomes a harmful and dangerous person for Islam, it is definitely necessary to treat him with reciprocity (*muqābala bi al-mithl*). The rulings of apostates in the hadith and *fiqh* are exclusively about this type of apostate. But if his survival is not dangerous for Islam, then one must not disturb him. In regard to the principle of canceling punishment due to uncertainty (*dar' al-hadd bi al-shubuhāt*), he might return to Islam again if approached with correct and logical methods.[105]

He also supported allowing a male *fitrī* apostate to repent.[106]

Mar'ashī Shoushtarī distinguished between two types of apostate: (1) one who is harmful for Islam; and (2) one who is not. The former is to be punished as stipulated in hadith and *fiqh*, but there should be no punishment for the latter. He clarified the former's subject in this way: "[one] who does not accept Islam intentionally and based on stubbornness". This restriction (*qayd*) plays no role in his ruling, for he paid attention to the probability of the apostate returning to Islam and thus emphasised dialogue and a convincing method, instead of a violent legal method. He was the first Shi'i jurist, at least in this approach, to remove the punishments traditionally meted out to non-harmful apostates. Although the concept of harmfulness needs more clarification and legal restrictions, it nevertheless opened a gate that was gradually fully opened by other jurists.

E. Sayfullāh Sarrāmī (b. 1961), an Iranian scholar and researcher of *fiqh* at the Qom seminary, published the first independent book on apostasy in Shi'i Islam: *Ahkām Murtadd az Didgāh Islām wa Huqūq Bashar* in 1997.[107] Including within its pages both Sunni and Shi'i literature, he analysed the *fatwas* of Shi'i jurists chronologically and found that Abū al-Salāh al-Halabī

Taqī al-Dīn ibn Najm (984–1055) had written that expressing *the slogan of disbelief* (*shi'ār al-kufr*) after Islam is the subject of apostasy. Al-Halabī explicitly mentioned that whatever is known as disbelief by means of demonstration (*istidlāl*) proves only disbelief (*kufr*), not apostasy.[108] In other words, he restricted the subject of apostasy in three ways: (1) expressing clearly not believing; (2) the slogan of disbelief (one's clear rejection of the *shahādatayn*) as opposed to ordinary disbelief; and (3) controversial theoretical details of belief that can be seen through demonstration do not cause apostasy. With these points, he shrank the domain of apostasy. Sarrāmī also highlighted the point of another jurist: apostasy is defined as expressing disbelief in God and his Prophet, as well as rejecting (*jahd*) the essentials of Islam either due to self-ignorance (*tajāhul*) or intentional disregard.[109] Sarrāmī followed these two jurists in terms of restricting the subject of apostasy.[110]

Shi'i *fiqh*'s classification of apostates as either *fitrī* or *millī* is undeniable, even though these terms are nowhere explicitly mentioned in any hadith. A *fitrī* apostate is one who chose Islam freely after reaching the "age of maturity" (different from puberty and may occur prior to it), meaning that he is capable of distinguishing between right and wrong (*sinn al-tamyeez*) (not only born of Muslim parents).[111] After restricting the subject of apostasy to *jahd* (intentional rejection after awareness of the truth), all of the penalties, including execution, are defensible and consistent with Qur'anic principles. He found no inconsistency between the relevant rulings with the foundation of human rights, in terms of the freedom of belief and expression, provided that *true divine guardianship* is considered.[112]

Sarrāmi's book has been among the most cited on this subject, for his goal was to collect the jurists' ideas, conceptual discussions and traditional argumentation for each detail in the hadith, *fiqh* and the Qur'an. He continued and completed Mar'ashī Shoushtarī's idea of restricting the subject of apostasy, as well as supporting decriminalisation in the case without *jahd*. It is one step forward. But he found no problem with executing an apostate with *jahd*, from either the viewpoint of the Qur'an or from the standards of human rights. His understanding of human rights and the Qur'anic principles related to religious freedom is problematic.

F. Muhammad Hussein Fadlallah (1935–2010), an Iraqi Shi'i authority (*marja' taqlīd*) who lived in Lebanon, in 1999 construed the punishments of apostasy to destroying one's Islamic identity through violating the social order or political rebellion against the state, which could be considered treason. However, discussing opposing thoughts is not forbidden. God did not officially proclaim that one could leave Islam, but neither did he say that people could not engage in free discussion and seek the truth.[113]

Fadlallah did not explain how he resolved this contradiction. If a Muslim researcher reaches a conclusion against Islam while seeking the truth and leaves Islam, then what happens to him or her?!

G. Mohammad Mehdi Shamseddine (1936–2001), an Iraqi jurist and president of the Lebanese Supreme Islamic Shi'a Council, wrote in 1999 that if a Muslim begins questioning or losing his faith, then he should refer his questions to Islamic scholars. If they are not resolved, he is not allowed to preach them. If he does, he will be excluded from the community and Islamic political society because Islamic attachments are both cultural and institutional, the institution of community, and the institution of society. If his apostasy changes into a political act against the society and state, he is to be executed for belligerence (*muhāraba*) and corruption (*ifsād fi al-ard*).[114]

Shamseddine divided apostates into three categories: (1) one who does not preach his non-Islamic idea – this type of apostasy is not a crime, and thus there is no punishment; (2) the apostate preaches his non-Islamic new ideas, but does not call for political action against the society and state – this is a crime, and its penalty is exclusion from community; and (3) the apostate becomes involved in political action against the society and state – this is a serious crime, and he should be executed. The first case is the decriminalisation of apostasy, the second case needs further clarification concerning its possibility and difference with the third case, and the third case is controversial because it contradicts the principle of religious freedom (i.e., criminalising non-violent acts against Islam).

Accepting repentance from all apostates, even from a male *fitrī* apostate, Shamseddine was the first contemporary Shi'i jurist to confirm an unlimited period for repentance (*istitāba*) for the apostate. In other words, he not only removed all such categorisations, but also denied that repentance had to occur within three days.[115] Shamseddine's *fatwa* on the latter point has a background in Shi'i *fiqh*[116] and is identical to preventing execution. This important *fatwa* is comparable to Nakha'ī's fatwa and those of his contemporary followers, such as Jāwīsh and Ṣa'īdī in Sunni *fiqh*.

H. Abdul-Karim Mousawi Ardebili (1926–2016) was a Shi'i authority (*marja' taqlīd*) and head of the Supreme Court (Chief Justice of Iran) (1981–1989). Although he published his book *Fiqh al-ḥudūd wa-l-ta'zīrāt*,[117] one of his students also published his recent discussions on the subject.[118] I outline a summary of it here. What is the primary principle in the discussion on apostasy? Killing humankind – as he or she is humankind – is forbidden. Permission to kill a person requires strong evidence. If apostasy is clearly proven, then the relevant ruling is implemented. In ambiguous cases, the person is legally assumed to be Muslim.[119] This is a helpful principle.

The apostasy manifested during the time of the Prophet, as seen in the Qur'an, differs from that seen during the times of the Imams as reported in the hadiths. There was no intellectual apostasy during early Islam, for such events were collective due to the primacy of political, economic or tribal motives. This was also true of people converting to Islam.[120] Ardebili found no punishment for apostasy in either the Qur'an or the Prophet's Tradition. In fact, any such penalties were the exclusive products of those hadiths collected after the Prophet's death.[121]

Apostasy would be *fitrī* type if all four of the following conditions were met: (1) at least one of the parents was Muslim and aware of Islamic teachings at the time of sexual intercourse; (2) this Islam continued until the child was born; (3) at least one parent remained Muslim until the child reached puberty; and (4) the child chose Islam freely and not because he was the child of a Muslim parent and then converted from Islam. If even one of these four conditions were missing, then the apostate would be considered *millī*.[122] Making it harder to consider one a *fitrī* apostate is one step towards minimising immediate execution with no chance of repentance.[123]

**I.** Hossein-Ali Montazeri Najaf Ābādī (d. 2009), in addition to being a Shi'i authority (*marja' taqlīd*),[124] and spokesman for the Assembly of Experts for the 1979 Iranian Constitution, was the most important and highest ranking figure among the semi-reformer jurists. I outline and analyse his ideas and *fatwas* in more detail here, as well as highlight the turning points in his evolving thought. By the 1990s, his ideas were close to those of the conservatives.[125]

In early 2000,[126] he significantly revised his opinion on two issues.[127]

Ruling 3210: the judgement of apostasy cannot be implemented upon one who rejects certain legal rulings that are construed to be "essentials of the religion" (e.g., considers the obligatory ritual prayers to be limited to the period of the dawn of Islam or the modest covering worn by Muslim women (*ḥijāb*) to be optional), because they are not proven and established for him and, as such, he has doubts and misgivings about their validity.

Ruling 3211: in addition to the conditions of maturity or puberty, a sound mind, the freedom of choice and one's intention for the judgement of apostasy to take effect, the person's rejection of Islam must be prompted by obstinacy and animosity. As such, one who reaches a different conclusion (about Islam's validity) based on (his or her own) research and rational proofs would be exempt from the punishment. In addition, it is not far-fetched to surmise that the origin of apostasy at the dawn of Islam was occasioned to deal with some political detractors' intrigues and plots against Islam and the Muslim community, and not due exclusively to changing their religion and manifesting it in public.

In 2004, he provided even greater clarity in his *Resāle-ye ḥuqūq* on the distinction between changing one's religion and apostasy. He formally acknowledged changing one's religion as one of the rights enjoyed by human beings:

> The Right to Change Religion: in reality, the freedom of thought or the right to change it exhibits carelessness and negligence in interpretation, for the genesis of a belief and remaining steadfast in it is caused by a specific mental process that falls outside the scope of human choice. What is accessible to humans (and what they are free to engage in) are the necessary preliminaries that enable one to do it, such as research, study, and mental exertion in order to discover the truth.
>
> Imposing any belief system on any person is neither possible nor proper, for discovering a viewpoint and remaining steadfast in it cannot be foisted upon anyone . . .
>
> Accordingly, every person has the right to practice his religion, regardless of its being true or not. However, while doing so he has no right to insult and ridicule the religion and viewpoints of others and what they hold sacred, or to distort and defame their religion. Mere reversion or change of religion and viewpoint due to animosity and spite are not grounds, in and of themselves, for subjecting one to any penal punishment, provided that there is no criminal punishment prescribed for such an act.
>
> Every person has the right to espouse an opinion and a belief system, make changes to it, disclose it openly, and solicit information on

> different viewpoints and ideas. None of these can be used to implicate him and thereby punish him for "apostasy", "causing mischief and corruption" (*fasād*), "insulting", "defamation" and similar offences.[128]

In 2007, he pointed out the following in his *Islām: Dīn-i feṭrat*:

> The ruling on apostasy applies to cases where the person deliberately plants and disseminates the seed of doubt and scepticism when he himself has already been convinced of [the truth of] Islam . . . The criterion of apostasy is not a change of conviction, because generally belief follows and is linked to the necessary preliminaries (which fall outside the scope of human choice). Rather, it is the intention to create mischief and corruption by way of oppression and cruelty . . . The judgement of apostasy is inapplicable to a person who, for instance, is unable to study the truths of Islam and falls under the influence of the proofs advanced by its opponents; or who, having no intention to conspire against Islam or shake the believers' conviction, gets embroiled in doubt and scepticism on the essential and self-evident rulings or the fundamentals of belief and, as a result of conjectures formulated while searching for truth, opposes certain aspects of religion on the basis of proofs and intellectual discourse.
>
> The decree of apostasy cannot be actualised in the following cases: a person's change of religion is motivated by doubts and he asks someone to dispel them – in such a case, it is obligatory to help him; one who is religiously illiterate; and one whose belief in Islam lacks a solid foundation (i.e., enough depth and sophistication to withstand the effects of doubts and misgivings).
>
> It appears to me that the basis of the ruling on apostasy or on exhibiting zealous hatred (*nāṣibī*) toward the Prophet's family is political and governmental in nature. This ruling has been understood and interpreted in the context of different times, places, issues, and circumstances.
>
> Establishing the crime of blaspheming the Prophet, Fāṭima, the twelve infallible Imams, and other prophets should be undertaken through categorical religiously sanctioned proofs or confession in a competent court and in a free environment. Moreover, an impartial judicial system's implementation of the ruling should not engender significant negative ramifications.

> The only possible way for a qualified judge to obtain a clear-cut intent to insult is by way of self-confession in an open environment. The judge is duty-bound to take into account the legal school of thought (*madhhab*), customs, and social conventions of the accused's region, because while there may be expressions that are generally construed to be insulting and abusive, they may not be so according to the standards of practice and social conventions in a specific locality. In the event of any doubt, the judge must refrain from implementing the punishment.
>
> A judge may pardon a person who has confessed to the crime of blasphemy in an impartial court, because the purpose of all punishments in such cases is to chastise and warn both the defamer and others. It may be appropriate to start with admonishing, instilling fear, intimidating, and then incrementally raising the punishment's severity. The decision to grant a pardon on certain grounds must be made by a qualified and just jurist who is attuned to the context of his time. The standard of determining whether blasphemy has reached the threshold of implementing a punishment is a function of the context of time (*zamān*) and place (*makān*).
>
> The label of "blasphemy" or "defamation" should not be abused to silence critics and/or prevent analyses and knowledge-based objections to religion. People in an Islamic society have a right to ask questions and research all aspects of faith, including monotheism (*tawḥīd*), and Muslim thinkers and researchers are obligated to respond to the critiques with sound logic.[129]

Finally, in 2008 Montazeri explicated his latest opinion in his *Ḥukūmat-i dīnī va ḥuqūq-i insān*:

> Choosing or renouncing a religion and a belief system do not fall under the rubric of apostasy. One who endeavors to search for the true religion and a belief system that is sound [in his view] will naturally select that particular belief system or will convert to it. In both situations, he sincerely believes that it is the truth irrespective of whether the others view it as false and deviant. The label of "apostate" applies to one who is not striving to reach the truth, but rather he knows it and, despite this, challenges it and is adversarial. The essence of the ruling of apostasy is based on hostility, adamance, and disavowal.

> The religious establishment must handle the situation of apostasy delicately, given that it is in tension with the rights of an Islamic society. As such, the crime of apostasy, like the other *ḥudūd* crimes, must be established in a competent religious court through clear-cut and unambiguous religious proofs or confession and carried out by the same impartial Islamic judicial system. Proving this particular crime is fraught with difficulty, because its modality demands certainty (*yaqīn*) in terms of the accused's views. However, this condition can never be met because one can never be privy to another person's inner intentions, as they cannot be attested to by the judge merely on the basis of his/her statements or acts.
>
> The minutest amount of doubt or ambiguity in establishing the crime of apostasy, as well as the other *ḥudūd* crimes and those that warrant discretionary punishment (*ta'zīr*), suspend the punishment's implementation . . . The subject of "apostasy" was broader in scope during the Prophet's time and that of the infallible Imams.[130]

Montazeri's latest opinions on blasphemy and apostasy could be outlined in this way:

1. Changing one's religion without any hostility, enmity or disavowal towards the truth does not, in and of itself, trigger any temporal punishment and, as such, has no association with the penal provisions for apostasy.
2. The label of "apostasy" cannot be applied to a person who rejects the essentials of religion while believing that this does not constitute a negation of prophethood.
3. The rejection of Islam depends upon enmity, hostility and disavowal as constituent components of the "subject of a ruling" (*mawḍū'*) and, as such, changing one's religion (or becoming an atheist) due to personal research and rational proofs precludes one from such a charge. The phenomenon of apostasy invoked at the dawn of Islam was associated with political rebellion and intrigue, and thus was not confined to the changing of one's religious belief and its proclamation. Judgements on apostates and those who are *nāṣibī*[131] are considered to be part and parcel of the political and administrative spheres bound by the context of their own particular time and place.
4. It is not obligatory for an apostate to convey his or her convictions to anyone. Moreover, such a person has an opportunity to repent, which is

between himself and God. This would invalidate the implementation of the three possible forms of punishment mentioned above.

5. A proper and impartial judicial system must adjudicate an alleged case of apostasy or blasphemy. If the person is found guilty, then the same court must implement the punishment, provided that no negative consequences will ensue from it.
6. The judge has to establish that the accused intended to denigrate and defame the Prophet. But he can only do so if the accused voluntarily and freely admits the truth of this charge. The judge must take into account the region's school of thought, culture and social conventions when determining the criterion of insult or offence.
7. Even if blasphemy has been established via personal confession in a competent religious court, the judge has the discretion to forgive the accused. All punishments related to defamation and slander must be carried out under the judge's supervision. Under certain circumstances, he can rescind the punishment and pardon the accused.
8. Scholarly objections and criticisms in an Islamic society should not be construed as defamatory, for these are allowed on any subject matter, even monotheism. The public is free to ask questions and research any aspect of the belief system.
9. With regard to implementing the punishment for certain offences mentioned in the Qur'an (*ḥudūd*) and others (*ta'zīr* (discretionary punishments to chastise and deter)), the slightest amount of doubt in establishing these offences suspends the punishment.

Montazeri has made the implementation of religiously sanctioned punishments for these two crimes extremely difficult and rare by narrowing their subject and situational context. The severe temporal punishment of apostasy can be applied only if an impartial religious judicial system can prove that the accused has renounced his faith out of animosity and stubbornness coupled with engaging in political intrigue and machinations. As for blaspheming the Prophet and other saintly figures (i.e., the Imams), the *ḥākim sharʿ*[132] has the discretion to pardon and waive the punishment even if the person is found guilty and convicted.

J. Mohammad 'Ali Ayāzī (b. 1954), an Iranian scholar of Qur'anic studies at Qom Seminary, wrote a book chapter on apostasy in *Azādī dar Qur'ān* in

2000, which is among the most cited books and contains some courageous new ideas. Just like his mentors Montazeri and Sarramī, Ayāzī restricted the subject matter of apostasy to *jahd*, meaning that the apostate is aware that Islam is true but nevertheless intentionally rejects it.[133]

Along with a few other semi-reformer jurists, he also believed that the repentance of all apostates, even that of a man who has been classified as *fitrī*, is accepted. He distinguished between request of repentance (*istitāba*), on the one hand, and accepting it while simultaneously removing the penalty, on the other hand. If the former is closed in some hadiths, the latter is open and without any obstacle.[134]

Ayāzi clarified that rejecting Islam because of these two causes does not constitute apostasy: (1) incorrect family training; and (2) his Islam was not based on awareness, but only in name without any reality behind it (*Islam ismī*).[135] In other words, just as Mousawi Ardebili contends, disbelief after real Islam, not that type of Islam that is "inherited" from the family without awareness, is the necessary condition for true apostasy. This is an important point.

He correctly mentions that the rulings of apostasy are not unchangeable and permanent in Islam. However, he reached this point from that innovative premise: therefore, its penalty is not *hadd*, but it is a *ta'zir* or governmental ruling and flexible with interests and harms.[136] Just as Sarrāmī had, he concluded, regarding these restrictions, that the penalty for apostasy does not violate religious freedom because it is totally exclusive to a hostile apostate.[137]

At least two innovative points in his book elevate Ayāzī to a position as one of the most progressive semi-reformer figures. First, a person who leaves Islam due to uncertainties (*shubuhāt*) without any evil intention cannot be charged with a crime, because uncertainty is involuntary and ignorance is not the same as guilt.[138] In other words, a crime requires two components: an evil intention and the rejection of the truth even though a person knows that it is true. The first component is a new point.

Second, execution is not the only solution to the problem of apostasy. Contemporary scholars of psychology and sociology, criminology and criminal law are to determine the best policy in this regard. Cultural preventions are far more influential than violent penalties and execution. Execution was the solution for another time and context, not for our time and context. Ayāzī emphasised that responding to the question of *why* (why does a person leave Islam?) is more important than discussing the penalty for apostasy.[139] This outstanding point is comparable with Mohamed Talbi. Acknowledging *fiqh*'s need for the social sciences when it comes to criminalising or decriminalising, as well as the type of penalty for the former, especially in the case of execution, is a very important point. If Ayāzī were to expand this point and activate its huge potentiality as much as possible, it could fundamentally change the problem of apostasy.

K. Mohammad Soroush Mahallāti (b. 1961), an Iranian scholar of *fiqh* at Qom Seminary, criticised[140] both the Sunni and Shi'i semi-reformer and reformist approaches as incorrect and unacceptable. He found that the penalty of apostasy was *ta'zīr* and that all of this section's hadiths, including the famous one narrated by Sunnis ("Kill the one who changes his religion") were governmental rulings and not divine *hudūd* punishments.[141]

Compulsion in religion is forbidden, unless if doing so serves a greater interest.[142] Although no governmental pressure is accepted for converting to Islam, serious obstacles have been created for those who want to leave it. Therefore, the proofs of religious freedom, such as "There is no compulsion in religion" (Q. 2:256), were specified (*takhsīs*) by the rulings of the penalty for apostasy.[143] The principle of proportionality between a crime and its penalty requires that an appropriate type of penalty be imposed on the apostate, and the ruler is responsible for both determining the type and implementing the penalty.[144]

The author concluded that the *fatwa* of Mohammad Fāzel Lankarānī[145] (Lankarānī Sr, 1931–2007) was innovative.[146] This jurist distinguished between disbelief and apostasy. If the problems and doubts reach the level of denying God and the Prophet's mission, then the rulings of apostasy are applied. But if they do not, he or she cannot be subjected to the rulings of an apostate but only excluded from Islam (i.e., he or she becomes a disbeliever).[147]

As I discussed, in Sarramī's book, Abū al-Salāh al-Halabī was the first jurist in the field of Shi'i *fiqh* to distinguish between disbelief and apostasy. A millennium later, Lankarānī Sr revived this distinction.

Although the penalty for apostasy has been one of two approaches in Shi'i *fiqh* since the beginning, the traditional approach was juridical and left it up to the judge's discretion. An approach in contemporary Shi'i jurisprudence known as "governmental ruling" (*al-hukm al-wilā'ī* or *al-hukm al-hukūmī*) denies the *hadd* punishment and supports *ta'zīr*, for this type of *ta'zīr* is in the hands of the ruler of an Islamic state, not a court judge. This type of ruling, which is flexible and includes a spectrum from forgiveness to execution, depends on the apostate's circumstances, the time and the ruler's decision as to whether it is in the interests of the Islamic state and/or Islam. It started out as a probability in Montazeri's early work[148] and was followed by others,[149] Ayāzī in particular, and some of Montazeri's students.[150] Soroush Mahallāti expanded it.[151]

L. Ahmad Qābel (1954–2012), an Iranian scholar of *fiqh* and student of Montazeri, discussed apostasy.[152] If the subject (*mawḍū'*) of "changing religion" manifests itself and is unplanned, then it is considered "involuntary" and falls outside the scope of religious obligations (*takālīf shar'iyya*). In other words, it would not fall under the scope of the jurisprudential discourse on apostasy. As such, changing one's religion is a neutral category that involves no reward or punishment. In the hadiths, four keywords pertaining to apostasy are confirmed: disbelief (*kufr*); polytheism (*shirk*); disavowal and rejection (*jahd*); and doubt (*shakk*). *Kāfir* connotes a person who knows the truth but nevertheless rejects it and defies it out of stubbornness and prejudice, and acts in a manner contrary to the truth. However, belief (*īmān*) and *kufr* are not two polarised ends of a scale, for there is a third category between them: those who reject faith because of faulty research or perplexity. Given that doubting is an "involuntary" act, it should not be equated with rejecting a manifestly clear truth about which one has complete confidence based on one's own study. There is no legal or rational basis for a legal ruling on matters of "doubt". As the discourse on apostasy does not cover this specific issue, which therefore cannot be part of this subject (of apostasy), it therefore falls outside the scope of this discourse.[153] "Involuntary" is an important point in restricting the subject matter of apostasy. This was taught by Montazeri and followed by Ayāzī. Qābel expanded, deepened and clarified it in the case of doubt.

The Qur'an does not mention temporal penal punishment for an apostate. Moreover, it advises forgiveness and prudence even towards those who are guilty of shaking the conviction of new converts by instigating sedition (*fitna*) among them via intrigue and various machinations. This was in line with that era's political context, rationally justified and conformed with the existing social conventions (*'urf*). In other words, it was a reasonable way of respond to the (Medinan) Jews' political intrigues and machinations in kind (*lex talionis*, identical retribution) against the young Muslim community.[154]

Mar'ashī Shoushtarī introduced the important principle of reciprocity (*muqābala bi al-mithl*) and Qābel expanded it. This viewpoint is comparable with that of the Sunni figure Sadiq al-Mahdi.

The Qur'an justifies execution as a penal punishment in only two identified instances: (1) premeditated killing (*qiṣāṣ*);[155] and (2) instigating "mischief and corruption in the land" (*fasād*), which is defined as endangering the lives and property of others. As such, when confronted with a supposed case of apostasy in which the criterion cannot be obtained through reason and supported by a transmitted proof (*dalīl naqlī*), then the penalty of execution can be implemented only if the act truly prompts "mischief and corruption in the land". Clearly, changing one's religion due to being influenced by deficient proofs and logic advanced by those who advocate and defend an opposing worldview, or on the basis of defective and feeble scholarship has no relation with "mischief and corruption in the land".[156] This good argument for restricting executions was started by Mahmoud Shaltut. Qābel continued: the criterion for establishing a true "subject of apostasy" is instigating "mischief and corruption" in the land, a crime that is to be punished by execution. Sentencing and killing a person on account of adopting a new religion, without any intent to mock or insult Islam, or to instigate "mischief and corruption" in the land would, according to the Qur'an, be equivalent to massacring humanity. The only exception would be if it could be established that the person's change of religion leads to an infringement on an inherent right of others. The Qur'an equates the unjust killing of one person with annihilating all of humanity.[157]

Returning to his first point, Qābel concluded that the ruling on apostasy, with all its restrictions and conditions, is political in nature and based upon the principle of "identical retribution". Its intent is to facilitate a reasonable relationship between Muslims and their opponents, like those who instigated sedition through intrigues or non-Muslim belligerents (*muḥārib*). This punishment was designed to ward off and inhibit any seditionist movements, like those incited by the Medinan Jews.[158]

In sum Qābel, just like Montazeri and Ayāzī, made a clear-cut distinction between deliberative and knowledge-based apostasy (*irtidād naẓarī wa 'ilmī*) and political and action-based apostasy (*irtidād siyāsī wa 'amalī*). The former carries no temporal punishment, whereas the latter calls for execution because it has the potential to spread a cancerous tumour in Muslim society.

M. Ahmad 'Ābedinī (b. 1959), an Iranian scholar of *fiqh* at the Isfahan Seminary (Iran) and one of Montazeri's students, discussed three points in his article[159]: the first point is his comparison between hypocrisy and apostasy. Both were disbelievers and tolerated during the Prophet's time, but after his death, two opposite policies became dominant: ease with hypocrites and toughness with apostates. The former were merged into the Muslim community and you do not hear about them after the Prophet's departure. You may even find them among government officials. The severe punishment for apostates was an administrative policy designed to remove political opponents and challengers. It contained no religiosity.[160] This point is comparable with Muhammad 'Abduh, even though it is analysed from a Shi'i perspective.

'Ābedinī critically mentioned a problem: the Imams were silent before this deviation and crisis and practically confirmed the ruling of apostasy. Why? The silence of the Companions, including 'Ali ibn Abi Tālib, proves the validity of these rulings. According to both the Sunni and Shi'i hadiths, 'Ali was severe and more intense when it came to punishing apostates. 'Ābedinī responded to this problem: first, the Imams demonstrated the criteria for us and repeatedly stated "Anything that contradicts the Qur'an, we did not say it" or "we do not say what our Lord did not say". According to this criterion, one cannot attribute to the Imams a ruling (executing the apostate) that was not mentioned in the Qur'an.

Second, the existence of a conflict of interests (*tazāhum al-masālih*) may require one to remain silent about the (official) ruling for a period of time, or not to reject it, or to mention it briefly to scare the criminal, whereas the real ruling is otherwise. If the Imams said that an apostate cannot be executed and therefore defied the government, the disbelievers, opportunists and others would exploit the situation. Based on these concerns, the Imams remained silent about such executions but also emphasised that "We do not say what our Lord did not say" (And our Lord said nothing about executing apostates!).[161]

After Ayoub's brief comparison between the penalty of apostasy during the time of Imam 'Ali and the other three caliphs, this is the first detailed engagement with this comparison. 'Ābedinī's first point requires the invalidity or lack of authoritativeness of all the hadiths attributed to the Imams. His second point is that if the authoritativeness of these hadiths is accepted, then they are justified. Although this justification is not impossible, its acceptance is difficult because it requires more clarification and more proofs that the events mentioned therein actually occurred.

We should keep in mind that this ruling (execution) refers to the age in which the people left the religion for reasons other than scientific uncertainty (*shubha*). Therefore, the hadiths on executing apostates are time-bound and limited to that period and do not fit our age, when scientific uncertainty is dominant and when Islam is supposedly inconsistent with the requirements of the age. The division into *fitrī* and *millī* and the variant rulings on them might return to negate the execution of a person who was probably truly uncertain. Anyway, the ruling of execution (in the Imams' hadiths) was suspended because of dissimulation and regarding the most important interest, or it was the ruling of that time and thus is not a constant (*thābit*) divine ruling for all times. In the other words, when the Imam was asked about the ruling for an apostate, he said: "is executed" (i.e., by the governments and the law of that time), but is this ruling correct or not? The Imam was silent about it. Or when the Imam said: "it is required to execute the apostate" it means during that period and with its specific conditions, and it does not include all apostates.[162]

This represents the continuation of the discussions of Mousawi Ardebili, Ayāzī and Qābel upon which 'Ābedinī expanded and further developed. Acknowledging that this age is dominated by uncertainty is a new point in 'Ābedinī's discussion.

No Imam ever sentenced an apostate to death, reported anyone's apostasy to a caliph, implemented this ruling or commanded their followers to do so, despite the existence of many apostates, such as Ibn Abi al-'Awjā' and other atheists (*dahrīyīn*). They attended the Imam's religious circles, loudly rejected the pilgrimage (*hajj*) and circumambulation (*tawāf*), and even Allah. If executing apostates were among the divine *hudūd* penalties, the Imams would have implemented it in all ways (*subul*), even reporting them to governments. History records no such action by the Imams after Imam 'Ali.[163]

Many stories about executing apostates have come down from the time of Imam 'Ali. After elaborating all of the hadiths in detail, we can say: some of them have problematic chains of transmission. Some of those who were killed were actual criminals and thus were executed for their crimes. Sunnis called them "apostates" to justify their execution, because they believed that all apostates had to be executed.[164] Although Ayoub and 'Ābedinī's justifications are close in the case of Imams, except for Imam 'Ali, their analyses of the historical and hadith proofs about him are completely different.

'Ābedinī concluded that the penalty for apostasy is restricted to a person who absolutely knows the truth but leaves the religion and rejects the truth due to obstinacy, to obtain property, calls others to disbelief and spreads his or her poisonous ideas. However, his analysis excludes two types of persons: (1) the ignorant and those with limited knowledge; and (2) scholars who have given priority to other religions via some wrong premises.[165] His conclusion is comparable to that of Sarrāmi, Montazeri, Ayāzi and Qābel.

In our age, a time when the uncertainties (*shubahāt*) are penetrating the mentalities of the world's youth, how can a religion revealed fifteen centuries ago prepare them for happiness or remove the inconsistencies between science and religion? As these questions have not arisen because of obstinacy, the ruling of execution is therefore negated.[166] This is exactly the conclusion that Golpaygāni reached.

N. Hussain Ahmad al-Khashin (b. 1966), a Lebanese scholar of *fiqh*,[167] published the first independent Arabic-language book on apostasy from a Shi'i perspective, *Al-fiqh al-janā'i fi al-Islām, al-ridda numūzijan*, in 2015. However, he excluded the cases of combined apostasy and belligerence (*muhāraba*), and apostasy designed to tempt Muslims to leave the religion by focusing his discussion on intellectual apostasy.[168]

Implementing the mandatories and leaving the prohibitions are necessary conditions of faith (*īmān*), not of being Muslim. All Muslims are not faithful (*mu'min*), but all faithful persons are Muslims. (This is relatively an innovative point.) Apostasy is the rejection of what is apparent (*zāhiri*) Islam, not of internal faith. Based on this criterion, a child is only attached to the apparent Islam of his or her parents or father. He or she chooses his or her internal faith only after puberty. Leaving Islam as a chosen faith is considered apostasy. A minor attached to a Muslim family even after puberty is not guilty of apostasy and subjected to execution for abandoning Islam, for such an attachment is not the criterion for apostasy.[169]

Apostasy is not leaving Islam, but in addition to becoming a disbeliever (*kāfir*). Islam and disbelief (*kufr*) are opposites, meaning that one cannot be both. Those who leave Islam because of doubt while in a state of searching for the truth or even experiencing stable uncertainty does not mean disbelief, because neither of these reaches the level of infidelity (*jahd*). When one reaches that level, one is an apostate. Throughout the history of Islam, the penalty for apostasy was not the ruling of the Lawmaker (*mawlawi tashrīʿī*) or a *hadd* punishment, but the administrative or governmental (*wilāʾī*) ruling or a *taʿzir* punishment. The punishment was applied not because of leaving Islam, but for rebelling against the Islamic system and joining the Muslims' enemies.[170]

Citing the aforementioned Golpayegānī's decision to negate the punishment of execution for apostasy, al-Khashin concluded that the timely absolute expression (*itlāq zamānī*) of executing an apostate is inapplicable to our time. Just as the penal code for theft (*hadd al-sirqah*) is suspended during a famine, the penalty for apostasy is suspended when suspicions and doubts (*al-shubuhāt wa al-shukūk*) are dominant.[171] This important point is comparable with that of ʿĀbedinī.

From the Qur'anic perspective, its general approach is free thought and free choice in belief as well as the negation of compulsion in the case of religion. The Qur'an supports no worldly penalty for apostasy, especially execution, and thus implicitly denies its validity. In addition, such an execution is rationally unjustifiable.[172]

Khashin explored all the Sunni and Shiʿi hadiths that support this penalty and concluded that they are problematic either in terms of their chains of transmission or content, or in both, and that they are "isolated hadiths" (*khabar al-wāḥid*). The issue of blood (life) cannot be proved by conjectural hadiths, for they cannot provide trust and assurance, and thus any "isolated hadith" that supports this penalty has no probative force and is not authoritative.[173] As he mentioned, this is close to Khwansārī's principle.

The best way to confront heresy (*zandaqah*) is dialogue, not the sword. None of the hadiths about ʿAli executing heretics is authentic. Heresy is divided into two types: (1) a purely intellectual attitude; and (2) destroying the Muslims' beliefs. Although there is no evidence for executing the former, there is for the latter and thus its implementation is accepted.[174]

Most of Khashin's points are compatible with those of Ayāzi, Qābel, ʿĀbedinī and other scholars[175] on these points, and he discussed them in both a disciplined *fiqhī* framework as well as via conventional *usūl al-fiqh*. His interpretation differs completely from Ayoub's in terms of Imam ʿAli's implementing the penalty for apostasy. Khashin's book can be introduced as a comprehensive Arabic-language book on this subject from the Shiʿi perspective. Of course, his justifying execution for the second type of heresy is problematic.

## Concluding Remarks

A. I selected ten Persians and four Arabs as the major representatives of the Shi'i semi-reformer approach. All of the former figures have resided in Iran except Muhammad al-Khālisī, who lives in Iraq. The latter includes two Iraqis (Mohammad Mehdi Shamseddine and Muhammad Hussein Fadlallah) who lived in Lebanon, and two Lebanese, one of whom lives in the United States (Mahmoud Ayoub), and the other who resides in Lebanon (Hussain Ahmad al-Khashin). Except for Ayoub, who studied in American universities, all of the others[176] are *'ulamā'* who studied in traditional Shi'i seminaries mostly in Qom and a few in Najaf (Khālisī and al-Husseinī al-Shirāzī). We can say that Qom is the centre of this particular approach.

B. The academic ranking of these scholars is high. Five of them are grand ayatollahs or Shi'i authorities (*marja' taqlīd*): Khālisī, Husseinī Shirāzī, Fadlallah, Mousawi Ardebili and especially Montazeri. Ayoub is a well-known scholar, and eight are *mujtahids* (jurists or scholars of *fiqh* and Qur'anic studies). I think this represents a weighty dossier for such a "young" and fresh approach.

C. Although the first ideas of this approach were published in 1953 and 1988, most of its works belong to the 1990s, a few to the 2000s, and one to the 2010s. Shi'i scholars published their independent works on apostasy in 1990s: Ayoub's first English-language article appeared in 1994; Mar'ashī Shoushtarī's first Persian-language book chapter in 1994; Sarrāmī's first Persian-language book in 1997; and Khashin first Arabic-language book in 2015.

D. At least twelve points restrict or remove execution for apostates in the semi-reformer approach:

First, leaving "attached Islam" (*al-Islam al-hukmi* or *al-ismī*) is not the same as committing apostasy, for that occurs if, and only if, a post-pubescent person voluntarily chooses Islam with complete awareness (*al-Islam al-haqiqī*) and, at some point in the future, clearly rejects it. The requirement of "real Islam" (*al-Islam al-haqiqī*) seriously minimises the cases of apostasy.

Second, allowing the male *fiṭrī* apostate to repent means that this option is available to all apostates, both male and female, and the *fitrī–millī* division is meaningless. This solution removes the main difference between Shi'i and Sunni *fiqhī* conceptions of apostasy.

Third, there is no limit, such as three days, for repentance because requesting apostates to repent (*istitāba*) is unlimited. Thus, they cannot be executed if they refrain from preaching and any public activity.

Fourth, collective apostasy during the community's early days was an absolutely political act. In contrast to the first caliph, Imam 'Ali never accused any of his political opponents in three civil wars of apostasy. As this is the permanent model for Shi'is, Shi'i *fiqh* is restricted to individual apostasy.

Fifth, the penalty is neither a *hadd* nor a judicial (*ta'zir*) one, but rather a political *ta'zīr* or governmental or administrative ruling. The ruler exclusively decides to either forgive or to punish via execution, imprisonment, exile, financial penalty or deprivation of social privileges or rights.

Sixth, there is a fundamental distinction between theoretical formulations of law and its practical applications. None of the Imams, except 'Ali, exercised any civil authority and thus only made legal pronouncements on hypothetical questions posed by their followers. The Imams' rulings on apostasy, especially on the Exaggerators (*Ghulāt*), were both theoretically systematic and unusually severe. While legal judgements may be harsh and uncompromising, they remain somewhat tentative and widely divergent. In other words, these theoretical harsh punishments were designed to prevent and, for this reason, the number of apostates punished by the Muslim rulers is very low. There was also the cautionary hadith: "Guard against (*idra'ū*) maximum penalties (*hudud*) by means of uncertainties (*shubuhāt*)", which practically prevents the implementation of this ruling.

Seventh, apostasy could occur because of a mistake, and thus neither execution nor any other punishment can serve as a solution. Such people may return to Islam due to cultural activities, advice and dialogue. If their survival does not harm Islam or the society, no punishment is acceptable, for punishment and execution are limited to dangerous apostates.

Eighth, apostates are divided to two types: (1) intellectual apostates; and (2) disavowal and hostile apostates. The former includes researchers who abandon Islam without enmity and those who, based on mistake, leave it. As these are not crimes, there can be no punishment, especially execution. Only the second type of apostate deserves to be punished, even executed. The Imams' hadiths exclusively discuss these people, not those who belong to the first group. In other words, the subject matter of apostasy is not simply leaving Islam, for the required component of its subject matter of apostasy – that its ruling is execution – is rejecting Islam, despite one's complete awareness of its truth, due to enmity and disavowal (*jahd*). According to the Prophetic principle of required precaution when implementing punishments, the judge must tolerate as much as possible when ruling on such a case.

Ninth, decriminalising intellectual apostasy by at least two justifications: (1) there is a clear distinction between disbelief (*kufr*) and faith – on its own, leaving Islam does not constitute apostasy, for that occurs only when one moves beyond doubt and reaches the level of rejection (*jahd*); and (2) changing religion because of doubt, uncertainty and disbelief based on unplanned research occurs "involuntarily". Involuntary action is not the subject of religious duty (obligation or prohibition) or of any punishment, including execution.

Tenth, the rulings of apostasy are neither unchangeable nor permanent divine rulings of Islam. Moreover, execution is not the sole solution for this problem. Contemporary scholars of psychology and sociology, criminology and criminal law can make suggestions about the best policy to pursue in this regard. Cultural preventions are far more influential than violent penalties and execution. Execution was the solution devised for another time and context, not for our own time and context. Responding to the question of *why* (why does a person leave Islam?) is more important than any legal discussion about how to penalise them.

Eleventh, both hypocrites and apostates are disbelievers. However, hypocrisy is not considered a crime and thus cannot be punished. The same is true of apostasy, as seen in the Qur'an and the Prophet's practice. The hadiths attributed to both him and the Imams are unacceptable because no acceptable hadith can contradict the Qur'an. The hadiths attributed to Imam 'Ali by both the Sunnis and the Shi'is have another problem: either their chains of transmission or indications (*dilāla*), or both, are invalid. The authentic hadiths of the other Imams that support punishing apostasy were issued in situations of dissimulation and in the context of striving to attain the most important interest, or it was the ruling of that period and thus is not a divine constant (*thābit*) ruling for all ages. Neither the Prophet nor the Imams ever classified anyone an apostate or executed anyone purely for apostasy. In contrast, the Imams dealt with apostates through dialogue and cultural challenge, not violence.

Twelfth, no "isolated hadith" (*khabar al-wāḥid*) is considered authoritative when dealing with critical issues, especially when a person's blood (life) is involved. All of the hadiths that support penalising apostasy are "isolated hadiths" and therefore absolutely invalid. Moreover, in any era when uncertainty is dominant, all penalties for apostasy are negated. The context in which apostasy (leaving Islam) was criminalised differs completely from the context of our own age.

E. These twelve points are not the same in terms of validity and helpfulness in removing or restricting execution. The first and last four points are necessary for any reform of the rulings on apostasy. Making the ruler responsible for handing down such a decision is identical to politicising Islam or the *shari'a*. The historical problem has been accusing political opponents of apostasy, and the fifth point facilitates this long-standing mistake. The sixth point is no more than an optimistic justification of the problem, and although the seventh and eighth points are a step forward, they decriminalise only the first type of apostasy. It is unclear whether this approach rejects execution. Most of them explicitly supported execution, and thus I called them semi-reformers. In terms of religious freedom, these scholars can be divided to three categories: (1) Ayoub, Ayāzī and Montazeri (in his last works) explicitly advocated religious freedom; (2) Sarrāmī and Soroush Mahāllatī supported *shari'a* rulings that conflict with religious freedom; and (3) the others were in between and did not explicitly express their ideas. Mar'ashi Shoushtari, Sarrāmi, Mousawi Ardebili, Montazeri, Ayāzī, 'Ābedini, and Khashin are almost on the same track in the last point.

## The Reformist Approach

This approach argues that religious freedom is a central principle that should be considered a criterion for accepting other teachings. Choosing a religion (or disbelief, agnosticism or atheism) and then leaving it, implementing its rulings and preaching its teachings are different elements of religious freedom and the core of human rights, which are inalienable and sacrosanct. Therefore, absolutely no punishment is acceptable for apostasy or leaving Islam, which means its absolute decriminalisation. The Qur'an supports this approach. The penalty for apostasy mentioned in the hadiths and *fiqh* are absolutely unacceptable as permanent rulings. The criteria of this approach are (1) decriminalising apostasy explicitly and (2) respecting religious freedom as the essential framework for any lawmaking. I have selected six figures and analysed their ideas chronologically.

A. Mehdi Bazargan (1907–1995), an Iranian intellectual,[177] wrote an article in 1993 titled "Is Islam a Danger to the World?",[178] in which he described individual apostasy in its historical context as something more than simple religious opposition or leaving monotheism. This crime was used to confront theological–political opposition and militant rebellion against the newly born community, or it was about violating their pledges and contracts and thereby committing transgression and rebellion. If not, how was it possible to permit or even command one to kill or issue the ruling of execution or any other violent punishment based on a ruling of faith and religious belief? According to the Qur'an, being a believer or a disbeliever is a private affair, one related directly to the Creator and dependent upon the individual's decision. This means that leaving Islam has no worldly punishment. In the case of blasphemy and insulting the saints and sacred affairs, the Qur'an advised only tolerance and preventing believers from staying in the company of blasphemers. How can we justify the huge threat and violent actions directed towards Salman Rushdie?[179]

Bazargan continued his debate: the reactions of senior religious figures in Iran and other Islamic countries against Rushdie brought him worldwide fame, public support and popularity, and wrongly gave Islam and Muslims the face of violence, ignorance and barbarism. Was it impossible to find a few powerful writers aware of Islam to respond to this ignorant person's baseless novel in a better way, such as with a novel or humour? That which is done with severity and violence, something that unfortunately continues, indicates our inability and weakness more than our righteousness and authority.[180]

Bazargan's third note, published after his death, explicitly rejected killing people for apostasy: "Basically, if one is supposed to execute a Muslim for leaving Islam and that this act becomes the cause of fear, harm and murder, then we are forcing the individuals to follow the religion and pretend religiosity. This clearly violates Q. 2:256, which states that 'There is no compulsion in religion', i.e., coercion and compulsion to the extent of execution occurs."[181]

This is the first explicit rejection of executing an apostate by a Shiʿi scholar and a non-*ʿulamāʾ* intellectual. Bazargan contextualised the relevant hadiths and *fatwa*s and focused on the Qur'anic principle of religious freedom as the permanent foundation of anything done in the name of "Islam". He is clear that we cannot accept any *fatwa* or ruling that explicitly contradicts the Qur'an. Bazargan's argumentation is simple, clear and far from any complexity or ambiguity. In reality, it is the start of establishing a new discourse, one that differs from the legal and old-fashioned *fiqh*-based discourse. His viewpoint is comparable with that of Muhammad Tawfiq Sidqī, his Sunni counterpart.

B. Ali Golzādeh Ghafourī (1923–2010), an Iranian liberal clergyman, scholar of Islamic law and member of 1979 Assembly of Experts for the Iranian Constitution,[182] mentioned during his 1996 interview that apostasy has been discussed in an imitative way without any new research, and thus needs reconstruction and revisiting. God is not a dictator who becomes angry if a person says something wrong. Prophets are not allowed to force human beings to do anything that, as they understand it, violates their reason, or to make rulings that sentence them to death for saying something that is thought to be against religion.

Received narrations and reports are called "God's ruling", but in reality, they are conjectural (*ẓannī*) not only in indication (*dilāla*), but also in transmission (*sudūr*). It is one's human right to follow one's knowledge and determine his or her way clearly. If he or she considers an issue to be imitative (irrational), then it is his or her right to ask questions (i.e., doubt and deny), for not doing so would mean that he or she disregards, even betrays, his or her mentality. If we prevent a person's thinking (and expression of those thoughts), it may change him or her into a pretentious and fawning person, even into a transgressor to him- or herself and others, or a traitor who would live in secrecy and practise dissimulation. We should conduct *ijtihād* on the principles and roots of our beliefs before discussing the derivatives of jurisprudence (*furu' al-fiqh*), such as apostasy.

Any system of thought that trusts itself knows that whenever human beings think, they will reach the results that original reformists discovered for improving humanity. A school or a system of thought that fears questions (and criticism) eventually causes people to open the gate of questioning and criticism, and perhaps question (doubt and criticise) everything. Anyway, doing so is actually a virtue, for it shows dynamism and growth. Those who are responsible for providing answers, especially to the young educated generation in this age of rapidly developing sciences and revisiting values, should investigate why and how these individuals leave their former beliefs and ask themselves why they could not convince, prepare and make this young dynamic generation aware of such things through correct discussions and choosing appropriate ways. Therefore, why should they not revisit their styles and approaches?

There is a big difference between obstinate people and those who search for the truth. The former, though rare, is a harmful person who wants to corrupt society and destroy its integrity. If he or she acts against the public interest, then society makes the final decision as to what to do with him or her. It is not the job of one person (i.e., the ruler). [183]

Golzādeh Ghafourī introduced and clarified the new discourse by first revisiting our understanding of God. God is not a dictator who becomes angry if a person says something wrong! We cannot find divine rulings through conjectural sayings (hadiths), for we need definitive and certain tools. Every person has the right to accept only reasonable teachings and challenge anything without any restriction. We are not allowed to blame those who remain unconvinced by traditional teachings. Theologians, jurists and scholars of traditional Islam should ask themselves what they did wrong while justifying and preaching Islam, for they are the ones who should revise their approaches, instead of compelling and accusing those who disagree with them, namely, dissidents and intellectuals, of apostasy and executing them. Dynamism and freedom of thought are essentials of this new discourse. Structural *ijtihād i*n epistemology and theology is preceded by minor *ijtihād* in legal and *fiqhi* rulings. Although Golzādeh Ghafourī was a scholar of Islamic law and in the vanguard of this new discourse, he only involved himself in the details of structural *ijtihād*'s practical procedures as a general prescription. His viewpoint is comparable with Mohamed Talbi, but does not have the same degree of academic accuracy and depth.

C. Mohammad Javād Mousawi Gheravī (1903–2005), an Iranian dissident jurist in Isfahan, published the second Persian-language book chapter on apostasy, but in the reformist framework in 1998. He wrote that the Qur'an contains no evidence for executing apostates. If this were an actual punishment, the Qur'an would have mentioned it. However, the Qur'an provides a clear statement on everything, especially of those rulings that deal with murder, which is the greatest or most important issue.

Such executions are based on a few weak hadiths that can only provide conjecture (*ẓann*). But what is needed, especially in issues related to blood (life) and killing, is definitive knowledge (*'ilm*). Conjecture is not authoritative (*hujja*). In the other words, these hadiths are "isolated" (*khabar al-wāḥid*) and contain various indications and signification that sometimes contradict each other. Comparing these hadiths with Judaism's ruling on apostasy reveals that it is probable that these hadiths – which are among the weakest in terms of their transmissions, have ambiguous indications and contradict the Qur'an – are calumnies from the Jews. Elaboration substantiates that these fake and fabricated hadiths contradict the Qur'an. *Hadd* punishments are restricted to what is mentioned in the Qur'an.

The apostate is asked to repent and return to Islam after resolving his or her uncertainties, even if doing so takes a long time. As compulsion is forbidden when one is thinking about converting to Islam, coercion cannot be used to force anyone to return to it after he or she abandons it. After this, he or she can repent and re-apostatise two more times and have his or her repentance accepted. If he or she does this a fourth time, his or her repentance is rejected.

Execution for apostasy is nothing but the employment of compulsion in the name of religion. Of course, the apostate, if he or she becomes a *muḥārib* (agent of belligerence), will be executed because of his or her *ḥirābah*. Killing a non-*muḥārib* apostate turns people away from Islam. Forgiveness is required in such cases.[184]

This is the outline of Gheravi's discussion. Apostasy is not a crime, and thus there is no worldly punishment for it. Punishing it makes people lose interest in Islam, so how does it benefit Muslims? Gheravi's concern is not religious freedom or the modern paradigm (although its consequence is modern), but rather a specific approach to the Qur'an. The Qur'an, the clear statement of *everything*, especially of rulings on killing individuals, is the unique source of Islamic law. And, as has been shown above, it contains no evidence for executing apostates. However, he did not clarify if all Qur'anic verses are the cause of definitive knowledge (*'ilm*).

Gheravi criticised the shortcomings of those hadiths that support executing apostates: (1) they are not authentic, which is problematic in Shi'i *fiqh*; (2) they are "isolate hadiths" (*khabar al-wāḥid*) and thus, by definition, can provide nothing more than conjecture; (3) conjecture is not authoritative (*ḥujja*), especially in issues related to blood and human life – these two recent points are exactly what Khwānsārī put forward sixteen years ago in Shi'i *fiqh*; (4) the hadiths that support execution were fabricated; and (5) were calumnies of the Jews. These two points, which are innovative among Shi'is, are close to Mohamed Talbi's research. Gheravi gave no evidence for his claim of fabrication, except that these hadiths contradict the Qur'an. His thought is comparable with Ahmad Subhi Mansour's in almost all details, but with fewer citations in the case of fabricated hadiths.

D. Abdolkarim Soroush (b. 1945), is the most well-known contemporary Iranian public intellectual[185] who stated in his 1999 article that if a person has the right to choose a religion, why does he or she not have the right to leave it? Is that right removed after choosing a religion? Is apostasy in and of itself enough for execution? Is the immediate execution of persons who abandon Islam the best solution for solving this problem? Can any belief cause a person to be excluded from the "circle of humanity"? Are human rights and social advantages dependent upon not changing one's sectarian or theological belief? The self-evident of the premodern age is not self-evident in our own age because of the change in reasonability. The jurists must revisit their self-evident hypotheses by conducting *ijtihād* on principles instead of just on derivatives (*ijtihād fi al-furou'*). This requires revisiting the jurists' epistemological and anthropological hypotheses. The modern world is not that of new derivatives, but of principles. If a thinker or writer criticises a belief, it is a mistake to condemn him or her on the assertion that he or she is insulting the sacred aspects and therefore deserves to be executed.

The rulings on apostasy are based on "isolated hadith" reports (*khabar al-wāḥid*). The reason for their authoritativeness (*hujjiyya*) is the rationale of reasonable people. But reasonable people, when confronted with implementing penalties to resolve issues concerning one's life and honour (*'ird*), are required to use caution or call for suspension (*tawaqquf*). Moreover, the issues of executing apostates, stoning, and so on cannot be proved by "isolated hadiths".[186]

Soroush continued what Golzādeh Ghafourī said, but with a better organised discussion. His work reached more people than did Ghafourī's. In addition, it was a focused criticism of *fiqh* and a written debate with Montazeri. Soroush's discussion is comparable with Mohamed Talbi's in terms of the new discourse. What he outlined briefly was a new Persian-language discourse.

His argumentation on the lack of authoritativeness of an "isolated hadith" (*khabar al-wāḥid*) is exactly the same argumentation made by Aḥmad Khwānsārī in 1981, and it was better organised than Gheravi's discussion on the same subject. His article was cited by most Iranian writers on apostasy, regardless of whether they accepted it or not.

E. Mohammad Mojtahed Shabestari (b. 1936), another well-known Iranian public intellectual,[187] is one of the prominent proponents of religious freedom. He summarises all the articles of the 1948 Universal Declaration of

Human Rights (UDHR) in three general and public principles: (1) freedom of thought, belief and expressing both; (2) the equality of all human beings as regards rights and obligations; and (3) the participation of all human beings in building humanity's social life.[188]

Although Shabestari has not written on apostasy independently, he obviously supports its absolute decriminalisation. He is clear about the right of freedom of religion: "If the UDHR recognizes the freedom of religion even to the extent of denying God and conversion, it means that no individual or state is allowed to force a person to confess God's existence or remain in a religion."[189] One can clearly extract his position on the absolute rejection of any punishment on apostasy, especially execution.

F. Abolghasem Fanaei (b. 1959), an Iranian scholar of the philosophy of ethics,[190] wrote in his 2010 book that the ruling on apostasy is unreasonable and irrational because of many proofs. This approach that the authoritativeness of a belief means that its content must conform to reality has nothing to do with humaneness or happiness, salvation in the next world, or in the praise and reward in this world or next world. What is involved in humaneness and, in consequence, to humanity's happiness is how to navigate freely and select a method of acceptance or rejection of beliefs. We can assume that sometimes apostasy is required both rationally and religiously. Free rational research on the principles of religion would be meaningless with such a ruling (execution for apostasy) and would constitute an imposition beyond the human ability.

The requirement of execution is rationally inconsistent with negating compulsion in religion. From an ethical perspective, we cannot attribute this ruling to God, because an ungeneralisable ruling is either invalid or fundamentally unethical. Muslims do not believe that the followers of other religions, or of no religion, are apostates.

This idea that the life, property and honour of disbelievers, polytheists and dissidents have no sanctity is exclusive to the worldview held by those people who have no regard for the sanctity of life, property and honour of the Shiʿis. This is based on the principle of reciprocity (*muqābala bi al-mithl*), which conflicts with the principle of justice and minimal ethical rationality.[191]

Fanaei not only absolutely decriminalised apostasy, but even went so far as to contend that such an action is required both rationally and religiously. Although some of his general claims need more clarification, his argumentation for rejecting execution and any kind of punishment for apostates is clear, well organised and strong. His approach is comparable with that of Hmida Ennaifer, his Sunni counterpart.

## Concluding Remarks

A. All of the Shiʿi reformists are Iranian. All but Mousawi Gheravī, who studied exclusively in Iran and at traditional seminaries, pursued their graduate studies in Western universities: Bazargan and Golzādeh Ghafourī in France, Soroush and Fanaei in the United Kingdom and Shabestari self-studied in Germany. Bazargan and Soroush are non-*ʿulamāʾ* Islamic scholars; the other four had a background of seminary education. None of them published an independent book on apostasy; Mousawi Gheravi wrote the second book chapter on it. The other five did not even write an independent article on apostasy. Shiʿi reformists began to publish their ideas from 1993; they published their last one in 2010. Half of them have now passed away. Although this "young" approach is an absolute minority within the Shiʿi community, it continues to grow among the graduate generation, academies and even seminaries.

B. This approach could be outlined in the following way:

First, we cannot breathe in the atmosphere of the premodern context. The rulings of apostasy in Shiʿi conservative *fiqh* are unacceptable, unreasonable, unethical and directly contradict the Qur'an's essential teachings.

Second, we need a new discourse to understand apostasy. *Ijtihād* in principle, instead of *ijtihād* in derivatives, requires a new epistemology, theology and a new understanding of Islamic teachings.

Third, the Qur'an mentions no worldly penalty for apostasy. In addition, it also condemns any compulsion and coercion in the case of religion and faith. Executing or punishing apostates in any way at all directly contradicts the Qur'an.

Fourth, premodern Islamic texts could have criminalised apostasy due to the principle of reciprocity; however, this principle no longer exists in the modern non-Islamic world. All of the hadiths that support it are "isolated" (*khabar al-wāḥid*), which cannot be considered authoritative in terms of penal codes, especially when it comes to execution. The definitive and certain evidence required for that ruling is missing. And so, the conclusion is clear: apostasy must be decriminalised absolutely.

Fifth, choosing, keeping, preaching and practising Islam, or not practising its teaching, leaving it, declaring this publicly and preaching against it peacefully are undeniable components of religious freedom, and religious freedom is an essential right of all human beings.

## *3 The Genealogy of the Book's Ideas and its Merits*

After reviewing the Sunni and Shiʿi literature on penalising apostasy and religious freedom, the focus now shifts to the genealogy of the author's ideas on this subject before, during and after writing the book, as well as the limitation of my research. Comparing with other scholars, I try to highlight the book's original contribution and the merits of the English translation to the original Persian text.

This section comprises four parts: an overview of the book, my earliest deliberations on apostasy, reflection on the book's ideas and, finally, the book's story.

### Overview of the Book

This book undertakes, first, to affirm certain positions and to negate others. As for the former, it attempts to establish first the freedom of religion, in particular the freedom to turn away from a religion (i.e., convert from Islam to other religions or atheism), is akin to the freedom to choose a religion at the outset; second, no temporal punishment or penal sanction is prescribed for one who rejects Islam's religious doctrines and the practices pertaining to any of its primary (*uṣūl*) or derivative (*furūʿ*) aspects and, in general, such categories as the essentials (*ḍarūriyyāt*) and issues upon which consensus has already been reached.

As for the latter, this negation applies these issues: (1) the blood of the apostate and blasphemer of the Prophet may be shed with immunity (*mahdūr al-dam*); (2) any worldly punishment for apostate; and (3) executing or severely punishing one who blasphemes the Prophet. If one is found guilty of this latter offence or of denigrating Islam's convictions, that person could be sentenced by a fair judicial system under what is called "hate speech".

The book has two parts. The first deals with the objections to and refutation of Moḥammad Fāzel Lankarānī's (Lankarānī Sr, 1931–2007)

November 2006 decree (*ḥukm*) that made it lawful to assassinate Rāfiq Taqī (1950–2011), who was residing in Baku, Azerbaijan. As a direct consequence of this decree, he was fatally injured in November 2011 and died shortly thereafter due to the multiple stab wounds inflicted on him by his assailants. This section contains the ensuing debate between myself and the jurist's son, Moḥammad Javād Fāzel (Lankarānī Jr, b. 1962), based on *ijtihād* in the foundations and principles. The reader will hopefully get a sense of the proofs advanced by both parties.

The second part examines the reaction to the decrees issued by certain groups of traditional jurists as regards a singer whose lyrics had prompted an upheaval; the release of a derogatory film against the Prophet on the Internet, which resulted in mayhem and blood-letting; and critically scrutinises and questions the unprecedented call for an inquisition in Shiʿism by the defenders of "suffocating the religionist", like Nāṣir Makārim Shīrāzī's *fatwa* against the author of the article "Imam [Ali]: Political Leader or Exemplary Role Model". This part concludes with a critical discussion on the limits of the freedom of religion and the prohibition of hate speech in merciful Islam.

## My Earliest Deliberations on Apostasy

In this part, I chronologically analyse what I published before this book and compare it with the writings of both semi-reformer and reformist Shi'i scholars. It includes four works (two interviews, an article and a letter) in five years since 1999.

A. My first critique of the legal punishment for apostates appeared in early 1999. At that time, I believed that the scope of temporal punishment was constrained on two fronts: (1) the subject of apostasy arises only in cases where rebellion and animosity are present. As such, a researcher who rejects some of Islam's essentials and necessities could not be punished as long as he or she surmises that his or her conclusions are true. Likewise, a person's verbal expression of "doubt" with regard to one of Islam's essentials is not grounds for implementing the rules. (2) The charge must be adjudicated in a fair judicial system so that the accused has the opportunity to defend him- or herself in an open court.[192]

This position could be classified as semi-reformer approach. The first point is compatible with Mar'ashī Shoushtarī and Sarrāmī. The second one was rarely discussed in this approach. Anyway, this is the first and the last work in the semi-reformer framework. I chose the reformist approach two years later.

B. In May 2001, after my release from prison, for the first time I advocated an absolute prohibition against implementing any temporal punishments for one found guilty of apostasy. I wrote:

> A study of the Qur'anic verses on apostasy reveals that:
>
> 1. Recanting one's faith is undoubtedly blameworthy, distasteful and reprehensible. This can be a result of one of two situations: a person's research and deliberation leads him (even if wrong) to deny the existence of God or the Hereafter, reject Islam, and/or doubt its validity, all of which can be labelled "deliberative and knowledge-based apostasy" (*irtidād naẓarī wa ʿilmī*). Or, one may renounce faith and reject the truth, despite knowing it to be true, in order to gain worldly benefits and pleasure or for political and other satanic temptations, as opposed to any personal doubts emanating from his own research and study. This may be called "political and action-based apostasy" (*irtidād siyāsī wa ʿamalī*).
> 2. The Qur'an prescribes no punishment in this life or the afterlife for one who apostatises as a result of his own deliberation and research. However, he will be deprived of the benefits and blessings that would have accrued as a result of finding the truth.
> 3. The Qur'anic punishment of eternal damnation in Hellfire is directed at and confined to those who apostatise due to political or other worldly temptations "after guidance has been made clear to him" (Q. 4:115, 47:25, 32).
> 4. The Qur'an has made (absolutely) no provision for this worldly consequence (e.g., execution or life imprisonment) to be inflicted upon an apostate.

In the same work, I draw the following conclusions on penalty of apostasy in Islam: the Qur'an prescribes no temporal punishment for one who professes a wrong (i.e., non-Islamic) religion or belief system; no force can be used to make him or her change his or her religion; likewise, whereas there is no temporal punishment for an apostate, a severe one awaits him or her in the Hereafter if his or her apostasy is linked with hostility and spite.

Based on the conventional methodology of *fiqh*, Sunni hadiths attributed to the Prophet, and by the Shiʿis to the Imams, are cited in support of executing an apostate on the assumption that their chains of transmission (*isnād*) are reliable. It might be said that if their indication (*dilālat*) is also complete, then there is no option other than to accept these hadiths along with the Qur'anic and rational absolute expressions (*iṭlāqāt*) and generalities (*ʿumūmāt*). However, there are three points to consider here:

First: assuming the validity of these proofs, is implementing the *hudūd* punishment operative only during the presence of the infallibles (the Prophet or the Imams), but suspended during the Twelfth Imam's occultation, or it is an absolute expression (*iṭlāq*), inclusive of both phases? In other words, is it one of the timeless rulings? The majority of Shiʿi jurists (some of whom claim that consensus was reached on this issue) contend that the *ḥudūd* punishments, one of which is said to be for apostasy (based on widespread opinion), cannot be implemented during the occultation. The importance of this point will be further elaborated upon in the light of the numerous objections raised today against punishing apostasy, as according to majority opinion, it is the Twelfth Imam's prerogative to initiate offensive jihad (*jihād ibtidāʾī*) upon his return. The subject of jihad and apostasy share a common point – Islam – for one is entering into Islam and the other is remaining within its fold.

Second: each hadith advanced as proof in favour of executing an apostate is a *thiqa* "isolated report" (*khabar al-wāḥid*),[193] which means that its validity and reliability rests upon the rationale of reasonable people (*sira al-ʿuqalāʾ*). On crucial and vital matters (i.e., the preservation of life), reasonable people would set such reports aside and demand high evidentiary standards: definitive and unequivocal (*qaṭʿī*) proofs in the form of an explicit Qur'anic verse or *mutawātir*[194] hadith. When it comes to killing the accused, the principle of caution (*qāʿida al-iḥtiyāt*) would call for prudence, especially given the great importance that the Lawgiver attaches to the sanctity of life. As such, this particular judgement would be suspended because it demands a definitive proof. In other words, one that is probable or less than certain (*ẓannī*) would not suffice.

Third: threatening one with death for not professing or returning to Islam, as well as for apostatising and abandoning Islam constitutes, without any doubt, a use of force in the matter of religion. Explicit verses (e.g., "There is no compulsion in religion", Q. 2:256) prohibit and negate such coercion. In addition, the hadiths cited conflict with the Qur'anic worldview, which means that the decree on executing an apostate must be rejected and dismissed. These verses do not lend themselves to specification or particularisation (*takhṣīṣ*) and qualification or restriction (*taqyīd*), because they express a rational ruling (like rational desirableness and the goodness of freedom of religion and belief system). Thus, such hadiths are considered invalid (i.e., the precise meaning of these hadiths are not clear for us) and should be relegated to those who are eligible; we should return them to the Imams in order to acquire clarity and remove ambiguities. Until that time, they cannot be implemented.[195]

I was the sixth and youngest Shi'i reformist to reject the penalty of apostasy absolutely. Bazargan, Golzādeh Ghafourī, Mousawi Gheravi, Soroush, Mojtahed Shabestari and I were of the same mind as regards the Qur'anic approach of rejecting any worldly punishment of apostasy. Although Mousawi Gheravi and Soroush criticised the authoritativeness of "isolated hadiths" (*khabar al-wāḥid*) in the case of critical issues such as loss of human life, I cited it to Aḥmad Khwānsārī, the first Shi'i jurist who made his argumentation on this subject. Questioning the legality of punishing apostasy during the Imam's occultation was an original point made by the reformist camp. I continued to emphasise Mojtahed Shabestari's view on religious freedom, which advocates human rights absolutely.

C. In 2001, I prepared and presented a succinct, two-page summary, "The Incompatibility of Traditional Jurisprudence (*Fiqh*) with the Universal Declaration of Human Rights (UDHR)", to Hossein-Ali Montazeri (1922–2009), one of my most revered mentors and teachers, for his legal opinion. After following up and waiting for a few months, it became clear that the resolution to this complex subject would not come about by invoking traditional *fiqh*. Rather, the answer must be sought by formulating a new jurisprudence (*fiqh jadīd*). My mentor compassionately encouraged me to seek out the answer, albeit with the admonition to be cautious while doing so.[196]

In the above letter (8 August 2001) to Montazeri, I had laid out the contradictions between the UDHR and traditional *fiqh* in six areas. The fifth area deals with freedom of belief and religion and the punishment for apostasy. Articles 18 and 19 of the UDHR, as well as the International Covenant on Civil and Political Rights (ICCPR), oppose the existing rulings of apostates and the restrictions placed on protected minorities (*ahl al-dhimma*), the People of the Book (*ahl al-kitāb*) in general, and atheists. Article 6, "arbitrary punishments, harsh punishments, and torture", deals with the conflict between the punishments prescribed for those whose blood it is lawful to shed with impunity (*mahdūr al-dam*), certain *ḥudūd* and *taʿzīrāt* punishments and penal retaliation (*qiṣāṣ*), on the one hand, and Article 5 of the UDHR, Articles 6 and 7 of the ICCPR, and the Convention on the Prohibition of Torture (1984), on the other hand.[197]

The explicit contradiction between traditional Islam and human rights in six areas was an innovative idea. Although my attempt to bring about my mentor Montazeri's engagement with human rights affairs was not successful at that time, a few years later its consequences would appear in his final books.

D. Below is an excerpt from my extensive interview in the summer of 2003 that dealt with apostasy under the subject of human rights:

> It is necessary to have the freedoms of belief and religion in order to afford the equality of rights and non-discrimination. The freedoms of belief and religion, of expressing belief and religion, of practicing religious rituals, of abandoning religious rituals; of changing one's belief and religion; and of propagating one's belief and religion are some of the items that fall in this category. Reason supports the freedom of religion and repudiates any temporal punishment for changing one's religion.
>
> Denying or restricting religious freedom and imposing penal punishments, such as execution and imprisonment coupled with torture, presents a visage of traditional Islam as being unreasonable and weak. Guarding the believers' beliefs is achieved by strengthening their understanding and appreciation of religion, not by repudiating the freedom of religion and belief system. Reason undoubtedly gravitates toward defending the freedom of religion as part of human rights . . . Today's "common sense" cannot accept that one can be punished and even executed in the absence of a competent court and due process in which the accused has no opportunity to defend himself against the accusations levelled against him.[198]

The attempts of Golzādeh Ghafourī, Soroush and Mojtahed Shabestari on the importance of considering human rights in *fiqh* were completed and expanded. The new discourse of removing any penalty for apostasy in the framework of human rights among Shiʿi thinkers is undeniable and continues to grow.

## Reflection on the Book's Ideas

This subsection provides the gist of my views that are elaborated in this work in three parts, in addition to distinguishing the book's innovative ideas or its merits. These parts are, respectively, rejecting any penalty for apostasy and blaspheming the Prophet; the freedom to critique religious beliefs co-joined with the prohibition of engaging in "hate speech", religious censorship and religious despotism (two sides of the same coin), and, finally, original ideas.

### On the Rejection of Penalising Apostasy and Blaspheming the Prophet

A. Islam has presented itself to the people, via clear-cut standards, as the true religion and possessor of sound beliefs. In addition, it has contrasted itself to the corrupt and harmful tendencies of falsehood. Islam envisions humanity's true prosperity as lying in following the true religion and its sound beliefs, and thus any digression from it is considered reprehensible. From Islam's perspective, people have the freedom to choose a religion and a belief system and cannot be compelled to accept the "true religion" and the "right belief system". Islam recognised the diversity of religions and beliefs after its revelation as the divine call to the true religion, in the sense that some responded and others persisted in error. The latter are divided into many groups and sects.

Those who knowingly decide to ignore this invitation out of stubbornness and obstinacy will be punished only in the afterlife. Islam's invitation to others is based on reasoned logic, peace and compassion, as opposed to violence and despotism. Faith pertains to the heart and, as such, it is impossible to force a person to change his or her religion. However, if his or her denial was due to spite and hostility, such a person will face a severe retribution in the afterlife. Given that Islam has inscribed the freedom of religion and faith, any hadith that sanctions killing or shedding an apostate's blood with impunity is incompatible with the noble Qur'an and must be rejected.

B. During the Prophet's time, no one was executed for apostasy. Those who were sentenced to death were guilty of other crimes. The killing of some people during the reigns of the first three caliphs in the so-called *ridda* (apostasy) wars was not endorsed by members of the Prophet's family (*Ahl al-Bayt*). The claim that Imam Ali (601–661), during his caliphate, executed those who had abandoned Islam lacks any credible evidence. Likewise, no Imam ordered such people to be executed. History records that the Umayyad and 'Abbasid rulers executed "apostates"; however, no reliable evidence supports the claim that the Imams endorsed such acts. In conclusion, nothing in the Shi'i corpus establishes that anyone was killed for apostasy due to a judgement rendered by the Imams or with their endorsement and satisfaction.

C. The subject and situational context of apostasy found in the hadiths or juridical works is wider in scope than just changing one's religion or leaving Islam, because at that time it was closely linked with joining Islam's opponents (i.e., the polytheists and unbelievers). These "apostates" not only left Islam, but also engaged in a propaganda campaign against it and joined the enemy's army. This constituted a form of political, cultural and military war against the Muslims. However, the present-day usage of "apostate" is restricted solely to leaving Islam without the additional conditions just stated or any concern over the "person's intention". In other words, this particular term was linked, in the religious judgements of Islam, to political crimes that are akin to non-Muslim belligerence. In contrast, in the intellectual context of our time apostasy is one of the components of humanity's cultural and religious freedom. Undoubtedly, these two contexts are quite distinct.

The Qur'an uses "apostasy" in reference to the hostile unbelievers who deliberately sought to turn Muslims away from their religion through propaganda and instrumentalising "apostasy" to deal a blow to Islam's prestige and image.

Abū Bakr (573–634), the first caliph, was the first to invoke this concept when some Muslims refused to remit their *zakāt* to the central government. The same practice continued under his two successors. In that period, the definition of apostasy was not confined to just exiting from Islam, but was undoubtedly coupled with practical opposition to the government's policies.

The ruling of killing apostates entered Shi'i jurisprudence from the Sunni schools of thought. The so-called prophetic tradition of "Kill the one who changes his religion" was a narration of the school of caliphates (Sunni Islam) from the Prophet; however, the school of the Household of Prophet (Shiʿi Islam) never narrated such a hadith originating from the Prophet.

This judgement, which was linked with political rebellion and joining the enemy by renouncing Islam, was gradually restricted to only changing one's religion. From the tenth century onward, narrations on this subject matter, in this most restrictive sense, have been attributed to the Imams although most of them have no chain of transmitters, contain unknown individuals in the chain or are weak.

If the explanation above fails to establish that the subject matter of "apostate" has undergone any alteration or change – although in my estimation this has been well established – at a minimum it generates ambiguity in terms of sustaining the situational context as it is understood today. The legal maxim of aversion (the lapse of the punishments (*ḥudūd*) in the presence of any doubt or ambiguity) would bar a "presumption of continuity" (*istiṣḥāb*) on sustaining the subject matter and, as a consequence, in sustaining the ruling. In accordance with the Prophet's command, the *ḥudūd* are suspended in the case of doubt and uncertainty, and which doubt can be stronger than that of an altered subject matter?

In actuality, from the tenth century onward a form of exaggerating the Imams' attributes – but not in the extreme – had progressed to such an extent that one could anticipate that any derogatory remarks made against them would result in capital punishment in the future. Moreover, hadiths were fabricated for that very purpose. Since such actions could not be justified without the same ruling for the Prophet, Shiʿi jurists were firmer and more united than their Sunni counterparts in killing those found guilty of blaspheming him.

D. The outcome of interrogating the issues of blasphemy and apostasy is:

- There is no reliable proof from the Qur'an, Sunna, consensus (*ijmāʿ*) or reason that can establish the validity of executing anyone accused of apostasy or blaspheming the Prophet. On the contrary, such actions violate both the Qur'an and human reason. Moreover, the negative effects of allowing such a practice would be numerous and, as such, would certainly weaken Islam.
- Only a sound judicial system can issue a judgement and supervise its implementation. The issuance of a ruling by a *mujtahid* who is qualified

to issue a legal opinion (*fatwa*) in the community without undergoing due process in the state's judicial system does not suffice.

- The Qur'an absolutely pronounces no death penalty on an apostate and a blasphemer of the Prophet. Traditionalist jurists, by employing derivative *ijtihād*, have arrived at this judgement and claimed consensus by relying on "isolated" (*khabar al-wāḥid*), or *muwaththaq*,[199] hadiths. The ruling on killing apostates and blasphemers is incorrect and cannot be implemented on account of the following seven proofs:

  First: the necessity of stopping the execution of an apostate or a blasphemer by invoking the secondary injunction (*ḥukm thanawī*) of "*wahn Islam*"[200] (i.e., implementing the punishment would impair or debilitate Islam; avoiding the harm or seeking public welfare or governmental injunction).

  Second: the necessity of suspending or stopping the *ḥudūd* punishment absolutely or at least the *ḥudūd* that would lead to killing a person during the Imam's occultation (since the mid-tenth century).

  Third: since the judgement on killing is based on *thiqa* "isolated reports" (*khabar al-wāḥid*), it is mandatory to exercise caution on matters that lead to shedding someone's blood (human life).

  Fourth: when dealing with vital and critical issues, all *thiqa* "isolated hadiths" (*khabar al-wāḥid*) are rendered non-probative and non-authoritative.

  Fifth: removing the death penalty for the apostate because of alteration of the subject matter of a ruling or situational context (*mawḍu'*).

  Sixth: hadiths that are contrary to explicit and univocal (*muḥkamāt*) Qur'anic verses are rendered non-probative and non-authoritative.

  Seventh: reason dictates that it is abominable to terrorise a person merely for abandoning Islam or insulting its holy personages.

In conclusion, given that no temporal punishment has been mandated for apostasy, executing anyone for insulting the Prophet, the Qur'an or any of Islam's other sacred objects is indefensible.

E. The right to life has no relationship to one's beliefs and convictions. As the results and consequences of one's faith will only appear in the afterlife, no reward or punishment should be assigned in this world, irrespective of the validity of one's faith. The prescribed punishments to be carried out in this world have to do with the commission of crimes. As no worldly punishment has been assigned for committing sins, apostasy by itself cannot be punished in any way, let alone by capital punishment.

Likewise, there is no worldly punishment for remaining an unbeliever and refusing to embrace Islam. A sound judicial system cannot convict and punish such people, because religion is a matter of the heart and personal choice. In addition, the Lawmaker did not proclaim any punishment in this world or in the Hereafter for erring in one's research and study. Of course, in the afterlife an apostate who rebelled and exhibited hostility and enmity to truth will receive a severe retribution.

## The Freedom to Critique Religious Beliefs Co-joined with the Prohibition of Engaging in "Hate Speech"

There are three essential conditions for "respect to be accorded to the believers and not the beliefs", on the one hand, and the freedom to profess Islam and the freedom of expression on the other: first, the freedom to critique religious beliefs; second, the prohibition on insulting another person's religious beliefs and atheism as constituting "hate speech"; and third, the general nullification of punishments for apostasy, especially capital punishment.

Further explanation: first, according to Islam there is no punishment whatsoever in this life or the afterlife for one who objects to and/or criticises religious beliefs, for one is free to do so. Second, insulting, ridiculing and belittling any religious beliefs (including Islam) are unworthy acts and violate the dignity of those who hold them. In addition, the Qur'an explicitly prohibits insulting atheistic beliefs (Q. 6:108). Third, in accordance with the second part of Article 20 of International Covenant on Civil and Political Rights, "Any advocacy of national, racial or religious hatred that constitutes incitement to discrimination, hostility or violence shall be prohibited by law." Insulting and belittling religious beliefs is an instance of "hate speech", which is currently considered a crime. The accused is to be summoned to a civil court in front of jury trial (a random selection of citizens) for adjudication. Undoubtedly, the punishment meted out would not be execution.

Failing to define the difference between "critique" and "insult", as well as belittling and mocking religious beliefs, has – and will continue to – generated conflicts and propelled violent extremist traditionalist believers to commit acts of cruelty. Mutual respect is an essential condition for a peaceful world. One should anticipate a harsh and extreme reaction from some Muslim traditionalists when their religious beliefs, scripture and/or Prophet are insulted and mocked. After all, Muslims comprise one-fourth of the world's population.

On the other hand, a culture in which a peaceful rivalry between religion and atheism can take place can be created, provided that a clear boundary separates critical analysis from insult. This boundary will be subject to time and place, along with the level of cultural maturity and development. In underdeveloped societies, many of the critiques could be construed as insults, and in developed societies one could perhaps categorise many of the insults as critiques. Establishing such ground rules requires serious theoretical research and fieldwork investigation. In any event, only coupling respect for religious beliefs and freedom of expression can bring about a peaceful and dignified world.

If believers do not have the right to impose their religious beliefs on others, then atheists do not have the right to impose their specific thoughts on others under the guise of universal norms and conventions. Alongside the Universal Declaration of Human Rights, there is a need for a universal declaration on obligations and human responsibilities for those who subscribe to a religious or an atheistic worldview under the category of a "covenant to obliterate all forms of violence, insults and hate speech".

Just as believers must nullify execution and all punishments for an apostate, atheists should proclaim and officially acknowledge that insulting and mocking religious beliefs constitute both a crime and an unworthy act. Both groups need to officially embrace the freedom to critique, as this undertaking is mutually beneficial. A healthy competition is attainable through mutual respect and is the only pragmatic method to defend adherents of all religions, ideologies and ideas.

## Religious Censorship and Religious Despotism: Two Sides of the Same Coin

Some Shi'i traditionalist authorities (*marāji' taqlid*) imagine that Islam in general and Shi'ism in particular can be safeguarded by preventing the spread of thoughts and ideas that conflict with widespread official Shi'i juridical positions. Even though they seem to have no objection to publishing such literature in specialised journals or discussing them in the academy or seminaries, scrutinising the more than four-decade record of the Islamic

Republic of Iran reveals that no such thing has actually happened. This is not merely an empty claim, for it can be fully substantiated.

Such *fatwa*s of these jurists and authorities (*marāji'*) present Shi'ism as extremely regressive and backward, fossilised and despotic, a belief system that can be sustained only by silencing its critics. Given that the available jurisprudence guarding the general populace's beliefs is so feeble – it would be destroyed as soon as it is exposed to and gains familiarity with fresh ideas – this leaves them with only one option to preserve "religious" conviction: to keep the general public's level of discernment and understanding of religion static and to divert their attention by beating their (i.e., the clergy's) laps in an emotional frenzy at the public gatherings for commemorating (the tragedy of Karbalā' in 680). Such a sickly jurisprudence can neither tolerate critical remarks on beliefs nor point to any affinity with the teachings of the Qur'an or the conduct of the Prophet and the Imams. As history shows, both of the latter were exponents of logic, debate and discourse.

The strategy of bullying and intimidating, being domineering and commanding, and muzzling any dissent was invoked by the Umayyads and conflicted with those of the Imams. Such jurists are preoccupied with training and breeding Iranian and non-Iranian students who resemble them: narrow- and closed-minded holders of fossilised ideas. Their stands and legal rulings on the freedom of expression actually help to weaken Shi'ism, and disgrace and humiliate the adherents of Ali, the Commander of the Believers. To date, no religion has progressed by imposing inquisition. The same will be true for Shi'ism, which is currently being pummelled from two directions: (1) "religious despotism" in the name of the Islamic Republic (of Iran); and (2) those jurists who advocate "religious suffocation/censorship" by donning the mantle of guardians of Shi'i Islam, but who, in reality, are debilitating it by means of their inquisition. Such an innovation (*bid'a*) disfigures the luminous visage of the school of *Ahl al-Bayt* by instituting sectarian suffocation/censorship, religious intolerance and religious despotism.

The freedom to express one's opinion on matters of religion and disseminate dissenting views is obligatory (*wājib*). Moreover, remaining silent in the face of *fatwa*s designed to muzzle all dissent, which result in people casting aspersions on the stature of Islam's religious sciences, as well as suspicion and misgiving against honest and principled Islamic scholars, is prohibited (*ḥarām*).

## Original Ideas

The ideas discussed in this book can be divided into two categories.

A. Ideas discussed by other Shi'i scholars earlier and later on expanded in terms of becoming more sophisticated and profound, as well their argumentations being revised and discussed in a better organised *fiqhi* framework. This category could be summarised by four points.

First, the Qur'an supports religious diversity and religious freedom, and restricts any punishment for apostasy to the next world. This view has reached consensus among Shi'i semi-reformers and reformists.

Second, there is no reliable evidence that the Prophet, Imam 'Ali and the other Imams executed anyone just for apostasy or even supported such a punishment. This is a clear proof that the practical Sunna does not support absolutely the execution of apostates. Most of the Shi'i semi-reformers, including Sarrāmī, Montazerī, Mousawi Ardebili and 'Abedinī, supported this important point.

Third, execution for apostates and/or blasphemers is exclusively based on some "isolated hadiths" (*khabar al-wāḥid*). There are at least three solutions here: (1) hadiths that contradict explicit and univocal (*muḥkamāt*) Qur'anic verses are rendered non-probative and non-authoritative. The vanguard of the Shi'i reformists in this solution were Bazargan and Mousawi Gheravi. (2) One must exercise caution on matters that lead to shedding someone's blood (human life). When dealing with vital and critical issues, all *thiqa* "isolated hadiths" (*khabar al-wāḥid*) are rendered non-probative and non-authoritative. Mousawi Gheravi and Soroush were among the first Shi'i reformists to use this solution. (3) Implementing the punishment would impair or debilitate Islam, meaning that it should be stopped by invoking the secondary injunction (*ḥukm thanawī*) of "*wahn Islam*". This is the practical solution of most of semi-reformers.

Fourth, removing the death penalty for the apostate because the subject matter of a ruling or situational context (*mawḍu'*) has changed. The first sparks of this most essential point in revisiting the penalty could be seen in the works of Golzādeh Ghafourī, Sorush, Mojtehed Shabestari, and later Montazeri, Fanaee and 'Ābedini.

B. The second category is this book's original ideas of this book, which can be presented in six points.

First, the necessity of suspending or stopping the *ḥudūd* punishment absolutely, or at least the *ḥudūd* that cause a person's death during the Imam's occultation. I revisited this contemporary conservative *fiqh* solution in the case of apostasy in contemporary Shi'i Islam.

Second, reason dictates that it is abominable to terrorise a person merely for abandoning Islam or insulting its holy personages. Using *wahn Islām* as a primary injunction as opposed to a secondary one, means that the Lawmaker never specified any penalty for apostasy. This essential solution is possible only based on rational principles that are accepted in Shi'i *uṣūl al-fiqh*.

Third, these three comparative inter-denominations of Islam (or Sunni–Shi'i) points are also original: (1) the ruling of killing apostates entered Shi'i jurisprudence from the Sunni schools of thought; (2) the so-called prophetic tradition of "Kill the one who changes his religion" was the product of Sunni Islam during the eighth and ninth centuries – Shi'i Islam has never narrated such a hadith originating from the Prophet; (3) from the tenth century onwards, narrations on the penalty for apostasy as well as blasphemy of the Prophet and even the Imams, in the most restrictive sense, have been attributed to the Imams, although most of them have no chain of transmitters, contain unknown individuals in the chain or are weak. The tenth to the twelfth centuries were a period of exaggerating the Imams' attributes, during which some Shi'is deliberately fabricated many such hadiths.

Fourth, blasphemy and apostasy are separate crimes in traditional Islam. Almost all of the Shi'i semi-reformers and reformists' works focused on apostasy and did not discuss blasphemy either absolutely or in detail. For the first time in Shi'i *fiqh*, blasphemy is now classified under "hate speech", the blasphemer's execution is rejected, and punishment is possible only by the judicial system. This light punishment can be suspended depending upon the level of the society's development.

Fifth, this is the first scholarly debate on the *fiqh* of apostasy between a conservative Shi'i and a reformist Shi'i scholar. In other words, this is a debate of two types of *ijtihad*: (1) *ijtihād* in derivations (*furū' fiqhiyya*); and (2) *ijtihād* in principles and foundations (*mabānī wa uṣūl*). Readers can therefore learn the argumentations in favour of executing apostates and blasphemers from a conservative perspective, and decriminalising apostasy and removing execution and any harsh punishments for blasphemers from a reformist perspective.

This book parallels the debate between 'Abd al-Mit'āl al-Ṣa'idī and 'Isā Manūn in Egypt in 1955, as recorded in *Al-Hurriyya al-Diniyya fil-Islam*.

Both of them were scholars of al-Azhar, the former a reformer and the latter a conservative. About six decades later, two *mujtahids* from the Qom Shi'i Seminary, Moḥammad Javād Fāzel Lankarānī (Lankarānī Jr) and myself, debated the same subject. Although al-Azhar's journal did not publish al-Ṣa'idī's response to Manūn's article, al-Ṣa'idī published the collection of these debates soon afterward in Cairo.

In my case, Lankarānī Jr had no problem when it came to printing and digitising his publications. On the reformist side, however, I have been absolutely banned from publishing (printed and digitalised in all formats, including books, articles, presentations and interviews) since 2009 in Iran. I have posted my debates on my website, which has also been filtered in Iran, first as articles and then as a book in Persian, their original language. As the original Persian-language work could not be circulated in Iran as a printed book, I was forced to publish it online. The book, which has been translated into Arabic and English, will be published at the same time, even though no publisher is permitted to publish the original text in Iran!

Sixth, classifying contemporary Sunni scholars in terms of their views on apostasy was started by Hmida Ennaifer and completed by Abdelmadjid Charafi. I expanded the classification to contemporary Shi'i scholars. This is the first such classification not only in English, but also in Persian and Arabic as well. In this book's Introduction, for the first time ever, the majority of the materials written by Shi'i scholars are compared with each other. In addition, it is a comprehensive comparative study of the penalty for apostasy and of religious freedom that focuses on the genealogy of thoughts both in Sunni and Shi'i Islam. This study highlights the original or innovative points of prominent Sunni and Shi'i thinkers. This comparative study could be continued and expanded as a book. I limited myself to presenting the first part of my research in the form of an introduction.

## The Book's Story

After introducing the book's ideas in the last subsection, I focus on the book's story. It includes four parts: (1) a brief summary as to why I wrote it and a discussion of its structure; (2) its limitation, namely, what the reader should and should not expect; (3) brief discussion of my later ideas that were not presented in the Persian book; and (4) on the substantially expanded Introduction in the English version of the book.

## A Quick Glance at the Book

This book seeks to prove that there are no punishments for apostasy and that one found guilty of blaspheming the Prophet cannot be executed. Alongside defending the right to freely critique religions, insulting the prophets or the scriptures is advanced as being among the criteria of "hate speech" that could be punished by recourse to the judicial system.

The book is divided into two parts: "Apostasy and Blaspheming the Prophet" and "Freedom of Expression and Hate Speech". The former contains two chapters. Chapter 1 includes three sections. The first section is devoted exclusively to the killing of Rāfiq Taqī (1950–2011), an Azerbaijani writer. On the basis of his articles, Lankarānī Sr (1931–2007) and other jurists residing in Qom issued a *fatwa* in early 2006 that he was guilty of apostasy and blaspheming the Prophet and, as a result, sentenced him to death. On 23 November 2011, Taqī died after being fatally stabbed in Baku. Four days later Lankarānī Jr (b. 1962), the late jurist's son, conveyed his joy and delight that his father's *fatwa* had been carried out. The first chapter deals with this ruling and other earlier incidents, as well as with the pronouncement of delight.

In an open letter on 28 November 2011 to my former classmate Lankarānī Jr, I denounced both the decree of death and the declaration of joy, and briefly critiqued the legal judgement of execution and killing someone who has been declared an apostate or a blasphemer. The text of this open letter constitutes the book's second section.

On 13 December 2011, Lankarānī Jr in his "Response to Doubts Surrounding Apostasy", which includes an introduction, six aspects and a few remarks, responded to my objections. This text, reproduced in full, constitutes the book's third section. He defended his father's *fatwa* forcefully and exhaustively, and considered the conservative juridical opinion on the lawfulness of killing an apostate and blasphemer, as well as subjecting them to capital punishment, to be correct.

Chapter 2, the most detailed part, consists of my second open letter to him in January 2012, "Treatise on Refuting the Punishment for Blasphemy and Apostasy". An elaborate treatment of the subject matter under the rubric of demonstrative jurisprudence (*fiqh istidlāl*), it comprises an introduction, ten sections and a conclusion. The proofs, all of which are based on the Qur'an, Sunna, consensus and reason, are presented and then examined in precise detail. The final outcome is that there is no punishment for an apostate, that killing either him or the blasphemer has no reliable evidence, and that executing the latter has no basis at all. Seven proofs, some of which are original, are cited to make this case.

Lankarānī Jr did not respond to this second open letter. In reality, he could not do so. His speech to Qom Seminary students on the need to aggressively defend Islam from malicious attacks and responses to two individuals' queries are reproduced in exactly the same form in Appendix 1.

This dialogue and debate clearly present the two different methods of research in contemporary jurisprudence: traditional *ijtihād* in the derivatives of *fiqh* (*ijtihād sunnatī fī al-furūʿ*) and *ijtihād* in the fundamentals and principles (*ijtihād fī al-uṣūl wa al-mabānī*). This debate, under the rubric of applied jurisprudence and the Islamic sources of criminal law, has produced some original points and perspectives.

Appendix 2 of the Part I contains three subjects: (1) the full translation of Rāfiq Taqī's October 2006 article, "Europe and Us" from the *Sanʿat* newspaper, which prompted the *fatwa* that led to his assassination; (2) two open letters written by Ghonā-ye Tabrīzī (a fictitious name of one of Taqī's Turkish defenders) that raise objections and criticise Lankarānī Jr's pronouncements – in his second letter, Lankarānī Jr responded to one of the points raised by Ghonā without mentioning his name; and (3) the translation of three interviews of Taqī conducted by his supporters prior to his assassination. These provide a useful glimpse into the thoughts that led to his killing.

The Part II pertains to a series of writings, composed from December 2011 to December 2013, on the relation between Islam and the freedom of expression. The first section comprises a short article on the freedom of expression and "hate speech".[201] The second component is an open letter, "Respected Jurists: Instead of Targeting the Effect, Target the Cause",[202] addressed to those jurists who had issued a dubious ruling on the lawfulness of shedding the blood of a singer[203] who had generated a public outcry.

The third section is an interview that took place in September 2012 after the film The *Innocence of Muslims* (with Arabic subtitles) was released on the Internet and the attendant mayhem and blood-letting under the title "Insulting the Prophet is a Form of 'Hate Speech'". The book's fourth and final section analyses and critiques the call for an inquisition in Shiʿism ("suffocating the religionist") by those claiming to be the vanguards of the faith, such as Shaykh Nāṣir Makārim Shīrāzī (b. 1927). He issued a terrifying and horrific *fatwa* against the author of the article “Imam [Ali]: Political Leader or Exemplary Role Model”.[204] The latter constitutes Appendix 3.

## The Book’s Limitations

This book comprises a collection of six pieces of different lengths written from November 2011 to December 2013. Most of the writings are responses that I felt obliged to make in the face of *fatwa*s and rulings, as well as other acts that were being foisted upon the public in the name of Islam in general or Shiʿi Islam as regards the freedoms of religion and of expression. In other words, various parts of it were composed to refute the fossilised and bigoted views being circulated in the name of religion by gathering competing views that have been set aside. The overall goal is to present a narrative that provides an equitable and knowledgeable response to the issue at hand. The ordering of the book’s contents is chronological and has taken shape organically.

The intended readers are jurists, *marājiʿ*, senior seminary scholars and students, academic professors and students of criminal law and criminology, and, in general, anyone who is interested in Islamic jurisprudential and legal discourses. An ordinary reader may find it somewhat laborious, because the language is specialised and coupled with widely used juridical vocabulary. Even then, he or she will not return empty-handed after studying it.

No discourse on religious freedom can be limited to the two vantage points that are the focus of this book (i.e., the freedom to turn away from religion and the freedom to reject its doctrine and ignore some of its fundamentals and practices). Other areas not covered here could include the freedom to proclaim one’s religious identity as well as to propagate one’s religious beliefs, study, publish, hold announced worship services, build places of worship and so on, from the point of view of different schools of thought, both Sunni and other Shiʿi schools, other Abrahamic (i.e., Judaism and Christianity) and non-Abrahamic religions (e.g., Zoroastrianism, Buddhism and Hinduism), and more recent ones (e.g., Babism and Baha’ism).

Although I have done my best to undertake an in-depth and meticulous examination of the subject matter from the Shiʿi Jaʿfarī perspective, along with an exhaustive analysis of the mainstream juridical opinions, I can make no such claim with regard to other Shiʿi (e.g., the Zaydi and Ismaʿili) and Sunni schools of thought. The first two sections of the Introduction provide the genealogy and history of thought on religious freedom and punishment for apostasy since the late nineteenth century.

The book's relevance is not confined to the discussion on Lankarānī Sr's *fatwa* to assassinate Rāfiq Taqī; rather, there is a resemblance to other edicts, such as the atrocious and savage killing of Ahmad Kasravi (b. 1890) by the fundamentalist *Fedāeyān-i Islām* (Devotees of Islam) on 11 March 1946 in court during his trial; the execution of Sudanese thinker and activist Mahmud Muhammad Taha (b. 1909) on 18 January 1985; the assassination of Egyptian writer Faraj Fawda (b. 1945) on 9 June 1992; Sunni and Shi'i *fatwas* against novelist Salman Rushdie (b. 1947) (including the February 1989 *fatwa* of Khomeini), and Egyptian scholar of the Qur'an Naṣr Ḥāmid Abū Zayd (1943–2010). The *shari'a* court declared this last figure to be an apostate but did not implement the traditional punishment. Unfortunately, the contemporary crisis of apostasy is not confined to these six well-known examples.

It is proper and constructive to write scholarly and well-researched responses to defamatory books, articles, films, cartoons and songs, as well as to raise and develop the public's cultural and religious literacy level. If a case truly is defamatory and an insult to believers, then one should follow it up by filing a complaint with the court. In any event, no judgement of capital punishment and allowing someone to shed the accused's blood with impunity can be passed during his absence and without allowing him the right of self-defence.

The brutal killing of Kasravi, the tragic execution of Taha, and, regretful assassination of Fawda did not eradicate their thoughts. The *fatwas* to kill Rushdie made him internationally famous and allowed Islam to be portrayed as a violent religion that opposes religious freedom and possesses fanatical tendencies. The court verdict of apostasy against Abū Zayd only increased the international attention paid to his works and thoughts. The bloody *fatwas* against Kasravi, Taha, Fawda and Taqī, as well as the legal rulings to kill Rushdie and Abū Zayd, must be publicly condemned to prevent their recurrence, for they only weakened and harmed Islam. Issuing such *fatwas* and legal opinions is a sign of weakness and the inability to provide a rebuttal. Condemning these *fatwas* and the subsequent killings should never be construed as justifying or defending of such problematic books or articles. A corrupt and unwholesome idea should be addressed by a scholarly response or by following the dictum that "falsehood fades into oblivion by abandoning its mention" (*al-bātil yamūt bi-tark dhikrihi*) and then, with dignity, ignore and tolerate their dissidence.

## Some New Thoughts since the Publication of the Persian Text

The English translation is being published more than five years after the original Persian book. During that time, I further elaborated on the expectations of religion, the changeability of law, Islamic jurisprudence, Islamic law and the *shari'a*. Although these issues are not directly related to the subject of this book, I mention them briefly at the end of the Introduction.

The expectations of religion could be classified into eight areas. The first four are theoretical and concern belief (i.e., giving the meaning of life and knowledge about God, the next life and the unseen world), and the second four are practical and ethical (i.e., guaranteeing ethics and morality and teaching the worship-related rituals, the boundaries of semi-rituals (e.g., what is permitted and forbidden in terms of drinking, eating and having sex), and the outline of some human interactions (*mu'āmalāt*). Politics, economics, administration and law are not components of religion expectations, for they are the result of human reason and humanity's historical experience and thus changeable and time-bound. One must always remember that there can never be any permanent or timeless law.

So-called Islamic law was the understanding of Muslim jurists derived from the Qur'an, the Sunna and premodern customs. This law fits neither within the modern era nor the contemporary nation-state context. What is related to this book is criminal law. So-called Islamic criminal law, which includes the premodern *hudūd* and *ta'zirāt* punishments, can in no way be termed Islamic criminal law in the present, for criminal law is absolutely secular in nature and determined by each country's parliament or similar institution. Criminology decides what is and is not a crime, and criminal law decides how the perpetrator is to be punished. In brief, it is not for religion, including Islam, to decide in place of criminology and criminal law. The *hudūd* and *ta'zirāt* discussed in the Qur'an and Sunna are time-bound rulings that were appropriate for the past, and neither source contains any evidence that they can be generalised beyond their original contexts and times. According to this reformist approach, blasphemy and apostasy cannot be criminalised. In addition, many proofs oppose execution absolutely or at least in non-murder cases. Thus, (1) neither apostasy nor blasphemy are crimes, and (2) execution is forbidden at least in these cases, if not absolutely.

In this approach, the *shari'a* is defined as Islam's permanent ethical values and moral norms or standards and is not considered to be identical to Islamic law. Moreover, *fiqh* is restricted to worship-related rituals, the boundaries of semi-rituals and the outlines of a few human interactions. Blasphemy and apostasy, as well as other subjects of criminal law, are not elements of *fiqh*.

## English Translation

The English translation is a full rendering of the original Persian book on blasphemy and apostasy. However, it has an added merit as it contains an expanded Introduction (with more than 75 per cent in new content), which provides an overview of the spectrum of views held by the Sunni and Shi'i scholars, embracing different approaches to the subject matter.[205]

I readily welcome all critiques on any aspect of this work. I invite those who are acquainted with Islamic jurisprudence, criminology, criminal law and human rights to share their constructive suggestions and criticisms to help me make the necessary corrections and enhance its quality.

I close this Introduction with a verse from the Qur'an: "I only want to put things right as far as I can. I cannot succeed without God's help. In Him I repose my trust, and to Him I turn" (Q. 11:88).

Mohsen Kadivar
Duke University, Durham, North Carolina
January 2020

## *Notes*

1. Muhammad al-Tāhir Ibn 'Āshūr, *Usūl al-Nizām al-Ijtimā'i fi al-Islām* (Tunisia: al-Shika al-Tūnisiyya lil Tawzī', 1985), 160.
2. Mohamed Talbi, "Religious Liberty: A Muslim Perspective", *Islamochristiana* 11 (1985): 101.
3. Wahba al-Zuḥaylī, *al-Fiqh al-Islāmī wa adillatuh* (Damascus: Dār al-Fikr, 1996), 6:181–186 and 7:621.
4. I intentionally did not select Abul A'lā Maududi (1903–1979), the prolific influential Pakistani activist and thinker, because he is accused of being one of the leaders of Islamic fundamentalism. Thus, there is no need to introduce him as a representative of the Muslim traditionalists and conservatives.

5. Moḥammed al-Ghazālī, *Huqūq al-Insān bayn Ta'līm al-Islām and I'lān al-Umam al-Muttahidah* (Cairo: Nihda Misr, 1963), 79–81.
6. Gamal al-Banna, *Kallā, Thumma Kallā . . . Kallā li-fuqahā al-Taqlid wa Kallā li-Adyā' al-Tanwir: Muhākima al-Fikr al-Misri* (Cairo: Dār al-Fikr al-Islāmī, 1994), 21.
7. Ibn 'Āshūr, *Usūl al-Niżām*, 171–172.
8. Yūsuf Al-Qaradāwī, *Malāmih al-Mujtama' al-Muslim Alldhi Nanshuduhu* (Cairo: Maktaba Wahba, 2012), 31.
9. Yūsuf al-Qaradāwī, *Jarima al-Radda and 'Uqaba fi Daw' al-Qur'an wa al-Sunna* (the author's website,1996), 30–32. '
10. Yūsuf al-Qaradāwī, *Fiqh al-Jihād* (Cairo: Maktaba Wahba, 2014), 197–198.
11. Ibid., 198–199.
12. For a good example of a conservative approach responding to the reformists, consult Fārūq Ibn 'Abdul-'Aleem Āl Mursī, *Fiqh al-Hudūd fi al-Sharī'a al-Islāmiyya: Jarimah al-Riddah: Dirāsa tafsīlīyyah lil-Jarimah wa al-'Uqubah wa Ahkām al-Qadā' al-Misrī al-Mu'āsir* (Egypt: Dār al-Falāḥ lil-Baḥth al-'Ilmī wa-Taḥqīq al-Turāth, 2008).
13. Translation used for all the Qur'anic verses: M. A. S. Abdel Haleem, *The Qur'an: A New Translation* (Oxford: Oxford University Press, 2005).
14. Muhammad Rashid Rida, *Tafsir al-Manār* (Cairo: Dār al-Manār, 1910), 5:327.
15. Muhammad Rashid Rida, *Tafsir al-Manār* (Cairo: Dār al-Manār, 1932), 11:139–140.
16. Muhammad Rashid Rida (ed.), *Majalah al-Manār*, monthly, Cairo, 9(7) (August 1906): 515–525; 10(12) (April 1907): 140; 11(8) (September 1908); 594–598; 11(9) (October 1908): 686–698; 11(10) (November 1908): 771–780. For more information about the critics of Sidqī, see Muhammad Tawfiq Sidqī, Rashid Rida and Tāhā Bushrā, *Hawār hawl al-Islām huwa al-Qur'an wadah*, ed. 'Abdul-'Aziz Hushām (Beirut: Jadāwil, 2011); Muhammad 'Ammarah (ed.), *al-Islam hal huwa al-Qur'an wahda?* (Cairo: Majjala al-Azhar, 2019).
17. Hassan Ibrāhim Hassan, *Tārikh al-Islām al-siyāsī wa al-dīnī wa al-thiqāfī wa al-ijtimā'ī* (Cairo: Maktaba al-Nihda al-Misriyya 1996), 281–288.
18. 'Abdul'Azīz Jāwīsh, *al-Islam dīn al-Fitrah wa al-Hurriya* (Cairo: Dār al-Kitāb al-Misrī, 2011), 231–239.
19. 'Isā Manūn, "Hukm al-Murtadd fi al-Shari'a al-Islāmiyya", *Majjala al-Azhar*, Cairo, March–April 1956, 884–892.
20. 'Abd al-Mit'āl al-Ṣa'idi, *Al-Hurriyya al-Diniyya fil-Islām*, Introduction by 'Ismat Nassār (Cairo: Dār al-Kitāb al-Misrī, 2012).
21. Ibid., 109–110.
22. Mahmoud Shaltut, *al-Islām,'Aqida wa Shari'a* (Cairo: Dār al-Shurūq, 2015), 281. In 1977, Subhi al-Sālih (1926–1986), the Lebanese thinker, chairman of the Supreme Islamic Council in Lebanon, and Secretary General of the Association of Lebanese 'Ulama, said, following Shaltut: "Although this isolated hadith (*khabar wāḥid*) is authentic, cannot be presented as the evidence for execution, as the researchers of Hadith reports and the jurists claim. An execution carried out on the basis of any hadith that does not reach the level of recurrent transmission (*tawātur*) conflicts with those Qur'anic and Prophetic statements that stress protecting human life and blood,

except in exceptional conditions that are determined by the consensus of Muslims. However, there is no such consensus on this matter, because Islam guarantees the religious freedom of all People of the Book, such as Jews and Christians, without compulsion and pressure. Therefore, during the premodern era such execution was the punishment for high treason and the result of religious scheming." Subhi al-Sālih, *al-Islam wa al-Mujtami' al-'Asri: Hawār Thulāthi pawl al-din wa Qadāyā al-Sā'a* (Beirut: Dār al-Ādāb, 1977), 262. He explained this in the same way in his other book, Subhi al-Sālih, *al-Islam wa Mustaqbal al-Hidarah* (Beirut: Dār al-Shaurā, 1982), 213–214.

23. Mahmoud Shaltut, *Tafsīr al-ajzā' al-'shara al-ulā min al-Qur'an* (Cairo: Dār al-Shurūq, 2004), 331–332.
24. Abdul-Hamid Mutawalli, *Mabādi Niżām al-Hukm fi al-Islam ma'a al-Muqārana bil-Mubtada al-Dastūryya* (Alexandria: al-Ma'ārif, 1978), 300–301.
25. 'Abdul-Karim 'Uthman's 1969 approach in *Ma'ālim al-Thaqāfa al-Islāmiyya* (Cairo: Mu'assisa al-Risāla, 1998), 62–63, was close to Mutawalli.
26. Muhammad Fathi 'Uthmān, *al-Fikr al-Islāmi wa al-Tatawwur*, 2nd edn (Kuwait: al-Dār al-Kuwaitiyya, 1969), 266–267.
27. Did 'Uthmān change his mind later? See Muhammad Fathi 'Uthmān, *Huqūq al-Insān bayn al-Sharia wa al-Qānūn al-Gharbī* (Cairo: Dār al-Shurūq, 1982), 104–105.
28. Sadiq al-Mahdi, *Nahw-i Marja'iyya Islāmiyya Mutijaddida* (Cairo: Maktaba al-Shurūq al-Dauliyya, 2006), 97–98.
29. These figures also can be categorised according to this approach: Shaykh Abdur Rahman (d. 2007), *Punishment of Apostasy in Islam* (Lahore: Institue of Islamic Culture, 1972); Mohammad Salim al-Awa (b. 1942), *Fī usūl al-Niżām al-Jinā'ī al-Islāmī* (Cairo: Nihda Misr, [1978] 2006); Abdul Hakīm Hassan al-'īlī, *al-Hurriyāt al-'Āmma fi al-Fikr wa al-Niżām al-Siyāsī fi al-Islām* (Cairo: Dār al-Fikr al-'Arabī, 1983); Rached Ghannouchi (b. 1941), *al-Hurriyāt al-'Āmma fi al-Daula al-Islāmiyya* (Beirut: Markaz Dirāsāt al-wahda al-Islāmiyya, 1993); Ali Gomaa (b. 1952), *al-Bayan limā yashghil al-Azhhān* (Cairo: al-Maqtam, 2005); Javed Ahmad Ghamidi (b. 1951), *The Penal Shari'a of Islam* (trans. Shehzad Salaam (Lahore: Mawrid, 2004).
30. Gamal/Jamal al-Banna was the youngest brother of Hassan al-Banna, founder of the Muslim Brotherhood.
31. Gamal al-Banna, *Ḥurrīyyat al-I'tiqād Fī al-Islām* (Cairo: Dār al-Anṣār, [1977] 1981; *Lasta 'alaihim bi Musaitir [Q. 88:22]: Qadiyya al-Hurriyya fi al-Islām* (Beirut: Mu'assasat al-Intishār al-'Arabī, [1985] 2011); *Kallā, Thumma Kallā; Khamsa Ma'āyīr li-Misdāqiyya al-Hukm al-Islāmī* (Cairo: Dār al-Fikr al-Islāmī, 1997) religious freedom was one of these five criteria; *Al-Islām, wa al-Hurriyya wa al-'Almāniyya* (Cairo: Dār al-Fikr al-Islāmī, 1997); *Ḥurrīyyat al-Fikr wa al-I'tiqād Fī al-Islām* (Cairo: Dār al-Fikr al-Islāmī, 1998); *al-Islam wa Ḥurrīyat al-Fikr* (Cairo: Dār al-Fikr al-Islāmī, 1999); *Tafnid Da'wa Hadd al-Ridda* (Cairo: Dār al-Fikr al-Islāmī, 2006).
32. Al-Banna, *Ḥurrīyyat al-I'tiqād Fī al-Islām*, 34.
33. Muhammad Sa'id al-'Ashmawi, *Usūl al-Sharia* (Cairo: Maktaba Madbūli, 2003), 127–129.
34. Muhammad Sa'id al-'Ashmawi, *Ma'ālim al-Islām*, 2nd edn (Beirut: Intishār al-'Arabi, 2004), 407.

35. Talbi, "Religious Liberty", 99–100.
36. Ibid., 101.
37. Ibid.
38. Ibid.
39. Ibid., 113.
40. Ibid., 102.
41. Ibid., 103.
42. Ibid., 106.
43. Ibid., 108–109.
44. Ibid., 109.
45. Ibid., 112.
46. Ibid., 113.
47. He is the chief editor of *Majalla al-Fikr al-Islami al-Mustaqbali.*
48. Hmida Ennaifer, "*Min al-Riddah ilā al-Imān ilā wa'i al-Tanāqud*", *Al-Hawār*, quarterly, Beirut, 2(7) (1987): 71–78.
49. Or 'Abd al-Majīd Sharafī.
50. Abdelmadjid Charafī, *Al-Islām wa al-Hidātha* (Tunisia: al-Dār al-Tunisiyya fi al-Nashr, 1991), 125–126.
51. Ibid., 126–130. In his other book, *al-Islam bayn al-Risālah wa al-Tārikh* (Beirut: Dār-al-Talī'a 2001), Charafī clarifies his position further.
52. The original book is in Arabic, Ahmad Subhi Mansour, *Hadd al-Ridda* (Beirut: Mu'ssisa al-Fikr al-'Arabi, 2008); translated as *Penalty of Apostasy: A Historical and Fundamental Study*, trans. Mustafā Sābet (Toronto: International Publishing, 1998).
53. Other advocates of this third approach are Abdullahi Ahmed an-Na'im (b. 1946), *Toward an Islamic Reformation: Civil Liberties, Human Rights and International Law* (New York: Syracuse University Press, 1990); Mohammed Abed Al Jabri (d. 2010), *Dimqrātiyya wa huqūq al- insān* (Beirut: UNESCO, 1994); Amel Grami (b. 1962), *Qadiyya al-Ridda fi al-Fikr al-Islāmī al-Hadīth* (Tunisia: Dār al-junūb lil-Nashr, 1996): Aiman 'Abdul Rasoul (1975–2012), "*Min baqāya al-turāth al-siyasi fi al-Islām: hadd al-ridda*", *Adab wa Naqd*, monthly, Cairo, 1998; Mohamed Charfi (1936–2008), *Al-Islam wa al-hurriyya: sū' tafāhum al-tārikhī* (Damascus: Dār Petra, 2002); Abdullah Saeed (b. 1960), co-author, *Freedom of Religion, Apostasy, and Islam* (Aldershot: Ashgate, 2004); Muhammad Shahrour (1938–2019), *Tajfīf Manābi' al-Irhāb* (Beirut: Mu'ssisa al-Dirāsāt al-Fikriyya al-M'aira, 2008); Taha Jabir al-Alwani (d. 2016), *Lā ikrāha fi al-dīn: ishkāliyya al-raddah wa al-murtaddin min sadr al-Islām ilā al-yaum* (Morocco: al-Markaz al-Thiqāfī all-'Arabī, 2014).
54. Half of them passed away during the 2010s; Ennaifer, Charafī and Mansour are still alive. It shows that this approach is far younger than the moderate reformer approach.
55. The general title for Shi'i authorities (*marja' taqlīd*) is "grand ayatollah" (*ayatollah al-'uzmā*) and "ayatollah" for a *mujtahid* or a jurist. I did not use these titles in my Introduction, but called the figures I discussed by their names and introduced all scholars including *'ulama'* briefly in terms of their academic positions in the traditional seminary or modern university, social and political positions, and so on.

56. Khomeini wrote two volumes of this book when he was in exile during the 1950s. It was published in Najaf (Iraq) twice during the 1960s and reprinted repeatedly during the 1970s and the 1980s without any revision.
57. Ruhollah Khomeini, *Taḥrīr al-Wasīla* (Damascus: Iranian Embassy in Syria, 1998). *Kitāb-i irth* under "Mūjibāt-i irth", No. 10; *Kitāb-i ḥudūd* under "al-qaul fi ḥukm al-irtidād", Nos 1 and 4; *Kitāb-i ḥudūd* under "ḥadd al-qadhf", ch. 3, subs. 1 and 2.
58. *Encyclopaedia of Islamic Jurisprudence According to the Doctrine of the Household [of the Prophet]*, 8:353–457. This is the official encyclopaedia of the Iranian Supreme Leader's office and represents the conservative Shi'i jurisprudence. Its chief editor, the jurist Mahmūd al-Hāshimī al-Shāhrūdī (1948–2018), was Chief Justice of Iran (1999–2009) and Chairman of the Expediency Discernment Council from 2017 until his death. In addition, he was one of the main writers of the Iranian Penal Code (*Qānoun mojāzāt Eslāmi*, 2013).
59. Mahmūd al-Hashimi al-Shāhrūdi (chief ed.), *Mawsú'a al-fiqh al-Islāmi tibqan li madhab Ahl al-Bayt* (Qom: Mu'assisa Mawsú'a al-Fiqh al-Islāmi, 2007), 8:353–354.
60. Ibid., 8:354–356.
61. Ibid., 8:356–357.
62. Ibid., 8:357–360.
63. Ibid., 8:360–364.
64. Ibid., 8:364–367.
65. Ibid., 8:367–371.
66. Ibid., 8:372–379.
67. Ibid., 8:379–380.
68. Ibid., 8:380–384.
69. Ibid., 8:384–385.
70. Ibid., 8:385–389.
71. Ibid., 8:389–391.
72. Ibid., 8:395–400.
73. bid., 8:400–405.
74. Ibid., 8:391–392.
75. Ibid., 8:392–394.
76. Ibid., 8:405–408.
77. Ibid., 8:410–417.
78. Ibid., 8:418–425.
79. Ibid., 8:425–454.
80. Ibid., 8:455.
81. Ibid., 8:455–457.
82. Or Khonsārī, Khansārī, Khvānsārī, Khvunsārī.
83. Ahmad Khwānsārī, *Jāmi'al-madārik fi sharh al-mukhtasar al-nāfi'*, ed. Alī Akbar Ghaffārī (Tehran: Maktabat al-Ṣadūq, 1976–81), 7:35.
84. Ibid., 7:109–113.
85. Mohammad Rezā Golpāyegāni, *Al-Durr al-Mandūd fi Ahkām al-Hudūd*, transcribed 'Ali Karīmī Jahromī (Qom: Dār al-Qur'ān al-Karīm, 1996), 3:324.

86. The Iraqi scholar Taha Jabir al-Alwani, mentioned al-Khālisi in addition to other muftis (a Sunni and a Shi'i), who agreed to issue a *fatwa* of apostasy for communists, responding to the request of Iraq's Ba'th political party. Baghdad executed many members of the Communist Party in 1963. (Alwani, *Lā Ikrāha fi al-Din*, 9–10).
87. Al-Khālisī, *Al-Islām sabīl al-sa'ādah wa al-salām* (Beirut: al-Mu'assisa al-Islamiyya lil-Nashr, 1987), 303.
88. Al-Shahīd al-Thānī, *Masālik al-afhām ilā tanqih sharāyi' al-Islām* (Qom: Mu'assisa al-Ma'ārif al-Islmiyya, 2004), 15:24–25.
89. One of them is Mohammad Mousawi Bojnourdī (b. 1943), a member of the Iranian Supreme Judiciary Council during the 1980s, *Fiqh Tatbiqī, bakh Jazā'ī* (Tehran: SAMT, 2008), 127.
90. Muhammad al-Husseinī al-Shirāzī, *Al-Fiqh, vol. 88: Kitāb al-hudūd wa al-ta'zīrāt* (Beirut: Dār al-'Ulūm, 1988), 270.
91. Ibid., 279–280.
92. He gained his PhD in the History of Religion from Harvard University in 1975. His books include *Redemptive Suffering in Islam: A Study of the Devotional Aspects of Ashura in Twelver Shi'ism* ((The Hague: Mouton, 1978); *The Qur'an and Its Interpreters* (New York: SUNY Press, 1984 and 1992); *Islam: Faith and History* (London: Oneworld, 2005); and *The Crisis of Muslim History: Religion and Politics in Early Islam* (Oxford: Oneworld, 2003).
93. Mahmoud Ayoub, "Religious Freedom and the Law of Apostasy in Islam", *Islamochristiana* 20 (1994): 75–91.
94. Ibid., 75.
95. Ibid., 88.
96. Ibid., 84–85.
97. Ibid., 87.
98. Ibid., 91.
99. Ibid., 81.
100. Ibid., 85.
101. Ibid.
102. Ibid., 86.
103. Ibid., 90.
104. The other scholar who should be mentioned as belonging to this approach is Abdulaziz Sachedina (b. 1942), professor and chair of International Institute of Islamic Thought in Islamic Studies at George Mason University, Fairfax, Virginia. Two of his book chapters are related to our subject: "Freedom of Conscience and Religion in the Qur'an", in *Human Rights and the Conflict of Cultures: Western and Islamic Perspectives on Religious Liberty* (Studies in Comparative Religion), co-authored with David Little and John Kelsay (Columbia, SC: University of South Carolina Press, 1988), 53–90; and 'Freedom of Religion and Conscience: the Foundation of a Pluralistic World Order", in *Islam and the Challenge of Human Rights* (Oxford: Oxford University Press, 2009), 185–208.

105. Muhammad Hassan Mar'ashī Shoushtarī, *Didgāhhāye No dar Huqūq Kiifar-eyī Islām* (Tehran: Nashr-e Mizan, 1994), 1:91–92.
106. Ibid., 1:85.
107. Sarrāmī was my classmate and discussant at Qom Seminary during the 1980s. In my capacity as director of the Islamic Thought section of the Strategic Research Centre during the 1990s in Qom, I suggested this topic to him. Sarrami researched it, and the Centre published his book. Muhammad Hassan Mar'ashī Shoushtarī was one of his advisory committee's three members.
108. Abū al-Salāh al-Halabī, *al-Kāfi fi al-Fiqh*, ed. Reza Ostādī (Esfahan: Maktaba al-Imam Amir al-Mu'minīn, 1983), 311.
109. Qutb al-Dīn al-Bayhaqī al-Kaydarī, *Isbāh al-Shi'a bi Misbāh al-Shari'a*, ed. Ibrāhim al-Bahāduri (Qom: Mu'assisat al-Imām al-Sādiq, 1995/6), 191. Sarrāmī (p. 220) narrated this quotation from Ali Asghar Morvarīd, *Silsilah al-Yanābī' al-Fiqhiyya* (Beirut: Mu'assisi Fiqh al-Shi'a, 1990), 9:171. The correct name of the author of *Isbāh al-Shi'a bi Misbāh al-Shari'a* is al-Kaydarī jurist of the sixth century (thirteenth century), not Salmān ibn al-Hassan al-Sahrashtī or al-Sahrdashtī jurists of fifth century (twelfth century). For more information, see Ja'far al-Sobhanī's introduction to al-Kaydarī, *Isbāh al-Shi'a*, 12–14.
110. Sayfullāh Sarrāmī, *Ahkām Murtadd az Didgāh Islām wa Huqūq Bashar* (Tehran: Markaz-e Tahqiqāt-e Esteratejik, 1997), 253–255, 264, 281.
111. Ibid., 265–282.
112. Ibid., 403–406.
113. Muhammad Hussein Fadlallah, *Qarā'ah Islāmiyya sari'ah li mafhumai al-hurriyya wa al-dimuqrātiyya fi jānib al-fikrī al-hidāri, al-Muntalq*, Islamic Union of Lebanese students, 65:4–21; its Persian translation by Majid Moradi, *Azadi va democracy: qarā'ti Eslāmi, Majalleh Oloum Siyāsi* 1(3) (Qom, 1999).
114. Mohammad Mehdi Shamseddine, *Al-ijtihād wa al-Tajdīd tī al-fiqh al-Islāmī* (Beirut: al-Mu'assisa al-Dawliyya, 1999), 234–240.
115. Ibid., 239.
116. Muhammad ibn al-Hassan al-Tūsī, *al-Khilāf* (Qom: Mu'assisa al-Nashr al-Islami, 1987), 5:356–357.
117. That is one of the references in this book, especially on apostasy during the time of the Prophet and Shi'i Imams.
118. Abdul-Karim Mousawi Ardebili, *Fiqh al-ḥudūd wa al-ta'zīrāt*, vol. 4 (including apostasy) (Qom: Enteshārāt-e Dāneshgā-e Mofid, 2009). This book was written in the late 1990s. The author taught the subject to the circle of his students during Ramadan (December 1999–January 2000) in the Qom Seminary. One of his students published his report of these sessions: Mohammad Javād Vara'ee, "*Ertedad negāhi nobāreh: taqrīri az mabāheth Ramazan 1420 of Ayatollah Mousawi Ardebili*", *Majalleh Hokoumat Eslāmi*, quarterly, 4(3) (1999): 9–26; 4(4) (2000): 74–110; 5(1) (2000): 77–111.
119. Vara'ee, "*Ertedad negāhi nobāreh*", 4(3): 13.
120. Ibid., 14–15 and 19.
121. Ibid., 20.
122. Ibid., 4(4): 90–91.

123. Yousef Saanei (b. 1937), an Iranian Shi'i authority (*marja' taqlīd*) and Attorney-General of Iran (1982–1985), wrote in his *fatwa*s of July 2000 that a person who doubts, is uncertain or rejects religion during his research and exploring the truth cannot be sentenced to apostasy. It is clear that such a person would not be executed or killed. In his *fatwa* of January 2000, he wrote: "The rulings of *fitrī* apostasy do not cover ignorant individuals if they do not commit other crimes" (Saanei, *Majma' al-masā'īl* (Qom: Mo'assese-ye Farhangi-ye Fiqh al-Thaqlain, 2008), 3:296–297, Nos 831 and 833).
124. The second figure of the 1979 Iranian Revolution. The Iranian Assembly of Experts selected him as the second leader of the Islamic Republic in 1986; however, Khomeini fired him illegally less than three months before his death. He had been under illegal house arrest for more than five years by January 2003, after disqualifying Khāmena'ī from becoming a Shi'i authority (*marja'taqlīd*) and calling it "the trivialization of the Shi'i *marja'iyya*".
125. There is a minor point here. In 1996, Montazeri added the following to his legal practical manual (*Tawḍīḥ al-masā'il*) – a booklet prepared for and circulated to his followers (*muqallids*): "Ruling 3213: It is not obligatory for the apostate to inform anyone of his or her apostasy. If he decides to repent then it is acceptable, for this is something between himself and God. Any assets earned after repentance belong to him, and he is entitled to remarry, even with his previous wife."
126. I came across these two legal rulings in the 2002 edition of Ayatollah Montazerī's *Fiqhī Manual* (available online) and followed up with an enquiry to his office. In the estimation of Sa'īd Montazeri and Moḥammad Ḥassan Movaḥḥedī Sāvejī, these revised legal rulings were issued sometime during the first half of 2000. Regretfully, we could not access Montazeri's *Fiqhi Manual* of 2000. However, pegging the date to 2000 for the revised rulings appears to be correct, given that the article by Abdolkarem Soroush, in which he raises objections to Montazeri's earlier legal rulings on apostasy, was published in *Kiyān* monthly, 46 (May 1999) (*Fiqh dar tarāzū: Ṭarḥ-e chand porsesh az Ḥazrat-e Ayatollah Montazeri*). In my interview of April 2011, I referred to this issue: "At that time I was in Evin prison, occupied with preparing my defence for the court hearing. However, I read each of the three correspondences between Montazeri and Soroush at a much later date and found most of the latter's objections to traditional jurisprudence in his scholarly article to be valid" (Kadivar, *Sūgnāme-ye faqīh-i Pākbāz*, Kadivar web-book, 2013, 218).
127. His opinion of 18 February 1999, states: "Islam never forces an unbeliever to embrace Islam, knowing full well that, in principle, religion and belief cannot be attained by coercion ('There is no compulsion in religion', Q. 2:256). However, if a previously practising Muslim openly announces his apostasy and questions the sacred aspects of religion, then, like a cancerous tumor, it will gradually spread to the healthy parts of the society. Moreover, it is likely that some of the political schemers against Islam and Muslim society will exploit the situation and thus, such a person would in reality be designated as one who is at war with God (*muḥārib*)." "*Dīn, mudārā, va khushūnat*", *Kiyān*, monthly, Tehran, No. 45, 1999; Hossein-Ali Montazeri, *Dīdgā-hā* (Qom: Office of Montazeri, 2002), 1:99.

128. Hossein-Ali Montazeri, *Resāle-ye ḥuqūq* (Qom: Arghavān-e Dānesh, 2004), 51–52.
129. Hossein-Ali Montazeri, *Islām: Dīn-i feṭrat* (Tehran: Sarā'i, 2006), 692–698.
130. Hossein-Ali Montazeri, *Ḥukūmat-i dīnī va ḥuqūq-i insān* (Tehran: Sara'i, 2007), 130–132.
131. See Glossary.
132. See Glossary.
133. Mohammad 'Ali Ayāzī, *Azādī in Qur'ān*, 2nd edn (Tehran: Mu'assese-ye Nashr va Tahqiqāt-e Żekr, 2016), 393.
134. Ibid., 399.
135. Ibid., 394, 396.
136. Ibid., 394–396.
137. Ibid., 399.
138. Ibid., 393–394.
139. Ibid., 397–398.
140. This research, conducted by the Office of the Assembly of Experts (*Dabirkhāne-ye Majles-e Khobregān*), was first published as the article, Mohammad Soroush Mahallāti, "*Ayā ertedād keifar-e hadd dārad? Ta'ammoli bar māhiyyat-e keifar ertedād*", *Majjalah Hukūmat Islāmī*, quarterly, Qom, 6(1) (19) (2001): 15–61 and then as the book Soroush Mahallāti, Mohammad, *Andisheh wa imān dar azādī* (Tehran: Rawzaneh, 2016).
141. Soroush Mahallāti, *Andisheh wa imān dar azādī*, 253, 257.
142. Ibid., 263.
143. Ibid., 246.
144. Ibid., 268.
145. The jurist who sentenced Rāfiq Taqī to death as an apostate in 2005.
146. Soroush Mahallāti, *Andisheh wa imān dar azādī*, 250–251.
147. Mohammad Fazel Lankarāni, *Jāmi' al-masā'il, Istiftā'āt* (Qom: Amīr al-'Ilm, 2004), 2:504.
148. The penalty for apostasy *might* originally have been a political and governmental ruling responding to the conditions of time, space and environment. Hossein-Ali Montazeri, *Dirāsāt fi wilāyat al-faqih wa fiqh al-dawlah al-Islāmiyya* (Qom: Markaz-al-I'lām al-Islami, 1988), 3:387. This probability could be seen in the unedited notes of the Iranian theologian Morteza Motahhari (1919–1979), which were published several years after his assassination. (Morteza Motahhari, *Yaddashthaye Ostad Motahhar*i (Tehran: Sadrā, 2000), 2:316).
149. 'Isā Velā'ī (b. 1950), *Ertedād dar Eslām* (Tehran: Nashr-e Nei, 2001), 270. It was the second independent book on apostasy published in contemporary Iran.
150. Mohammad Fāzel Meybodi (b. 1955), "*Ensān, adyān, wa irtidād*", first in *Aftāb*, monthly, Tehran, 23 (March 2004); then in *Shari'at, 'Urf, wa 'Aqlāniyyat* (Tehran: Hermes, 2015); and Abolfazl Mousavaian Mousavian (b. 1955), "*Keifar Mortadd Hokmi Siasī*", *Majalleh-ye 'Elmi-ye Motale'āt-e Fiqh va Hoqouq-e Eslāmī*, quarterly, Semnan, 1(1) (2009): 145–171.

151. Muhammad 'Ali Al-Taskhirī (b. 1948), former Secretary-General of the World Forum for Proximity of Islamic Schools of Thought (*al-Majmaʿ al-ʿAlami lil-Taqrīb bayn al-Madāhib al-Islāmiyya*), "*Hukm al-riddah wa madā Insijāmihi maʿ huriyyah al-iʿtiqād*", *Risalat Al-taqrab*, bimonthly, Tehran, 14(67) (2008): 137–156, summarised the book by Soroush, *Mahallāt*, followed him, and concluded: "We prefer the approach of *taʿzir* as governmental ruling (*wilāʾi*) because of its strong argumentations and evidence. It neither violates any consensus nor denies any hadith. It is consistent with how the Prophet treated the hypocrites and apostates. It does not specify (*takhsīs*) the Qur'anic universals that never accept specification. It is in harmony with rational and textual rulings. In addition, it is consistent with the humanistic approach to Islam."
152. It is composed from his 2005–2007 writings. Qābel passed away soon after due to brain cancer following a delay in diagnosis due to his illegal imprisonment. His complete works, *Majmūʿe-ye āsār-i Aḥmad-i Ghābel*, e-book, were published under my supervision in 2013. Publication of his works has been banned in Iran since 2009.
153. Aḥmad Qābel, "*Aḥkām-i jazāʾī dar Sharīʿat-i Muḥammadī*" (e-book at his web-page, 2013), 80–84, 91–107.
154. Ibid., 88–89.
155. See Glossary.
156. Qābel, "*Aḥkām-i jazāʾī dar Sharīʿat-i Muḥammadī*", 76–79.
157. Ibid., 15.
158. Ibid., 148–150, 153.
159. Ahmad ʿĀbedinī, "*Auqūba al-Murtadd: Dirasa Jadiadh fi al-Mulabasāt wa al-Zurūf*", trans. Hassan al-Hāshimī, *Majjala al-Ijtihad wa al-Tajdid*, quarterly, Beirut, 3(9/10) (2008): 109–145. The original Persian copy of the article could not be published in Iran because of censorship!
160. Ibid., 117.
161. Ibid., 120.
162. Ibid., 119.
163. Ibid., 120.
164. Ibid., 123.
165. Ibid., 129.
166. Ibid., 139.
167. Khashin studied in Qom Seminary and at Islamic Āzād University in Tehran. He is a member of the board of trusties of the institutions of Muhammad Hussain Fadl Allah in Lebanon.
168. Hussain Ahmad al-Khashin, *al-Fiqh al-janāʾi fi al-Islām, al-ridda numūzijan* (Beirut: Mu'assisa al-Intishār al-ʿArabī, 2015), 23–28.
169. Ibid., 47–72.
170. Ibid., 82–105.
171. Ibid., 137–150.
172. Ibid., 169–195.
173. Ibid., 196–307.
174. Ibid., 309–332.

175. Although Khashin studied in Iran, he cited none of these scholars in his book.
176. I mean "*main*" graduate studies.
177. He was a prolific writer on scientific Islam and Qur'anic studies, head of the University of Tehran's first engineering department, a long-time pro-democracy activist, and interim prime minister after the 1979 Iranian Revolution.
178. Bazargan wrote his article originally in French and sent it to *Le Monde* on 3 November 1993. *Le Monde* published a summary of it (almost one quarter of the article) on 19 April 1994 ("L'islam est-il un danger international?"). His political party, Nehzat-e Azādi-ye Iran (The Freedom Movement of Iran), published the Persian translation of the whole article, with an introduction, in a declaration on 5 May 1994. Because of Iranian media censorship, Bazargan sent it to the Iranian weekly *Kayhan Havāi,* which was circulated outside the country. It was published on 7 September 1994, with the long critical comments of the governmental editor. The German weekly newspaper *Die Zeit* published its summary on 23 September 1994 under the title "*Der Koran predigt weder Terrorismus noch Despotie: Glauben Privatsache*".
179. Mehdi Bazargan, "*Aya Eslam yek khatar-e jahāni ast?*" in *Ta'ābir-e khodkhasteh az Eslām: ghabāri bar chehreh-ye tabnak-e din*, weekly *Kayhan Havāi*, Tehran, 7 September 1994.
180. Mehdi Bazargan, "*Pasokh be Kayhan Havāi*", in *Ta'yyon-e hauzehāy-e tamaddoni va chārchoubhā-ye mashrou' barāye tabligh-e Eslām, Kayhan Havāi*, weekly, Tehran, 21 December 1994.
181. Mehdi Bazargan, "*Dovvomin pasokh be Kayhan Havāi*", in *Akharin mobahetheh ba Mehdi Bazargan: Nazdiki fi bāvarhāy-e Nezam-e solteh bā ddourī jostan az esālathā! Kayhan Havāi*, weekly, Tehran, 22 February 1995.
182. Golzādeh Ghafourī was the most distinguished cleric who openly opposed and did not vote for the guardianship of the jurist in the Constitutional Assembly. Elected as the representative of Tehran during the first round of the Parliament, he resigned in June 1981, believing that the Islamic Republic had fundamentally gone astray. Later on, that same year, two of his sons were executed and his daughter and son-in-law were executed in 1988 in prison. All of these young university students were political activists. Ghafourī continued to write and revise his books at his home, in seclusion and in a sombre state.
183. Ali Golzādeh Ghafourī, *Payām Hājar*, weekly, Tehran, 18(276), 26 July 1996. He discussed this in the same way in his books *Qazā dar Eslām*, 114, 198–202; and *Zarourat baznegari feqhi*, 66, 418–419 (Tehran: n.p., n.d.).
184. Mousawi Gheravi, *Feqh-e Estedlālī dar Masā'e-el Khelāfi*, trans., from Arabic to Persian Ali Asghar Gheravi (his son) (Tehran: Negāresh, 1998), 602–644. (Its original Arabic draft has not been published yet.) Also see Appendix 3 towards the end of this book.
185. Soroush is a pharmacologist, as well as a researcher of analytic philosophy and Persian Sufism, especially Rumi. For more information about his ideas, see Adbolkarim Soroush, *Reason, Freedom, and Democracy in Islam: The Essential Writings of Adbolkarim Soroush*, trans., ed. with Introduction M. Sadri and A. Sadri (Oxford: Oxford University Press, 2000); and Adbolkarim Soroush, *The Expansion of Prophetic Experience:*

*Essays on Historicity, Contingency, and Plurality in Religion*, trans. Nilou Mobassar, ed. with Introduction Forough Jahanbakhsh (Leiden: Brill, 2008).

186. Adbolkarim Soroush, *Fiqh dar tarāzū: Ṭarḥ-e chand porsesh az Ḥazrat-e Ayatollah Montazeri, Kiyān*, monthly, Tehran, 46 (1999): 14–21.
187. Shabestari studied at Qom Seminary. While serving as the imam of the Islamic Centre in Hamburg (1969–1978), he learned German and self-studied modern Christian theology. During the first round of the Iranian Parliament after the Revolution (1980–1984), he was elected as one of the representatives of Tehran. He taught and researched at Tehran University's School of Theology (1984–2006), focusing on theology and mysticism.
188. Mohammad Mojtahed Shabestari, *Naqdi bar qarā'at-e Rasmi az Dīn: bohranhā, Chaleshhā va vāh-e Halhā* (Tehran: Tarh-e Nō, 2000), 201.
189. Ibid., 226.
190. He teaches in Mofid University's Department of Philosophy in Qom, Iran.
191. Abolghasem Fanaei, *Akhāq Deen-shenāsi* (Tehran: Negāh-e Mo'āser, 2010), 488–489.
192. Mohsen Kadivar, "*Marzhā-ye āzādī az manẓare-e dīn*", *'Aṣr-e mā*, biweekly, Tehran, 13 January 1999, 10 February 1999 and 23 August 1999; later in my book *Dagdage-hā-ye ḥukūmat-i dīnī* (Tehran: Ney, 2000), 494–543. The third part of the interview and the book were published while I was incarcerated in Tehran's Evin prison.
193. See Glossary.
194. See Glossary.
195. Mohsen Kadivar, "*Āzādi-ye 'aqīde va madhhab dar Islam va asnād-i ḥuqūq-i bashar*", presented at the first international Conference of Human Rights and the Dialogue of Civilizations, Tehran, Mofid University, with the collaboration of UNESCO and the International Center for the Dialogue Civilizations, 2 May 2001; *Majmū'e-ye maqālāt-i hamāyesh-e bayn al-melalī-ye ḥuqūq-e bashar va goftegū-ye tamaddon-hā* (the conference's collected articles, Mofid University, Qom, 2001, 243–265); *Aftab*, monthly, Tehran, 23 (March 2003): 54–63; Kadivar, *Ḥaqq al-nās* (Tehran: Kavīr, 2008), 181–215. Its English translation appears as "Freedom of Religion and Belief in Islam", in Mehran Kamrava (ed.), *The New Voices of Islam: Reforming Politics and Modernity – A Reader* (London: I. B. Tauris, 2006), 119–142; Kadivar, *Human Rights and Islam*, trans. Nikky Akhavan, Series In Translation: Modern Muslim Thinkers (London and Edinburgh: Institute for the Study of Muslim Civilizations, Agha Khan University and Edinburgh University Press, forthcoming).
196. Kadivar, "*Ḥuqūq-i bashar va roshanfekri-ye dīnī*", *Āftāb*, monthly, Tehran, 27 (August 2003): 54; later in Kadivar, *Ḥaqq al-nās*, 135; and Kadivar, *Sūgnāme-ye faqīh-i Pākbāz*, web-book, 39.
197. Kadivar, "*Ḥuqūq-i bashar va roshanfekri-ye dīnī*"; Kadivar, *Ḥaqq al-nās*, 86–117; and Kadivar, *Sūgnāme-ye faqīh-i Pākbāz*, 38.
198. Kadivar, "*Ḥuqūq-i bashar va roshanfekri-ye dīnī*", *Āftāb*, monthly, Tehran, 26 (July 2003), and 27 (August 2003); later Kadivar, *Ḥaqq al-nās*, 125; Kadivar, "Human Rights and Intellectual Islam", trans. Nilou Mobassser, in Kari Vogt, Lena Larsen

and Christian Moe (eds), *New Directions in Islamic Thought: Exploring Reform and Muslim Tradition* (London: I. B. Tauris, 2009), 56.

199. See Glossary.
200. See Glossary.
201. Written for St Antony's College, Oxford University.
202. Collectively written by Abdolali Bazargan, Siddīqi-ye Wasmaqī, Ḥasan Yousefi Eshkavarī and myself in May 2012.
203. Shahin Najafi.
204. Written by Ali Asghar Gheravi (b. 1946), the son of Mohammad Javād Mousawi Gheravi.
205. The preface of the original Persian monograph was written in July 2014. I merged the translated preface completely to my English Introduction.

# Part I

# *Blasphemy and Apostasy*

# 1
# *The Background of the Treatise*

### *1 Legal Rulings (*Fatāwā*) on Assassination and Statement of Delight at its Implementation*

1 Legal rulings condemning Rāfiq Taqī to death for apostasy or blaspheming the Prophet issued by Morteză Banī Fazl and Mohammad Fāzel Lankarānī (Lankarānī Sr.) on 22 November 2006
2 The Killing of Rāfiq Taqī and Legal Ruling of Five Years Ago – Issued by Mohammad Fāzel Lankarānī (Lankarānī Sr) in 2011
3 The statement of delight and rejoice by Mohammad Javād Fāzel Lankarānī (Lankarānī Jr) upon implementing the judgement on apostasy against Rāfiq Taqī issued on 27 November 2011

### *Legal Rulings (*Fatāwā*) on Execution*

### **Morteză Banī Fazl**

Morteză Banī Fazl, a member of the Assembly of Experts [in Iran] representing the eastern province of Azerbaijan and a teacher at the Qom Seminary, announced: "[Rāfiq Taqī], a journalist in the republic of Azerbaijan, has been condemned to death on the charges of apostasy and causing 'mischief and corruption'." He added, "I will reward the person who dispatches him to perdition and death."[1]

## Mohammad Fāzel Lankarānī (Lankarānī Sr)[2]

Lately, an article written by the apostate Āzarī journalist Rāfiq Taqī was published in *San'at*, a newspaper of the Republic of Azerbaijan. It has caused indignation and anger among the Muslims residing in that region. I am enclosing the article with its Persian translation for you.

The writer of this article endeavours to analyse the differences between Europe and the Middle East and their religions, Christianity and Islam, respectively. It concludes that the former is superior to Islam in all aspects, and that the latter is inferior and worthless. In a section of the article, he addresses the revered Prophet Muhammad with repulsive words and undeserved insults and mocks all of Islam's sacred aspects. He ends the article by asserting that he has written it knowingly and intentionally and will write again in the future.

Moreover, the same newspaper has repeatedly denigrated and attacked Islam's sacred aspects by publishing a few pages from the disgusting *Satanic Verses*.

*Question*: what is the Muslims' [religious] obligation regarding this intolerable issue?

Your followers (*muqallids*) from Azerbaijan.

*Answer*: if such a person was a born [native] Muslim, then his aforementioned confession would render him an apostate. If he was an unbeliever, then it would constitute blaspheming the Prophet. In both situations, if he has made such a confession then it is obligatory upon everyone who has access [to him] to kill him. The same ruling applies to the responsible party of the aforementioned newspaper who published such ideas and beliefs knowingly and with intent. May God protect Islam and Muslims from the evil of its enemies.

"They desire to extinguish the light of God with their mouths, but God will perfect His light, even though the disbelievers are averse." (Q. 61:8)

Mohammad Fāzel Lankarānī (Lankarānī Sr)
25 November 2011

## *The Killing of Rāfiq Taqī and the Legal Ruling (*Fatwa*) of Five Years Ago – Issued by Mohammad Fāzel Lankarānī (Lankarānī Sr) in 2011*[1]

The Republic of Azerbaijan's Salman Rushdie has been killed. Rāfiq Taqī, famously known by that designation for blaspheming the Prophet, was killed yesterday by an anonymous person.

Detested by the people of Azerbaijan for his unprecedented blaspheming of the Prophet, they had sought a legal ruling from Lankarānī Sr, who right away sentenced him to death. Yesterday, Rāfiq Taqī was killed by an anonymous person while getting off a bus.

Once this information became public, the newspapers reported that Rāfiq Taqī was admitted to the hospital last week after receiving seven stab wounds; he died during the afternoon of Wednesday, 23 November 2011.

Rāfiq Nāẓir Ūghlū Taqī Zādeh (famously known as Rāfiq Taqī-lī), previously a member of the Azerbaijan Union of Journalists, was expelled in 2004 after the publication of his offensive *'Āshūrā'* piece in which he considered Baku's Tāzeh Pīr mosque as the best place for satisfying one's lust and passion and used pornographic terms in his description. He reduced the people's commemoration of the *'Āshūrā'* ceremonies [to mark the martyrdom of Ḥusayn b. 'Alī in 680] to one of merrymaking and pleasure-seeking.

In a similar vein, his publication of "Europe and Us" in 2006 sparked a major outrage in the Muslim community. After receiving the Azerbaijan Muslims' protests, the government arrested him and sentenced him to three years' imprisonment. He was released after two years due to a presidential pardon.

While at the hospital, Rāfiq Taqī accused a religious [fanatic] group and the Islamic Republic of Iran of this attack. On Tuesday, the Embassy of Iran in Azerbaijan denied any involvement and published its denial in Azerbaijan's newspapers. It alleged that this is a Zionist and American plot [designed] to rupture the relations between the two countries, a plot that is doomed to failure. Up until now, there has been no official reaction to this incident from the [Azerbaijani] government.

Based on the reporting of Pārsīneh, Rāfiq Taqī was killed precisely five years after the issuance of Lankarānī Sr's legal ruling (*fatwa*) on 25 November 2011, in which he was sentenced to death after the publication of his "Europe and Us" in the *San'at* newspaper.

## *Lankarānī Jr's Statement after the Implementation of the Legal Ruling on Apostasy against Rāfiq Taqī*

"Do they not know that whosoever opposes God and his Messenger, surely for him shall be the fire of Hell, wherein he will abide eternally? That is the great disgrace." (Q. 9:63)

Muslims and religiously observant people of Azerbaijan!

We thank God, the Subduer, whose hand of requital appeared from under the sleeves of the zealous Muslims who dispatched to Hellfire a wicked person for insulting and abusing the sacred visage of Islam and the honourable Prophet.

Undoubtedly, the one who carried out this divine ruling and brought delight and joy to the Muslims' hearts will receive recompense and a bountiful reward from God.

The enemies of Islam should know that free and young honourable Muslims will not grant permission to the arrogant world powers and international Zionism to implement their sinister plots to insult Islam's sacred aspects. Rather, these Western-influenced and "sellers of religion" will receive their due punishment for their shameful acts.

I would like to extend my congratulations to the Muslim world, especially to the zealous people of Azerbaijan.

In memory of the late Shi'i grand jurist Lankarānī Sr, I petition God to honour and raise his station, for He was the one who issued the legal ruling making it lawful to execute this atheist and apostate.

Mohammad Javād Fāzel Lankarānī (Lankarānī Jr)
27 November 2011

## *Notes*

1. *Bāy Bek-i Āzarbaijān*, monthly, No. 44, 22 November 1986, provides an elaborate and diligent critique of human rights violations in Iran, which was sourced by the newspaper, *Jumhūri-ye Islāmī*.
2. Website of Mohammad Javād Fāzel Lankarānī (Lankarānī Jr).
3. Website of Lankarānī Jr, 26 November 2011. However, only the first paragraph is quoted in the newspaper, *Jumhūr-ye Islāmī* (24 November 2011), sourcing the *Pārsīneh* website, however, no such text exists on its website. As such, the information must have been taken from the website of Lankarānī Jr.

## *2 Objections to the* Fatwa *of Assassination*[1]

Mohsen Kadivar

Dear Javād Fāzel Lankarānī (Lankarānī Jr),

I petition the Almighty God to endow you with health, safety and success. I fondly remember the many years during which we both benefited from our professors, who have passed away and are resting peacefully in the presence of the Merciful God. I hope that like your late father, in your capacity as the heir of his deep jurisprudential understanding and *marja'iyya*, you will call for the seminaries to remain independent.

The motive for my imposition pertains to the crucial issue that was dealt with during our student days: preserving the people's life, along with Islam's and Shi'ism's honour and dignity. In your statement of 26 November 2011, you express delight and joy at the assassination of "a wicked person for insulting and abusing the sacred visage of Islam and the honourable Prophet" and for Lankarānī Sr's *fatwa* "making it lawful to execute this atheist and apostate".

Your father issued the following legal ruling, dated 25 November 2006, in response to a query from some of his followers on their religious responsibility to the writings of the Āzerī journalist Rāfiq Taqī:

> If such a person was a born [native] Muslim, then his aforementioned confession would render him an apostate. If he was an unbeliever, then it would constitute blaspheming the Prophet. In both situations, if he has made such a confession then it is obligatory upon everyone who has access [to him] to kill him. The same ruling applies to the responsible party of the aforementioned newspaper that published such ideas and beliefs knowingly and with intent.

Your statement and your father's legal ruling continue the legal ruling of the late Khomeini regarding the distasteful and foolish book *Satanic Verses*, the only difference being that the author was living in the West and is still living [there] under the protection of the British police. The Azerbaijani author, however, was assassinated and died five days ago at the hospital from the stab wounds he received.

Undoubtedly, you must be aware that these are not the only two persons who have shown disrespect to and defamed the visage of the Prophet, the Qur'an and Islam. On a daily basis and in different languages, there are those who cast aspersions and insults upon religions in general and Islam in particular in the print and other media, as well as in hearsay and gossip circles. It is unlikely that you or other jurists and *marāji'* are aware of even a fraction of these insults, even [if they are uttered] solely in the Persian language.

Based on the above *fatwa*, are all the authors and publishers of such insults and disrespect adjudged "apostates" or "blasphemers of the Prophet"? If so, in both scenarios it would be obligatory upon everyone who has access [to them] to kill them. If the believers and followers of your late father and other *marāji'* who espouse the same path desire to act upon their religious obligation, then they would be required to kill such people (or, in modern parlance, commit an act of terrorism) by themselves or arrange for agile and athletic persons to carry out their religious obligation.

## Objections to the Assassination *Fatwa* and the Lawfulness of Shedding Blood with Impunity (*mahdūr al-dam*)

The following objections are in order:

1. Calling for the execution of an apostate or a blasphemer and shedding their blood lack any reliable Qur'anic justification. Rather, the Qur'an's very tenor goes against such a legal ruling.[3]
2. Even if one were to assume that the chain of transmission is sound and the substance of the hadiths contained in the two sections (of blasphemy and apostasy) legitimise execution, they cannot be invoked as a basis for establishing the validity of the *fatwa* for assassination or execution because they could not withstand the following strong and solid proofs:
   (a) Many leading jurists, such as Muḥaqqiq Ḥillī (d. 1277)[4] and Ibn Idrīs Ḥillī (d. 1202),[5] have conditioned the implementation of *ḥudūd*[6] punishments and offensive jihad upon the presence of the Prophet or the infallible Twelfth Imam.
   (b) The justification for both legal rulings (i.e., the lawfulness of executing an apostate or a blasphemer) is based on *thiqa* "isolated reports" (*khabar al-wāḥid al-thiqa*).[7] As such, its probative force and reliability rests upon rational beings. On a matter so crucial and vital, in contrast

to other issues, rational beings would not find such hadith reports sufficient. Two of the most important issues are the "right to life" and the "preservation of life", both of which can be breached only by fulfilling high evidentiary standards: definitive and unequivocal (*qaṭʿī*) proofs in the form of an explicit Qur'anic verse or a *mutawātir*[8] hadith.

One cannot issue a legal death penalty ruling on the basis of "isolated reports" (*khabar al-wāḥid*) for such a ruling requires definitive and categorical proofs. Exercising caution on the "shedding of blood" (i.e., human life), especially given the great importance that the Lawgiver attaches to the sanctity of life, would demand that no such ruling be issued against anyone without a clear-cut (as opposed to a more probable (*ẓannī*)) proof. Muḥaqqiq Ardabīlī (d. 1585) writes, "Killing is a grave matter because the Lawgiver has placed special importance on life's preservation, for it is the axis of religious obligations (*takālīf*) and prosperity (*saʿāda*). Accordingly, He has made it mandatory to preserve life. This principle cannot be abandoned even in the case of a preemptive strike to preserve one's own life. Although human reason may provide some support for this, the preservation of life deserves all possible precautions and considerations."[9]

Aḥmad Khwānsārī (d. 1985), an eminent jurist emphasises, "The reliability of an 'isolated hadith report' (*khabar al-wāḥid al-thiqa* or *ʿādil*) that has been attested (*tawthīq*) to by the *rijāl* (science of hadith transmitters) scholars or contains upright narrators [in the chain of transmission] is not devoid of objection, in the estimation of rational people based on their norms (*bināʾ al-ʿuqalāʾ*), when it comes to relying on it for matters that deal with [passing a judgement on] human life. Moreover, there is a need to exercise intense care in the case of human life. Do you not observe that rational beings could consider a *thiqa* report on crucial issues to be insufficient, while at the same time [consider it] as sufficient for non-vital issues?"[10] Likewise, Muḥammad b. Ḥasan Fāḍil al-Hindī (d. 1725) regarded carrying out the penal punishments for *ḥudūd* that require execution to be the exclusive provenance of the infallible [Twelfth] Imam, based on the principle of caution.[11] The ruling to justify the punishment for apostasy is based on a few "isolated hadith reports" (*khabar al-wāḥid*) that should be dismissed, because they fall short of the evidentiary standards for a ruling that requires execution.

Accordingly, the principle of caution mandates that the ruling for apostasy not be confirmed.[12]

(c) It is inevitable that proclaiming one's blood is lawful to shed incites lawlessness and encourages believers to violate the law [of the land]. Establishing and implementing any ruling, especially when it involves a person's life, has to be limited exclusively to a competent court. Each country's constitution has incorporated the characteristics of such a court, and the Universal Declaration of Human Rights has specified these standards with great clarity.

In a competent court, the accused and his attorney would have the right of self-defence, and an impartial fair council would oversee the activities of such an open court. Based on the customary or conventional (*ʿurf*) understanding, a jurist or a *marjaʿ* is not viewed as a competent court. A death sentence can never be implemented outside the judicial system and without going through the three levels, namely, a trial court, an appellate court, and the Supreme Court. Entrusting the implementation of such a ruling to unauthorised individuals directly contravenes the norms of human rights. Moreover, delegating this responsibility to the citizens would spread chaos and lawlessness, which lead to public disorder. This is unanimously regarded by the jurists as "corruption".

(d) Issuing such a *fatwa* against an apostate or a blasphemer of the Prophet disfigures the face of Islam, Shiʿism and jurisprudence. It also associates them with violence, terrorism and narrow-mindedness. One of the accusations levelled against Islam with great frequency by its opponents and critics is its harsh, violent and illogical mode of dealing with dissenters and those holding "unorthodox" views. We live in an era of cultural ascendancy, of competition among ideas and religions, and it requires us to use a method that is cultured, strong in logic and proofs, respectful in disputation, and understandable by a contemporary audience when defending religion and ideas: "Invite to the way of your Lord with wisdom and goodly exhortation, and dispute with them in the most dignified manner" (Q. 16:125).

Fear can be instilled in the hearts of some by issuing such *fatwa*s, but certainly no one would be attracted to Islam on account of this. In fact, such an approach would prevent its credibility and dignity from rising. Such violent *fatwa*s essentially defame Islam and result in the killing of those who hold "unorthodox" views or, [sometimes] make them famous. How can one possibly believe in a religion that kills and sentences to death those who criticise or oppose it without allowing the accused any recourse to the legal right of self-defence or to have a public court hearing? How do these kinds of *fatwa*s measure up to the standards set by the merciful Messenger? Do they have any relationality to them [at all]?

If a citizen objects to the alleged aspersions or insults to his religion made by another citizen, then he is responsible for filing a complaint in a competent legal system, retaining an attorney, preparing a dossier, endeavouring to prove the act or crime in court, and seeking the appropriate punishment. If disrespecting and insulting one's religious beliefs is not a crime according to the country's civil laws, then the *marja'* or his honourable followers should either (1) make a case to the Supreme Court or Constitutional Court (if available) or (2) rebut the insults by writing articles and contributing pieces to newspapers to bring about a change in public norms and customs so that such activities can be construed as shameful and unacceptable.

## Strategies to Confront the Insults and Mockery of Religious Beliefs

Cultivating and building an international culture based upon mutual respect and acceptance is an ongoing process, one that requires proper conduct and etiquette that are in harmony with the highest standards of ethics and religion. Some of its characteristics include moderation, compromise and tolerance, on the one hand, and respect for the beliefs of others and refraining from exhibiting contempt, insulting or ridiculing the other. Alongside following the international human rights standards, a document on shared duties and responsibilities needs to be prepared and secure international currency. Such a proclamation should contain no allowance for insulting and defaming the religious beliefs of anyone. But at the same time, it must allow people the freedoms to criticise them and to raise scholarly objections without any fear of being punished. Also, it should incorporate the freedoms to change one's religion and to propagate one's faith without any negative consequences. Assassinating a so-called erring person is indefensible in all circumstances.

In our times, we should oppose the insulting and ridiculing of religious beliefs by (1) officially recognising the freedom of religion; (2) respecting other people's religious beliefs; (3) prescribing no temporal punishment for changing one's religion and for disseminating one's faith; and (4) prosecuting in accordance with the civil law anyone who insults and defames another person's religious beliefs. Entrusting a sharp instrument to one who is drunk with fanaticism must be strictly avoided.

In contrast to you, not only am I not jubilant at the execution of this impudent Azeri citizen, but I am also ashamed at this savage and cowardly deed done in the name of Islam, Shiʿism, *marjaʿiyya* and *fatwa*. [I say this] regardless of the effects of his [Rāfiq Taqī] actions and the torrent of insults and aspersions that he cast upon the Prophet and Islam. In my estimation, you are advocating the worst possible way of defending Islam and Shiʿism at this point in time. We follow the infallible Imams, all of whom are exemplary models with impeccable character, nobility and compassion. A fresh look at the bases of anthropology, cosmology, epistemology, ethics and exegesis confirm that the process of *ijtihād*[13] that produces such *fatwa*s is nothing but the parroting and regurgitating of the past (i.e., taking ideas and practices out of their original time and place-sensitive contexts). One may call this by any name one chooses; however, it cannot be called the *ijtihād* of the *Ahl al-Bayt* school.

I would be grateful for your critique of my scholarly analysis and counsel, for it will help open up the channel of discourse, which is in keeping with the approach of the Jaʿfarī school of jurisprudence. If not, I remain grateful to you for giving consideration to some of the critiques put forth by one of your classmates.

The sacrifice of the doyen of the martyrs, Ḥusayn b. ʿAlī, and his dear ones was made to preserve the school of the merciful Prophet from transmuting and degenerating into the school of the merciless Umayyads. A discerning contemporary jurist, in the place of disfiguring the radiant visage of the merciful Islam, ought to actualise "enjoining the good and forbidding the evil" (*amr bi-l-maʿrūf wa-l-nahī ʿan al-munkar*). [I believe that] its best application at this point in time is to be found in earnestly striving against religious despotism and unjust guardianship and governance. In this regard, an allusion suffices for one who is familiar.

Mohsen Kadivar
28 November 2011

## *Notes*

1. Open letter sent to Lankarānī Jr, available at: www.kadivar.com_and http://www.rahesabz.net, 28 November 2011.
2. See Glossary.
3. Also see Kadivar, *Ḥaqq al-nās*; Kadivar, "*Āzādi-ye 'aqīde va madhhab dar Islam va asnād-i ḥuqūq-i bashar", in Majmū'e-ye maqālāt-i hamāyesh-i bayn al-melalī-ye ḥuqūq-i bashar va goftegū-ye tamaddon-hā* (Qom: Intishārāt-i Dāneshgāh-i Mofīd, 2001), 204, 205.
4. Ja'far b. Ḥasan (Muḥaqqiq Ḥillī), *Sharā'i' al-Islām*, ed. Ṣādiq al-Shīrāzī (Tehran: Istiqlāl, 1989), 1:344.
5. Ibn Idrīs al-Ḥillī, *al-Sarā'ir al-ḥāwī li-l-taḥrīr al-fatāwā* (Qom: Mu'assasat al-Nashr al-Islāmī, 1989), 2:25.
6. See Glossary
7. See Glossary
8. See Glossary
9. Aḥmad b. Muḥammad al-Ardabīlī, *Majma' al-fā'ida wa-l-burḥān fī sharḥ Irshād al-adhhān*, ed. Mujtabā al-'Irāqī, 'Alī Panāh al-Ishtihārdī and Ḥusayn al-Yazdī (Qom: Mu'assasat al-Nashr al-Islāmī, 1983), "Kitāb al-ḥudūd", 13:90.
10. Khwānsārī, *Jāmi' al-madārik*, "Kitāb al-ḥudūd", 7:35.
11. Muḥammad b. Ḥasan Fāḍil al-Hindī, *Kashf al-lithām fī sharḥ Qawā'id al-aḥkām* (Qom: Mu'assasat al-Nashr al- Islāmī, 1995), 10:477.
12. For greater elaboration, see Kadivar, *Ḥaqq al-nās*, 181–216.
13. See Glossary.

# *3 Response to Doubts Surrounding Apostasy*[1]

## Mohammad Javād Fāzel Lankarānī (Lankarānī Jr) (Son of Mohammad Fāzel Lankarānī (Lankarānī Sr))

Imam Ali says, "You witness the breach of God's covenant, and yet do not get enraged, although you fret and frown at the breach of your forefathers' traditions."[2]

I have recently received letters on the issue of Khomeini's ruling on Salman Rushdie's apostasy, in which he condemned the latter to death, and also Lankarānī Sr's edict against Rāfiq Taqī's apostasy and blaspheming of the Prophet.

In one of the letters, a person with a traditional seminary (*ḥawza 'ilmiyya*) training and author of a number of works has brought forth certain scholarly points and jurisprudential objections on the ruling of an apostate's execution. The issues and objections raised are a rehash of the past; my expectation was that he would bring forth a fresh and new perspective to pave the way for engaging in serious discourse. Instead of responding to each letter independently, for which I lack the time, it may be more befitting to provide a single comprehensive response and, for this, I extend an advance apology. I hope that those who adore religion, logic and sound argumentation, even to a limited extent, will discover the truth and acknowledge it.

It is necessary for me to state right at the outset that no Muslim gets any joy from observing another person's deviation and the ensuing negative aftermath. In addition, no Muslim is delighted by the killing of another human being, in and of itself. Rather, that which causes joy and pleasure is implementing the divine ruling and obeying His command, a point that has been underlined in the infallible Imams' invaluable statements, especially those of Imam Ḥusayn, as one of the end goals of religion, which is a source of abundant temporal and spiritual blessing.

Quṭb al-Dīn al-Rāwandī (d. 911) relates a statement from the Prophet in his *Lubb al-lubāb*, "Implementing one of the *ḥudūd* punishments on Earth is more meritorious than sixty years of worship."

Before I provide a detailed response, I must state explicitly and forthrightly that the ruling that condemns an apostate to death is one upon which there is consensus between the early and the later Shi'i and Sunni jurists. No doubt has been expressed about its validity. It is only in the recent past that a very small number of scholars, not exceeding the fingers on one's hand, have raised doubts; however, they are not comparable to the hundreds of past and current eminent jurists. I will show with clarity that this ruling is regarded as one of the essential (*ḍarūrī*) elements of religion and that jurists acknowledge that there is no *ijtihād* on such matters.

We should announce in unison, resoundingly and with pride, to everyone that only the Divine Law is lofty and true and, therefore, that all rules or proclamations that oppose it have no merit. No person or group has any authority or competence to issue laws for the people, for only God [has the right to] do so. All Muslims ought to know that condemning an apostate is a definitive and indisputable divine ruling that was acted upon during the Prophet's time as well as that of the infallible Imams and thereafter.

Now, let me briefly elaborate upon the various scholarly aspects and components of making a case in favor of this ruling by dividing the discussion into six sections: (1) killing an apostate and the Qur'an; (2) killing an apostate and the Hadith; (3) killing an apostate and creating chaos and anarchy; (4) does this ruling weaken and debilitate religion?; (5) is the infallible [Twelfth] Imam's presence required to implement the *ḥudūd*?; and (6) is mandating the killing of an apostate compatible with the Prophet's merciful character?

## Killing an Apostate and the Qur'an

a. Some have conjectured that this ruling has no Qur'anic basis and have even asserted that it contradicts the spirit of the Qur'an! It appears to me that this thought first originated among the Sunnis. By way of introduction, it is necessary to say that the Qur'an contains no explicit proof on this issue and that if we were to rely exclusively on it to establish apostasy's punishment, as well as set aside the hadiths, consensus (*ijmā'*), and essentials of religion, then it would be fraught with difficulty. However, the following points should be taken into account:

*Issue 1*: Is it true that no jurist or exegete has argued for this case on the basis of the Qur'an? Those who oppose this ruling are essentially claiming that no historical scholar has ever done so. This mindset is the result of either a lack of (1) rigour and diligence in studying the Qur'an's verses, or (2) information and/or deficient knowledge. To clarify further,

i. One can invoke Q. 2:54, among other proofs, to establish that an apostate deserves to be killed: "Moses said to his people, 'O my people! You have wronged yourselves by taking up the calf [as your god]. So repent to your Creator and kill yourselves. That will be best for you in the sight of your Creator.' Then He accepted your repentance. He is the Ever Relenting and Most Merciful." A large number of Israelites, after being delivered from the pharaohs of the time and prevailing over them, succumbed to worshipping the "speaking" calf and grew distant from monotheism after Moses had gone to Mount Sinai to receive the Tablets. Upon his return, he proclaimed, "You have wronged yourselves by this deviance and must seek repentance and kill (*qatl*) yourselves." What is meant by *qatl* here is not to combat the lower self and lustful desires, but the literal killing and annihilation of the self. It is clear that the divine order of "killing" was issued because of the Israelites' apostasy and stumbling, even after they had witnessed God's miracles and signs.

From this verse, one can conclude the following: (1) the subject matter of apostasy among the Israelites is linked to killing, which is the punishment for such a violation; and that (2) by relying upon the [the interpretive device of] "presumption of continuance" (*istiṣḥāb*) of a previous divine ruling, one can consider this ruling as valid in Islam, and set aside the issue of abrogation (*naskh*). Even if one does not accept the "presumption of continuance", the first point suffices to validate our claim.

Shihāb al-Dīn al-Ālūsī (d. 1854) writes in his Qur'anic exegesis, "'To repent' (*tawba*) here means 'to kill', be it pertaining to this particular group or as a general and an invariable rule on *tawba* for the apostate in the *shari'a* of Moses."[3]

The exegesis of Q. 2:54 points out that the following is attributed to Imam Ali: He is held to have remarked that the Israelites had asked Moses about the nature and modality of this *tawba* and that the latter stated, "Those who are guilty of worshipping the calf should kill each other." This led to the killing of blood brothers [and sisters], parents, and children; God interjected and commanded that they stop it.[4]

The only remaining objection that the opponents can raise is to say that the verse is about worshipping a calf and that as it pertains to a collective apostasy, it cannot be used to derive a ruling for an individual apostate. To refute [this contention], one can look at the contextual meaning of *tawba* in the verse – it is obligatory for each person individually to seek repentance. We can employ this to argue that killing an apostate is an individual legal ruling and, as such, the apostasy of each person is the subject matter that is linked to killing.

ii. Fakhr al-Dīn al-Rāzī (d. 1209) writes in his exegesis of the following verse, "Whosoever among you renounces his religion and dies as a disbeliever, their deeds will come to nothing (*ḥabaṭat aʿmālu-hum*) in this world and the Hereafter, and they are the inhabitants of Hellfire, where they remain" (Q. 2:217), that "What is meant by effacing or the perishing of the deeds (*ḥubūṭ al-aʿmāl*) in this world is that the person must be overpowered and killed. In the event that this is not possible, then he must be engaged in combat and killed. No believer has the right to help and assist him or voice any praise about him. His marriage is annulled without a need to recite the divorce formula, and he is not entitled to inherit from a Muslim."[5]

It is clear that Fakhr al-Rāzī has employed the generalised meaning of *ḥubūṭ al-aʿmāl*, namely, that absolutely all acts that were performed physically or verbally in this world, and can be extended to include even declaration of one's faith comprising the dual testimony, which made his blood sacrosanct [in the first place] and endowed him with the status of being ritually pure (*ṭāhir*). In some reliable traditions, Imam Ṣādiq (d. 765) is reported to have said, "Testifying that there is no god but God and affirming the Messenger of God spares one's blood and enables one to marry [a Muslim] and receive inheritance [from a Muslim]." The meaning derived from this hadith is that in the absence of the dual testimony of faith, one's blood is no longer sacrosanct and the permission to marry and inherit is nullified.

Abū al-Qāsim al-Khūʾī (d. 1992) wrote, "There are numerous hadiths in which uttering the dual testimony of faith is the basis for one entering the fold of Islam, thereby making his blood sacred and entitling him to marry and inherit [from a Muslim].

> Perhaps it is because of this that Shaykh Ḥasan al-Ṭūsī (d. 1067) ruled that a pilgrimage (hajj) performed by a Muslim would be rendered void upon [his] becoming an apostate. In my estimation, this generalization of the Qur'anic verse is valid."[6]

This argumentation enables us to respond to two objections:

*First Objection*: "The nullification of one's deeds" (*ḥubūṭ al-a'māl*) does not apply to this world but is restricted to the Hereafter, where the apostate will not be entitled to any recompense or reward.

*Response*: This is an unfair objection, for in actuality God voids all the deeds of an apostate that have any religious connotation (e.g., prayers, fasting and other acts of worship of any consequence in both this world and the Hereafter). In addition, even the permission to marry a Muslim is withdrawn. As such, the "nullification of deeds" represents a form of worldly punishment.

In other words, this "nullification of deeds" is comprehensive in scope, for it is not limited to good deeds that would have been recompensed in the Hereafter. The connotation is as if he had performed no deeds at all and had never accepted the dual testimony of faith. Thus, that which sanctifies his blood (i.e., embracing Islam) is rendered void and this "absence of sanctifying his blood" is the subject matter for worldly punishment. Accepting this premise, even without acknowledging the validity of killing the apostate in this world, would utterly destroy the opponents' claim that the Qur'an does not mention any temporal punishment for the apostate and that no verses can be invoked as categorical or highly probable proofs in this regard.

It is stated in the exegesis *Kanz al-daqā'iq wa baḥr al-gharā'ib* that "abandoning and renouncing Islam entails [the] loss of [all] worldly benefits".[7] The author has interpreted the "loss of benefits" as worldly, which is a conventional and ordinary meaning. That is, the "nullification of deeds" is inclusive of both this world and the Hereafter. Moreover, this universal meaning of *ḥubūṭ al-a'māl* appears in the hadiths pertaining to other types of violations, such as drinking wine and adultery; however, it seems that both this life and the Hereafter are explicitly specified only in the case of apostasy. Thus, it merits the kind of generalization that we have made.

*Second Objection*: In Q. 2:217, the restriction of "death" is used in this context: ". . . he dies as an unbeliever (*kāfir*) . . ." This stipulation shows that the "nullification of deeds" becomes actualised for the temporal and the Hereafter domains only if one dies in a state of unbelief (*kufr*). In other words, the "nullification of deeds" occurs only when one dies as an unbeliever while still in a state of apostasy. Thus, one cannot employ this verse to argue that apostasy by itself causes the "nullification of deeds" in both worlds.

*Response*: First, some verses speak about polytheism (*shirk*) or apostasy (*irtidād*) without stipulating that death actualises the "nullification of their deeds", such as ". . . Were they to ascribe partners to God, all their deeds would have come to nothing" (Q. 6:88) and ". . . And whoever rejects faith, his deeds will come to nothing . . ." (Q. 5:5). It has been established in Islamic legal theory that the "principle of the absolute expression (*muṭlaq*) over the restricted (*muqayyad*)" does not apply in a case where both are positive sentences, harmonious and no contradiction exists between them. The outcome in such a situation is that the verse is positing one particular among other particulars of an apostate. As such, Q. 2:217 provides only one possible application for an apostate wherein dying in a state of apostasy is not a specific characteristic sought or intended by God.

Second, if we accept the application of the principles of the absolute and the restricted as valid in this case, the restriction would have to be considered a stipulation of avoidance in the sense that it alludes to not having repented (*tawba*) after becoming an apostate.

Third, if we accept this phrase as a restrictive clause, then it is meaningless to talk about the "nullification of deeds" in this world, for the verse points out that the apostate will cause his good deeds to be blotted out during his temporal life. Thus, in order for the "nullification of deeds" to have efficacy, we must say that the only criterion is apostasy and non-repentance. If it is said that up until death no judgement should be passed upon him, then the "nullification of deeds" in this world has no meaning.

iii. Shams al-Dīn Sarakhsī (d. 1090) writes under the section of apostasy that "the basis for the mandate to kill is His Word, 'submit', in the verse on apostasy" (Q. 48:16).[8]

iv. Zayn al-Dīn b. ʿAlī (Shahīd II) (d. 1558) alludes to two verses after having indicted apostasy as the most abominable, heinous, atrocious and extreme type of unbelief from the perspective of retribution: "Whosoever among you renounces his religion and dies as a disbeliever, their deeds will come to nothing (*ḥabaṭat aʿmāluhum*) in this world and the Hereafter . . ." (Q. 2:217), and "Whoever seeks a religion other than submission (*islām*), it will not be accepted from him; and he will be one of the losers in the Hereafter" (Q. 3:85). He binds to these two verses a prophetic hadith: "It is not permissible to shed the blood of a Muslim except in one of three situations: unbelief after believing, adultery after being a chaste person, or the premeditated unjust killing of another." This suggests that he considers killing mandatory as the outcome of these two verses, even though he does not say so explicitly.[9]

v. In addition to generalising the meaning of the "nullification of deeds" to be inclusive of this life and the afterlife, one can resort to the phrase in the same verse ". . . persecution and sedition (*fitna*) is worse than slaying . . ." (Q. 2:217). Two positions have been adopted on the meaning of "*fitna*": unbelief (*kufr*) and apostasy (*irtidād*). That is to say, the *fitna* initiated by unbelievers who embrace Islam and then recant in order to encourage Muslims to do likewise is far graver than killing a person. Accordingly, apostasy is far more serious and repugnant than killing a human being. Can one not derive from this the permissibility of killing an apostate? If a premeditated killing can rationally and religiously call for killing the murderer under the law of identical retribution (*qiṣāṣ*),[10] then why cannot one do so for apostasy, which is far more serious?

Note that my intention is not to use this verse to prove the necessity of killing an apostate; rather, it suffices to demonstrate that it is possible for apostasy to be a potential subject (*mawḍūʿ*) for the killing. Why is it so improbable to believe that statements attributed to the Prophet or the infallible Imams on killing an apostate can be linked to this verse? It is important to note that based on this verse, every act of apostasy, without exception, is *fitna* and therefore the most abominable act.

vi. In addition, one can use this verse to prove the following point: "The recompense of those who wage war against God and His Messenger and strive to spread mischief and corruption on Earth is that they be killed or crucified, or have their hands and feet amputated on opposite sides, or [be] banished from the land. That is their disgrace in this world; and there is a tremendous torment in store for them in the Hereafter" (Q. 5:33). Shaykh Ṭūsī writes, "The intended group comprises those who had apostatised and were subsequently overpowered and received this punishment. The occasion for this verse's revelation pertains to a group of men from the ʿUrayna tribe who entered Medina and embraced Islam. They got severely sick with bloated and inflated bellies."[11] As it became unbearable for them to stay there, the Prophet allowed them to leave and sent a camel and a driver with them. When they recovered from the illness, they apostatised, killed the driver and stole the camel. Upon learning of this, the Prophet dispatched a contingent of twenty individuals. His men overpowered them, and he had them killed on the charge of apostasy. The commentary of the *al-Tāj al-jāmiʿ li-l-uṣūl*, which deals with the Prophetic hadith, confirms that the occasion of Revelation was this particular incident. This is also the consensual opinion of the early and later Sunni scholars.[12]

vii. Hadiths are invoked on the authority of Imam Ali pertaining to Q. 4:137 to prove the ruling on killing an apostate. In *Daʿāʾim al-Islām*, Imam Ṣādiq relates on the authority of Imam ʿAli: "Do not allow the apostate to exceed three days of grace for repentance. If he has not repented until the fourth day, then kill him." Then he recited the verse, "As for those who believe [and] then reject the faith, then believe again [and] then reject the faith again, and then increase in disbelief, God will not forgive them, nor will He guide them to a path" (Q. 4:137).

Obviously, the Imam derived a clear proof from this verse by using an approach that mandates the killing of an apostate. Although it is possible that we may be unable to fathom the argument and proofs, it is clear that the necessity of killing an apostate is derived from this verse.

One can make a case that this verse points out that rejecting the apostate's repentance and pleas for guidance can be generalised as inclusive of this world and the Hereafter. However, there is a relationship between the non-acceptance of one's repentance and the issue of killing him because there exists no case in the jurisprudential literature where the apostate's repentance is rejected and he is simultaneously released on his own recognizance.

The conclusion of the discourse is as follows: The opponents' claim that the punishment of apostasy cannot be implemented without an explicit Qur'anic text (*naṣṣ*) or a hadith report that generates certainty (*yaqīn*) is remote from the principles of *ijtihād* and jurisprudence. All jurists are aware that one of the most fundamental discussions in Islamic legal theory is establishing the probative force (*ḥujjiyya*) of the apparent or obvious (*ẓawāhir*), inclusive of the apparent meaning of the Qur'an and the Hadith. Moreover, the Uṣūliyyūn have ruled that absolutising and generalising a word is one of the specific applications of the apparent [meaning], and no scholar until now has considered it mandatory to have an explicit Qur'anic text or hadith to deduce a legal ruling. In any event, one should not categorically and dogmatically reject the absence of a Qur'anic proof for killing an apostate, even though it is fraught with difficulty. In other words, when the hadiths provide clear proofs in favor of killing an apostate then, at a minimum, the verses can be used as corroboration.

*Issue* 2: Response to the opponents' claim that the Qur'an's spirit and general tenor is not compatible with killing an apostate:

a. The claim that it contravenes the Qur'an's spirit is a colossal one and is essentially outside the scope of the proofs that can be advanced. In other words, they have resorted to something that cannot be extracted. In opposition, we can make a counterclaim that its spirit is compatible with the legal ruling on apostasy. In any event, grasping onto the "spirit" is a spiritless and feeble argument and is of no benefit to either side.
b. A close study of the verses reveals that the worldly repercussions and punishment, as a result of apostatising, are very severe. The Qur'an specifies eight of them: nullification of the deeds in this world and the Hereafter; being grouped among the "losers" on the Day of Resurrection, with no

possibility of remedying the situation; not entitled to God's forgiveness; deprived of God's guidance, for "How shall God guide a people who disbelieved after having believed?" (Q. 3:86); enter the Hellfire; remain in the Hellfire forever; Satan will adorn evil deeds, make them [appear to be] appealing, and will inspire them with distant and grandiose hopes and aspirations [to make them forget God]; and the curse of God, the angels and humanity will descend upon them until the Day of Resurrection, for "They are those whose recompense is that upon them shall be the curse of God, the angels, and the people combined" (Q. 3:87).

These consequences prove that the Qur'an proclaims that apostasy is not only a sin, but a major sin and, in actuality, one of the most calamitous and gravest of all the major sins.

With the presence of all these harsh repercussions in the Hereafter and some in this world, how can one accept that the Qur'an's spirit is incompatible with the apostate's receiving a severe worldly punishment? How would the advocates of freedom and the right to express all types of thoughts and beliefs justify the harsh consequences for the apostate in the Hereafter? In other words, based on this type of thinking, apostasy is incapable of becoming a "subject matter" either for worldly punishment or for the Hereafter. They consider apostasy protected under the freedom of thought and human rights. If so, then it follows that since there is no abhorrence (*qubḥ*) in the commission of apostasy, it negates the possibility of any worldly or otherworldly punishments. The advocates of freedom of religion are required to also accept that there is no otherworldly punishment because of the absence of any *qubḥ*. Otherwise, if they admit that there is inherent *qubḥ* in the act, then what is the basis of their aversion for accepting worldly punishment?

One can assume that the hadith reports from the Prophet and the Imams regarding the killing of an apostate are founded upon the Qur'an's recorded inevitable and customary harsh worldly punishments for apostasy.

*Issue 3*: Do those who clamour that the Qur'an has prescribed no worldly punishment for the apostate also reject the explicit Qur'anic punishments for the *ḥudūd* crimes, such as adultery, theft, belligerency (*muḥārib*), and spreading mischief and corruption on Earth? Certainly those who compose works and express an opinion under the pretext of institutionalising freedom and human rights reject the *ḥudūd* punishments. If not, then they need to explain why they cannot also accept the punishment for apostasy, even though the latter is far more repugnant and reprehensible than adultery and theft.

*Issue 4*: Even if one were to accept that the Qur'an mentions no worldly punishment for the apostate, it does not puncture the validity of the legal ruling because there are many detailed legal rulings derived for such issues as pilgrimage, prayers and *zakāt* that are also not mentioned in the Qur'an.

In reality, one cannot envision a separation between the Qur'an and the statements of the Prophet and the Imams, for the truth of the Qur'an cannot be uncovered without them: "We have sent down to you the Reminder so that you may make clear to the people that which has been sent down to them" (Q. 16:44). The Qur'an must be understood through the mediation of the Prophet and the Imams, for "Whatsoever the Messenger gives you, take it; and whatsoever he forbids you, abstain (from it)" (Q. 59:7). Clearly, Muslims are obliged to comply with whatever the Prophet advances as his interpretation of the verses or of any other subject.

Thus, if there are hadiths in which the Prophet or the Imams (who are the "speaking Qur'an" and its true exegetes) condemn the apostate to death, then acting upon them is equivalent to acting upon the Qur'an. Paying attention to the phrase *lan yaftariqā* (both of them (the Qur'an and the *Ahl al-Bayt*) will never separate) in the *ḥadīth al-thaqalayn* (the two precious weights) makes it categorically clear to those who possess understanding and discernment that the Qur'an is inseparable from the *Ahl al-Bayt* and vice versa. Moreover, they do not possess the capacity to be otherwise. On the basis of this hadith, arguments and proofs taken from the Qur'an while disregarding and ignoring the hadiths, or its converse, are both void and rejected.

## Killing an Apostate and the Hadith

Having examined that the Qur'an mandates the killing of an apostate, we now do the same in a summary fashion by invoking the hadiths. Those who are opposed to using them to validate this punishment are afflicted with certain doubts and conjectures:

a. They fancy that the hadiths in support of mandating such killings are rare and few.
b. They imagine that these hadiths are "isolated" (*khabar al-wāḥid*) and cannot be relied upon because their probative force is based upon the attestation of rational beings who would generally consider it inappropriate and repugnant to act upon them on matters that are vital, such as killing and execution.

## Response to Conjecture 1

(a) The topic of an apostate's punishment has been broached in connection with five subject areas of jurisprudence: the Book of Purity (*Kitāb al-ṭahāra*); the Book of Marriage (*Kitāb al-nikāḥ*); the Book of Hunting and Slaughtering (*Kitāb al-ṣayd wa-l-dhibāḥa*); the Book of Inheritance (*Kitāb al-irth*); and the Book of *Ḥudūd* (*Kitāb al-ḥudūd*). If one were to undertake a brief overview of all the hadiths dealing with apostasy contained within these books, they would clearly realise that there are more than twenty of them. Shaykh Muḥammad b. Ya'qūb al-Kulaynī (d. 941) gathered twenty-three hadiths in his hadith work under the chapter "Fixed Punishments for an Apostate" (*Ḥadd al-murtadd*).[13] Most of them fall in the category of "sound" (*ṣaḥīḥ*),[14] and jurists have employed them as evidence in the above-mentioned five subjects. These hadiths are not only sound in terms of their chain of transmission (*sanad*), but they are also attested to by scholars to have been related by the infallible Imams; without any hesitation, we can say that these hadiths have reached a threshold of widespread transmission in meaning (*tawātur ma'nawī*)[15] and *tawātur ijmālī*.[16]

On other topics of substantive law, the eminent jurists have considered ten hadiths on any one topic sufficient to reach the level of *tawātur*,[17] let alone twenty-three. In the event that a hadith reaches this level, then there is no need to even interrogate the chain of transmission. This matter is clear and indisputable among the jurists.

(b) A jurist cannot rely on only a portion of the hadiths when deducing or proving an issue; rather, he must examine all of those that are pertinent to the subject. Scrutinising the hadiths on the topic of apostasy results in the following five groupings:

*Group I*: Hadiths that prove with great clarity and precision the necessity to kill an apostate.

a. A *ṣaḥīḥ* hadith related by Muḥammad b. Muslim on the authority of Imam Bāqir (d. 733): "I asked Abū Jaʿfar about apostasy and he replied, 'If a Muslim turns away from Islam or shuns it and rejects what was revealed to the Prophet (i.e., a *fiṭrī* apostate), then his repentance cannot be accepted and it is obligatory to kill him. His marriage is annulled and his estate is to be distributed among his children.'"[18]
b. The fifth hadith regarded as *ṣaḥīḥ* in the same chapter is related by Jamīl b. Darrāj on the authority of Imam Bāqir or Imam Ṣādiq, who was asked about a person who had apostatised. "He should be encouraged to repent. If he does so, then it should be accepted; otherwise, he should be killed." This hadith clearly demonstrates that the apostate deserves the punishment of execution.
c. The tenth hadith on the authority of Imam Kāẓim (d. 799), who was asked, "What is the ruling on a person who has converted to Christianity?" to which he replied, "He should be killed."
d. The eleventh hadith, in which ʿAmmār Sābāṭī relates that he heard Imam Ṣādiq say, "Any Muslim who apostatises and disavows Muhammad's prophethood and belies it, then his blood is lawful for every Muslim who heard him say that."
e. ʿAbdallah b. Abī Yaʿfūr asks Imam Ṣādiq about Bazīʿ, who conjectures and claims that he is a prophet. He replied, "If you have heard him say this, then you should kill him."
f. The ruling on the necessity of killing an apostate has also been recorded in the books of Sunni scholars, such as Manṣūr Nāṣif, author of *al-Tāj al-jāmiʿ li-l-uṣūl fī aḥādīth al-Rasūl*. On the authority of the Prophet: "The blood of a Muslim who testifies that there is no god but God and I am His Messenger cannot be shed except under three circumstances: premeditated and unjust killing [resulting in *qiṣāṣ*], adultery, and abandoning the community by recanting Islam."[19] He points out that this hadith has been related in *Ṣaḥīḥ Bukhārī*, *Ṣaḥīḥ Muslim*, *Nasāʾī*, *Abū Dāwūd* and *Tirmidhī*. Clearly, the Prophet makes it clear that a person who renounces Islam and thus becomes an apostate can be killed. Thereafter, he relates from ʿIkrima that Imam Ali killed a group of Muslims who had recanted and adds that all the Sunni books of hadith other than

*Ṣaḥīḥ Muslim* recount this hadith from Ibn ʿAbbās on the authority of the Prophet: "Whoever changes his religion must be killed."[20]

*Group II*: Hadiths cited to support and establish that a female apostate should not be killed clearly demonstrates that this is supposed to be an exception to a generally accepted ruling on the legality of executing an apostate.

*Group III*: Those who persist in committing major sins are condemned to death, whereas apostasy is not only a major sin but without a doubt one of the most grievous enormities of all major sins. The jurists are united that even if an apostate is not to be killed on his first reversion from Islam, he must be killed at the third or fourth instance. A hadith from Imam Kāẓim is invoked to substantiate this: "Those who commit major sins must be killed at the third instance."

Likewise, an adulterer who has been convicted of this sin twice should be killed when it recurs for the third time. Certainly, it is the same in the case of apostasy. Jamīl b. Darrāj has clarified this matter in the fifth hadith related in the same chapter. The point is that the jurist ought to look at the subject of apostasy from this angle as well. That is, even if one were to assume that no clear-cut hadiths prove the necessity of killing an apostate, by this method we can still establish the killing of an apostate, albeit on the condition that his apostasy is repeated.

*Group IV*: Hadiths that establish a corollary that reciting the dual testimony of faith makes one's blood sacrosanct and prohibits its shedding, validates marriage with a Muslim, and entitles one to inherit from a Muslim. As such, in the absence of the dual testimony of faith, one's blood would no longer be inviolable. Khūʾī has stated that many hadiths make the dual testimony of faith the basis for sanctifying blood, allowing marriage, and inheriting. The conclusion is that one who apostatises would forfeit the protection that was provided as a result of being a Muslim.[21]

*Group V*: Hadith reports in which Imam Ali implemented the punishment of apostasy.

Hadith 1: Imam Ṣādiq relates that a Muslim had converted to Christianity and wore a cross around his neck. They brought him to Imam Ali, who told him, "If your intention is to marry, then we can arrange what is needed to facilitate it. If you desire to inherit from a Christian and think that you could not do so if you remain a Muslim, then we will provide you with [an] inheritance." However, the convert did not accept. The Imam asked him, "Have you truly converted to Christianity?" to which he replied that he had. The Imam exclaimed, "God is greater" (*Allāh akbar*), and he countered, "Jesus is greater" (*al-Masīḥ akbar*). At that moment, the Imam gave the order to kill him.[22]

Hadith 2: Imam Ṣādiq relates that a tribe came to Imam Ali and addressed him as their lord, *al-salāmu 'alay-ka yā rabba-nā* (peace be upon our Lord), to which the Imam reacted fiercely and demanded that they repent. They refused. Thus, he dug two trenches and a connecting path between them. When they persisted in the false belief, he threw them into a trench and set the other one on fire to kill them.[23] Here is an instance where the standard of apostasy is applied in the case of exaggerating (*ghuluww*) the attributes of the Imams.

Hadith 3: Imam Ṣādiq relates that a number of people testified to Imam Ali against a person from the Tha'laba tribe, which had converted from Islam to Christianity. The Imam asked him, "Do you accept their testimonies?" to which he replied, "Yes, but I am renewing my pledge to Islam." The Imam said, "If you had denied their testimonies, then I would have severed your head instantly because your denial would show that your second claim (of having reverted to Islam) was also false, and thus I would have had to implement the ruling of apostasy on you."

This hadith confirms that there were such cases during Imam Ali's caliphate and that in numerous instances he implemented the ruling of apostasy. No contextual sign (*qarīna*) suggests that this was a particular instance or an "objective case" (*qaḍiyya fi wāqi'a*). In fact, the hadith's apparent meaning proves that the Imam implemented a general ruling on apostasy. The Sunni Hadith corpus also contains instances in which the Prophet gave an order to kill a group that had apostatised. I have already alluded to this.[24]

Based on the collective evidence of the five hadith groups, can one not derive a definitive and clear conclusion that an apostate is condemned to death? Do not the hadiths mandating, only in the case of an apostate, his estate be distributed to his inheritors, and his (former) wife undergo a widow's waiting period prove the necessity of killing him?

Those who reject the killing of an apostate would also need to reject the following rulings: embracing Islam is the cause of preservation and sanctification of one's blood; an apostate's marriage is annulled due to apostasy; his estate is distributed to his inheritors; the animal slaughtered by him is unlawful for human consumption; and all of the other rulings regarding apostates specified in the books of substantive law. The deniers cannot opt to reject only the killing of an apostate and accept the rest.

In my estimation, based on the evidence gathered from the different groups of hadiths cited above, there is no room for any doubt or hesitation that the necessity of killing an apostate is among Islam's well-established and definitive rulings. Please note that these hadith reports were not exclusively related during the time of Imam Ali's caliphate or during the Medinan period of the Prophet in order to preempt one from speculating that such a ruling is political or governmental and thus only valid for a particular period. Rather, they are related by the infallible Imams, such as Imam Bāqir, Imam Ṣādiq, Imam Kāẓim, and Imam Riḍā (d. 819) and thus demonstrate with glaring clarity that this ruling is timeless and perpetual, [and therefore] valid until the Day of Resurrection. These hadiths are instances of actual events and present a general rule on apostasy.

## Response to Conjecture 2

Those who claim that the hadiths pertaining to apostasy are "isolated reports" (*khabar al-wāḥid*) and, as such, cannot be relied upon as a proof text on critical issues should take note of the following:

a. I have demonstrated with clarity and confidence that these hadiths rank as *tawātur* in meaning or are *ijmālī* and, as such, are absolutely beneficial.
b. Even if we assume that the hadiths are "isolated" (*khabar al-wāḥid*), there is no difference in the punishment's application in terms of crucial and non-crucial matters. This has been the opinion of many distinguished and eminent Akhbārī and Uṣūlī jurists. Jurists from the early and later periods, as well as from the inception of jurisprudence up to and including today, have relied, as testified by their works, on trustworthy "isolated reports" (*khabar al-wāḥid*) for issues that pertain to the loss of life, property, worship, and politics. I have deliberated on this issue in great detail elsewhere.[25]
c. On the subject of the "necessity to execute an apostate", Shaykh Ṭūṣī clearly says that there is a "consensus of the *umma*" on this matter. In other words, it is not only the juridical consensus of the Sunni and Shi'i scholars, but rather of the entire *umma*. The interpretation of such a

ruling reaches the rank of an essential (*ḍarūrī*) decree. As such, the basis of this ruling is not based only on "isolated hadiths" (*khabar al-wāḥid*); rather, consensus is incorporated into it.

d. What are the criteria for distinguishing crucial from non-crucial matters? In the discourse on *khums* and *zakāt*, connected with an individual's property and other similar matters with grave financial implications, "isolated reports" (*khabar al-wāḥid*) are invoked as proofs. Should not assigning a religious decree on an extremely substantial property fall under "crucial" matters?

   On the issue of *zakāt*, undeniably a Qur'anic concept, the Qur'an does not provide any details on the specifics and conditions for levying the rate of one-tenth or one-twentieth. Thus, the only recourse is to cite "isolated reports" (*khabar al-wāḥid*)

   Likewise, the sacrificing of an animal during the hajj rituals that has been decreed at Mina illustrates that the jurists do not act exclusively on the basis of an "isolated hadith report" ("There is no sacrifice except in Mina"). Rather, they also take into account the reasoning and qualifications provided by other jurists, especially the ancient ones, as well as the absence of any hindrance at that time. Thus, what objection could there be to employing "isolated reports" in a similar manner, even if it be on such crucial matters as executing an apostate?

e. It is claimed that jurists have exercised caution (*iḥtiyāt*) on matters of the loss of life, guarding chastity and property. But as I have demonstrated elsewhere, many of them issued no such *fatwa* (to exercise obligatory caution). Rather, they considered implementation of the punishment as extremely preferred and highly recommended.[26]

f. Even if the hadith reports, Qur'anic verses and consensus independently do not provide sufficient proof, there is no doubt that collectively they do produce the necessary confidence and assurance for the jurist to issue a decree.

## Killing an Apostate and Creating Chaos and Anarchy

Some have argued that establishing and implementing judgements, especially pertaining to life and death, must be done through a just judicial system so that neither a culture of anarchy and lawlessness will be fostered, nor will believers be encouraged to violate the civil law. There are several points to consider here:

a. Would advocates of such a position accept a convicted apostate's punishment if it were established and certified by a competent court? Apparently, their objection is to the very ruling on apostasy and, as such, is not dependent on deriving a judgement from a competent court.

b. A jurist or *marja'* has no right to give an opinion on apostasy until and unless he first obtains confidence on the truth of the matter. If Khomeini had issued such an opinion regarding Salman Rushdie, it was only after the subject of apostasy was totally confirmed and undeniable for him. The same applies to Lankarānī Sr concerning Rāfiq Taqī, for the former arrived at this conclusion after having reviewed several of his translated works from their original language into Persian. Could not a fully qualified jurist, who has fulfilled numerous conditions before attaining this rank, establish the subject matter of apostasy? Does the philosophy of setting up a court involve anything other than obtaining and confirming the subject matter with clarity? Does the court fabricate and make up a law, or is its mandate to apply and implement the existing law? Are not the judicial system's three levels designed to ensure the correct formulation of the subject matter with great confidence?

c. The fundamental question is "What constitutes a competent court for you?" If the rulings issued are not compatible with the deceptive slogans of human rights, then it becomes an unjust and incompetent court. If so, then most of the Islamic judgements would have to be considered faulty and be discarded! Instead, a just court is defined as one that competently applies the reliable religious rulings, that is to say, a court that implements and acts upon the ordinances and *shar'ī* standards. Clearly this criterion is best fulfilled and with precision in the person of the jurist.

   The jurist is able to apply the divine ordinances after confirming them with great accuracy, as this is one of the areas emphasised for gaining proficiency in jurisprudence. To act as a judge was one of the important posts of the Prophet and the infallible Imams. As for the qualified jurists, they are required to have the ability to exercise *ijtihād* and it is enjoined that none other than a *mujtahid* can be appointed to the post of a judge.

d. Is it the ruling itself or its implementation that fosters anarchy? Is the execution of an apostate not a divine ruling? Is it not a violation and a rejection of a divine ruling to waive it due to its incompatibility with the standards and criteria of contemporary human rights? Should we discard the divine rules and instead pay heed to the apparent pleas of human rights advocates? Would this not constitute the worst possible approach and the most hideous form of anarchy?

Is it proper for us to encourage the implementation of divine laws or the Universal Declaration of Human Rights? Can the latter, which bestows freedom upon homosexuals, guarantee success and prosperity for humanity? The protesters should either accept Islam or this charter, because combining both is impossible. In fact, if they do so it would lead to the negation of Islam. I am amazed at those who are so concerned about not violating this charter but care so little about preserving the dignity of Islam. Not only are they not angered by the idle talk of the exponents of human rights, but instead they defend them. Imam Ali says, "You witness the breach of God's covenant, and yet do not get enraged, although you fret and frown at the breach of your forefathers' traditions. God's matters have been coming back to you; but you have made over your place to wrong-doers and thrown towards them your responsibilities, and have placed God's affairs in their hands. They act on doubts and tread in [fulfilment of] desires."[27]

e. Islam has set out clear criteria and conditions for implementing the *ḥudūd* punishments, even for those who are mandated to carry it out. One should be mindful that, at times, the public welfare demands that those tasked with implementing a specific legal ruling be the public at large. In the case of apostasy or blaspheming the Prophet, all Muslims (both male and female) are religiously responsible for carrying out this obligation. The philosophy behind such a command is to serve as a deterrent for the public by underlining the fact that apostasy is so reprehensible and repugnant in God's sight that it merits a particularly grave punishment. The decree on the apostate or the blasphemer is preventive, for its purpose is to defend the divine legal corpus of Islam. Given that both Islam's fundamentals and secondary aspects accord with human reason and logic, it does not allow one to reject the truth of Islam after it has been clearly proven or confirmed, which is also the case with one who insults and defames the most sanctified person of Muhammad.

This type of ruling is not designed to attract others towards Islam, and thus there is no reason to be concerned that its implementation would prevent others from embracing Islam. Rather, it is a fortress that guards Muslims from harm and restrains them from damaging Islam by their own actions. On the one hand, it prevents Muslims from hastily leaving

Islam and compels them to reflect some more and ponder and, on the other hand, it has forever closed the door employed by the unbelievers to strike at Islam (from within) by fostering apostasy.

f. Some have objected that issuing the decree of execution and terror for blasphemy and apostasy deforms the visage of Islam and Shiʿism, as well as jurisprudence, by portraying them as prone to violence, being dreadful and closed-minded, and so on. This is true if one introduces Islam only by this method and without explaining the specifics and conditions that must be fulfilled before the apostate can be punished, and also by only elaborating upon one aspect while neglecting all of the ruling's other aspects and details. Instead, the public ought to be informed that, as a general rule, logic and human reason are dominant in Islam and that a Muslim can bring his misgivings or queries about Islam to the jurists (who are the proofs (*ḥujja*) from God) for clarification. If, despite this, he stubbornly defies Islam and then suddenly recants and circulates this information to the public, only then can such a harsh punishment be applied.

In reality, apostasy itself is a case of promoting religious chaos and disorder. Why is it that those who write about anarchy are so oblivious to this fact? This ruling on executing an apostate or a blasphemer has been in existence ever since the dawn of Islam, and at no point has it ever been the cause of defacing the visage of Islam. From the time that the (European) colonialists began expounding upon human rights (and, in actuality, this was the start of confronting Islam), they have protested with incredulity by asking, "What kind of a ruling is this?" This objection is motivated by their desire to spread wicked and false information about Islam and has ended here on this point, namely, that Islamic rulings "are in conflict" with human reason, freedom and dignity.

Why should we Muslims be so simple-minded and naive that we fall prey to deception under such assertions? One day they claim, under false pretences, that Islamic rulings are incompatible with reason; another day that they are incompatible with freedom; and still the next day say that they disregard human dignity.

Clearly, one should never judge a partial legal ruling, and even that from its outward appearance (i.e., capital punishment), as a standard of good and praiseworthy (*ḥusn*) and abominable and blameworthy (*qubḥ*)! In other words, it is not proper to introduce the issue of *ḥusn* and *qubḥ* with regard to a particular legal ruling; rather, it is in the context of the aggregate connected with the type of criterion formulated to render a judgement. Why do you consider it valid and respectful for one who has "tasted" and "touched" the truths of religion, who has been convinced of its evidences and proofs, to stubbornly reject and deny them and yet consider it illogical and violent to mete out the well-deserved punishment? Would you have any regard for someone who denies the Sun's presence on a sunny day? Why do you view apostasy as a type of reflection of thought and ideas, and present it as a type of fully-fledged competition of thought? Apostasy is a type of denial of reality that is impossible to deny.

It is taken for granted that one should enter the field of thought with logic, the best disputation and solid proofs. However, how should one react to a person who rejects this method? If one denies the obvious and conspicuous truths and poses a danger for the rest, then what does human reason dictate? An apostate is a sick and an abominable person whose "abomination" (emanating from his whims, caprices and love for the material world) is contagious and could spread in the society and religion. As such, he must be punished.

Those who object to the punishment invoke "Invite to the way of your Lord with wisdom and goodly exhortation, and dispute with them in the most dignified manner" (Q. 16:125) to substantiate their argument. In all fairness, can this verse be applied in the case of apostasy? What is its relationship with apostasy? Have you not observed that God proclaims in the verses on apostasy that an apostate is someone who cannot receive His guidance or forgiveness? Should such a person, who is the subject of such harsh treatment, be included in this verse? Clearly, this verse pertains to someone who has not yet adopted the straight path, although such efforts are underway. However, one who is already on it and then leaves it and, driven by animosity and whim and caprice, opposes it, cannot possibly be included in this verse. Can a murderer be included here by dealing with him through wisdom, goodly exhortation, and disputation? I do not think that any sane person would accept the claim that this is the sole approach that can be used in all circumstances, even in a case where one is massacring people.

We mentioned previously that the ruling on apostasy is not designed to attract others towards Islam; rather, it is an internal requital designed to prevent the spread of the unbelievers' intrigues into the Muslim body.

If one desires to present Islam, one should take into account its totality and multiple perspectives, like the advancement of reason, knowledge, ethics, societal affairs and politics, and public administration. Why do they not announce that Islam has issued no legal ruling of execution against a native-born unbeliever (*kāfir aṣlī*) who has never wavered in his native belief?

## Does this Ruling Weaken and Impair Religion?

Some people claim that issuing such decrees impairs and weakens Islam. However, we should first identify the criterion of what constitutes the weakening of Islam. In this regard, there are four possibilities:

a. An act is considered to be impairing religion when all rational beings in all times and places agree that the act is unpleasant and harmful. Under this assumption, there are two prospects:
   i. Rational beings in all times and places would not accept it as proper to heap insults upon individuals and things that more than one billion people hold sacred. They would consider such a person worthy of being punished in proportion to the gravity of his insults and the consequences of its impact upon the public. That is to say, if the insults mislead Muslims or are exploited by the enemies to destroy or weaken Islam, then the response would be more severe.
   ii. Assume that rational beings do not regard an apostate or a blasphemer as deserving of punishment, even though the Legislator (*Shāriʿ*) has said that they are, that is, one who recants Islam after embracing it deserves a severe punishment; however, a native-born unbeliever who remains an unbeliever is not subject to any temporal punishment.

      All jurisprudents are united in their agreement of the universal principle that on some issues the Legislator has the prerogative to declare rational beings' conclusions incorrect but that He would not denigrate a rational ruling. This is an instance of separating the "rationality" (*ʿaql*) from "rational beings" (*ʿuqalāʾ*), a subject that has been dealt with at great length outside of jurisprudence.

b. The criteria of what constitutes "impairing or weakening of Islam" is something that does not agree with humanity's natural disposition and therefore is detested. In this situation, obviously no one will abhor the punishment meted out to an apostate or one who blasphemes the Prophet, the most impeccable and honoured person.

c. If the criterion of what statement or action constitutes "impairing Islam" is defined by the non-religious, then many Islamic rulings on worship and its details, human inter-relations (*mu'āmalāt*), politics, and even some matters dealing with ethics would be labelled as "impairing Islam". Even enjoining the good and forbidding the evil could be viewed as "impairing Islam", if doing so were to be considered as interfering in another person's life. Likewise, jihad and martyrdom in the path of God would be considered a cause of debilitating Islam.

d. The criterion of what constitutes an act that is "impairing Islam" is one that requires no vindication in human reason or hadith reports. In my opinion, this is perhaps the right definition. However, we have clearly demonstrated that the ruling on executing an apostate or blasphemer of the Prophet has both a clear rational and textual (hadith) basis. As for the former, reason accepts that the Creator and Sole Owner of everything, of which humans are a part, can issue such a legal ruling that pertains to the subject of worldly punishment. In such a case, it cannot be considered either repulsive or abominable.

In other words, the most fundamental question is whether reason could support that God can issue such a judgement. Some of the critics of apostasy, eager to advance their point, assume that the criteria on rationally deduced legal rulings are based upon the goodness (*ḥusn*) of justice (*'adl*) and the repugnance (*qubḥ*) of oppression (*ẓulm*). (Khomeini deliberates upon this in some of his works.) If this is the case, then the issuance of a legal ruling on killing an apostate or a blasphemer raises no rational objection that it is repulsive or oppressive. In actuality, they would accept that no oppression was perpetrated, based upon the premise that it was God, the true Creator of humanity, who had issued such a ruling. Moreover, reason is able to corroborate the validity of such a legal ruling with the sinner who deserves the punishment. As for traditional proofs, the Legislator has elaborated these through the hadith reports.

Under the subject of "impairing Islam", people seem to have forgotten that it is grouped under "secondary status" (*'unwān thānawī*) like hardship (*ḥaraj*) and urgency (*iḍṭirār*), harm (*ḍarar*) and dissimulation (*taqiyya*). It has been established that such subjects are not valid and applicable in all instances. For example, in the case of dissimulation the subject would be suspended in a situation where blood could be spilled, for "There is no *taqiyya* when it leads to spilling of blood" (i.e., if it results in shedding of innocent blood).

In some instance, the issue of "impairing Islam" could not be formulated into a subject for a legal ruling. For example, occasions that demand extreme and harsh measures against unbelievers and polytheists that would lead to their killing. In such a case, no jurist would rule that if this would result in impairing Islam's image, then it is not obligatory. This point can be readily attested to by one who has familiarity with the science of jurisprudence. Accordingly, in the case of apostasy the subject of "impairing Islam" has no relevance, although one could temporarily suspend the punishment of "stoning the adulterer" if it leads to "impairing Islam". However, a ruling that is essentially designed to deal forcefully with the unbelievers, polytheists and deviants who are scornfully rejecting and exploiting the situation, and thereby producing greater hatred and distance between themselves and the Muslims, cannot be blocked by raising the issue of "impairing Islam".

## Is the Infallible [Twelfth] Imam's Presence Required to Implement the *Ḥudūd*?

Some people claim that many eminent jurists have conditioned the implementation of the *ḥudūd* punishments or the launching of an offensive war on the presence of the Prophet or the infallible (Twelfth) Imam. However, in my opinion this conclusion is based upon faulty research and the reality is actually quite the opposite. Such early prominent jurists as Shaykh Mufīd (d. 1022),[28] Sallār al-Daylamī (d. 1056–1057),[29] Abū al-Ṣalāḥ al-Ḥalabī (d. 1055),[30] Ibn Zuhra (d.1189),[31] Ibn Saʿīd,[32] Shaykh Ṭūsi,[33] 'Allāma Ḥillī (d. 1325),[34] Muḥammad b. Makkī (Shahīd I) (d. 1384),[35] Muḥaqqiq al-Karakī (Muḥaqqiq II) (d. 1533) in his commentary of *Sharāʾiʿ*, Shahīd II in *Masālik al-afhām*, and Fāḍil Miqdād (d. 1423) in *al-Tanqīḥ al-rāʾiʿ*, consider both of these to be permissible and legally sanctioned during the occultation of the Twelfth Imam. True, some of the expressions of Ibn Idrīs in *Sarāʾir* and other jurists, such as Ṣaymarī and Ibn Fahd, are advanced to reject this claim. However, Muḥammad Bāqir Shaftī (d. 1844)[36] has brought expressions and phrases from the end part of Ibn Idrīs' book to show that not only was he a popular exponent of this permissibility, but also that his expressions can be used to infer his insistence on its permissibility.

Thus, what sources sustain the claim made by some that many of the past distinguished jurists considered implementing the *ḥudūd* punishments conditional upon the presence of the infallible (Twelfth) Imam? Muḥaqqiq Ḥillī ought to be grouped under those who suspended passing a judgement on this and not as being against the ruling, a view shared by Khū'ī and Khwānsārī. The latter two also regarded Ibn Idrīs as having shared this position.

Muḥammad Ḥasan al-Najafī (author of *Jawāhir*) (d. 1850), the "pivot of jurisprudence of the times", writes, "There is no dissent, except that which has apparently been reported by Ibn Zuhra and Ibn Idrīs. But it is not established; rather, it is possible that it merits and necessitates quite the opposite."[37]

## Is Mandating the Killing of an Apostate Compatible with the Prophet's Merciful Character?

Some people ask what is the congruence between such harsh *fatwas* and the visage of the merciful Messenger?

a. This kind of interpretation and expression does not accord with the dignified stature of *ijtihād* and the techniques employed to derive legal rulings. Rather, it resembles a slogan. This is akin to saying that if God is the Most Merciful, then why did He create Hellfire where some will suffer (eternal) chastisement? As such, in principle, all of the *ḥudūd* punishments during the time of the (Twelfth) Imam's presence and his absence must be rejected.
b. According to historical accounts, during the Prophet's time some former Muslims were convicted of apostasy. How can this be reconciled with the trait of "merciful Messenger"? How can ". . . harsh against the disbelievers, merciful to one another" (Q. 48:29) be interpreted? Should the apostate, despite apostatizing, be allowed to enter the fold of the Muslims? This clearly cannot be the case. According to the tenor of the Qur'an, is an apostate not worse than an unbeliever?
c. Executing an apostate is the cause of mercy for Muslim society, and not confronting him would lead to its injury. Why is the "mercy" attached to and explained in relation to a specific person be independent of

others or the religion? In other words, they have failed to provide a proper understanding of "merciful Messenger", for he is a mercy for all of humanity, as opposed to for each individual person.

## Some Final Thoughts and Reminders

a. The legal ruling on apostasy is not confined to Islam, for it is present in other religions as well. This conclusion can be derived from: "Surely it has been revealed to you and to those before you that if you ascribe partners [to God, then] your work will surely become worthless and you shall be among the losers" (Q. 39:65). Moreover, Q. 2:54 makes it clear that the punishment during the time of Moses was execution. As such, the Bible states that Christians and Jews who recant their faith are also subjected to the prescribed punishment.
b. On the basis of the collective proofs, the subject for execution can only be established when the apostate discloses his apostasy. After he divulges it and it becomes public knowledge, then he will be executed.
c. According to the Qur'an, punishment in this life and the afterlife is contingent upon the person embracing Islam on the basis of knowledge and awareness and then rejecting it "after guidance has been made clear to them" (Q. 47:32). Thus, one who has doubts or is so influenced by negative propaganda that he rejects Islam would be exempt from the ruling on apostasy. Some jurists, however, opine that this issue requires further deliberation before a conclusion can be issued. Lankarānī Sr has said, "Youth who have just attained the age of puberty and are doubtful about the validity of Islam should be given time and must not be judged as apostates."
d. Does an apostate's repentance have any effect in this life? This issue has been discussed at great length in the books of jurisprudence and exegesis. For our purposes, the assumption is that, at a minimum, an apostate who does not repent certainly deserves to be executed.
e. At the outset, the killing of an apostate does not require a juridical ruling. Therefore, any Muslim can implement it. A hadith attributed to ʿAmmār Sābāṭī states: "If the shedding of blood (i.e., taking of human life) has become lawful, then anyone who hears him (recant Islam) can carry it out." However, caution dicates that it be done under the supervision of a qualified jurist.

f. It is worthy to note: why has Islam not prescribed the punishment of execution for a native-born unbeliever who continues in his unbelief, contrary to its ruling against an apostate? The reason is that a Muslim who declares his apostasy from within the Muslim community is declaring war against Islam. It is, therefore, natural to deal harshly with him, in contrast to a native-born unbeliever (who has not embraced Islam).

g. The expression used to negate the punishment of execution for apostasy is, "The scholars have differing opinions in defining the essentials of religion . . ."

   i. The essentials of religion are those on which there is unanimity between the Shi'is and Sunnis, and thus there is no need for proofs or even consensus to demonstrate their validity.

   ii. Assuming that there are differing opinions on defining these essentials, those hadiths on the subject of apostasy make clear two instances that constitute apostasy: (1) abandoning Islam or denying the prophethood of Muhammad; and (2) denying the Day of Resurrection. Some hadith reports relate that a *zindiq* who had denied the Day of Resurrection was brought to Imam Ali and that the Imam gave the order to kill him.

   In any event, denying Muhammad's prophethood or the Day of Resurrection constitutes apostasy and, at a minimum, should be accepted without any dispute. Moreover, the title of "essentials" is not a subject by itself, for its only function is in determining instances for its application. If this can be reached with clarity and confidence from the hadiths, then there should be no hesitation in executing the apostate, regardless of whether the confirmation falls under the category of "essentials" or not.

h. Some who have misgivings about the ruling on apostasy object to the method of *ijtihād* that is prevalent in the seminaries and argue that a new method of *ijtihād* should be formulated on the basis of anthropology, cosmology, and new Qur'anic hermeneutics. Whether this claim is true or not requires an independent study and falls outside the scope of this work. What I have penned here is in conformity with the *ijtihād* method that scholars have used for a thousand years. Therefore, there should be no doubt about the necessity to execute an apostate. In addition, this necessity is neither time-bound nor limited to politics and state, although the latter could be one instance of apostasy. The proposed new method of *ijtihād* would result in changing many legal rulings and thus lead to nothing but the destruction of Islam and taking shelter under the aegis of man-made laws. Over and beyond this, using such a new method will efface the heritage of the *Ahl al-Bayt* and its jurisprudence.

In closing, the following issue still remains open: Is a qualified jurist allowed to use his discretion to delay or nullify the implementation of this punishment decreed by God for the apostate on the grounds of public welfare (*maṣlaḥa*) or in those cases that this subject (apostasy) finds many particulars (this hypothesis would not occur if this ruling (punishment of apostasy) was actualised from the beginning)? In certain hadiths on apostasy, Imam Ali is reported to have said: "On matters of *ḥudūd*, once established, even I cannot suspend its implementation." In any event, this subject demands careful deliberation, and I would like to use this opportunity to announce that the *Markaz-i Fiqhī-ye A'imme-ye Aṭhār*, an institution that specialises in jurisprudence, is ready and equipped to engage in a debate on this subject. Islamic scholars and jurisprudential experts who wish to participate, independent of the political furor and tumult and any predisposition toward the West, could engage the subject matter under this framework.

This constitutes a brief defense for the validity of the legal ruling on apostasy. However, it should be obvious that a more detailed deliberation demands a better opportunity.

May God bestow us with the capacity to understand reality and Islam and to act upon them, God willing.

Peace upon those who follow the path of guidance.

Mohammad Javād Fāzel Lankarānī (Lankarānī Jr)
13 December 2011

## *Notes*

1. Issued on 13 December 2011, see website of Lankarānī Jr, available at: http://www.lankarani.com/far.
2. Muḥammad b. al-Ḥusayn Sharīf al-Raḍī, *Nahj al-balāgha: Selection of Sermons, Letters and Sayings of Amīr al-Mu'minīn 'Alī b. Abī Ṭālib*, trans. S. A. Reza (Rome: European Islamic Cultural Centre, 1984), Sermon 106.
3. Shihāb al-Dīn al-Ālūsī, *Rūḥ al-ma'ānī* (Beirut: Dār Ihyā' al-Turāth al-'Arabī, n.d.), 1:260.

4. See commentary, Jalāl al-Dīn al-Suyūtī, *al-Durr al-manthūr* (Beirut: Dār al-Fikr, 2011), 1:169.
5. Fakhr al-Dīn al-Rāzī, *al-Tafsīr al-kabīr*, first print (Egypt) (Beirut: Dār al-Fikr, 1981), 6:40.
6. Abū al-Qāsim al-Khū'ī, *al-Tanqīḥ fī sharḥ 'al-'Urwat al-wuthqā'*, transcribed al-Mīrzā 'Alī al-Gharawī al-Tabrīzī (Qom: Dār al-Ḥādī li-l-Maṭbū'āt, 1990), "Kitāb al-ṭahāra", 3:84.
7. Muḥammad b. Muḥammad b. Riḍā al-Qummī, *Kanz al-daqā'iq wa baḥr al-gharā'ib* (Qom: Jāmi'e-ye Mudarassīn, n.d.), 1:516.
8. Shams al-Dīn Sarakhsī, *Mabsūṭ* (Beirut: Dār al-Ma'rifa, n.d.), 10:98.
9. Zayn al-Dīn b. 'Alī (Shahīd II), *Masālik al-afhām* (Qom: Mu'assasat al-Ma'ārif al-*Islāmiyya*, 2004), 15:22.
10. See Glossary
11. Abū Ja'far Muḥammad b. al-Ḥasan al-Ṭūsī (Shaykh Ṭūsī), *al-Mabsūṭ*, ed. Muḥammad Taqī al-Kashfī (Tehran: al-Maktabat al-Murtaḍawiyya li iḥyā' al-Āthār al-Ja'fariyya, 1999), 2:121.
12. Manṣūr 'Ali Nāṣif, *Al-Tāj al-jāmi' li-l-uṣūl fī aḥādīth al-Rasūl* (Beirut: Dār al-Jīl, n.d.), 3:19.
13. Muḥammad b. Ya'qūb al-Kulaynī, *al-Kāfī*, ed. 'Alī Akbar al-Ghaffārī (Tehran: Dār al-Kutub al-Islāmiyya, 1968), 7:256.
14. See Glossary.
15. See Glossary.
16. See Glossary
17. See Glossary.
18. al-Kulaynī, *al-Kāfī*, 7:256, hadith No. 1.
19. Nāṣīf, *al-Tāj al-jāmi'*, 3:17, 18.
20. 'Ali b. Abi Bakr al-Haythami, *Majma' al-zawā'id wa manba' al-fawā'id*, ed. Muḥammad 'Abd al-Qādir Aḥmad 'Aṭā (Beirut: Dar al-Kutub al-'Ilmiyya, 2001), 6:261.
21. al-Khū'ī, *al-Tanqīḥ*, 3:84.
22. Ḥusayn al-Nūrī al-Ṭabrisī, *Mustadrak al-Wasā'il* (Qom: Mu'assasat Āl al-Bayt, 1988), 18:163.
23. al-Kulaynī, *al-Kāfī*, 7:256, hadith No. 8.
24. Refer to *al-Tāj al-jāmi'*, 3:17, 18.
25. Mohammad Javād Fāzel Lankarānī (Lankarānī Jr), *Durūs khārij-i uṣūl* (2008/9), lesson 77, 4 April 2008.
26. Refer to my book, *Talqīḥ-i maṣnū'ī* (Qom: Markaz-i Fiqhi-ye A'imme-ye Aṭhār, 2006).
27. Sharīf al-Raḍī, *Nahj al-balāgha*, Sermon 106.
28. Muḥammad b. Muḥammad b. Nu'mān (Shaykh Mufīd), *al-Muqni'a* (Qom: Mu'assasat al-Nashr al-Islāmī, 1990), 810.
29. Sallār al-Daylamī, *al-Marāsim al-'alawiyya fi-l-aḥkām al-nabawiyya*, ed. Maḥmūd Bustānī (Qom: Haramayn, 1984), 260.
30. Abū al-Ṣalāḥ al-Ḥalabī, *Al-Kāfī fī al-fiqh*, ed. Riḍā Ustādī (Isfahan: Maktabat al-Imam Amīr al-Mu'minīn al-Āmma, 1982/3), 421.

31. Abū al-Makārim 'Izz al-Dīn Ḥamza b. 'Alī b. Zuhra al-Ḥalabī, *Ghunyat al-nuzū'*, ed. Ibrāhīm al-Bahādurī (Qom: Mu'assasa Imām al-Ṣādiq, 1996), 436.
32. Yaḥyā b. Sa'īd al-Ḥillī, *al-Jāmi' li-l-sharā'i'*, ed. Ja'far Sobhani (Qom: Mu'assasa Sayyid al-Shuhadā', 1985), 548.
33. Shaykh Ṭūsi says this clearly in *Mabsūṭ* and alludes to it, with some justification, in *al-Nihāya* (Beirut, Dār al-Kitāb al-'Arabī, 1980), 301.
34. Ḥasan b. Yūsuf ('Allāma Ḥillī), *Taḥrīr al-aḥkām al-shar'iyya*, ed. Ibrāhīm al-Bahādurī (Qom: Mu'assasa Imām al-Ṣādiq, 1999), 2:242; *Qawā'id al-aḥkām*, 1:525; *Irshād al-adhhān*, 1:352; *Mukhtalaf al-Shī'a* (Qom: Mu'assasat al-Nashr al-Islāmī, 1992), 4:478.
35. Muḥammad b. al-Makkī (Shahīd I), *al-Durūs al-sharī'a* (Qom: Mu'assasat al-Nashr al-Islāmī, 1991), 2:47.
36. Muḥammad Bāqir Shaftī, *Risāla fī taḥqīq iqāmat al-ḥudūd fī hādhi-hi a'ṣār*, ed. Pazhūheshgā 'ulūm va farhang-i Islāmī (Qom: Daftar Tablīghāt-i Islāmī Hawze-ye 'Ilmiyye, 2006), 144.
37. Muḥammad Ḥasan al-Najafī, *Jawāhir al-kalām fī sharḥ Sharā'i' al-Islām*, ed. 'Abbās Qūchānī (Tehran: Dār al- Kutub al-Islāmiyya, 1988), 21:394.

# 2
# *Treatise on Refuting the Punishment for Blasphemy and Apostasy*[1]

## *Preamble*

Dear Mohammad Javād Fāzel Lankarānī (Lankarānī Jr),

I acknowledge receipt of your correspondence via email, dated 13 December 2011. I am grateful to you for accepting my offer to join me in this critical discourse on the subject of implementing the death penalty for blasphemy and apostasy. I hope that the outcome of this scholarly discourse will bring about greater clarity and refinement of the subject and move it closer to reality. Your objections and critiques of my letter, in which I objected to your late father's issuance of the "terror *fatwa*" and your expression of joy and delight at its implementation, is useful and important because, regrettably, your view is commonly held in the seminaries and warrants scrutiny.[2] In this treatise, while subjecting your central claim to critical analysis, I endeavour to bring to light the futility of the endless proofs and groundless justifications that you had advanced under the rubric of traditional Islam and current *ijtihād*, as well as your negligence in failing to take precautions to preserve the principle of the sanctity of life. I invoke the Qur'an, as well as the Sunna of the Prophet and the Imams, within the framework of the *ijtihād* adopted by the school of *Ahl al-Bayt* (i.e., the merciful Islam).

Your central claims are:

1 and 2: A *fiṭrī* apostate and blasphemer's blood can be shed with impunity (*mahdūr al-dam*)
3 and 4: An apostate (*fiṭrī* unconditionally and *millī* after refusing to repent) and blasphemer are subject to the death penalty.
5: Every jurist who is qualified to issue legal rulings is recognised as *ḥākim shar'*.[3]
6: There is consensus on the obligation to kill an apostate; it is an essential part of religion; and the narrations adduced to prove such a ruling are mostly *ṣaḥīḥ*[4] and beyond reproach, as they are related through multiple independent chains of transmission that are either verbatim (*mutawātir lafẓī*) or fully capture its meaning (*mutawātir ma'nawī*).

I anticipate that the readers of our discourse will consist of distinguished scholars, seminary and university students, lawyers, and especially those members of the young generation who are extremely annoyed and irritated with the arrogance of the jurists.

I will strive to zero in on and deconstruct your exposition with humility,[5] with a response that takes the form of an introduction, two parts: Part I (Chapters 1 and 2) and Part II (Chapters 3, 4 and 5), and a Conclusion. This chapter comprises ten sections:

Section I: Issuing a Ruling on the Death Penalty by a Process that Falls Outside the Sphere of a Competent Court, and Subsequently Bestowing upon the General Public a Mandate to Implement it Will Engender Lawlessness and Anarchy.
Section II: Claiming the Validity of the Death Penalty for Blasphemy and Apostasy is based on One Deficient "Isolated Report" (*khabar al-wāḥid*).
Section III: Refuting the Claim that Most of the Hadiths on Apostasy are "*tawātur* in Meaning or in their General Tenor".
Section IV: Refuting the Claim of Consensus (*ijmā'*) and the Necessity to Implement the Death penalty for Blasphemy and Apostasy.
Section V: No One, during the Time of the Prophet, Imam Ali and the other Imams, was Sentenced to Death Solely for Apostasy.
Section VI: Opinions of Eminent Jurists on the Absolute Cessation of the *Ḥudūd* Punishments or those that Necessitate the Death Penalty

and Injury, and Suspension during the Time of the Twelfth Imam's Occultation.

Section VII: "Isolated Reports" (*khabar al-wāḥid*) are Non-Probative (non-*ḥujjiyya*) in Matters of Critical Importance.

Section VIII: Issuing *fatwa*s on Killing an Apostate or a Blasphemer Weakens and Impairs (*wahn*) Islam.

Section IX: Alteration of the Subject (*mawḍūʿ*) of Apostasy and Objecting to the Perpetual Applicability of the Death Penalty for Blasphemy and Apostasy.

Section X: The Incompatibility of Executing a Blasphemer or an Apostate with Explicit Qur'anic Verses.

Mohsen Kadivar
February 2012

*Introduction*

In brief, I call your attention to three objections from your correspondence:

## Downgrading an Explicit Divine Covenant (*'ahd maqṭū'*) to a Doubtful Divine Ruling

You begin the introduction with an excerpt from *Nahj al-balāgha*, Sermon 106, in which Ali says, "You witness the breach of God's covenant, and yet do not get enraged, although you fret and frown at the breach of your forefathers' traditions."[6]

You have surmised that the "breach of covenant" refers to implementing the *ḥudūd* punishments or other divine rulings. Moreover, you claim that the dissenters are worried that implementing them would violate the West's Universal Declaration of Human Rights and, as such, have maintained that Ali is referring to the dissenters while simultaneously invoking his statement to defend your father's ruling as an instance of fulfilling the divine covenant.

In actuality, this is the exact opposite of Ali's intent, for you are the one who is trying to defend your father's position. Although the Qur'anic usage of "God's covenant" (*'ahd Allāh*) includes God's rulings and commands, it is far broader than that. In fact, the clear-cut touchstone is the primordial covenant of affirming monotheism,[7] not to follow in Satan's footsteps, and to worship God by adhering to the Straight Path.[8] Breaching the divine covenant has been elucidated in both Q. 13:20 and Q. 13:25. In his Sermon of Shiqshiqiyya, Ali has contrasted the pledge that God has obliged the scholars not to "acquiesce in the gluttony of the oppressors and the hunger of the oppressed"[9] with great clarity.

Clearly, the "divine covenant" found in Sermon 106 is identical to the one found in the Sermon of Shiqshiqiyya and in the Qur'an. Therefore, at no point can it be lowered to a secondary level of implementing the *ḥudūd* punishments, which are contested in terms of being perpetually relevant and applicable. You have co-mingled an explicit divine covenant with a doubtful legal ruling on *ḥudūd*, and have equated a minor component of religion and knowledge of Islamic jurisprudence (i.e., a subset of the *shari'a*), which is a human endeavour (and thus can produce no more than a probable ruling) as equivalent to the splendid divine covenant. You have used it as a prelude to transpose and invert its actual meaning in order to defend your father's position.

## Confusing a Factual Divine Legal Ruling with an Apparent Divine Ruling

You assert that "We should announce in unison, resoundingly and with pride, to everyone that only the Divine Law is lofty and true and, therefore, that all rules or proclamations that oppose it have no merit. No person or group has any authority or competence to issue laws for the people, for only God [has the right to] do so." I say with gentleness that there is no need for you to screech this out with such a resounding tone, for what is required here is the presentation of solid and profound proofs. Regrettably, such a thunderous assertion is the result of your unfair delineation of the scholarly disputation as one of either for or against the factual divine rulings.

Some of the past jurists have opined that the disputation over killing an apostate or a blasphemer is adjudged as an "apparent (*ẓāhir*) divine ruling" and a *ḥujja shar'īyya* (religiously valid proof) for themselves and their followers. However, the "actual divine ruling" is privy only to Him, and therefore no jurist can claim to have attained it. How were you able to equate your father's probable and presumptive (*ẓannī*) legal deduction to the actual divine ruling so decisively? Did you receive a revelation? Were you inspired? Such dogmatism contains no religious or rational argument. My objection is not with the actual divine law, but rather with your faulty deduction. To be sure, any law or pronouncement that conflicts with the actual divine law has no value. But with regard to a conflict over an apparent legal ruling, which actual divine order and divine law is being breached? Contrary to your claim, it is not one that is essential and mandated due to consensus, but rather, as will be explained in greater detail, one that remains contested. No opinion deserves any preference or superiority over others just because more people support it, for the criterion is the strength of the arguments and not number of claimants.

In other words, our debate concerns whether imposing the death sentence on one accused of apostasy and/or blaspheming the Prophet constitutes an apparent legal ruling or not. Other issues are related to this debate, for example: if one accepts this legal order, is it immutable and perpetually effective, or just a temporary apparent legal ruling? If the jurists of a particular time deduced it properly, could they have meant it to be temporary in nature and therefore, since its duration has expired and thus is now abrogated?

Incidentally, *qānūn* is a shared term in the juridical and legal lexicons. In order to avoid co-mingling the meaning attached to it, one must clarify that the *qānūn* referenced by you is a religious legal ruling, whereas in law it refers directly to customary law, agreements, and contracts.

## Determining the "End Goals of Religion" on the Basis of *Mursal*[10] Hadith

You wrote:

> It is necessary for me to state right at the outset that no Muslim gets any joy from observing another person's deviation and the ensuing negative aftermath. In addition, no Muslim is delighted by the killing of another human being, in and of itself. Rather, that which causes joy and pleasure is implementing the Divine Ruling and obeying His command, a point that has been underlined in the infallible Imams' valuable statements, especially those of Imam Ḥusayn, as one of the end goals of religion, which is a source of abundant temporal and spiritual blessing.
>
> Quṭb al-Dīn al-Rāwandī (d. 911) relates a statement from the Prophet in his *Lubb al-lubāb*, "Implementing one of the *ḥudūd* punishments on Earth is more meritorious than sixty years of worship."

Your revision and correction of your reasoning for expressing joy and delight [at the killing of Rāfiq Taqī] is a step in the right direction. Undoubtedly, gaining God's pleasure by implementing the ethical standards and religious legal criteria is a source of happiness. Spreading justice and ensuring security for the people and arranging for their gainful employment and prosperity is a source of pleasure because they are precursors to realising noble religious objectives. But among all of the laws and norms that have been neglected, is it only in implementing the death penalty for blasphemy and apostasy (an action that is disputed and contested) that one can find happiness? And even more, by bringing as evidence statements attributed to Imam Ḥusayn that are generally uttered by preachers and mosque leaders? Incidentally, the phrase *'uttilu al-ḥudūd* (nullifying or suspending the *ḥudūd*) is used to refer to the Umayyads' deviation.[11] However, first, the *ḥudūd* of God found in the Qur'an and Sunna refers to the divine boundaries and limits, both of which are broader in scope and include the religious legal limits. Second, even if we assume that such narrations are authentic, are they the ultimate end goals of religion?

One sign of drifting away from the Qur'an's spirit is downgrading the clear-cut aims and ultimate goals to implementing legal punishments on the basis of weak hadiths with an unsound chain of transmission.[12] What a stark contrast there is between gaining proximity to God and His pleasure, rising in excellence, attaining prosperity, and spreading justice and equity versus implementing the *ḥudūd* punishments. And that also under the category of "one of the end goals of religion". A hadith with an unsound chain of transmission is not permitted in jurisprudential discussion, let alone in defining the ultimate goals of religion, which is a matter of theological and philosophical deliberation. In the latter, even a *thiqa* "isolated hadith" (*khabar al-wāḥid*) cannot be entertained, let alone a *mursal*[13] hadith. A religious worldview formed on the basis of *mursal* hadiths from *Mustadrak* cannot produce an outcome better than the work of this same traditionist (*muhaddith*).[14] Straying from the spirit of the Qur'an would bring about such a misfortune: so, learn a lesson, O you who understand (*ūlū-l-albāb*).

## *Notes*

1. Websites of Mohsen Kadivar, see at: www.kadivar.com, and Jaras at: http://www.rahesabz.net, 2 February 2012.
2. I wrote a detailed letter, given the importance of human life and my objections to the legal rulings and judgements that were the cause of weakening and defacing Islam and Shiʿism, with the hope of preventing a repetition of such rulings. In 1999 a number of dissenters, such as Dariush and Parvāneh Forūher, Mohammad Mukhtārī and Mohammad Jaʿfar Puyandeh, were killed by intelligence service officials. This act of terror was justified in proclamations and on Iranian TV on the basis of three legal rulings issued by jurists proclaiming that they were killed in response to the charges levelled against them of apostasy and causing mischief and corruption on Earth. At that time, I had strongly objected to the religious validity of such a ruling and had stipulated: "Terrorism is prohibited in Islam, and no jurist or *marjaʿ* is able to issue a ruling that is contrary to the Shariʿa." The illegitimate court that deals exclusively with issues pertaining to the clerical class sentenced me to one year in prison for this objection and another six months for objecting to the actions of the Islamic Republic (see Zahrā Rūdī, *Bahā-ye āzādī* (Tehran: Ney, 2000)).

   The principal players in that illegitimate court have secured lofty positions for their deference: Prosecutor General for the whole country, the Supreme Court and Prosecutor Committee member of the 90th session of the eighth term of the Parliament who was infamous for defending the programme, Cherāgh-i Sīmā, Director of Archives, Consultant to the Judiciary, etc.

In addition to my objection I had brought forward proofs, not to mention that recent circulated documentary evidence shows that Rāfiq Taqī had confessed in the court that he was a Muslim, apologised for offending Muslim sensibilities, and made it clear that he had no intention of denigrating Islam (see Appendix 2). Therefore, the act of terrorism will need to be justified through other channels. This case is still open and is under investigation to determine the basis of the judgement.

3. See Glossary
4. See Glossary
5. You write: "In one of the letters, a person with a traditional seminary (*ḥawza 'ilmiyya*) training and author of a number of works has brought forth certain scholarly points and jurisprudential objections on the ruling of an apostate's execution. The issues and objections raised are a rehash of the past; my expectation was that he would bring forth a fresh and new perspective to pave the way for engaging in serious discourse. Instead of responding to each letter independently, for which I lack the time, it may be more befitting to provide a single comprehensive response and, for this, I extend an advance apology."

   It appears that you received two letters: one from myself dated 28 November 2011 and another one under a fictitious name of Ghonā-ye Tabrīzī dated 30 November 2011, the full content of which appears in Appendix 2. In response to my friendly and kind letter, you have replied with an arrogant and haughty tone. If you were of the same rank as the traditionist Nūrī (author of *Mustadrak*), then you would have had familiarity with the Qur'an and noticed the verse: "When you are offered a greeting, respond with a greeting that is better, or at least return it [in the like manner]" (Q. 4:86). I will not digress into such unethical tangents, as I have a lot to say in a scholarly manner to respond to your claims.

   We were classmates in the classes of the late Ahmad Pāyānī studying *Makāsib* during 1985 and 1986. This is what is stated in the biography about me that was issued by his office on its website: ". . . a few seminary professors took private classes [from the ayatollah] and were able to finish the level of *saṭḥ* [equivalent to Masters level] in a short period of time. In 1982, he assessed that they can enter *dars al-khārij* [advanced level of studies to be able to undertake *ijtihād*] in *fiqh* and *uṣūl*. In addition, they studied the *Makāsib* in private sessions with Pāyānī."
6. Sharīf al-Raḍī, *Nahj al-balāgha*, Sermon 106.
7. Q. 7:172.
8. Q. 36:60–61.
9. Sharīf al-Raḍī, *Nahj al-balāgha*, Sermon 3.
10. See Glossary.
11. Muḥammad b. Jarīr al-Ṭabarī, *Ta'rikh al-umam wa-l-mulūk* (Beirut: Mu'assasat al-A'lamī, 1983), 3:306.
12. Quṭb al-Dīn Sa'īd b. Hibatullah Rāwandī, *Fiqh al-Qur'ān*, ed. Aḥmad al-Ḥusaynī al-Ishkawarī (Qom: Maktabat al-Mar'ashī al-Najafī, 1985), 18:9, chapter "al-Ḥudūd", hadith 10, No. 21843.
13. See Glossary
14. Nūrī al-Ṭabrisī, *Faṣl al-khiṭāb fī tahrīf kitāb Rabb al-arbāb* (Tehran?: n.p., 1881).

## *Section I: Issuing a Ruling on the Death Penalty by a Process that Falls Outside the Sphere of a Competent Court, and Subsequently Bestowing upon the General Public a Mandate to Implement it, will Engender Lawlessness and Anarchy*

In this section, my aim is to respond to two questions: (1) can one issue judgements on blasphemy and apostasy outside the orbit of a competent court?; and (2) can one delegate the responsibility for carrying out the punishment that is, in principle, the mandate of judicial functionaries, to "anyone who has access to the convicted"? One who replies "Yes, it is" to both of these questions is actually issuing a *fatwa* in favour of anarchy and disorder, which is certainly not the Lawgiver's intent.

This part is divided into four sections:

### Under Which Jurist's Jurisdiction is a Judicial Ruling Issued?

*Question 1*: Under which jurist's jurisdiction is a judicial ruling issued? In Shi'i jurisprudence, the accepted principle is: "Implementing the *ḥudūd* rests with the one who is entrusted with issuing judicial judgements." In other words, the *ḥākim shar'* is responsible for applying the *ḥudūd* (e.g., the death penalty, cutting off the hand and flogging). But who is this person during the Twelfth Imam's occultation? Although many jurists have applied this mandate to themselves in the general sense through indirect deputisation (by the Twelfth Imam), others have totally suspended either all of these punishments or at least those that involve the death penalty. Those who hold the former opinion need to clarify whether every just jurist can function as a *ḥākim shar'*. Or does this post require, in addition to jurisprudential expertise and a just character, governmental and political authority, at least to the extent that would allow these punishments to be implemented? It should be clear that, based on this standard, every jurist is only a potential *ḥākim shar'*.

In the absence of a *ḥākim shar'*, every just jurist is empowered to establish the *ḥudūd*. However, once a fully qualified *ḥākim shar'* issues a judicial opinion, no other just jurist is permitted to reject or violate it unless he can prove that the former has erred in adducing the arguments and proofs upon which he based his judgement.

If the *ḥākim shar'* subscribes to the guardian-jurist's all-comprehensive authority (*wilāya muṭlaqa*), then he has arrogated to himself a leadership role in politics and judgeship. Thus, in principle, issuing a judicial ruling, particularly one dealing with the *ḥudūd*, is his sole responsibility or that of those whom he designates.

If the ruler has not issued a judgement, then the other jurists are obligated to undertake one of the following:

a. If the ruler is not fully qualified for such a post (i.e., he has not yet attained the station of full *ijtihād*), if his integrity and justness have been questioned at any time, if his management (of the country) is disputed, or if he does not meet the standards of a *ḥākim sharʿ*, then other jurists who do fulfil these conditions may issue a legal judgement and establish the *ḥudūd*.
b. If the one issuing the judgement categorically disagrees with the intellectual basis of the jurist's all-comprehensive authority (*wilāya muṭlaqa*) or his political authority and mandate, and therefore regards the latter's rulership as religiously illegitimate and so cannot accept his judgements, then he may issue, without any fear of repercussion, a judgement if the political leader has failed to do so.

If the jurist subscribes to the guardian-jurist's (*walī al-faqīh*) all-comprehensive authority and considers him to possess the necessary qualifications to issue a *fatwa*, then the former cannot issue a judicial ruling or establish the *ḥudūd* punishments before obtaining the *walī al-faqīh*'s permission to do so, either before the issuance of the *fatwa* or afterwards by gaining his affirmation. In other words, issuing a judgement calling for the death penalty in these two cases (blasphemy and apostasy) without the ruler's consent is tantamount to negating his authority and guardianship.

Could such a jurist residing in another place, say Iran, issue a legal judgement of death for the citizen of another country? Just saying that religious law rejects any geographical boundaries is not a cogent response, for such an undertaking constitutes a clear interference in the latter country's internal affairs and a rejection of its judicial sovereignty and autonomy. Furthermore, that country would be entitled to file a grievance with the officials of the country in which the jurist resides. In the above scenario, issuing a legal judgement by one who does not have an official governmental mandate (even if he is a qualified jurist), would lead to an international conflict and, in some respects, could be considered a breach of national sovereignty.

Your late father was one of the few jurists who embraced the jurist's all-comprehensive authority advocated by his mentor, the late Khomeini.[1] On 30 July 1990, he acknowledged that Iran's present ruler, Khāmena'ī, enjoys a "lofty scholarly position, excellence in jurisprudence, and competence and qualification for fully-fledged *ijtihad*".[2] This same leader (i.e., Khāmena'ī) replied categorically, when asked, "Does a qualified jurist during the period of [the Twelfth Imam's] occultation have the authority to implement the *ḥudūd*?" that "Implementing the *ḥudūd* during the occultation is obligatory, but the authority and mandate for this rests exclusively with the leader of the Muslims (*walī al-amr al-Muslimīn*) [i.e., Khāmena'ī]."[3]

How can one rationalise sentencing an apostate or a blasphemer to death by a jurist who has acknowledged his faith in the *walī al-amr al-Muslimīn*? Even if one were to accept that the jurist's all-comprehensive authority does not recognise national boundaries and thus there is no difference between Azerbaijani and Iranian Muslims, the fact remains that issuing a legal ruling on *ḥudūd* rests exclusively with the *walī al-amr*. No one else has the right to issue such a ruling, unless your father had secretly received Khāmena'ī's permission to do so, or unless Khāmena'ī had delegated this part of his responsibilities to your father, or unless your father changed his opinion on politics or its criterion: "The family ought to know what is in the household." In any event, the conflict between your father's opinion and his action is more evident than the luminosity of the Sun.

## Issuing a Judicial Order is the Exclusive Mandate of a Competent Court

Up to this point, the discussion has revolved around legal orders issued by the jurists from a jurisprudential perspective but who are not the *walī al-amr*. We will now examine the issue from the judiciary's perspective.[4] Issuing a judicial order is limited to a competent court, defined as one that has been promulgated by the law to resolve matters on the basis of fairness and equity, and within the legal framework. The law is enshrined by parliament and, additionally, those international covenants to which it is a signatory render them as part and parcel of the respective country's constitution. From this perspective, joining and signing such a pledge requires the endorsement at the highest level of government, such as parliament or the president, and within the confines of the constitution. The courts are to implement such agreed-to international covenants as if they were part of the nation's constitution.[5]

A jurist's *fatwa* is not law, and a (fully qualified) ruler's order cannot be considered law or superior to the law, for their substance can take effect only after Parliament's legislative branch approves it. In addition, the judge cannot invoke any justification from sources outside the law,[6] for his duties are limited to the following: rendering his judgement after organising and giving a framework to the claims and proofs provided by the litigants and their lawyers; investigating the evidence and oaths; and summoning and verifying the witnesses' testimony. In the past, when the conditions and situations were far simpler, he was also entrusted with obtaining a judgement.

However, in our complex contemporary world, both functions are restricted to a competent court. Today, a jurist's mandate is limited to deducing religious rulings from detailed proofs (i.e., issuing a *fatwa*). Observing court procedures is not just a formality, but a conventional necessity to discovering the truth behind the rubric of equity and justice. The accused has a right to protest the lower court's judgement. In such a situation, the higher court would review the case afresh under a different judge. If he still objects to that court's ruling, he can take his case all the way to the Supreme Court. Ultimately, the sentence can be implemented, but only after it has gone through all of the stages and has been signed off by the highest official.

Clearly, the intricate stages of investigation (e.g., objecting to the judge's ruling and requesting a fresh review of the case) was not anticipated in Islamic jurisprudence. Undoubtedly, the judge's tenure of office is not incompatible with that of a specialist in jurisprudence. If he is a *mujtahid* or aware of the jurisprudential standard, he could issue the judgement with greater discernment. However, the primary prerequisites for issuing a judgement are mastery of the law, implementing the punishments with care and diligence, experience, and observing justice and fairness. Jurists who hold that only they can issue a ruling must first officially be appointed to this post and only then can fulfil their responsibility to the best of their ability. Given that the jurist is trained to discern and deduce the true judgement, there is no reason to assume that he would be any good at identifying the subject matter.

Iran's current legal system has not identified apostasy and conversion to another religion (or to none at all) as crimes, and thus no punishment has been contemplated.[7] However, Article 262 of the statutes stipulates that the punishment for blaspheming the Prophet is death (legislated in May 2013).

The Universal Declaration of Human Rights and the International Covenant on Civil and Political Rights were accepted in 1975 by Iran's two assemblies. As these have not been abolished, they are still effective. The higher court's commutation of the lower court's regressive sentence of death for Ḥasan Yousefī Eshkavarī and Hāshim Āghājarī on a trumped-up charge of apostasy to several years in prison was the result of pressure exerted by the public and various international human rights institutions. This was a good learning experience and an eye opener.

Even thirty years after the revolution, most of the judges are not *mujtahids* but have been authorised by a (boan fide?) *mujtahid* to issue and implement *ḥudūd* judgements. The fundamental difficulty here is not to affirm or reject the general designation of judges, but rather the implementation of the Islamic criteria by those who have only a general understanding of *fiqh* and thus cannot be expected to deduce a religious ruling when civil law is silent on a matter. In such a context, it is even more imperative to pay heed to customary law and provide greater supervision for its proper implementation. The benefit of exercising caution in the matter of calling for the death penalty in such a scenario is all the more evident.

*Question 2*: Can the judicial functionaries, who alone are entrusted with implementing the death penalty for blasphemy and apostasy, delegate this responsibility to anyone who has access to the one convicted? The previous question pertained to issuing a judgement out of the sphere of a competent legal system, whereas this one deals with allowing someone who is outside the sphere of the judicial system to implement the death penalty. Responding to the first question automatically answers the second one. Traditional jurisprudence emphatically forbids anarchy and disturbing the social order. Letting anyone who has access to the accused apostate or blasphemer to kill him or her can only give rise to disorder and anarchy.

It is important to point out at this juncture Montazeri's opinion, recorded in the chapter dealing with the source of sound judgement and defining the subject (*mawḍūʿ*) of apostasy, so that we can appreciate the extent of his caution:

> The religious establishment must handle the situation of apostasy delicately, given that it is in tension with the rights of an Islamic society. As such, the crime of apostasy, like the other *ḥudūd* crimes, must be established in a competent religious court through clear-cut

> and unambiguous proofs or confession and carried out by the same impartial Islamic judicial system. Proving this particular crime is fraught with difficulty, because its modality demands certainty (*yaqīn*) in terms of the accused's views.
>
> However, this condition can never be met because one can never be privy to another person's inner intentions, as they cannot be attested to by the judge merely on the basis of his/her statements or acts.
>
> The minutest amount of doubt or ambiguity in establishing the crime of apostasy, as well as the other *ḥudūd* crimes and those that warrant discretionary punishment (*ta'zīr*), suspend the punishment's implementation.[8]

In addition, Montazeri responded to a question about implementing the Islamic penal code and human rights: "In case of doubt over the judgement or subject matter of the allegation, the court has no right to implement the punishment and needs to again review the circumstances surrounding it and the merits of the confession and testimony."[9]

## Disorder Resulting from Allowing the General Public to Carry Out the Death Sentence

You claim:

> One should be mindful that, at times, the public welfare demands that those tasked with implementing a specific legal ruling be the public at large. In the case of apostasy and blaspheming the Prophet, all Muslims [both male and female] are religiously responsible for carrying out this obligation. The philosophy behind such a command is to serve as a deterrent for the public by underlining the fact that apostasy is so reprehensible and repugnant in God's sight that it merits a particularly grave punishment. The decree on the apostate and the blasphemer is preventive, for its purpose is to defend the divine legal corpus of Islam. Given that both Islam's fundamentals and secondary aspects accord with human reason and logic, it does not allow one to reject the truth of Islam after it has been clearly proven or confirmed, which is also the case with one who insults and defames the most sanctified person of Muhammad.

> This type of ruling is not designed to attract others toward Islam, and thus there is no reason to be concerned that its implementation would prevent others from embracing Islam. Rather, it is a fortress that guards Muslims from harm and restrains them from damaging Islam by their own actions. On the one hand, it prevents Muslims from hastily leaving Islam and compels them to reflect some more and ponder and, on the other hand, it has forever closed the door employed by the unbelievers to strike at Islam [from within] by fostering apostasy.

Your claim is exposed to serious objections:

a. The death penalty for an apostate (which I will elaborate on in the second section) is based on only one narration that, moreover, has issues with its chain of transmission and indication (*dilāla*).[10] Given this reality, how can you introduce it as a "divine judgement"? Given that discernment and recognition of blasphemy and apostasy require expertise and that ordinary people cannot determine the relevant limits and parameters, then certainly allowing everyone to render such a judgement on the basis of what he or she hears is most improper and incorrect, even if some unreliable traditions apparently support this position. Moreover, it is improper for the *ḥākim shar'* to delegate his responsibility to the general public instead of the court functionaries, for this deprives the accused person of his or her chance to repent.

In addition, any minor deviance from the standard is not permitted. Does assassinating the accused or the convicted by stabbing him while he is distracted conform to the criteria of Islam? Was killing Muammar Qadhafi (d. 2011), the tyrant of Libya, based on the edict of the Egyptian Yūsuf al-Qaradāwī, by tearing off his clothes and inserting a knife into his anal orifice, in harmony with the luminous *shar'*? On the Day of Judgement, jurists like your late father and Qaradāwī will be taken to task in the court of divine justice for inciting their followers and disciples to kill, which is contrary to the *sharī'a*. Even as Imam Ali lay dying, he advised those around him to treat his assassin, Ibn Muljim Murādī, with fairness and not rip him to pieces.[11] What is more egregious? Killing a saint of God or denigrating and blaspheming him?

b. Your claim that it is in the public interest (for the general public to carry out the punishment), even if such an approach, effective in the past, would have the complete opposite effect in the modern world due to how everything is now so closely interconnected. Ask yourself this: if this is a divine approach, then has it helped contain the spread of, as well as lower the incidence of, blasphemy and apostasy? My disagreement with you on the issue of blasphemy and apostasy has to do with the method and approach, as opposed to considering it repugnant to denigrate the Prophet and the person's instant departure from Islam. What lesson would the public draw if, after sentencing the apostate to death, the number of people denigrating the saints, rejecting the *shari'a*, and leaving Islam were to increase? Do you not think that an enlightened and broad-minded and insightful *mujtahid* ought to revisit his process of formulating a *fatwa* by taking into account the changes that occurred over time and keeping in mind the lofty aims of the *shari'a* and of preserving the sanctity of religion?

c. Execution and violence do not prompt one to pause and think about the "lesson" to be learned. It might have an apparent temporary effect; however, it does nothing to sustain true faith. If the apparent religious expression and assertion bear no relationship with the inner conviction, then of what use is it? People's faith cannot be actualised or preserved by violence, the death penalty, and imposing strictures. If it could be, then the Wahhabis in Saudi Arabia and the Taliban in Afghanistan would have been far ahead of others in this aspect. Such an approach can only engender an increase in the number of those feigning belief, as well as hypocrisy and duplicity, not to mention fomenting hatred for the *shari'a*'s rulings.

## Human Rights are Not in Conflict with Islam

You write:

> Is it the ruling itself or its implementation that fosters anarchy? Is the execution of an apostate not a divine ruling? Is it not a violation and a rejection of a divine ruling to waive it due to its incompatibility with the standards and criteria of contemporary human rights? Should we discard the divine rules and instead pay heed to the apparent pleas of human rights advocates? Would this not constitute the worst possible approach and the most hideous form of anarchy?

Is it proper for us to encourage the implementation of divine laws or the Universal Declaration of Human Rights? Can the latter, which bestows freedom upon homosexuals, guarantee success and prosperity for humanity? The protesters should either accept Islam or this charter, because combining both is impossible. In fact, if they do so it would lead to the negation of Islam. I am amazed at those who are so concerned about not violating this charter but care so little about preserving the dignity of Islam. Not only are they not angered by the idle talk of the exponents of human rights, but they actually defend them.

## Response

First, my objection is to both the judgement and its method of implementation.

Second, I do not view the death penalty for such cases as "divine law", but rather as a fallible jurisprudential deduction of past jurists and their present-day emulators. I will elaborate later upon the deficient proofs put forward to prove this ruling. "Divine law" is equivalent to the "actual (*wāqiʿī*) divine order". The target of my sharp criticism is the apparent (*ẓāhirī*) divine orders (i.e., *fatwa*s of the jurists). Jaʿfarī *fiqh,* which is fallible and prone to containing errors, cannot be viewed as sacred. In other words, any given *fatwa* may be wrong. This is why I object to the *fatwa* on blasphemy and apostasy. The corollary of your statement is that you are following the "school of consecration" by considering any disagreement with your father's *fatwa* as equal to "negating the actual divine law". How is this anything other than consecration?

Third, you claim that one cannot reconcile the human rights charter with Islam and that accepting the former is equivalent to negating Islam. Your knowledge about this charter is revealed by your claim that it has gifted freedom to homosexuals. If you had read this charter even once, you would not have made such a baseless assertion.

Which of its articles or covenant have given this supposed freedom? I entreat you to declare loudly and to the whole world the extent of your understanding of the charter as a board member of the Assembly of Teachers (*Jāmiʿat al-Mudarrisīn*) of the seminaries in Qom and as the son of the jurist who considered the death penalty proper for an apostate. How can one beat the drum of the charter's "incompatibility" with Islam when you have absolutely no idea of its content? To be sure, this charter conflicts with the type of "Islam" advanced by your father. Your understanding of Islam – confined, as it is, to the customary conventions of the Arabs at the time of Qur'an's revelation, the neglect of the criteria of its revelation, and just mimicking the past jurists and regarding their *fatwa*s as "actual divine law" – is, of course, incompatible with human rights.

You are correct in saying that the "Islam" of Muḥammd Bāqir Shaftī, Faḍlullāh Nūrī (d. 1909) and Lankarānī Sr conflicts with the human rights charter. However, in the "Islam" of Ākhund Mullā Mohammad Kāẓim Khorāsānī (d. 1911), Mullā 'Abdullah Māzandarānī (d. 1912), Mīrzā Nā'īnī (d. 1936) and Hosein-Ali Montazeri, all human beings are entitled to the natural and human rights by virtue of being human. My dispute with you has to do with two conceptions of Islam, namely, Islam versus Islam: the exoteric and outer Islam (kernel) and its husk with its ultimate goals. You have construed the apparent conjectural legal orders as "divine laws" and as contradictory to human rights, whereas I hold that the "actual divine laws" cannot be in conflict with the people's natural rights.

## *Notes*

1. Mohammad Fāzel Lankarānī (Lankarānī Sr), *Tafṣīl al-sharī'a fī sharḥ Taḥrīr al-wasīla*, "Kitab al-amr bi-l-ma'rūf wa-l-nahī 'an al-munkar" (Qom: Markaz Fiqh al-A'immat al-Aṭhār, 2009), 130–132.
2. 'Alī Khāmena'ī, *Durar al-fawā'id fī ajwibat al-qā'id* (Beirut: Dār al-Wasīla, 1992), rulings 12 and 13. For more information on the role of Lankarānī Sr in confirming the candidacy of Khāmena'ī, see Kadivar, *Ibtizāl-i marja'iyyat-i Shī'e: istīzāḥ-i-marja'iyyat maqam-i rahbarī Hojjatoleslam va-l-Muslimīn Sayyid 'Alī Khāmena'ī*, May 2014, online at: www.kadivar.com, 120, 121, 188–196.
3. 'Alī Khāmena'ī, *Ajwibat al-istiftā'āt* (Beirut: Dār al-Ḥaqq, 1995), 24, question 66.
4. See Raḥīm Nowbahār, *Aṣl-i qazā'ī būdan-i mujāzāt-hā: Taḥlīl-i fiqhī-ye ḥaqq bar muḥākime-ye 'ādilāne* (Tehran: Mu'assase-ye muṭāle'āt va pazhūhesh-hā-ye ḥuqūqī shahr dānesh, 2010).
5. Article 9 of the Civil Code of Iran states: "Treaty stipulations which have been, in accordance with the Constitutional Law, concluded between the Iranian Government and another government, shall have the force of law." Article 77 of the Iranian Constitution states: "Treaties, international undertakings, and other agreements of a similar nature must be approved by the National Consultative Assembly."

   In international relations, the validity of the treaty has priority over internal laws, and the discretion of the country is determined in opposition to those limits. Nāṣer Kātūziyān, *Kulliyāt-i ḥuqūq* (Tehran: Tehran University, 1968), 2:210. For greater elaboration, see his *Qānūn-i madanī dar naẓm-i ḥuqūqī konūnī* (Tehran: Nashr-i Mīzān, 2005), 31.

6. Regrettably, Article 167 of the Constitution of Iran states that in the absence of a civil ruling, the judge is permitted "to deliver his judgement on the basis of authoritative Islamic sources and authentic fatwas". On most aspects of Islamic law, there are diverse opinions. Giving each judge the leeway to use his own judgement or rely upon the legal rulings of someone else would seriously impair the implementation of justice and create chaos. This was one of the causes of the Constitutional Revolution of 1905–1911, for the public was annoyed and exhausted with the contradictions and thus aspired for a more just system. Article 167, as well as Articles 5, 57 and 110, are possible sources of lawlessness and quite dangerous. However, it is possible to read Article 167 in a different way:

   Today, many judicial systems in the world have become totally transparent and are inclined to invoke and give preference to the opinion of legal experts over their own. International Courts likewise, rely on the same experts when they have no choice other than to give a ruling against a country's human rights violations.

   Article 167 opens the path for experts to expand their scope of legal discretion and entertain outside legal experts. In this regard, this Article says, "The judge is bound to endeavour to judge each case on the basis of the codified law. In case of the absence of any such law, he has to deliver his judgement on the basis of authoritative Islamic sources and reliable fatwas." What is meant by "reliable fatwas" are the opinions rendered by the eminent jurists. However, it cannot be confined just to that for the following reason. On the one hand, Article 167 endows the judges with the responsibility to render a judgement on all aspects of law and not to confine himself to only those aspects that have been addressed by *fiqh*. But, on the other hand, we all know that new issues have been cropping up in the areas of business and modern society, which has led to the appearance of conflicting rules regarding which no jurist has given an opinion or there is no scope for its formulation in present-day jurisprudence. Thus, either the judge refrains from rendering an opinion, as he has no sound basis, or he is given permission to rely upon the expertise of other reliable scholars and researchers in the field. The first possibility is negated by Article 167: "He, on the pretext of the silence of or deficiency of law in the matter, or its brevity or contradictory nature, cannot refrain from admitting and examining cases and delivering his judgement." Thus, the only viable option open to him is the second one. Undoubtedly, the judge is not duty-bound to defer to any particular opinion and his opinion would carry the stamp of finality. However, he can marshal other experts' opinions to corroborate his own position. Whatever the judge brings forth has the force of law and provides some justification. Thus, there are many factors that lead a judge to reach a final conclusion, and one of the most important ones is to consult experts in the field. Besides, even those responsible for enacting civil laws can benefit from these experts. (Kātūziyān, *Qānūn-i madanī*), 19.

7. The Islamic penal provisions were formulated and enacted by the Judicial Council of the Parliament with the goal of experimenting with them from 1991. They have been extended six times so far. On 21 April 2013, an amended version of the Islamic penal provision was enacted in an open session. However, once again and without any specifics or outside input, just like the previous case, its term was limited to

five years. The following catches one's attention in the revised version: "Article 220: Whatever *ḥudūd* punishments that have not been mentioned in this rule would be implemented on the basis of Article 167 of the Constitution" (*Rasmī* (newspaper), 27 May 2013). Although the death penalty for an apostate is not explicitly mentioned in the laws, the judge has the discretion to implement this punishment by basing it on the *shari'a*. The Islamic penal provisions have foundational problems with respect to rights and are themselves causing the weakening of Islam. See my article, "*Mujāzāt-i mokhālefān bā qavānīn-i falle-ī, murūrī ijmālī bar mohemtarīn qavānīn-i kayfarī-ye jumhūrī-ye Islāmī-ye Īrān*", available at: www,kadivar.com, March 2010.

8. Montazeri, *Ḥukūmat-i dīnī*, 131.
9. Hosein-Ali Montazeri, *Pāsokh be porsesh-hā-ye peyrāmūn mujāzāthā-ye Islāmī va ḥuqūq-i bashar* (Qom: Arghawān-i Dānesh, 2008), 85.
10. More elaboration will be forthcoming in Part II.
11. Sharīf al-Raḍī, *Nahj al-balāgha*, Letter 47.

## *Section II: Claiming the Validity of the Death Penalty for Blasphemy and Apostasy is Based on One Deficient "Isolated Report"* (khabar al-wāḥid)

You have issued a legal ruling to the effect that: "First of all, killing an apostate does not require a juridical ruling. Therefore, any Muslim can implement it. In a hadith attributed to 'Ammār Sābāṭī, 'If the shedding of blood (i.e., taking of human life) has become lawful, then anyone who hears him [recant Islam] can carry it out.' However, caution dictates that it be done under the supervision of a qualified jurist."

### Response

I regard this as a dangerous "terror *fatwa*" that is null and void from the perspective of both *shar'* and reason, and have warned you that its only possible aftermath is anarchy and social disorder. Your cited narration of 'Ammār Sābāṭī, which will be discussed below, is unreliable. Do not trivialise any believer's life and faith by such an incorrect and incomplete understanding of such narrations. It is intriguing that the permission conferred upon the general public to assassinate such a person is accompanied by no more than a recommendation to consult a *mujtahid* before doing so. If the Legislator had not prescribed caution in matters of "shedding blood" and Ali had not said, "Never shed blood [without justification]",[1] what would you have done?

Subscribing to the notion that anyone can kill an apostate or a blasphemer and that neither a judicial order nor a court official is required to implement this death sentence entails the following problems: it is not an essential part of religion; no consensus on it has been reached; and the narrations are not *mutawātir* but rather "isolated reports" (*khabar al-wāḥid*) whose chains of transmission and proofs have been strongly contested by various prominent jurists.

### Interrogating the Death Penalty for Apostasy

Permission to kill an apostate by anyone who is able to do so rests upon only two narrations.

a. A narration by Sahl b. Ziyād: "Some of our companions had written to the father of Ḥasan b. 'Alī (al-'Askarī) (d. 874) [i.e., the Tenth Imam,

ʿAlī b. Muḥammad (al-Hādī) (d. 868)]: 'May our life be sacrificed for you. 'Ali b. Hasaka claims to be your representative, describes you as eternally pre-existent, and states that he is your interlocutor and your prophet. He alleges that you have commanded him to be the leader, inviting people to this path . . .' The [Imam] replied: 'Ibn Hasaka (may God curse him) is a liar . . . I seek refuge in God from one who says this and I disavow it. Thus, dissociate yourselves from them (may God curse them), hamper their progress, and block them in constricted area. And if one of you finds them alone, smash their heads with a rock.'"[2]

b. It has been related by the three shaykhs (i.e., al-Kulaynī, Ṣadūq (d. 991) and Ṭūsī) regarding ʿAmmār al-Sābāṭī: "I heard Abū Abdallah say, '[For] every Muslim who apostatizes and repudiates and rejects Muhammad's prophethood, it is lawful for the one who hears him say these things to kill him. His wife will be irrevocably divorced upon his apostasy, his estate should be distributed among his heirs, his wife should exercise the *ʿidda* period for a deceased husband, and the leader must kill him and reject his repentance.'"[3]

## Analysis of Hadith 1

First, this hadith's chain of transmission is weak. Second, the proof cited, assuming that it is true, could be applied to religious exaggeration (*ghuluww*) and not apostasy because it deals with a personal matter (i.e., it pertains to a particular person whom the Imam has given permission to execute). In both instances, it cannot be generalised and thereby made applicable to every apostate.

## Analysis of Hadith 2

This hadith is more pertinent, for the phrase "it is lawful for the one who hears him say these things to kill him" grants a blanket permission to everyone to kill the apostate. This is the only reliable narration on this subject, and the three shaykhs have cited it. Some have graded it as *muwaththaq*.[4] However, other jurists and eminent *rijāl* experts, four of whom are cited below, object to ʿAmmār Sābāṭī and his narration.

a. Muḥaqqiq Ardabīlī categorically objects to this penalty after invalidating the chain of transmission containing ʿAmmār Sābāṭī: ". . . It is not clear whether the permission to kill the apostate is granted to anyone who hears his denial; rather, what is *mashhūr* (well-known) is that carrying out the death penalty for apostasy rests with the Imam, as intimated toward the end of the hadith. Thus, the beginning of the hadith is not in harmony with the end. Likewise, there is a probability that the clause 'whoever hears him say this' refers to the Imam's deputies. Thus, this issue requires further reflection."[5]

b. Muḥammad Taqī al-Tustarī (d. 1996), in his esteemed research on biographers, has brought forth eighty reports attributed to 'Ammār Sābāṭī that his companions did not implement. From this, he concludes that in all likelihood "most of the words employed [in the narration] are entangled and ambiguous, lacking in coherence and order."[6]
c. Khū'ī records from the works of Muḥsin Fayḍ Kāshānī (d. 1680) and Muḥammad Bāqir al-Majlisī (d. 1699): "The narrations related by 'Ammar were not practised, for there were so many errors that no narration from him is free of incoherence and disorder."[7]
d. It is likely that 'Ammar Sābāṭī has blended the issue of blaspheming with apostasy and has supplemented the ruling of each with the other.[8]

Moreover, this is the only hadith in which the permission to kill the apostate appears by itself, as opposed to being made in the presence of the Imam (competent court). For instance, the authentic hadith of Barīd al-'Ajlī: "It is upon the Imam to kill him."[9] In principle, the notion that people can on their own decide to carry out this particular religious decree has never been established.

In the narration attributed to Fuḍayl b. Yasār, instead of carrying out the punishment when he witnessed two Muslims prostrating to idols, he reported it to Ali and asked about his religious obligation in this matter.[10] According to Shaykh Ṭūsī's *fatwa*, if one kills an apostate without the Imam's consent, then although he is not liable for the convicted apostate's death, he must nevertheless be subjected to a discretionary punishment because he did this without the Imam's consent.[11]

Shahīd I has made this crystal clear: "The mandate to implement the death penalty for an apostate rests with the Imam or his designated deputy. If someone else embarks upon it or makes haste in carrying it out, although he would not be charged for the apostate's death because he had been sentenced to death penalty, he would nevertheless have committed a sin, which makes him liable to a discretionary punishment." Relying upon Shaykh Ṭūsī's *fatwa*, he adds: "It is far-fetched that 'Allāma Ḥillī[12] considered it lawful for anyone who heard a Muslim say something that would render him an apostate to kill that person."[13] Shahīd II also believed that one who kills an apostate outside the orbit of a competent court has committed a sin: "Executing an apostate rests with the *ḥākim shar'*. If one does so without the Imam's consent, then he has committed a sin."[14] Muḥaqqiq Ardabīlī raises serious objections to the chain of transmission and indication of the narration attributed to 'Ammār Sābāṭī.

Fāḍil al-Hindī, who has responded to each and every proof adduced by those who favour executing an apostate, concludes: "Implementing the *ḥudūd* punishments rests with the *ḥākim shar'*."[15] The author of *Jawāhir* concurs that carrying out this particular sentence is the provenance of the Imam and considers it a sin for anyone else to kill him; however, doing so would not result in *qiṣāṣ*,[16] he has clarified that "Implementing the death penalty for apostasy is lawful only for the Imam."[17]

*Outcome*: Taking into account the sanctity of life and the need to exercise caution in such a matter, sentencing an apostate to death based upon the single narration by 'Ammār Sābāṭī, the chain of transmission and text of which have been contested, is both wrong and unethical. This assessment stands even though some past jurists gave similar rulings (and erred in their judgement). Therefore, allowing anybody to carry out the death penalty is void of a reliable religious proof in the Qur'an and Sunna, consensus and reason. This ruling reveals that some of the honourable jurists relied upon a defective "isolated report" (*khabar al-wāḥid*) and thus understood the issue incorrectly.

## Analysis of the Death Penalty for Blasphemy

a. 'Alī b. Ja'far relates from his brother Imam Kāẓim that Governor Ziyād b. 'Ubaydallāh Ḥārithī of Medina sent an emissary to bring Imam Ṣādiq to his court. Inside the court, the Imam observed that the city's jurists were discussing a person who had written something that denigrated the Prophet. They adjudged that he should be disciplined with a discretionary punishment and beating. The Imam objected, "Should there not be a difference between [denigrating] the Prophet and others [in terms of the severity of the punishment]?" The governor replied that he would abide by the Imam's *fatwa*. The latter related, through a chain linking to the Prophet, that, "My followers are like me [when it comes to implementing the punishment for blasphemy]. Anyone who hears one insulting and denigrating us is obliged to kill the blasphemer who used foul language and not to defer to the governor. It is also required that the governor kill anyone who insults us when the matter is presented to him."[18]

b. Hishām b. Sālim on the authority of Abū 'Abdallah, who asked, "What is the status of one who insults and denigrates you?" He replied, "One who has the closest access is obliged to kill the blasphemer before the case reaches the governor."[19]
c. Narration from *Da'ā'im*.
d. A narration reported by 'Alī b. al-Ḥadīd on the authority of Imam Kāẓim, who ruled against Muḥammad b. Bashīr for having blasphemed him: "It is lawful for whoever hears the denigration and insult to kill him, just as is the case with one who blasphemes the Prophet."[20]

## Analysis of the Four Narrations

*First narration*: the narration attributed to 'Alī b. Ja'far has a deficient chain of transmission.[21] It was common knowledge that Muḥammad Bāqir Majlisī regarded the chain linking al-Kulaynī to 'Alī b. Ja'far as weak. Shaykh Ṭūsī gave a similar opinion.[22]

*Second narration*: Majlisī regards the one on the authority of Hishām b. Sālim as *ḥasan*.[23] Fāḍil Hindī brings forth two objections: one with regard to its chain of transmission and considers it *ḥasan*; and, second, with regard to its indication considers it particularistic, meaning that they cannot be generalised from the point of view of proofs.[24]

*Third narration*: found in *Da'ā'im al-Islām*, this *mursal* tradition is almost identical to the second narration, albeit with some changes in certain words.[25]

*Fourth narration*: Muḥammad b. 'Umar al-Kashshī (d. 951/2) regards this one from 'Alī b. Ḥadīd as weak due to the latter's unfavourable reputation when it came to transmitting hadiths (detailed reasons for this will be provided in Part III), even though, from the perspective of indication, it supports the intended outcome.[26]

From the above four narrations, granting permission to anyone who hears the blasphemer insult the Prophet and the Imams to kill him instantly is as follows: hadith 3 is *mursal*, and hadiths 1 and 4 are *daʿīf*.[27] Thus, they cannot be relied upon as proofs in issuing a *fatwa*. Hadith 2 is *ḥasan*, but its chain of transmission is defective and there is a likelihood that it is an "objective case" (*qaḍiyya fī wāqiʿa*) (i.e., it was meant for a specific case and thus cannot be generalised). In any event, this is the only evidence available to justify this particular assertion. And yet it contains many faults in its text and chain. Your father did not rely upon the hadith, which required the person to refer the case to the Imam or his deputy. Rather, he acted upon ʿAlī b. Jaʿfar's unreliable hadith to support his position that the case should not be deferred to the ruler and invoked this as his foundational argument to surmise that the general public should carry out the death penalty.[28]

## What is the Position of the Jurists on One who Denigrates the Prophet?

We will discuss the issue surrounding the obligation to kill one who blasphemes the Prophet (and the Imams) in the next section. As for the *fatwa*s, Shiʿi jurists have adopted two positions:

1. Any member of the general public can kill this blasphemer: Shaykh Ṣadūq was the first one to express this opinion: "It is lawful to immediately carry out the death penalty."[29] Sayyid Murtaḍā (d. 1044), in his elaborate discussion and citation of proofs, decrees that one (inclusive of Muslims and protected minorities) who blasphemes the Prophet should be killed right away, regardless of his religion. He believes this to be the opinion solely of the Shiʿis, for the Sunnis had decreed that a Muslim blasphemer must be killed, but that a non-Muslim blasphemer who belongs to one of the protected minorities (*ahl al-dhimma*) must be subjected to one of the discretionary punishments, the severest of which is death. Sayyid Murtaḍā justifies his stance on apostasy for a Muslim on the grounds that he has denigrated the Prophet, and on the protected minorities for breaching their contract of indemnity with the Muslims.[30] Abū al-Ṣalāḥ al-Ḥalabī held that one who blasphemed the Prophet and the Imams ought to be killed by the ruler, as well as the opinion that the ruler has no right to punish a believer who hears the blasphemer's denigration and kills him.[31]
2. The punishment for one who blasphemes the Prophet can be carried out only with the Imam's permission. This was the position of Shaykh Mufīd[32]

and 'Allāma Ḥillī.[33] Ibn Zuhra[34] believed that the Shi'is had reached a consensus on this position: "It is not permissible for the one who hears [the denigration] to kill before obtaining permission from the *Ṣāhib al-amr*." Substituting "blasphemy" or "breach of the agreement by the religious minorities" for "apostasy" would produce the same result. In other words, sentencing an apostate to death has no independent and reliable proofs. All of the objections to killing an apostate can be applied to a blasphemer. The claim of consensus by the two dissenting groups here (i.e., a and b) is indicative that the consensus is *ijmā' madrakī*[35] (i.e., the origins of the *ijmā'* are available in jurisprudential sources for scrutiny).

Most Shi'i jurists regard having no fear of causing harm to one's life or property or of other believers as one of the conditions for killing an apostate. According to Muḥaqqiq Ardabīlī, even when the fear of harm is suppositional, carrying out the punishment is probably not obligatory.[36] Undoubtedly, not carrying it out due to the fear of losing one's life or property will tarnish the person's honour and dignity.[37] However, one should ask "Is preserving Islam's dignity not more important than the executioner's dignity?" Is the principle of not weakening Islam not the same as the obligation to preserve its dignity, which is one of the important matters?

*Result*: Implementing the death penalty for blasphemy is supported by a sole tradition from Hishām b. Sālim, one that has a contested chain of transmission and indication. Even if this narration were upgraded from *ḥasan* to *saḥīḥ*, it is highly likely that it was meant for a particular case. Given that taking extra precautions in the matter of the loss of life and the possibility of spreading disorder and corruption is imperative, it follows that allowing members of the public to carry out the punishment would only accentuate this problem. As such, the verdict of the death penalty (which has no Qur'anic proof or consensus and possesses no more than one faulty narration) is contrary to *shar'*. In particular, the further proofs presented below will show that such a ruling is contrary to the Qur'an's explicit teachings.

*Outcome of Part II*: The death penalty for blasphemy and apostasy is supported by no more than two "isolated hadiths" (*khabar al-wāḥid*), both of which have strongly contested chains of transmission and indication. Such an important judgement cannot be supported by such extremely weak and shaky proofs. Thus, pronouncing the death penalty for blasphemy and apostasy in the absence of reliable proofs contradicts the *shar'*, debilitates Islam and violates the Qur'anic dictates.

## *Notes*

1. Sharīf al-Raḍī, *Nahj al-balāgha*, Letter 53.
2. Abū Ja'far Muḥammad b. Ḥasan al-Ṭūṣī (Shaykh Ṭūṣī), *Ikhtiyār ma'rifat al-rijāl* (aka *Rijāl al-Kashshī*), ed. Mīr Dāmād al-Astarabādī and Mahdī al-Rajā'ī (Qom: Mu'assasa Āl al-Bayt, 1984), 2:804, No. 997.
3. Muḥammad b. 'Alī b. al-Ḥasan b. Mūsā b. Bābawayh (Shaykh Ṣadūq), *Man lā yaḥḍuruh al-faqīh*, ed. 'Alī Akbar al-Ghaffārī (Tehran: Maktabat al-Ṣadūq, 1972), 3:89, hadith No. 333; *al-Kāfī*, 7:257–258, hadith No. 11; Abū Ja'far Muḥammad b. Ḥasan al-Ṭūṣī (Shaykh Ṭūsī), *Tahdhīb al-aḥkām*, ed. Ḥasan al-Mūsawī al-Khirsān (Tehran: Dār al-Kutub al-Islāmiyya, 1970), 10:136–137, hadith No. 541; Abū Ja'far Muḥammad b. Ḥasan al-Ṭūṣī (Shaykh Ṭūṣī), *al-Istibṣār*, ed. Ḥasan al-Mūsawī al-Khirsān (Tehran: Dār al-Kutub al-Islāmiyya, 1970), 4:253, hadith No. 957; al-Ḥurr al-'Āmilī, *Wasā'il al-Shī'a* (Qom: Mu'assasa Āl al-Bayt li Iḥyā al-Turāth, 1993), 28:324, hadith No. 3.
4. See Glossary
5. Aḥmad al-Ardabīlī, *Majma'al-fā'ida wa-l-burhān*, 13:320.
6. Muḥammad Taqī al-Tustarī, *Qāmūs al-rijāl* (Qom: Mu'assasat al-Nashr al-Islāmī, 1998), 8:19–31.
7. Abū al-Qāsim al-Mūsawī al-Khū'ī, *Mustanad al-'Urwat al-wuthqā*, transcribed Murtazā Boroujerdi (Qom: Manshūrāt Madrasa Dār al-'Ilm, 1993), 6:150.
8. 'Abd al-Karīm Mūsawī Ardabīlī, *Fiqh al-ḥudūd wa-l-ta'zīrāt* (Qom: Intishārāt Dāneshgāh-i Mufīd, 2005), 4:362.
9. Ḥurr al-'Āmilī, *Wasā'il*, 10:248, 249, hadith No. 1.
10. Ibid., 28:339, hadith No. 1.
11. Ibid., 7:284.
12. Khomeini, *Taḥrīr*, 2:236.
13. Shahid I, *al-Durūs*, 3:574.
14. Zayn al-Dīn b. 'Alī (Shahīd II), *Ḥāshiyat al-irshād*, contained in Muḥammad b. Makkī (Shahid I), *Ghāyat al-murād*, ed. Rezā Mukhtārī (Qom: Markaz al-Abḥāth wa-l-Dirāsāt al-Islāmiyya, 1994), 4:286.
15. Fāḍil al-Hindī, *Kashf al-lithām*, 10:662.
16. Muḥammad Ḥasan al-Najafī, *Jawāhir*, 42:190.
17. Ibid., 42:166, 167.
18. Ḥurr al-'Āmilī, *Wasā'il*, 28:212, 213, hadith No. 2.
19. Ibid., 28:337, hadith No. 1.
20. Ṭabrisī, *Mustadrak*, 18:106, hadith No. 2.
21. Al-Ḥurr al-'Āmilī, *Wasā'il*, 28:217, hadith No. 6.
22. Muḥammad Bāqir al-Majlisī, *Mir'āt al-'uqūl fī sharḥ akhbār Āl al-Rasūl* (Tehran: Dār al-Kutub al-Islāmiyya, 1984), 23:414.
23. See Glossary.

24. Muḥammad Bāqir Majlisī, *Malādh al-akhyār fī fahm tahdhīb al-akhyār*, ed. Mahdī al-Rajā'ī (Qom: Maktaba al-Mar'ashī al-'Āmma, 1986), 16:166.
25. Ibid., 16:282.
26. Fāḍil al-Hindī, *Kashf al-lithām*, 10:662.
27. See Glossary.
28. Mohammad Fāzel Lankarānī (Lankarānī Sr), *Tafṣīl al-sharī'a fī sharḥ Taḥrīr al-wasīla* "Kitab al-ḥudūd" (Qom: Markaz-i Fiqh al-A'immat al-Aṭhār, 2006), 406.
29. Muḥammad b. 'Alī b. al-Ḥasan b. Mūsā b. Bābawayh (Shaykh Ṣadūq), *al-Hidāya* (Qom: Mu'assasat al-Imām al-Hādī, 1997), 295.
30. al-Sharīf al-Murtaḍā 'Alam al-Hudā 'Alī b. al-Ḥusayn, *al-Intiṣār* (Qom: Mu'assasat al-Nashr al-Islāmī, 1995), 480–483.
31. Abū al-Ṣalāḥ al-Ḥalabī, *Al-Kāfī fī al-fiqh*, 416.
32. Shaykh Mufid, *al-Muqni'a*, 743.
33. al-Ḥalabī, *Ghunyat al-nuzū'*, 438.
34. 'Allāma Ḥillī, *Mukhtalaf al-Shī'a*, 9:452.
35. See Glossary.
36. Ardabīlī, *Majma' al-fā'ida*, 13:170.
37. Lankarānī Sr, *Tafṣīl al-sharī'a*, 405.

## *Section III: Refuting the Claim that Most of the Hadiths on Apostasy are* "Mutawātir *in Meaning or in their General Tenor"*

Given that the fundamental proofs adduced in favour of the death penalty for both blasphemy and apostasy are narrations, this section will critically examine the reliability of their chains of transmission. The primary question is: "Are these narrations at the level of *mutawātir*, which means that their chains of transmission do not need to be interrogated?" If not, how many of the reliable "isolated reports" (*khabar al-wāḥid*) are *ṣaḥīḥ* and *muwaththaq*, and to which Imam are they attributed? Thus, we will first examine the narrations that mandate death penalty for apostasy and then those related to blasphemy.

### Analysis of the Hadiths on Apostasy

In this section, four issues will be discussed.

You make two claims: the hadiths are *tawātur* and most of them are authentic:

> [T]here are more than twenty of them. Shaykh Muḥammad b. Ya'qūb al-Kulaynī (d. 941) has gathered twenty-three hadiths in his hadith work under the chapter "Penal Punishments for an Apostate" (*Ḥadd al-Murtadd*).[1] Most of them fall in the category of "sound" (*ṣaḥīḥ*), and jurists have used them to prove the punishments for apostasy under the above-mentioned five subjects. These hadiths are not only sound in terms of their chain of transmission (*sanad*), but they are also attested to by scholars to have been related by the infallible Imams; without any hesitation, we can say that these hadiths have reached a threshold of widespread transmission in meaning (*tawātur ma'nawī*)[2] and *tawātur ijmālī*.[3] On other topics of substantive law, the eminent jurists have considered ten hadiths on any one topic sufficient to reach the level of *tawātur*, let alone twenty-three. In the event that a hadith reaches this level, then there is no need to even interrogate the chain of transmission. This matter is clear and indisputable among the jurists.

An in-depth analysis will demonstrate that the narrations are deficient in terms of their chains of transmission and lack authenticity.

## Two-thirds of the Narrations Pertaining to the Death Penalty for Apostasy have a Deficient Chain of Transmission

i. To begin with, the chapter from *Kāfī* referred to above contains only fifteen narrations specifically dealing with apostasy; the rest pertain to other subjects: claiming prophethood, denigrating the Prophet and exaggerating (*ghuluww*) (the Imam's attributes). If one were to include "exaggeration" as a criterion, then the total number of narrations would reach eighteen. The death penalty is not mentioned in three instances, and thus the total number of narrations adduced for this penalty drops to fifteen.

In any event, Muḥammad Bāqir Majlisī has categorised these twenty-three hadiths as follows: *mursal* (incomplete chain of transmission) (hadith No. 7); *majhūl* (unknown narrator(s)) (hadiths Nos 4, 13 and 14); *ḍaʿīf* (weak) (hadiths Nos 5, 8 and 23); *ḍaʿīf ʿalā al-mashhūr* (acknowledged to be weak) (hadiths Nos 2, 6 and 15–17); *ḥasan* (sound) (hadiths Nos 3, 18 and 20–21); *ḥasan ka al-ṣaḥīḥ* (almost ranks as *ṣaḥīḥ*) (hadith No. 1); *muwaththaq* (trustworthy) (hadiths Nos 10 and 12); *muwaththaq ka al-ṣaḥīḥ* (almost ranks as *ṣaḥīḥ*) (hadith No. 22); and *ṣaḥīḥ* (hadiths Nos 9, 11 and 19).[4] Majlisī, who is quite lenient when interrogating the chains of transmission and thus has a threshold for categorising a hadith as reliable that is far below that of other jurists, estimates that only three of the twenty-three hadiths are *ṣaḥīḥ*. If we were to add the *muwaththaq*, *muwaththaq ka al-ṣaḥīḥ* and *ḥasan ka al-ṣaḥīḥ* hadiths, then only seven could be categorised as reliable; the other sixteen would be categorised as unreliable (i.e., inclusive of *mursal, majhūl, ḍaʿīf, ḍaʿīf ʿalā al-mashhūr* and *ḥasan*). In other words, the number of reliable hadiths is less than one-third of the total hadiths presented in this chapter. As such, your claim that "Most of them [hadiths] fall in the category of *ṣaḥīḥ*" has been arrived at with minimal research and is no more than exaggeration and pompous talk. Likewise, your claim that the past jurists acted upon the hadiths is baseless.

ii. The total number of hadiths on the death penalty and invoked in jurisprudential discussions for apostasy is twenty-one, all of which have been gathered in *Wasāʾil al-Shīʿa* and *Mustadrak* from *Kutub al-Arbaʿa* and other sources. Your claim that most of the narrations (be they from *Kāfī*, *Wasāʾil* and *Mustadrak* on the issue of apostasy) are *ṣaḥīḥ* is wholly incorrect, as any close study will show. In the best scenario, the total number of *ṣaḥīḥ* hadiths is no more than six. Moreover, even if one were to add the *muwaththaq* hadiths (viewed as reliable by past jurists), the total number would still reach no more than eight. Only half of them appear in *Kāfi*. Those that appear in *Kāfi* are narrations by 'Alī b. Ja'far from Imam Kāẓim, Muḥammad b. Muslim from Imam Bāqir, Ḥasan b. Maḥbūb from Imams Bāqir and Ṣādiq, and 'Ammār Sābāṭī from Imam Ṣādiq. The rest are Ḥusayn b. Sa'īd from Imam Riḍā (*Tahdhīb* and *Istibṣār*), Muḥammad b. Muslim from Imam Bāqir (*Faqīh*), 'Ibād b. Ṣuhayb from Imam Ṣādiq (*Tahdhīb* and *Istibṣār*), and Sakūnī from Imam Ṣādiq (*Faqīh*). Of the other thirteen narrations on the death penalty for apostasy, eight of them are *mursal* and five are *ḍa'īf*. In other words, less than one-third of the narrations on this subject are *ṣaḥīḥ*.

## Non-*mutawātir* Hadiths Do Not Permit or Mandate the Death Penalty for Apostasy

iii. Your claim: "Without a doubt, these hadiths overall have reached a threshold of widespread transmission in meaning (*tawātur ma'nawī*). On other topics of substantive law, the eminent jurists have considered ten hadiths on any one topic sufficient to reach the level of *tawātur*, let alone twenty-three" is a distortion for the following reasons: a *mutawātir* hadith should produce a real or conventional certainty and provide confidence. In addition, its proof and probative force should be incontestable. Attaining a consensus on *tawātur* requires numerous reports and is not pegged at a specific number. Rather, the essence of *tawātur*[5] is the report's transmission by a number of independent chains of transmission, not a particular number, and to such an extent that it could not possibly have been fabricated through collusion.[6]

Claiming that a decisive *tawātur* can be reached with the affirmation of its absolute truthfulness (not just a probable satisfaction) with only ten narrations is presumptuous. Generally, such a small number cannot produce confidence that no collusion was involved, for this is true only when the report is so decisive that its authenticity is above any doubt. As for your claim that one can attain the threshold of *tawātur* with ten narrations that are considered *mursal*, *musnad*, *ṣaḥīḥ* and *ḍa'īf*, it is baseless. Which jurist ever said that the level of *tawātur* can be reached on any subject with only ten narrations? How can certainty and *tawātur* be reached by relying upon *mursal, majhūl*[7] and *ḍaʿīf* hadiths? It is extremely negligent to consider twenty or so hadiths, two-thirds of which are *ḍaʿīf*, as capable of producing *tawātur* even in terms of meaning and general tenor and *ijmālī*. Or, eight *ṣaḥīḥ* and *muwaththaq* 'isolated reports' (*khabar al-wāḥid*) (even with twenty-one reports) do not, in general, generate decisive confidence unless for some other reason they are irreproachable. A person who attains confidence on a report's decisive truthfulness through non-conventional means has no probative value for one who does not value those particular means.

iv. The jurists have examined the validity of the chains of transmission as regards apostasy, and it is clear that none of them ever claimed that it has reached the level of *tawātur*. To be sure, which jurist regarded the narrations on apostasy as *mutawātir*? Even your late father never claimed that the narrations have attained a level of *tawātur* in meaning and *ijmālī* (assuming that you, in principle, are trying to articulate his position), let alone other jurists. He examined[8] the ruling on the death penalty for a *fiṭrī* apostate without giving him an opportunity to repent (in order to mitigate the punishment) from the perspective of the chain of transmission and indication, and concluded that it is nothing more than a well-known (*mashhūr*) *fatwa*.[9]

## The Narration by Jamīl b. Darrāj is *Ḍaʿīf*, not *Ṣaḥīḥ*

You have graded the narration by Jamīl b. Darrāj[10] as *ṣaḥīḥ*, whereas it is, in reality, *ḍaʿīf* due to the presence of ʿAlī b. Ḥadīd b. Ḥakīm Madāʾinī.

Shaykh Ṭūsī, at a minimum of three times, has forcefully graded the hadith as weak.[11] Al-Khūʾī provided the following evaluation: "What can be obtained is that it is not possible to adjudge him to be reliable."[12] Likewise, Majlisī considered him as weak and provided the following elaboration: "It is far-fetched to assume that Jamīl acted on the basis of his *ijtihād* because it is a form of analogy (*qiyās*), unless if it is *qiyās al-awlā* ('analogy of the superior', a valid form of *qiyās* accepted in Shiʿism)."[13]

By the way, the problems associated with ʿAmmār Sābāṭī's narration, the only hadith that specifies the death penalty for apostasy, were brought forth in Part II. Moreover, ʿAbdallah b. Abī Yaʿfūr's hadith has to do with one who claims prophethood, which is an entirely different issue. On what basis do you adduce such a narration as proving with "great clarity and precision the necessity to kill an apostate"? Every judgement of the death penalty does not have to deal with apostasy.

## The Error of Grasping on to the *mafhūm laqab*[14]

You write: "Hadiths that establish a corollary that reciting the dual testimony of faith makes one's blood sacrosanct and prohibits its shedding, validates marriage with a Muslim, and entitles one to inherit from a Muslim. As such, in the absence of the dual testimony of faith, one's blood would no longer be inviolable."

The most important hadith cited as proof to support this group's position is attributed to Ḥumrān b. A'yan: "It is agreed upon by all that one who expresses belief in Islam by his outward statements or actions like prayers, fasting, and hajj render his blood sacrosanct; entitles him to inheritance; and permits him to marry. Consequently, he departs from unbelief and attaches himself to belief."[15] The subject matter of such hadiths is "sanctification of blood". The argumentation and the inference laid out by you are as follows:

| | |
|---|---|
| Premise 1: | It is implied that negation of the judgement (of sanctifying blood) resides in the subject matter (of Islam). In other words, by rejecting Islam one also forfeits the sanctification of his blood. |
| Premise 2: | Rejecting Islam is the same as apostasy, and thus an apostate's blood is not sacrosanct. |
| Result: | The meaning of one's blood not being sacrosanct is the same as *mahdūr al-dam* (i.e., his blood can be shed with impunity). Thus, an apostate's life can be taken. |

## Critique

This type of argumentation and inference is absolutely deficient. The first premise rests on *mafhūm laqab*, that is, the negation of the noun that is the subject matter of the ruling, which is the weakest of all implications. This is because the title (*laqab*) has no implications[16] for the subject matter of the ruling by itself indicates that the ruling attaches to the subject matter, let alone when it appears as a restriction (*inḥiṣār*). Confirming both (i.e., attaching to the subject matter and its restriction) requires an external contextual indicator (*qarīna*), and this constitutes non-authoritativeness (non-*ḥujja*) of the *mafhūm laqab*. In general, restricting the sanctification of blood to Islam is a recipe for catastrophe and is extremely dangerous. I say with brevity here and will elaborate on it later on in the work: every person, by virtue of being a human being, makes his blood sacrosanct, and thus shedding it requires a decisive proof.

The second proposition is deficient as well. As one's rejection of Islam has two possibilities, a native-born unbeliever and an apostate, it is not limited to an apostate. The first person could potentially be a non-monotheist or a monotheist non-Muslim. It logically follows that since your argumentation for the non-sanctification of a non-Muslim is absolute (*muṭlaq*), their blood is also not sacrosanct.

## Examination of the Narrations on the Death Penalty for Blasphemy

First, the narration sentencing a blasphemer to death is an "isolated report" (*khabar al-wāḥid*) as opposed to a verbatim *mutawātir*. Second, it being *mutawātir* in meaning or *ijmālī* is not actualised. Third, most of the relevant narrations on this matter are unreliable. Fourth, the lawfulness of shedding the blood of a blasphemer with impunity (*mahdūr al-dam*) lacks any reliable narration, which was discussed in the previous section. The first three issues will be explored below.

Altogether, the Shi'i sources relate ten narrations for executing a blasphemer. Of these, four are *mursal* and four of the remaining six hadiths are *ḍa'īf*. In other words, only two of them are regarded by some jurists as *ṣaḥīḥ* in their chain of transmission: the narration by Hishām b. Sālim attributed to Imam Ṣādiq, and the one by Muḥammad b. Muslim attributed to Imam Bāqir. Fāḍil Hindī[17] and Muḥammad Bāqir Majlisī[18] categorise the first narration as *ḥasan*. Regarding the second narration, which has been recorded in *Kāfī* and *Tahdhīb*, the jurists express three opinions.

1. *Ḥasan*: Muḥaqqiq Ardabīlī,[19] Muḥammad Bāqir Majlisī,[20] Fāḍil Hindī,[21] the author of *Jawāhir*[22] and Muḥaqqiq Golpayegānī.[23]
2. *Ṣaḥīḥ*: Muḥaqqiq Khū'ī.[24]
3. *Majhūl*: Muḥammad Bāqir Majlisī.[25]

It should be clear from this that the categories of *tawātur*, inclusive of verbatim (*lafẓī*), meaning and general tenor (*ma'nawī*), and *ijmālī*, are actually non-existent. Only two hadiths are viewed by some jurists as reliable as regards their chain of transmission. As such, the death penalty for blasphemy rests exclusively on two "isolated reports" (*khabar al-wāḥid*) that are seriously contested from the perspective of their chain of transmission.

### Notes

1. al-Kulaynī, *al-Kāfī*, 7:256.
2. See Glossary.
3. See Glossary
4. Majlisī, *Mir'āt al-'uqūl*, 26:396–403.
5. Muḥammad Bāqir al-Ṣadr, *Buḥūth fī 'ilm al-uṣūl*, transcribed Maḥmūd Hāshimī (Najaf: n.p., 1976), 4:327, 332.
6. Zayn al-Dīn b. 'Alī (Shahīd II), *al-Ri'āya fī 'ilm al-dirāya*, ed. 'Abd al-Ḥusayn Muḥammad 'Alī Baqqāl (Qom: Maktabat al-Mar'ashī al-Najafī, 1988), 62.
7. See Glossary.
8. Mohammad Fāzel Lankarānī (Lankarānī Sr), *Tafṣīl al-sharī'a fī sharḥ Taḥrīr al-wasīla*, 692–704.
9. Ibid., 692.
10. Ḥurr al-'Āmilī, *Wasā'il*, 28:328, hadith No. 3
11. Shaykh Ṭūsī, *Tahdhīb*, 3:95, end of hadith No. 435: "He was extremely weak and cannot be relied upon"; *Istibṣār*, 3:95, end of hadith No. 325: "He was extremely weak"; ibid., 1:79, end of hadith No. 112: "The narration is weak, and his reliability has been impugned by the author of *al-Iḥtijāj*."
12. Abū al-Qāsim al-Khū'ī, *Mu'jam al-rijāl al-ḥadīth wa tafṣīl ṭabaqāt al-ruwāt* (Najaf: Mu'assasat al-Imām al-Khū'ī, 1993), 12:331.
13. Majlisī, *Malādh al-akhyār*, 16:273
14. A method for understanding an implied text, one example of which is known as "*laqab*", the weakest form of proving a case.
15. al-Kulaynī, *al-Kāfī*, 2:26, hadith No. 5.
16. See Muḥammad Kāẓim al-Khurāsānī, *Kifāyat al-'uṣūl* (Qom: Mu'assasa Āl al-Bayt li Iḥyā al-Turāth, 1989), 212.
17. Fāḍil al-Hindī, *Kashf al-lithām*, 10:662.
18. Majlisī, *Malādh al-akhyār*, 16:282.
19. Ardabīlī, *Majma' al-fā'ida*, 13:170.
20. Majlisī, *Mir'āt al-'uqūl*, 23:415.
21. Fāḍil Hindī, *Kash al-lithām*, 10:541.
22. Muḥammad Ḥasan al-Najafī, *Jawāhir*, 41:433.
23. Mohammad Reza Golpayegānī, *Taqrīrāt al-ḥudūd wa-l-ta'zīrāt*, transcribed Muḥammad Hādī al-Muqaddas al-Najafī (Qom: n.d.), 1:280.
24. Abū al-Qāsim al-Khū'ī, *Mabānī takmilat al-minhāj* (Najaf: Mu'assasat al-Khū'ī al-Islāmiyya, 1976), 1:321.
25. Majlisī, *Malādh al-akhyār*, 16:167.

## *Section IV: Refuting the Claim of Consensus (*ijmāʿ*) and the Necessity to Implement the Death Penalty for Blasphemy and Apostasy*

You have reiterated two claims several times: consensus on the necessity to execute apostates has been reached and this is an essential ruling of religion. These claims, along with that of the consensus on executing blasphemers, will be examined in this part.

### Examining the Claim of Consensus on the Necessity to Kill Apostates

Shaykh Ṭūsī claims that the community had reached consensus of the *umma* on the issue of sentencing apostates to death.[1] Ibn Zuhra claims that this was limited to the Shiʿis.[2]

First, there is no doubt that some past jurists considered that consensus of the *umma* had been reached on this specific issue.

Second, up until the last century, Shiʿi jurists considered this claim as one on which there was a consensus and it was free from any controversy. The question is whether one can invoke such a consensus as an independent source to discover the infallible Imam's instruction.

The author of *Jawāhir* says that the consensus is of two types:[3] "acquired directly" (*ijmāʿ muḥaṣṣal*) and "reported" (*ijmāʿ manqūl*), as in the case of obtaining confidence via an explicit hadith text (*naṣṣ*). In other words, the latter is an *ijmaʿ madrakī*[4] that has the same value and reliability as the proofs advanced to reach the asserted consensus. In this case they are narrations, and a consensus obtained through this channel cannot be invoked as an independent proof. If such narrations had not been present in the hadith chapter, would such a consensus have been reached? In addition, a directly acquired consensus cannot be attested to by mere claims, for in some cases the presence of even one dissenter could breach the consensus and reduce it to a *mashhūr fatwa*.

It is striking that you have acknowledged the presence of contemporary dissenters: "It is only in the recent past that a very small number of scholars, not exceeding the fingers on one's hand, have raised doubts; however, they are not comparable to the hundreds of past and current eminent jurists." In your estimation, are these dissenters, despite their small number, not part of the Islam's scholarly community?

## Examining the Death Penalty for Apostasy as an Essential Component of Religion

You state: "I will show with clarity that this ruling is regarded as one of the essential (*ḍarūrī*) elements of religion and that jurists acknowledge that there is no *ijtihād* on such matters." In addition, you have defined religion's essentials as "those on which there is unanimity between the Shi'is and Sunnis, and thus there is no need for proofs or even consensus to demonstrate their validity".

## Critique

First, the word essential (*ḍarūrī*) does not appear in any of the narrations.

Second, in many of the early scholars' statements, this word was not used. In fact, Yaḥyā ibn Sa'īd and Muḥaqqiq al-Ḥillī were among the first to use it.[5]

Third, rejecting a *ḍarūrī* is irrelevant in terms of apostasy so long as it is not co-joined with the prophetic mission.[6]

Fourth, what is the basis of your definition of *ḍarūrī*?

## Is the Ruling on Executing Apostates Part of the Essentials of Religion?

First, where is your proof for such a claim? Moreover, expanding the scope of these essentials would only produce more cases of apostasy!

Second, this penalty for apostasy is, according to you, an essential component of religion and thus, also according to you, no one has a right to exercise *ijtihād* on it and thus it requires no proof or consensus to validate it. If so, in principle, no one should raise this subject in the jurisprudential literature or undertake *ijtihād* on it. And you, likewise, should not get embroiled in it. And yet from the outset until today, Shi'i jurists have deliberated on the issues of narrations and consensus pertaining to apostasy. It therefore follows, based upon your criterion, that no jurist regards the death penalty for apostasy as an essential aspect of religion. It is ironic that despite your extravagant claims, your own father does not adduce such a claim and that, moreover, he, like other jurists, advanced proofs via relating narrations on this issue instead of seeking refuge in the claim that it is an essential part of religion.[7]

In any event, it appears that categorising this penalty as an essential aspect of religion is unique to you. Your dissenters are not your disciples or followers (*muqallids*) to willy-nilly accept your evaluation and not undertake *ijtihād* on the subject matter. In addition, based upon your claim that those jurists who reject this penalty are, in actuality, negating an essential part of religion, it follows that they have become apostates. That is, by categorising this penalty as an essential element of religion, you have sentenced those who disagree with you on this matter to death.

## Examining the Claim of Consensus on Killing Blasphemers

Among the *mutaqaddimīn*,[8] Ibn Zuhra[9] and Sayyid Murtaḍā[10] have labelled the consensus on the death penalty for apostasy as "indecisive". Among the *muta'akhkhirīn*,[11] 'Ali Ṭabāṭabā'ī (d. 1947) says, "The claim of consensus has been made in the community's statements, and this is a valid proof."[12] The author of *Jawāhir* also writes, "There is consensus on both of these issues."[13] Just like the inadmissibility of an *ijmā' madrakī* on the death penalty for apostasy, here too it would not be allowed as an independent proof to discover the infallible Imam's statement. Furthermore, this issue has not been defined as an essential of religion.

## Summary

The ruling on killing apostates and blasphemers lacks a reliable proof from the Qur'an; and there is no presence of a *mutawātir* narration, either verbatim, in meaning or *ijmālī*. In addition, less than one-third of the twenty-one relevant narrations are reliable as regards the chains of transmission. Moreover, an *ijmā' madrakī* is inadmissible as an independent proof to discover the infallible Imam's statements. Hence, on the basis of conventional *ijtihād*, the death penalty for apostasy and blasphemey relies upon few *thiqa* "isolated reports" (*khabar al-wāḥid*) and is consolidated with an *ijmā' madrakī*, the invoking of which will be analysed in other parts of this book.

## *Notes*

1. Shaykh Ṭūsī, *al-Mabsūṭ*, 7:281.
2. al-Ḥalabī, *Ghunyat al-nuzū'*, 380.
3. Muḥammad Ḥasan al-Najafī, *Jawāhir*, 41:605.

4. See Glossary.
5. Ardabīlī, *Fiqh al-ḥudūd*, 4:65.
6. Khū'ī, *Mustanad al-'urwat al-wuthqā*, "Kitāb al-Zakāt", 1:10; *al-Tanqīḥ*, "Kitāb al-Ṭahāra", 2:58–64.
7. Lankārānī Sr, *Tafṣīl al-Sharī'a*, 678–714.
8. See Glossary.
9. al-Ḥalabī, *Ghunyat al-nuzū'*, 438.
10. Sharīf al-Murtaḍā, *al-Intiṣār*, 482.
11. See Glossary.
12. 'Alī al-Ṭabāṭabā'ī, *Riyāḍ al-masā'il* (Qom: Mu'assasat al-Nashr al-Islāmī, 1992), 13:531.
13. Muḥammad Ḥasan al-Najafī, *Jawāhir*, 41:432.

## Section V: No One, during the Time of the Prophet, Imam Ali, and the Other Imams, was Sentenced to Death Solely for Apostasy

You repeatedly invoke narrations, both their text and the commentary upon them, from the two Sunni hadith works, *Kitāb al-tāj al-jāmiʿ li-l-uṣūl* and *Kitāb al-muḥāriba*, as proofs to substantiate your claim that apostates were killed during the Prophet's time at his direction. You make a similar claim with respect to Imam Ali during his caliphate by invoking hadiths from both Sunni and Shiʿi sources. You also insist that this penalty was applied even during the time of the other Imams on their explicit command, or at least with their implicit consent and satisfaction.

Incidentally, Jewish and Christian Orientalists, who rely primarily on Sunni hadiths as well as exegetical and historical sources, agree with your assertion that the Prophet and the Rightly Guided Caliphs followed this practice. Their motive for doing so is to establish that Islam is an inherently violent religion that does not allow for freedom of belief. Is there any reliable evidence in the Shiʿi sources that the Prophet, Imam Ali or other Imams actually ordered this penalty for apostasy or blasphemy?

A general review of the relevant chapters in *Wasāʾil* and *Mustadrak* reveal that seventeen narrations reported that Imam Ali ordered the killing of apostates. However, most of them deal with the Exaggerators (*Ghulāt*). They also contain one narration that Imam Ṣādiq ordered this fate for an apostate. On the issue of blaspheming the Prophet, there are two hadiths: one related by ʿAlī b. Jaʿfar[1] and another one in the *Daʿāʾim*, in which the Prophet supposedly sentenced a person from the Hudhayl tribe to death.[2] Based on the study and research of Majlisī, only one narration out of the twenty can be considered *ṣaḥīḥ*[3] – and even that pertained to a specific case adjudicated by Imam Ali. Thus, it cannot be generalised or extrapolated.[4] Of the two hadiths attributed to the Prophet, one is *ḍaʿīf* and the other is *mursal*. Consequently, one cannot establish with any degree of confidence, at least by relying upon Shiʿi sources, that the Prophet or the Imams sentenced anyone to death for either of these deeds.

You have made three grandiose claims concerning the execution of apostates: the Prophet, Imam Ali and the other Imams explicitly ordered this punishment. Of these three, only the last one can be supported and considered valid.

1. No one during the time of the Prophet was killed solely on the charge of apostasy. Rather, it was for some other transgression.
2. The *Ahl al-Bayt* did not endorse those killed during the reigns of the first three caliphs (632–656) under the title of *ahl al-ridda* (the people of "apostasy").
3. No reliable evidence indicates that Imam Ali executed anyone for apostasy during his caliphate.
4. The other Imams never ordered anyone to be executed for abandoning Islam.
5. No one disputes that the Umayyad and 'Abbasid caliphs sentenced people to death for apostasy. However, no reliable proof substantiates that these executions were carried out in accord with the Imams' instructions or implicit consent.

*Result*: No Shi'i sources substantiate the claim that the Prophet or the Imams ordered the execution of apostates or that this was done with their consent and satisfaction.

Below is a brief elaboration on these five assertions:

## At the Time of the Prophet

I hereby summarise the findings of two contemporary jurists:

a. Montazeri writes: "The subject of 'apostasy' during the Prophet's time and even that of the Imams was far broader in scope than changing one's religion or proclaiming this in public"[5] and "Historical reports, which show that certain people were sentenced to death and subsequently killed on the Prophet's order was not due to their assault or solely because of their disbelief or apostasy, but rather to their involvement in killing [the Muslims], or actively fighting them, persecuting them, or inflicting harm [upon them] via espionage or other violations that will be pointed out later."[6]

He scrutinises the historical reports in which the Prophet sentenced people to death and categorises them into five groups. This is his finding for the first group:

Even if we accept the veracity of the report that the Prophet sentenced a number of people to death, he did not do so solely because

> of apostasy. Rather, there were additional facts to consider: murdering someone, espionage, or actively fighting the Prophet and the Muslims. Moreover, in those days apostasy was not confined to changing one's religion or belief system, for anyone who left Islam or killed a Muslim was immediately regarded as a belligerent and an enemy of Islam who would immediately offer his support to the enemy. According to ancient Arab tribal custom, every person and tribe had to affiliate and bond with other tribes for self-preservation. As such, anyone who left Islam was viewed as a belligerent.[7]

I quote here the result of his study and research for the third group, as it is of great relevance and importance:

> The third group deals with the claim that the Prophet ordered the death penalty solely because of apostasy. The *Sunan* of Dār al-Quṭnī (d. 995) states, "It is said that during the Battle of Uhud, a Muslim woman apostatized and that the Prophet ordered others to seek her repentance and to kill her if she refused [to return to Islam]."[8] This narration has been reported through a number of channels. In one of them, Muḥammad b. 'Abd al-Malik Anṣārī is present. One can read in the margins: "Aḥmad and others have said that Muḥammad b. 'Abd al-Malik used to fabricate narrations."[9] The same text of this hadith is related through another one by way of Jābir b. 'Abdallah however, in the margins it says that 'Abdallah Udhīna is mentioned in the chain of transmission, about whom Ibn Ḥubān writes: "Under no circumstances can one rely upon hadiths related by him." 'Ali b. 'Umar Dār al-Quṭnī says, "His narrations should be abandoned"[10] and Ibn 'Adī writes, "[Any] hadith related by 'Abdallah Udhīna should be repudiated . . ."[11] Another narration with Jābir b. 'Abdallah in the chain says that Umm Marwān apostatized and that the Prophet ordered others to explain Islam to her. If, after that, she refused to repent, then she should be killed. However, in the margins of the same book it says, "Mu'ammar b. Bakkār is present in the chain of transmission. 'Uqīlī [Muḥammad b. 'Amr] and Zīl'ī have determined that he composes hadith based upon conjecture and delusion. Muḥammad b. 'Abd al-Malik is also present. Bayhaqī, who relates this hadith through two channels, says that both of them are *ḍa'īf*."[12] Apparently, these three

hadiths deal with the same subject. As their respective chains of transmission are weak, they cannot be relied upon.[13]

b. Al-Mujīz (Ardabīlī) writes:

> Some books of narrations, exegesis, and history have recorded the incidents in which some individuals during the time of the Prophet left Islam. Most of these reports do not possess a sound chain of transmission. I did not find in them any person who embraced Islam with conviction and subsequently decided to leave it solely for finding faults in its dogma or rulings. The reason for leaving Islam was associated with some crimes, like murder and spying for the enemy. As a result, the criminals would flee to the lands of the unbelievers and polytheists and stay there until they died, fearing the implementation of the Islamic ruling. Upon closer examination and reflection, it becomes clear that those identified as apostates were, in all cases, guilty of economic and political crimes or other criminal activity. In no single decisive case did the Prophet ever order someone's death for leaving Islam solely due to doubts about the belief system, without the person being involved in one of the other forbidden acts. Thus their so-called act of apostasy was linked with crimes. In fact, some of them had never embraced Islam, which means that their supposed apostasy could not have been the cause of their death.[14]
>
> Some Sunni jurists have given a death penalty fatwa for a female apostate on the basis that after conquering Mecca, the Prophet ordered the death of two enslaved female singers who had been affiliated with Abū Jahl. He supposedly did so because they denigrated him in their songs. Shaykh Ṭūsī writes, "This [judgement] is neither correct nor valid, because they were not Muslim. Rather, it was because they were unbelievers who denigrated the Prophet and blasphemed him in their songs."[15]

Taking the above analysis into consideration, you will have discovered that in your zeal to defend your late father, you have tarnished and soiled the Prophet's visage by relying upon weak (*ḍaʿīf*) hadiths from Sunni sources. This negligence in invoking the saintly figures to establish your proof, especially the Prophet, reflects your failure to exercise the expected caution obligatory in important and crucial matters. And what issue can be more important that the Prophet's stature?

## During the Reign of the Three Caliphs

A group of Muslims are held to have become apostates during the period of the Prophet's first three political successors. However, in most instances the reason for this ascription was their refusal to pay the *zakāt* (to the central government). However, this does not constitute apostasy, for in no way does it sever their attachment to Islam. Rather, their non-compliance was due to their misgivings about handing it over to the caliph.[16] Imam Ali did not support him during the *ridda* wars.

Shaykh Ṭūsī writes:

> Those who were categorized as "people of *ridda*" were of two kinds: (1) those who had reverted to unbelief, like Musaylama, Ṭulayḥa, 'Unsā, and their supporters. Without a doubt or dissent, by leaving Islam they became apostates; and (2) those who refused to remit the *zakāt* while remaining faithful to Islam. [Some of the Sunnis] have grouped both of them under "people of *ridda*", even though the second group, in the estimation of the Shi'is [and most Sunnis], were not apostates.
>
> *Ridda* means to abandon a truth to which one had been committed and espoused. By this action, the person becomes an apostate. Thus, apostasy is of two types: (1) abandoning Islam for disbelief; and (2) neglecting something (e.g., not remitting the *zakāt*) while remaining faithful to Islam. Clearly, the latter cannot be labelled as an apostate [in the technical sense] because not fulfilling or refusing to fulfil a financial obligation does not turn one into an apostate. Some have argued that such people should still be labelled as such because they consider it permissible to withhold the *zakāt* and that one who believes in such a "right" should be labelled an unbeliever. This is incorrect in light of the clarification just provided: they did not consider its non-payment permissible, but rather had [certain] misgivings and apprehensions [about handing it over to the caliph].[17]

## During the Caliphate of Imam Ali

Ardabīlī write:

> During this period, one encounters many narrations in Sunni and Shi'i sources containing stories about some Muslims embracing a false belief and doctrine. Not only are the chains of transmission of some of these narrations weak, but they also give off the stench of fabrication by the enemies of Islam and political opportunists, among them such people as Mu'āwiya b. Abī Sufyān (d. 680) and the Umayyads, who sought to disparage Imam Ali, inspire the people to hate him, dishonour him, and lower his status.[18]

Your claim that Ali executed apostates during his caliphate is based on three Shi'i narrations and a few Sunni ones. As for the former, the two that are related to this issue are weak and unreliable.

Hadith 1: it is graded as a *mursal*.[19]

Hadith 3: related on the authority of 'Amru b. Shimr from Jābir.[20] Majlisī regards the chain of this narration as weak and explains the drawbacks of using it as a proof, "Perhaps killing is prescribed because this constitutes a denial, assuming he does not repent and his apostasy is established by witnesses, and there is an objection here. Likewise, the order of Ali, 'I will not accept your return' does not necessarily mean that he must be killed. Perhaps he was reproving him lest he were to carry this out, because the apparent meaning in both contexts suggests that he only made these two utterances as an equivocal and ambiguous threat."[21]

Hadith 2: related on the authority of Hishām b. Sālim. First, it pertains to exaggerating (*ghuluww*) in matters of faith, and trying to link it to apostasy is fraught with great difficulty. Second, according to Majlisī[22] and Fāḍil Hindī,[23] it is ranked as *ḥasan*. Third, and contrary to your opinion, Fāḍil Hindī believed that this hadith could be applied as proof, but only in special cases (*qaḍiyya fī wāqi'a*), and certainly could not be generalised. Fourth, "isolated reports" (*khabar al-wāḥid*) with a sound chain of transmission on important and critical issues, as well as those that involve the loss of life, are non-probative and thus were not invoked by the jurists.

I have already dealt with the dubious nature of the relevant hadiths from Sunni sources during Ali's caliphate.

## During the Time of the Other Infallible Imams and the 'Abbasids

Ardabīlī asserts: "There is no evidence that any of the [eleven] Imams after Ali ordered the killing of any specific person for leaving Islam or believing that the *sharīʿa* is deficient. To be sure there are narrations of this type, but all of them are weak and unreliable from the perspective of chain of transmission and indication."[24] The Umayyad and 'Abbasid caliphs did implement this punishment during their reigns; however, no reliable evidence exists to confirm that this was done at the Imams' behest. Second, without such a confirmation, the actions of oppressive caliphs cannot be invoked as proof for the followers of *Ahl al-Bayt* or, rather, for any Muslim at all.

*Result*: No reliable evidence proves that the Prophet, Imam Ali or the other Imams ordered people to be executed solely for apostasy. The death penalty meted out to the apostates under the first three caliphs, as well as under the Umayyads and the 'Abbasids, cannot be advanced as proofs in the school of *Ahl al-Bayt*.

### *Notes*

1. Ḥurr al-ʿĀmilī, *Wasāʾil*, 'Ḥadd qadhf,' Bāb 25, hadith No. 2.
2. al-Ṭabrisī, *Mustadrak*, "Ḥadd qadhf", Bāb 23, hadith No. 1.
3. Ḥurr al-ʿĀmilī, *Wasāʾil*, "Ḥadd murtadd", Bāb 4, hadith No. 5.
4. Shaykh Ṭūsī, *Tahdhīb*, 10:143.
5. Montazeri, *Ḥukūmat-i dīnī*, 132.
6. Ibid., 88, 89.
7. Ibid., 91.
8. 'Alī b. 'Amr al-Dār al-Quṭnī, *al-Sunan*, ed. Majdī b. Manṣūr b. Sayyid al-Shūrā (Beirut: Dār al-Kutub al-'Ilmiyya, 1996), 3:119, hadith No. 121.
9. Ibid.
10. Ibid.
11. Ibid., hadith No. 125.
12. Ibid., 3:118, hadith No. 122.
13. Ibid., 3:96, 3:97.
14. Ardabīlī, *Fiqh al-ḥudūd*, 4:4.
15. Shaykh Ṭūsī, *al-Mabsūṭ*, 7:282.
16. Ardabīlī, *Fiqh al-ḥudūd*, 4:5.

17. Shaykh Ṭūsī, *al-Mabsūṭ*, 7:267, 268.
18. Ardabīlī, *Fiqh al-ḥudūd*, 4:17.
19. al-Ṭabrisī, *Mustadrak*, "Ḥadd murtadd", Bāb 1,18:163, 164, hadith No. 4.
20. Ḥurr al-'Āmilī, *Wasā'il*, "Ḥadd murtadd", Bāb 3, 28:328, hadith No. 4 (obtained from *al-Kāfī* and *al-Tahdhīb*).
21. Majlisī, *Malādh al-akhyār*, 16:273, 274.
22. Ibid., 16:282.
23. Fāḍil al-Hindī *Kashf al-lithām*, 10:662.
24. Ardabīlī, *Fiqh al-ḥudūd*, 4:29.

## *Section VI: The Absolute Cessation of the* Ḥudūd *Punishments or Those that Necessitate the Death Penalty and Injury, and Suspension during the Time of the Imam's Occultation*

Many of the early jurists opined that implementing the *ḥudūd* and calling for jihad are considered to be the exclusive prerogative of the Prophet and the Imams. For instance, Muḥaqqiq Karakī writes in his treatise on the Friday prayer that: "The Imāmī jurists are united [in their belief] that [only] a just, fully-fledged jurist can issue fatwas and indirectly represent the infallible Imam wherever necessary. However, many of them made two exceptions: on the matter of jihad and the *ḥudūd*."[1] The exceptions have been thoroughly interrogated and analysed by past jurists.

A good number of jurists hold that they have been entrusted with implementing the *ḥudūd* punishments, to the extent possible, during the Imam's occultation. Shaykh Mufīd was the first jurist to articulate this position with clarity: "Implementing the *ḥudūd* rests with *al-Sulṭān al-Islām*, i.e., the person who has been designated by God: the Imams and their deputies and the judges explicitly appointed by them for the particular task. The Imams have delegated this responsibility to the jurists when it is possible for them to do so."[2]

Many other jurists believe that implementing the *ḥudūd* punishments and declaring jihad during the occultation period is not permissible or has been suspended, based on the principle of caution in the matter of loss of life and the weaknesses in the proofs cited. They regard these matters as exclusive to the infallible Imam and his explicitly appointed deputies. A cursory look in this matter reveals that, at a minimum, fourteen Shiʿi jurists (most of whom enjoy high distinction) subscribe to this view.

Muḥammad Bāqir Majlisī lays out the four different positions of his time:

> There is a difference of opinion on whether a jurist, during the occultation, can implement the *ḥudūd*. Many jurists believe that a fully qualified just jurist can implement all of the *ḥudūd* punishments, including cutting off the hand, execution, stoning, and hanging by rope, during this period. [The second group] believes that the non-fatal *ḥudūd* punishments can be implemented. [The third group] advocates that anything that results in injury cannot be implemented.

> Some jurists belong to [the fourth group], which holds that implementing the *ḥudūd* is the sole prerogative of the infallible Imam or his specially appointed deputy. As such, the jurist has no mandate in this area. This opinion, however, is not free from objection. Research on this matter is not necessary, because every jurist will derive his own opinion and act upon it.[3]

In brief, jurists who are absolutely opposed to implementing the *ḥudūd* during the occultation comprise (1) those who have issued an explicit *fatwa* that the jurists have absolutely no mandate to implement them; (2) jurists who believe that they have a limited mandate in the area of *ḥudūd* as long as the punishment does not lead to death or cause injury; and (3) jurists who believe that their implementation has been suspended during the Imam's occultation. In reality, the first and third groups are the same.

## Full Suspension of the *Ḥudūd* during the Imam's Occultation

The following eight eminent jurists believed that only the infallible Imam or his specially appointed deputy could implement the *ḥudūd* punishments: Shaykh Ṭūsī,[4] Qāḍī 'Abd al-'Azīz b. al-Barrāj (d. 1088),[5] Shaykh Ḥasan al-Ṭabrisī (d. 1154),[6] Quṭb al-Dīn Rāwandī,[7] Yaḥyā b. Sa'īd al-Ḥillī[8] and Ibn Fahd Ḥillī.[9] In this regard, I would like to quote two of them:

Ibn Idrīs al-Ḥillī:

> Only the Ruler of the Age (*sulṭān zamān*) or one who has been appointed by God or designated by the Imam can implement the *ḥudūd*. No one else is permitted to carry them out under any circumstances . . . because a consensus has been attained among the Shi'i jurists and all Muslims that only the Imams, as well as the rulers appointed by them for this task, can implement the *ḥudūd* or hand down a sentence. No one else is permitted to undertake it under any circumstances. This consensus cannot be repealed by an "isolated report" (*khabar al-wāḥid*), but would require another consensus of the same calibre or categorical evidence from the Qur'an or a *mutawātir* hadith.[10]

While adding some more details, Ibn Idrīs says categorically and with forthrightness that implementing the *ḥudūd* during the occultation is prohibited. He supports his position by invoking both the consensus of the Muslims and the Shiʿis. He believes that either consensus can be breached only with another opposing consensus, an explicit Qur'anic verse or a *mutawātir* hadith. An "isolated report" (*khabar al-wāḥid*) cannot do this. According to him, those who believe that implementing the *ḥudūd* is permissible during the occultation have only an "isolated report" to support their position.

Ibn Idrīs (along with Shaykh Mufīd and Shaykh Ṭūsī) hold that the jurists have been delegated to pass judgements on disputed issues and implementing judicial rulings during the occultation, as long as there is no fear of harm and injury befalling them. Clearly, this means making judgements on issues other than the *ḥudūd*. At the end of the *Sarā'ir*, he states that during the Imam's presence, there is no difference between the validity of a judgement issued by him and one issued by his designated deputies.[11]

Aḥmad Khwānsārī states:

> As for implementing the *ḥudūd* during the Imam's absence, it is generally recognized that doing so is not permissible. Some have gone so far as to claim the existence of a consensus on this matter. Others have said that it is permissible for well-versed and upstanding jurists who are intimately aware of the *shariʿa* to implement the *ḥudūd* during this period . . . It is not far-fetched that this matter is one of those that falls under the exclusive purview of the infallible Imams and their special designates, as is the case of jihad against the unbelievers, which is prohibited without permission from them or their appointed deputies.[12]

In his explanation, Khwānsārī alludes to the point that the famous opinion that the *ḥudūd* punishments have been suspended during the Imam's occultation has attained consensus. He bases this claim on the statements of Ibn Zuhra and Ibn Idrīs. He believes that the dissenting side (i.e., most likely Shaykh Mufīd, ʿAllāma Ḥillī, Shahīd I and II, Muḥaqqiq Karakī, the author of *Jawāhir* and others) have relied upon ʿUmar b. Ḥanẓala's *maqbūla*.[13] He brings forth and briefly scrutinises the five proofs advanced from narrations by those who advocate implementing the *ḥudūd* punishments during this period.

1. Implementing the *ḥudūd* does not come under the rubric of enjoining the good and forbidding the evil (*amr bi-l-ma'rūf wa-l-nahī 'an al-munkar*) as a collective obligation, and thus is not connected with attaining juridical consensus. Without a shadow of doubt, implementing the *ḥudūd* results in bodily injury. Given this reality, only the Prophet, Imams and their explicitly appointed deputies can implement them.
2. 'Umar b. Ḥanẓala's *maqbūla* makes no mention of implementing the *ḥudūd* punishments.
3. Ḥafṣ b. Ghiyāth's narration, even if considered authentic from the perspective of its chain of transmission, would still present difficulty for proving the case because, according to it, doing so is in the hands of the one who governs. It is not possible to surmise from this narration that it is permissible for the judge (*qāḍī*) to implement the *ḥudūd* because a judge, in this context, refers to one who has been appointed by the infallible Imam to adjudicate people's cases.
4. The narration called the "*mashhūra* of Abī Khadīja"[14] pertains to adjudication and removing personal enmity and hostility. It has nothing to do with *ḥudūd*.
5. The Twelfth Imam's rescript (*tawqī'*) in response to a question on newly occurring situations (*al-hawādith al-wāqi'a*) provides a directive. It is likely that the definite article (*alif* and *lām*) in the word *al-ḥawādith* refers to a kind of contract and thus alludes to the same issue that must have been mentioned in that very letter that was sent (to the Imam). However, since we have no access to that letter and are ignorant of exactly what "issue" was raised, this narration cannot be invoked to confirm this claim.

Khwānsārī articulates the rational proof advanced by those who are in favour of implementing the *ḥudūd* punishments during this period as follows: first, suspending them will lead to the perpetuation of sin and the spreading of vice, both of which the Legislator clearly detests. Second, it is both fitting and appropriate to implement them whether the Imam is present or absent, for the resulting benefit accrues not to the one who upholds them, but rather to the one who is punished or to some of the believers. In both situations, the only option is to implement the *ḥudūd*.

His ultimate response to address the above-mentioned objections: the formulation of the mentioned proofs necessitate the *ḥudūd*'s implementation in every age, without the need for any authorisation or appointment from the infallible Imam. The corollary of this claim is that *ḥudūd*'s implementation was obligatory even prior to receiving ʿUmar b. Ḥanẓala's *maqbūla* or Abī Khadīja's *mashhūra* and *tawqīʿ*. Moreover, based upon the same logic and proof, the responsibility for carrying out these punishments could fall on the just believers (*ʿudūl muʾminīn*), and even on the morally depraved and sinners (*fussāq*) when the jurists are unable to fulfil their responsibility in this regard. This sequence is similar to the one provided for protecting the property of the derelict and the absentee when the jurists are unable to do so.

The objections to the above reasoning are self-evident. If those who are unaware of the legal matters of faith were to implement the *ḥudūd*, the result would be an enormous amount of chaos and disturbance. Thus, it is not far-fetched that during the occultation their implementation would be restricted to the infallible Imam and his specially appointed deputies, just as in the case of jihad against the unbelievers.

## Discontinuation of the *Ḥudūd* in Cases Leading to Death or Injury during the Occultation

Two jurists from this group write:

> Bahāʾ al-Dīn Muḥammad ʿĀmilī (d. 1621) writes, in *Jāmiʿ ʿAbbāsī*: "The jurists disagree on whether a fully qualified jurist can implement the *ḥudūd* during the infallible Imam's absence [and thus] without his permission. A fully qualified jurist, as will be pointed out later, is able to implement the *ḥudūd* absolutely (*muṭlaq*), however, there is disagreement among the jurists whether it can be done during the Imam's occultation. The stronger view is that he can, provided that doing so does not lead to death, harm, or injury."[15]

You are aware that Bahāʾ al-Dīn, who was unable to complete his book, only composed five chapters of the section on "worship". However, his student Niẓām al-Dīn Sāwujī (d. 1628) completed his work from chapter six onward, which includes the subject under discussion.[16] What is meant by Bahāʾ al-Dīn when he invokes *muṭlaq* is that it not be confined to the category of slaves and their families. In his estimation, the stronger opinion is impermissible, and he therefore prohibited the jurists from ordering punishments that result in injury or death, such as the amputation of one's hand, execution and stoning. He only permitted the inflicting of floggings and punishments that do not cause harm or injury. This is a rare opinion.

Fāḍil Hindī, when asked if a fully qualified jurist could issue legal opinions, replied, "This is the view expressed in the *Mukhtalif*, as you are aware, while others have considered it absolute, based on the proof texts. (And in the event that implementing the *ḥudūd* leads to execution or stoning, then it is restricted to the Imam only), based upon the principle of caution in the matter of loss of life, although they might be permitted to enact the *ḥudūd* as a matter of public interest."[17]

Citing the principle of (required) caution when it comes to loss of life (*dimā'*), Fāḍil Hindī restricts the *ḥudūd*'s implementation that leads to the execution of the convicted exclusively to the Imam. From the perspective that he considers that the jurist is authorised to implement the *ḥudūd* to promote the public interest, clearly there is no scope for rehabilitation if he is killed. The only difference between Fāḍil Hindī and Bahā' al-Dīn is that the former allowed implementation of the *ḥudūd* punishments that correlated with injury, that is, cutting of the bodily organs, during the Imam's occultation whereas the latter did not.

## Suspension of the *Ḥudūd* during the Occultation

Four jurists supported this stance: Muḥaqqiq Ḥillī, 'Allāma Ḥillī, Muḥaqqiq Ardabīlī and Mīrzā Qommī (d. 1816).

Muḥaqqiq Ḥillī writes in two of his works:

> Is it mandatory [to implement them] if doing so would cause injury or death? Some have said "yes" and others have said "no". It appears that the latter position is correct: during the Imam's presence, the *ḥudūd* can be implemented only with his permission or that of his designate appointed for this task . . . It is said that well-versed jurists are permitted to implement the *ḥudūd* during the Imam's absence, just as they are mandated to adjudicate between people, but only as long as they are safe from any harm from the temporal ruler. In this situation, the people are obliged to help them [Muḥaqqiq Ḥillī cites this as a typical opinion of Shaykh Mufīd and his followers].[18]

> If it leads to injury or death, then it is permissible only after obtaining the Imam's permission or that of his designate. Likewise, the *ḥudūd* should be carried out only with permission. It is said that the husband is allowed to carry out the *ḥudūd* punishments on his wife and children. It is said that the jurists should establish the *ḥudūd* during the occultation as long as they are safe from harm. In such a situation, it is mandatory for the public to help them.[19]

Muḥaqqiq Ḥillī, who undoubtedly excels as one of the leading three Shiʿi jurists, writes in both of his books (which still feature in contemporary jurisprudential discussions) that if "enjoining the good and forbidding the evil" leads to death or injury, then just like the *ḥudūd* punishments, it would be restricted to the infallible Imam or his specially designated deputy. He alludes to the dissenters' (Shaykh Mufīd and his followers) point of view by describing what he refers to as "frail and weak opinion".

The prolific ʿAllāma Ḥillī, in all of his works, with the exception of *Muntaha al-maṭlab*, argues in favour of implementing the *ḥudūd* during the Imam's occultation. In the *Muntaha*, he surprisingly relates three contradictory *fatwa*s, separated by only a page: prohibited ((2) below), suspended ((1) below) and permissible ((3) below). He writes:

> (1) Only the Imam or his designate is allowed to implement the *ḥudūd* . . . Shaykh Mufīd narrates on the authority of Ḥafṣ b. Ghiyāth, who says that he asked the Imam whether a judge or the ruler should establish the *ḥudūd*. The Imam replied that the one who holds the reins of power (the ruler) should do so. This confirms for the two shaykhs [Mufīd and Ṭūsī], based on the narration by this transmitter, that the jurists are allowed to implement the *ḥudūd* during the Imam's absence but I have reservation about this and thus favor suspension.[20]
>
> (2) Only the Imam or the one whom he permits to [do so can] implement the *ḥudūd*.[21]
>
> (3) Shaykh [Ṭūsī] says that the well-versed jurists can implement the *ḥudūd* during the Imam's absence, just as they are mandated to adjudicate between people, provided that they are safe from any harm from the ruler. In this situation, the people are obliged to help them, based upon the narration related by Ḥafṣ b. Ghiyāth from the Imam:

> "I asked who should implement the *ḥudūd*, the ruler or the judge?" to which he replied, 'The *ḥudūd* must be implemented by the one who holds the reins of power (the ruler).'" This confirms that the jurists should implement the *ḥudūd*, just as they are to adjudicate other cases for the people. He also bases it on the fact that suspending the *ḥudūd* punishments during the Imam's occultation when one is able to apply them will cause corruption and moral decadence, and therefore it is permissible [to apply them], and this is a strong argument in my opinion.[22]

In explaining his reasoning for suspension (i.e., the first *fatwa*), he relates the narration of Ḥafṣ b. Ghiyāth from Shaykh Ṭūsī's work and says that the two shaykhs (Mufīd and Ṭūsī) relied upon this hadith to reach the definitive conclusion that the *ḥudūd* can be implemented during the Imam's occultation. However, he was hesitant about this and opted for its suspension.

In his third *fatwa* he presents verbatim the opinion of Muḥaqqiq Ḥillī, which he had classified as a "frail and weak opinion", with its attribution to Shaykh Ṭūsī. Thus, two proofs are adduced in favour of implementing the *ḥudūd*: (1) the jurists have accepted the narration of Ḥafṣ b. Ghiyāth cited by Ṭūsī as reliable, and because adjudging cases by the jurists has been recorded, it therefore follows that implementing the *ḥudūd* is established for them; and (2) as suspending their implementation will result in spreading moral decadence, it is permissible to implement them. Here he categorically says that he finds this opinion to be the stronger one.

Muḥaqqiq Khwānsārī articulates and responds to their rational arguments (but without mentioning 'Allāma Ḥillī by name). The uneasiness and ambiguity created by these conflicting *fatwa*s is not a hidden matter. His first *fatwa*'s categorical prohibition in this regard cannot be reconciled with his next *fatwa*, which advocates suspension. How does someone who has reached a conclusion of prohibition or suspension come to regard the opinion of its permissibility as the stronger one? Second, on what basis can one claim that Shaykh Mufīd and Shaykh Ṭūsī reached their determination of permission on the basis of the narration from Ḥafṣ b. Ghiyāth?

Muḥaqqiq Ardabīlī scrutinises the opinion of the 'Allāma found in his *Muntaha* and surmises that 'Allāma favoured suspension: "Perhaps the reason for this hesitation is that [the narration of Ḥafṣ b. Ghiyāth] is not sound combined with the possibility that the Imam was forced to say 'the one who holds the reins of power' – as seems to be the case – or the possibility that the Imam is observing dissimulation (*taqiyya*) by not being candid and unequivocal. Thus, the presumption of non-permissibility is strong."[23] Ardabīlī argues that 'Allāma favours suspension based on three pieces of evidence: the non-reliability of the hadith narrated by Ḥafṣ b. Ghiyāth; "the one who holds the reins of power" refers to the infallible Imam; and the clear response in favour of the ruler suggests that he was practising *taqiyya*. It is, therefore, unworthy of acceptance.

He argues that based on his scholarly research, the verdict is strong for prohibiting the *ḥudūd*'s implementation in the absence of a reliable proof in its favour. On the basis of this contextual indicator, he was grouped with those who were undecided and ambivalent on this issue. He advances several proofs to show that the narration cited by 'Allāma Ḥillī to support implementing the *ḥudūd* punishments by the jurists during the Imam's absence is unreliable for a number of reasons, let alone cause one to believe that narrations of 'Umar b. Ḥanẓala and Abī Khadīja can resolve this issue. He ends his discourse with "*fa-ifham*", thereby indicating that these two narrations remain disputed. This assessment is consistent with his wavering and being indecisive, as mentioned above.

Mīrzā Qommī writes:

> Question 477 . . . Thus, this is valid when we regard the implementation of the *ḥudūd* punishments during the occultation as something permissible. In such a case, the mandate would fall on the just jurist. In my estimation, this issue of implementing the *ḥudūd* during the Imam's absence requires further reflection and should therefore be suspended. However, the *ḥākim shar'* is permitted to implement the discretionary (*ta'zīr*) punishments. If he cannot fulfil his mandate, then others can discipline the sinner under the rubric of "enjoining the good and forbidding the evil" in whatever manner possible. In fact, it becomes obligatory for them to do so in the sequence of what is easier.[24]

Mīrzā Qommī, like 'Allāma Ḥillī, opines that the *ḥudūd* must be suspended during the occultation, but also leaves the door open for implementing the discretionary punishments, which certainly are less severe than the *ḥudūd* punishments.

Ḥasan Mudarris (d. 1937) can be placed in the first category, based on the opinion of his colleagues cited below:

> On 13 May 1910, Mullā Mohammad Kāẓim Khorasānī and Mullā 'Abdullah Māzandarānī wrote a letter to the National Consultative Assembly to explicate the *mujtahid*'s role as it pertains to Article 2 of the Constitution: ". . . responsibility of the honourable members . . . As for the laws pertaining to judiciary under the subject of disputes, *qiṣāṣ*, *ḥudūd*, and others, the issuance of the judgement is the special mandate of the noble *ḥukkām shar'* (pl. of *ḥākim shar'*). The honourable assembly members have no option other than to forward those cases to the just *mujtahids*, who are empowered by the government to implement the judgement without any interference or discretion . . ."[25]

Ḥasan Mudarris was the committee's most influential and effective member despite his short life. On 2 September 1911, the first criminal law, "Temporary law on fundamental criminal procedures", was registered by the parliament's Judiciary Committee under his leadership. Even though the fundamental rights in criminal procedure were borrowed from foreign laws and statutes, they were not in conflict with Islamic jurisprudence. Mudarris confirmed this compatibility of Article 2 of the Constitution on 9 July 1912: "I was a member of the National Consultative Assembly (national and international) and, to the extent possible, made a contribution. 'Necessity makes forbidden things permissible.' Punishments that have been laid out for transgressions, which would be addressed in civil and criminal courts are in accordance with the noble *shari'a*, and issues related to its implementation are also not in conflict with the Islamic law."

In the aforementioned law and the general penal provisions of 1925, there is absolutely no mention of amputating body parts, flogging, stoning and other *ḥudūd* punishments. Even though Article 207 of the present provision states: "Sodomy, as it pertains to unmarried women and those who are *maḥārim* (within the prohibited degree of marriage) and those who are coerced. If this crime is proven in accordance with the Shari'a, then the punishment is death. Otherwise, it will be adjudicated in public courts in accordance with the punishment outlined in the Articles below . . ." However, in general, *ḥudūd* punishments have been specified within the context of imprisonment and financial penalty: "It appears that eminent jurists like

Mudarris embraced, in his own handwriting, the lack of conflict between the *shari'a* and the penal provisions of his own time. Thus, he effectively espoused that in matters of crime that necessitate the *ḥudūd*, the Islamic penal punishments should not be implemented, just like the proponents of suspension [during the Imam's absence]."[26]

*Result*: There is no consensus on implementing the *ḥudūd* punishments during the Imam's occultation; rather, there is a clear and strong prohibition side by side with permission.

Numerous eminent Shi'i jurists advocate that implementing the *ḥudūd* is absolutely prohibited or that permission is granted only if it does not lead to death or cause bodily harm or injury. Some of those who are unable to formulate a definitive decision have opted to pause and indefinitely postpone adopting any stance on this matter, which is equivalent to suspending the *ḥudūd*.

The author of *Jawāhir* deemed permission to implement the *ḥudūd* as having been settled. However, taking into account what has been discussed above, his characterisation of the opinion held by those who favour pausing and not rendering a decision, or else advocating the suspension of the *ḥudūd*'s implementation during the Imam's absence, as having failed "to fathom the 'taste' of *fiqh*" or as "strange and bizarre" cannot withstand serious scrutiny.[27] He has used the same phrase regarding those who reject the general guardianship of the jurists (*wilāyat al-faqīh*).[28]

Muḥammad Bāqir Shaftī attempts to reconcile the positions of those who opposed, had paused and advocated its discontinuation, and those who permitted its implementation.[29] He considers the prohibition issued by Ibn Idrīs and Ṭūsī as being confined to their own time, and has taken the designation of the "Imam", in the words of Ibn Barrāj, Ṭabrisī and Rāwandī, as broader and applicable to the general class of jurists. Muḥaqqiq's stance of pause and reflection, due to the usage of *ḥākim* in the *ḥudūd* discussion, is read as an implicit permission.

Shaftī's argument and justification is incomplete. First, the discussion of Ibn Idrīs towards the end of his *Sarā'ir* deals with the reliability of the judges' knowledge and expertise during the Imam's presence and not at all times. In such a situation, his claim of having attained consensus is perfectly true. In addition, there is no doubt that the Shi'i jurists have been mandated to adjudicate disputes and implement judgements during the Imam's occultation. However, gathering Ibn Idrīs' various opinions makes it clear that he regards the scope of juristic authority pertaining to carrying out such judgements as limited to issues that exclude *ḥudūd*.

Second, extrapolating from the text that the "appointment" and "his designate" refer to a general deputyship lacks any contextual indicator and proofs. Third, when used in books dealing with *ḥudūd*, *ḥākim* refers to a "designated *ḥākim*" during the infallible Imam's presence, as opposed to just any *ḥākim*. These three points confirm the compatibility of his *fatwa*. If this were not the case, his *fatwa* would have been refuted in some other work.

In order to reconcile the *fatwa*s of all advocates and opponents, Shaftī has attempted to ascribe them to eminent Shi'i jurists. Contrary to his conclusion, however, the opinion of those who oppose implementing the *ḥudūd* during the Imam's occultation, as well as the opinion of those who, after his time, adopted a stance of suspension – such as Aḥmad Khwānsārī – is stronger and more profound than those who advocate permission, regardless of their numerical strength.

## *Notes*

1. 'Alī b. Ḥusayn (Muḥaqqiq al-Karakī), *Rasā'il*, ed. Muḥammad al-Ḥasūn (Qom: Maktabat al-Mar'ashī al-Najafī, 1988), 1:142, 143.
2. Shaykh Mufīd, *al-Muqni'a*, 810.
3. Muḥammad Bāqir Majlisī, *Resāle-ye ḥudūd va qiṣāṣ va diyāt*, ed. 'Alī Fāḍil (Qom: Nashr-i Āsār-i Islāmī, 1983), 58.
4. Abū Ja'far Muḥammad b. al-Ḥasan al-Ṭūsī (Shaykh Ṭūsī), *al-Ṭibyān*, ed. Aḥmad Ḥabīb Quṣayr al-Āmilī (Beirut: Dār Iḥyā al-Turāth al-'Arabī, 1989), 7:407 (commentary on 24:2).
5. Qāḍī 'Abd al-'Azīz b. al-Barrāj, *al-Muhadhdhab* (Qom: Mu'assasat al-Nashr al-Islāmī, 1986), 1:341, 342; 2:518.
6. Al-Ḥasan al-Ṭabrisī, *Majma' al-bayān fī tafsīr al-Qur'ān* (Beirut: Mu'assasat al-A'lamī li-l-Maṭbū'āt, 1995), 7:219.
7. Rāwandī, *Fiqh al-Qur'ān*, 2:372.
8. Yaḥyā b. Sa'īd al-Ḥillī, *al-Jāmi' li-l-sharā'i'*, 548.
9. Ibn Fahd al-Ḥillī, *Muhadhdhab al-bāri' fī sharḥ al-Mukhtaṣar al-nāfi'*, ed. Mujtabā al-'Irāqī (Qom: Mu'assasat al-Nashr al-Islāmī, 1987), 2:326, 327.
10. Ibn Idrīs al-Ḥillī, *al-Sarā'ir*, 2:24, 25.
11. Ibid., 3:545, 546.
12. Khwānsārī, *Jāmi' al-madārik*, 5:411–413.
13. 'Umar b. Hanẓala says, "I asked Imām Ṣādiq whether it was permissible for two of the Shi'is who had a disagreement concerning a debt or a legacy to seek the verdict of the ruler or judge. He replied, 'Anyone who has recourse to the ruler or judge, whether his case be just or unjust, has in reality had recourse to *tāghūt* [i.e., the illegitimate

ruling power]. Whatever he obtains as a result of their verdict, he will have obtained by forbidden means, even if he has a proven right to it, for he will have obtained it through the verdict and judgment of the *tāghūt*, that power which God Almighty has commanded him to disbelieve in.'" ("They wish to seek justice from illegitimate powers, even though they have been commanded to reject them" (Q. 4:60)). 'Umar b. Hanẓala then asked: "What should two Shi'is do then, under such circumstances?" Imām Ṣādiq answered: "They must seek out one of you who narrates our traditions, who is versed in what is permissible and what is forbidden, who is well acquainted with our laws and ordinances, and accept him as judge and arbiter, for I appoint him as judge over you." Hamid Algar, *Islam and Revolution* (Berkeley, CA: Mizan Press, 1981), 92–93.

14. Abū Khadīja, one of the trusted companions of Imām Ṣādiq relates: "I was commanded by the Imām to convey the following message to our friends [i.e., the Shi'a]: 'When enmity and dispute arise among you, or you disagree concerning the receipt or payment of a sum of money, be sure not to refer the matter to one of these malefactors for judgment. Designate as a judge and arbiter someone among you who is acquainted with our injunction concerning what is permitted and prohibited, for I appoint such a man as judge over you. Let none of you take your complaint against another of you to the tyrannical ruling power.'" (Algar, *Islam and Revolution*, 96).
15. Bahā al-Dīn al-'Āmilī (and Niẓām al-Dīn Sāwujī), *Jāme'-i 'Abbāsī* (Tehran: Farāhānī, n.d.), 162.
16. Some have recorded the names of his student Muḥammad b. 'Alī 'Āmilī (d. 1647) and his nephew and student Zayn al-'Ābidīn Ḥusaynī as part of the group who completed the *Jāme'-i 'Abbāsī*. However, the most important and famous one is Niẓām al-Dīn Sāwujī. Mohammad Ra'īs-zāde, "Madkhal-i Jāme'-i 'Abbāsī", *Dāneshnāme-ye jahān-i Islām*, 9, Tehran, 2005.
17. Fāḍil al-Hindī, *Kashf al-lithām*, 10:477.
18. Muḥaqqiq al-Ḥillī, *Sharā'i' al-Islām*, 1:312, 313.
19. Muḥaqqiq al-Ḥillī, *Al-Mukhtaṣar al-nāfi'* (Tehran: Mu'assasat al-Bi'tha, 1990), 115.
20. Ḥasan b. Yūsuf al-Muṭahhar al-Ḥillī ('Allāma Ḥillī), *Muntahā al-maṭlab* (Mashhad: Majma' Buḥūth al-Islāmiyya, 2007), 15:244–45.
21. Ibid.
22. Ibid., 2:995.
23. Ardabīlī, *Majma' al-fā'ida*, 7:545.
24. Mīrzā Abū al-Qāsim Qommī, *Jāmi' al-shitāt*, ed. Murtaḍā Raḍavī (Tehran: Kayhān, 1992), 1:394–395.
25. Mohsen Kadivar, *Siyāsatnāme-ye Khorāsānī* (Tehran: Kavīr, 2006), 259–261.
26. Moṣṭafā Moḥaqqeq Dāmād, "*Ḥudūd dar zamān-i mā ejrā yā ta'ṭīl?*" *Taḥqīqāt-i ḥuqūqī* (Dāneshgāh-i Shahīd Beheshtī), Tehran, Nos 25 and 26 (summer 1999): 76.
27. Muḥammad Ḥasan al-Najafī, *Jawāhir*, 21:394–397.
28. Ibid., 21:397.
29. Shaftī, *Maqāla fī taḥqīq iqāmat al-ḥudūd*, 144.

## *Section VII: "Isolated Reports" (*khabar al-wāḥid*) are Non-probative (non-*ḥujjiyya*) in Matters of Critical Importance*

So far, we have attempted to establish and prove the following: the ruling on sentencing apostates or blasphemers to death has no Qur'anic basis; the cited narrations are not *mutawātir*; the narrations supporting it are *thiqa* "isolated reports" (*khabar al-wāḥid*); the claim of consensus is untenable because it is an *ijmā' madrakī* validated on the basis of the narrations cited; permission to kill apostates or blasphemers has no stronger proof than one *thiqa* "isolated report"; and there is no evidence that the Prophet, Ali or the other Imams issued such a decree in these two cases. It is now time to examine the validity of employing an "isolated report" as proof for this issue.

### Argumentation on the Basis of Non-probative (non-*ḥujjiyya*) "Isolated Report" (*khabar al-wāḥid*) on Matters of Critical Importance

Premise 1: The most important evidence, in actuality the only evidentiary proof, for a *thiqa* "isolated report's" (*khabar al-wāḥid*) validity is the conventions and practices of rational beings (*sīrat al-'uqalā'*).[1]

Premise 2: Rational beings do not rely upon conjectural *thiqa* 'isolated reports' (*khabar al-wāḥid*), which have a likelihood of being false; rather, they seek certainty on such vital and critical matters. In other words, *thiqa* 'isolated reports' in such matters is non-probative.[2]

Premise 3: The life of a human being constitutes an important and critical matter. Thus, issuing a death sentence based on a *thiqa* "isolated report" (*khabar al-wāḥid*) is not sustainable.[3] Muḥaqqiq Ḥillī writes, "It is dangerous to rely on an 'isolated report' on issues that calls for death."[4]

*Result*: the basis for issuing a punishment of killing requires a decisive and unquestioning transmitted proof (i.e., an explicit Qur'anic text or a *mutawātir* hadith), a *thiqa* "isolated report" (*khabar al-wāḥid*) that is co-joined with definitive contextual indicators, or a decisive rational proof. In other words, such a decree cannot be issued merely on the basis of a *thiqa* "isolated report", even if the narration is *saḥīḥ* and all of the transmitters are considered *thiqa*.

## Critical Analysis of the Proofs Adduced by the Opponents

Your rebuttal of my stance can be summarised as follows:

a. If the basis upon which rational beings act on a *thiqa* "isolated report" (*khabar al-wāḥid*) is that it produces confidence, there is no difference between critical and non-critical matters. If a matter requires unquestioned obedience (*ta'abbudī*), then rational beings would not distinguish between critical and non-critical matters. The outcome is that rational beings assign trust and confidence in "isolated reports" – be it on critical or non-critical issues.
b. What are the criteria for distinguishing critical from non-critical matters? How can one consider killing an apostate a critical matter, whereas the daily prayers are considered non-critical? Given that the *shari'a* requires four witnesses to prove adultery and that only two are needed to prove murder, on what basis is murder considered more critical than adultery? In principle, there are no such criteria to distinguish one from the other because all matters are important. The issues of *khums* and *zakāt*, which are connected with the individual's wealth and the place for sacrificing the animal during the hajj, are very important; however, they are confirmed by "isolated reports" (*khabar al-wāḥid*) only.
c. All or most of the chapters dealing with punishments (i.e., *diya*, *qiṣāṣ* and *ḥudūd*) are established by "isolated reports" (*khabar al-wāḥid*) only.
d. No one to date has deliberated on the division between critical and non-critical matters in the context of the validity of presenting an "isolated report" (*khabar al-wāḥid*) as evidentiary proof. As such, to advocate this division would therefore be contrary to *ijmā' murakkab* (composite consensus).
e. If we accept the premise that the practice and conduct of rational beings (*sīrat al-'uqalā'*) assigns probative value to "isolated reports" (*khabar al-wāḥid*) but only in cases dealing with non-critical matters, then what are we to say of those who have used other proofs (i.e., not relying on rational beings), to confirm an "isolated report"? These proofs are absolute and can be generalised. That is, it is not confined to critical matters.

### Critique

I do not accept your rebuttal as sound for the following reasons:

a. Rational beings act upon a *thiqa* "isolated report" (*khabar al-wāḥid*) because they have attained confidence in its veracity, even though there is a chance that it may be false. This is the threshold required to attain confidence in non-critical issues. As for critical matters, the customary practice of rational beings is to raise the threshold and, as such, obtain a level of confidence that is decisive, certain and beyond any possibility of being false. In other words, one can attain confidence in a *thiqa* "isolated report" in the case of non-critical matters, but not in the case of critical matters. As such, your statement that there is no difference between critical and non-critical matters is incorrect.
b. This discussion is not about the "importance of the *shariʿa*", and thus there is no need for you to engage in such a passionate dispute and argumentation. Rather, the issue is one of defining "importance" according to rational beings, regardless of whether they are believers or not. For rational beings, human life and the human being itself occupy the top tier of importance; honour and dignity would be on the second tier. Imam Ali's inspiring and stunning epistle to Mālik Ashtar, "Beware! Abstain from shedding blood", confirms and validates the same rational beings' conclusion. The proof text on the prohibition of robbing people of their honour and dignity manifests the same truth. Shaykh Ansāri's assertion, "Important matters in the estimation of the Legislator, like the death penalty and chastity"[5] or Akhund Khorāsānī's "Important matters like the death penalty and chastity, and other such matters",[6] officially recognise this same "importance" in the *shariʿa* according to rational beings. Clearly, if we look at the issue from the perspective of the legal ruling, then whatever we can prove and establish as having been decreed by the Legislator is, without exception, critical. The need for four witnesses to prove adultery, as established in the *shariʿa*, has nothing to do with the issue of critical importance in the estimation of rational beings. Thus, the *Ahl al-Bayt* school has rejected analogy (*qiyās*).
c. You claim that the corollary of discarding the principle of relying upon "isolated reports" (*khabar al-wāḥid*) amounts to rejecting most or all of the penal provisions because most of the proofs for *qiṣāṣ*, *ḥudūd* and *diyāt* are based on "isolated reports". If it is proven with reliable proofs that certain things practised up until now were considered to be valid religious legal rulings whereas in actuality they are not, then undoubtedly those items must be set aside. What inherent sanctity do *ḥudūd*, *qiṣāṣ* and *diyāt* possess that you are so concerned about losing them?

Things that Muḥammad is known to have prescribed for perpetuity as lawful or prohibited on the basis of reliable proofs must remain effective until the Day of Judgement. However, what relation does this have with the derived rulings, which are only presumptive (*ẓannī*) and have proven to be unreliable? The legal rulings are nothing more than a means and a path, not the end goal. The jurists' *fatwa*s are meant to help one walk this path, but are not sacrosanct in and of themselves. It goes without saying that rational beings hold the jurists responsible for investigating and analysing everything that is relevant to the penal provisions. God willing, their rulings agree with the will of the Wise Legislator. However, imitating past jurists and considering doing so to be *ijtihād* is definitely against caution and *ijtihād*. Moreover, the validity of "isolated reports" as regards the acts of worship is beyond question because their importance is a recognised religious mandate. But such an understanding of "importance" has no connection with those matters that rational beings consider critical.

d. You claim that, in the past, jurists were either in favour of or against adducing, without any restriction, "isolated reports" (*khabar al-wāḥid*) as proofs on critical matters and thus any dissent would constitute a breach of *ijmāʿ murakkab*: in reality, such a consensus has no validity because it is an *ijmāʿ madrakī*, meaning that the conclusions of both groups have been deduced from different proofs. In the words of al-Ghazālī, we likewise have the right to both revert to and to examine those same proofs.[7] You express concern about examining and revising penal rulings, which is equivalent to closing the doors of *ijtihād*. This is more abhorrent than suspending the *ḥudūd* or introducing changes into the penal provisions. Furthermore, this subject falls under *uṣūl* and thus is not part of *fiqh*. It is open to question and unresolved whether it can even be considered a technical consensus, let alone be considered a breach of an *ijmāʿ murakkab*.
e. Given that the basis of considering an "isolated report" (*khabar al-wāḥid*) being probative is based solely on the determination by rational beings, if one opts to adduce other proofs that he considers reliable then in the context of critical and non-critical matters, they cannot be entertained as absolute and unrestricted. Through this approach, one can at most gain proofs of a general nature. In addition, it is an obligatory caution not to rely upon such proofs for matters that could lead to the loss of a human being's life.

## The Necessity of Exercising Caution on Matters that Lead to Death

You have said, "Contrary to what you have heard before, namely, that jurists have advised caution in matters of the loss of life, chastity, and property, I have shown that many of them issued no such fatwa (to exercise obligatory caution). Rather, it was a strong and a forceful recommendation."[8]

Alongside my appreciation for your treatment of artificial insemination in your book on contemporary issues, allow me to be forthright in saying that what you claim in your books to have established, namely, that "there was no consensus and the absence of obligatory caution pertains to matters of chastity" as opposed to the "absence of obligatory caution on critical matters". You provide in great detail numerous statements of those jurists who favour obligatory caution and precaution in matters of chastity and then subject them to critical analysis. However, you have not broached the subject matter of the lack of necessity of caution in critical matters in this section, let alone proven or established it.

Rather, you have done just the opposite. You have acknowledged a difference between the loss of life (*dimā'*) and chastity (*furūj*), "In the chapter on [the] loss of life, because *qiṣāṣ* and the execution or implementing the *ḥudūd* is conditional upon obtaining some of the factual information, as long as this has not been obtained, one cannot decree the death penalty or implement *qiṣāṣ*. However, the chapter on 'Marriage' or 'Chastity' mentions no such specificity."[9] The source of this is attributed to Muḥaqqiq Nā'īnī, "Certainly, the presumption of permissibility does not apply in matters of wealth. On the contrary, it is necessary in such cases to observe caution, as in matters that lead to loss of life or on chastity. He has approximated this position through the well-known principle expounded by him, namely: 'In cases where there is a ruling of license (*tarkhīṣ*), this [permission] is contingent upon a matter of fact. But where this fact is not definitively established, it must be assumed to be absent.'"[10] In your response you acknowledged that at a governmental level, especially when dealing with the loss of life, this can be grouped under "secondary injunction": "There is no *taqiyya* when it comes to the loss of life."

It is patently clear that there is no connection between chastity and the loss of life, except for the fact that some jurists list the former under the heading of "critical matters". The loss of life, being a specific and independent subject, mandates caution. In other words, the invalidity of a *thiqa* "isolated report" (*khabar al-wāḥid*) as proof in critical matters like the loss of life mandates obligatory caution. Thus, even those who do not limit the validity of "isolated reports" to non-critical matters favour caution in this particular case. This elaboration shows that your claim is baseless and contrary to reality.

## *Notes*

1. I first broached the subject of the validity or lack thereof of an "isolated report" (*khabar al-wāḥid*) for critical matters at a conference, "Human Rights and the Dialogue of Civilization", at Mufīd University, Tehran, in April/May 2001. The paper was titled, "Freedom of Belief and Religion in Islam and its Basis in Human Rights". That same year, it was published in the conference collection of papers. In February/March 2003, it was printed in the *Āftāb* magazine for the second time (March 2003, 23:54–63). The English translation was done in 2006 and finally published in 2008 in my book, *Ḥaqq al-nās: Islām va ḥuqūq-i bashar*.

You acknowledge in your advanced classes dealing with Islamic legal theory that after investigating a few articles (without specifying the source), you decided to bring forth the subject of critical matters in your class: "I am discussing this because, at times, this issue crops up in some articles, and if we or others do not provide an appropriate response, then we might as well discard half of *fiqh*! And some of those who pursue this issue are aware of this conclusion that we would have to set aside all the sections dealing with punishments, as well as many of the rulings on *khums* and *zakāt* and jihad. We have many rulings dealing with jihad that have been established on the basis of an 'isolated report' (*khabar al-wāḥid*). How then can we say that the matters of property and life are part of critical matters and, as such, 'isolated reports' are of no benefit here?" Lankarānī Jr, *Dars-i khārij-i uṣūl* (27 January 2009), session 57.

In the end, you allocated one full session of the class to the subject, "Investigating the issues of customary practice of rational beings and the validity of an 'isolated report' (*khabar al-wāḥid*) in critical and non-critical matters." I alluded to the same subject in my brief rebuttal of the fatwa on killing [Rāfiq Taqī], which you dismissed as "outdated and a rehash of the past." Moreover, you clamour that "there is nothing new" in my treatment of the subject but yours is unparalleled in terms of its importance and originality: "In the past ten years, this subject has been analysed by some who have left important imprints and have attributed it to certain past eminent jurists holding the view that the test of rational beings can be applied only to ordinary and non-critical matters if the proof is based on an 'isolated report'. If we accept this, then we would not be able to prove critical matters such as murder and apostasy, because they are based on an 'isolated report'. We will investigate this subject matter. Pay close attention, as the subject is vital and not tackled in any other place." Lankarānī Jr, *Dars-i khārij-i uṣūl* (5 April 2009), session 77.

You want to have your cake and eat it too! As far as I know, (praise be to God) you are the first honourable professor, based on your own testimony, to have dealt with a subject and tried to refute it after having read some articles (without specifying them). Let me say at the outset that I am sincerely grateful to you for your formulation and critique. You correctly acknowledge the importance of this subject matter and that half of *fiqh* would be transformed and undergo substantive change, especially in the area of punishments. Your anxiety that this would have a great impact on *khums* and *zakāt* is also totally understandable. However, the crux of the matter is the following: Why do you not reference your dissenters' perspective so that the students can compare your proofs with others to reach their own determination of the strengths and weaknesses of the arguments?

2. Khwānsārī, *Jāmi' al-madārik*, 7:35.
3. *Majma' al-fā'ida*, 13:90; Khwānsārī, *Jāmi' al-madārik*, 7:35.
4. Muḥaqqiq Ḥillī, *Al-Sharā'i'*, 4:114.
5. Murtaḍā b. Muḥammad Amīn al-Anṣārī, *Farā'id al-uṣūl*, ed. Turāth al-Shaykh al-A'zam (Qom: Majma' al-Fikr al-Islāmī, 1998), 2:137.
6. al-Khorāsānī, *Kifāyat al-uṣūl*, 354.
7. Abū Ḥāmid Muḥammad al-Ghazālī, *Iḥyā 'ulūm al-dīn*, ed. 'Abd al-'Azīz 'Izz al-Dīn Sayrawān (Beirut: Dār Iḥyā al-'Ulūm, 1990), 1:24.
8. Mohammad Javād Fāzel Lankarānī (Lankarānī Jr), *Talqīḥ-i maṣnū'ī* (Qom: Markaz-i Fiqhi-ye A'imme-ye Aṭhār, 2006), 32.
9. Ibid.
10. Ḥusayn Ḥillī, *Dalīl al-'urwat al-wuthqā*, ed. and annotated Ḥasan Sa'īd Tehrānī (Najaf: n.p., 1962), 1:203.

## *Section VIII: Issuing* Fatwas *on Killing an Apostate or a Blasphemer Weakens and Impairs (*wahn*) Islam*

This section comprises four points for deliberation.

### Impairing (*wahn*) Islam Means to Deface its Visage so that it Becomes One of Violence, Repugnance and Ferociousness; One that is Distant from Mercy and Compassion

You reject my objection on this matter by providing four possible methods of determining what defaces or impairs Islam. You then discard the first three and embrace the fourth to support your argument that these *fatwas* do not deface Islam's visage.

a. An act is considered to impair religion when all rational beings at all times and places agree that it does.

   Your response: one who blasphemes the Prophet, who is revered by more than a billion Muslims, deserves punishment according to rational beings. Second, there is a possibility that the Legislator proscribes the rational ruling derived by humans pertaining to blasphemy and apostasy.

b. The criteria of what "weakens or impairs Islam" is that which disagrees with humanity's natural disposition and is therefore detested.

   Your response: human nature is not repulsed by punishing one who blasphemes the Prophet.

c. The criteria of what constitutes "defacing" should be determined in accordance with the perspective of non-believers.

   Your response: if that is so, then the atheist would find most Islamic legal rulings, inclusive of acts of worship and human interrelations in Islam to be repulsive.

d. Criteria of *wahn*

   You assert: "The criteria of which acts 'impair Islam' requires no vindication in human reason or hadith reports." This is how you have defined the correct meaning of *wahn* and, based on this, concluded that it is rational for God, given that He is the True Master, to prescribe a worldly punishment for the apostate and the blasphemer.

   Reason also dictates that both of them deserve to be punished. In addition, the transmitted reports from the Legislator have specified the type of judgment.

## Response

What constitutes *wahn*, just like *ḍarūrī* (essential) is deduced from a totality of proofs and, as such, goes beyond the the Qur'an or transmitted narrations. To identify an instance of *wahn* at any particular time, the conventional practice of rational beings in that particular age must remain the yardstick. In our own time, the majority of rational beings, both believers and unbelievers, would regard the following acts as defacing the visage of Islam: enslaving the women and children of those who fight against the Muslims in a war; stoning, executing apostates, burning a living person [to death], hurling a person from a high altitude, demolishing a house with the occupants inside and crucifying; amputating one's hand, foot or finger and flogging; carrying out *qiṣāṣ* (the traditional "eye-for-an-eye" mentality); throwing acid in one's face; and a husband striking his wife.

Most of these actions, which can be found in the section on punishments, can clearly be said to deface Islam's visage by making it appear to be violent, repulsive, brutal, and distant from mercy and compassion. And so instead of honouring and respecting the divine rulings, such rulings repulse people and make them fear Islam.

To be sure, the standard of what constitutes "defacing and impairing Islam" has changed over time, due to changing customs and conventions. Thus, based on the outlook of contemporary rulers and their people, both believers and unbelievers, one can surmise that they would not accept such violent punishments. In general, the era of physical punishment has been replaced by one of imprisonment, social boycott, fines and rehabilitation.

Undoubtedly, enslaving individuals, especially women and children, is repugnant and non-defensible. Although this practice was acceptable by the reasoning standards of the past, it has been condemned by our own era's reasoning standard. "Reasoning" does not mean a ruling by reason that is totally independent, but rather one that is connected to its own time. Yes, the standard of rational beings has changed over time, as the (formally) discontinued practices of slavery and physical punishment show.

An increase in the number of incidents viewed as defacing Islam at any given time implies that there has been erosion in the rational justification of Islam. This gradually accentuates the cleavage between religion and reasonableness. Such a severe contrast is due to three possibilities: (1) the foundation and principles of reasonableness have diverged from the truth; (2) our definition and elaboration of religion is wrong; and (3) neither of them is reliable. Undoubtedly, generalising a ruling in every case is not correct, for in each domain one needs to take into account the practices and conduct of rational beings and the principal tenets of religion.

After researching this subject from several perspectives, I concluded that all of the criteria that I have specified above are present in the Universal Declaration of Human Rights. I have candidly written that the standards and conduct of rational beings in the modern period, in comparison with the *fatwa*s of pre-modern jurists, are superior.[1] This does not pertain to the divine rulings, so there is no justification for you to indulge in such a loud campaign of sensationalism and sloganeering about "sacrilege" in this regard. This superiority relates to those *apparent* legal rulings that have incorrectly been attached to the Ja'farī school of thought, and therefore it has no connection with the *actual* divine judgements.

The presence of elements that produce this type of *fatwa*s in books is not a rebuke of the Qur'an and Sunna, for they were well-founded and valid – but at a different time and in a different place. If any fault exists, it has to be attributed to those jurists who removed specific Qur'anic verses and narrations from their contexts and de-historicised them, clamoured for their generalisation (*ta'mīm*), and made them absolute (*iṭlāq*) and perpetually relevant (*dawām*). If the *fatwa*s of Shaykh Mufīd, Ṭūsī, Shahīd I and Shahīd II were sufficient and appropriate in their own times for the objectives set out, one is not justified in imitating them and their rulings within the context of a very different time and place, one in which the standards of rational people have substantially changed. Merely relating the opinions of past jurists and prefixing "caution" (*aḥwaṭ*) or "preferable" (*awlā*) does not constitute *ijtihād*.

Insulting and denigrating any person is repugnant, and even more so when it is done to the Prophet, who is revered by one-fourth of the world's population. One must respect the sacred aspects of each faith. Insulting, vilifying and blaspheming them are unacceptable practices and, in some cases, deserve punishment. However, today such actions do not reach the threshold of ordering one's death, and even more so that anyone who hears that sacrilege can kill the person independent of the judiciary. It is impossible to show the merciful Prophet's grandeur by means of such violence. As such, that which defaces Islam's visage and is terrifying is the above-mentioned death sentence and the right of one person to kill another based upon what he or she has heard, as opposed to allowing a competent court to hear the case, issue a judgement, and punish the accused in accordance with it.

In the case of merely apostatising (i.e., not linked with any crimes), any form of temporal punishment would deface Islam, not to mention execution or permanent imprisonment accompanied by harsh acts such as whipping the person at the time of the five daily prayers. Based on the standards of rational people living today, punishing apostasy in any way violates the inherent right of the freedom of religion. Hence, what is at issue here is the very notion of temporal punishment and, even more so, allowing someone to kill any person who has been deemed guilty of apostasy by a jurist as opposed to a competent court.

## *Wahn* as "Secondary" (*ḥukm thānawī*) and "Primary Injunction" (*ḥukm awwalī*)

*Wahn* as a "secondary injunction" would prevent the ruling's application if it were considered to deface and weaken Islam; and as a "primary injunction", it would provide an indicator of an error in the ruling's (killing an apostate or a blasphemer) deduction. You endeavour to subtly distract the non-meticulous reader:

> Under the subject of "impairing Islam", people seem to have forgotten that it is grouped under "secondary status" (*'unwān thānawī*) like hardship (*ḥaraj*) and urgency (*iḍṭirār*), harm (*ḍarar*) and dissimulation (*taqiyya*). It has been established that such subjects are not valid and applicable in all instances. For example, in the case of dissimulation the subject would be suspended in a situation where blood could be spilled, for "There is no *taqiyya* when it leads to spilling of blood" (i.e., if it results in shedding of innocent blood). Likewise, in some instances the issue of "impairing Islam" could not be formulated into a subject for a legal ruling.
>
> Those occasions that demand extreme and harsh measures against unbelievers and polytheists would lead to their killing. In such a situation, no jurist would rule that if this resulted in impairing Islam's image, then it is not obligatory. This conclusion is commonly accepted in jurisprudence. Accordingly, in the case of apostasy the subject of "impairing Islam" is of no relevance, although one could temporarily suspend the punishment of "stoning the adulterer" if it leads to "impairing Islam". However, invoking a

ruling designed to deal forcefully with the unbelievers, polytheists and deviants who are scornfully rejecting and exploiting the situation, and thereby producing greater hatred and distance between them and the Muslims, cannot be blocked by raising the subject of "impairing Islam".

## Response

A ruling that impairs Islam can be approached from two perspectives:

One, as a "secondary status", meaning that although the ruling's implementation would be suspended as long as it impairs Islam, the original ruling would remain untouched. In light of the difficulties and problems faced by Muslims after a film on stoning was distributed internationally, many of the traditional scholars working for the Islamic government (of Iran) suspended that practice in order to protect Islam's honour and dignity.

The late Khomeini supposedly also consented to this judgement. Thus, can we not do likewise for blasphemy and apostasy based upon the same principle? Contrary to your view, the answer is "yes". From the perspective of traditional jurists, stoning and executing an apostate or a blasphemer are all legal rulings and part of the *shari'a*. However, implementing these judgements today would impair Islam's visage. As such, preserving Islam's dignity in general, when compared with implementing one subsidiary ruling, is undoubtedly far more important. As such, the rulings on blasphemy and apostasy cannot be implemented until *wahn* no longer exists in their implementation.

You distinguish between stoning, and blasphemy and apostasy by arguing that the latter's essence and quiddity deals with unbelievers and deviants. Latching on to this rationale is merely conjectural, something upon which a jurist does not rely. If one is to entertain this, then it can be argued that that the essence and quiddity of stoning, given the severity and coarseness of the punishment, when applied to those who engage in an act that violates chastity would stand as a lesson for others. It should be clear that such a discourse enters the area of juristic preference (*istiḥsān*),[2] which Ja'farī *fiqh* rejects.

Montazeri favoured suspending the implementation of those judgements that impair Islam's visage under the rubric of secondary injunction:

> It is possible that some of the punishments, due to the insufficient explanation of their objectives or incorrect implementation, cause

people to be cynical of the Shari'a's fundamentals and impair Islam's image. In such a situation, the judgement's philosophical underpinnings must be explained to, and accepted by, the public before it can be implemented. If this has not been done, then its implementation must be suspended . . . If implementing the *ḥudūd* in a particular time or place will negatively affect an individual or an Islamic society, then it must be suspended temporarily.[3]

Even if, under normal circumstances, implementing the *ḥudūd* provides numerous benefits to the society, on the condition that the crime is proven through the method provided by the Shari'a . . . however, the ruler can suspend their implementation if, under special circumstances, the public welfare demands that they be abandoned [temporarily]. In a *thiqa* "isolated report" (*khabar al-wāḥid*) of Ghiyāth b. Ibrāhīm, Imam Ali is reported to have said: "I do not implement the *ḥadd* punishment on a person while he is inhabiting enemy-ruled land until he exits from there, out of fear [that] this would push him in the direction of seeking the enemy's protection and forging an alliance with them." If implementing even some of them would engender revulsion (in a particular locality, or in all of the regions, or during a particular time) against Islam and its rulings, thereby weakening Islam's foundations, then the ruler or his designate of the region's judiciary is obligated to suspend their implementation for as long as necessary.[4]

Second, the ruling could be considered to fall under "primary injunction" (in contrast to a "secondary injunction"), in the sense that there has been a change in the standards and conduct of rational beings such that *wahn* targets the original legal injunction itself, not its implementation in a particular time and place. A temporal punishment, in particular killing apostates and especially allowing anyone who has heard him (apostatise or blaspheme) to kill him, in and of itself leads to *wahn*, that is, the original ruling (of killing an apostate or a blasphemer) was the result of an erroneous deduction that occurred right at its base. Even if no errors were made, it was still limited to a specific time when it was conventional to render such punishments. Clearly this is not the case today. That is, the injunction was temporary.

The Legislator has prescribed no specific temporal punishment for changing one's religion and no temporal or afterlife punishment for erring in one's research. But one who apostatises out of animosity and stubbornness will be punished severely in the afterlife.

In the case of narrations on the death penalty, even if the principle of restricting the probative force of solitiary reports to non-critical matters is not accepted, the indicators (*adilla*) of prohibiting *wahn* would negate the validity of narrations on the death penalty for an apostate under "primary injunction". In my estimation, invoking the prohibition of *wahn* under the rubric of "primary injunction" is a contextual indicator of an error in the ruling's deduction (of killing an apostate) from the proofs pertaining to killing apostates.

## Contemporary *Ijtihād* is Far Away from the Standard of the Prophet's Mercy

a. You responded to my assertion that such types of *fatwa*s have no association with the merciful Prophet as follows: "This kind of interpretation and expression does not accord with the dignified stature of *ijtihād* and the techniques employed to derive legal rulings. Rather, it resembles a slogan . . . they have failed to provide a proper understanding of 'merciful Messenger', for he is a mercy for all of humanity, as opposed to for each individual person."

### Critique

First, you are correct in assessing that the merciful Prophet's "standard" is far away from that of present-day *ijtihād* and the techniques and proofs employed to derive legal rulings and therefore, any claim of conforming to such a "standard" is more of a slogan. This disparity is precisely why *fiqh* has become so backward. The Prophet said, "O Lord, my people treat this Qur'an as something to be shunned and forsaken" (Q. 25:30). Removing the Qur'an or minimising its role from the process of *ijtihād* and jurisprudential techniques is common. In the Qur'an, each human being is entitled to honour and nobility by virtue of just being a human being, even prior to embracing a religion. This right does not increase or decrease. Just as air and sunlight are accessible to everyone – unbelievers and believers – faith plays no role here. Can you appreciate the large gap that exists between this "standard" and that which you named as part of *ijtihād* and deep jurisprudential understanding?

Second, religious rulings are derived from the totality of the Qur'anic verses and the Sunna. This is equivalent to the Qur'an's spirit because of embracing the totality of the proof-texts instead of being selective.

b. You claim:

> This ruling on executing an apostate and a blasphemer has been in existence ever since the dawn of Islam, and at no point has it ever been the cause of defacing the visage of Islam. From the time that the [European] colonialists began expounding upon human rights (and, in actuality, this was the start of confronting Islam), they have protested with incredulity by asking, "What kind of a ruling is this?" This objection is motivated by their desire to spread wicked and false information about Islam and has ended here on this point, namely, that Islamic rulings "are in conflict" with human reason, freedom, and dignity.
>
> Why should we Muslims be so simple-minded and naïve that we fall prey to deception under such assertions?

## Response

Objectionable *fatwa*s have been scrutinised ever since humanity learned to discern and understand the cosmos. Even the human being itself has undergone a change. This change of discernment, eventually co-joined with the advancement of knowledge and technology, resulted in military, economic and political power. Western civilisation's two tracks, knowledge and colonialism,[5] have a reality and cannot be ignored.

The concept of human rights is a relatively new ethical outlook that can, like any other good concept, be abused to advance colonial interests. The fact that previous and present superpowers and their allies have/still misuse it should never prevent us from accepting the reality that many of our own scholars and jurists have been/are heedless of the divinely endowed natural rights, which they did/do not take into account when formulating their legal rulings. Should we reject this concept just because the philosophy and logic of human rights come from classical-era Greeks and non-Muslims?

Are you forgetting that "Grasp the truth even if it be from a hypocrite" is part of the Shi'i worldview? What about the claims of past jurists: "We are the children of proofs"? Did not Ali instruct us to "Pay attention to what is being said and not [to] who is saying it"? and also "Take wisdom from wherever you find it, for whenever wisdom is in the bosom of a hypocrite it flutters therein until it comes out and settles in the bosom of the believer and his associates."[6] And his statement, "Wisdom is the lost treasure of a believer, so get it even if it be from the hypocrites."[7] Accepting the truth, even if it has been discovered by a non-Muslim, does not mean that one is gullible or simplistic, for truth is not bound by geography. Be in tune with the times to avoid being confounded by the onslaught. Do not sanctify conventions and customs prevalent at the time of Revelation. Legal rulings are a path to attaining the divine goals of religion, and thus the focus should remain on striving to reach that end.

## Unbelief and Apostasy have No Temporal Punishment

a. You point out, "If one desires to present Islam, one should take into account its totality and multiple perspectives, like the advancement of reason, knowledge, ethics, societal affairs and politics, and public administration. Why do they not announce that Islam has issued no legal ruling of execution against a native unbeliever (*kāfir aṣlī*) who has never wavered in his native belief?"

### Response

You have alluded to the right principles. One should take into account the totality of Islam when introducing it. But should one not also do the same thing when deducing a ruling? A deduced *fatwa* on killing an apostate could not have been issued if the jurists were also focused on the religion's ultimate divine objectives and contextualising the text from the vantage point of mercy and human dignity, as well as doing this with an eye on reforming the world and human beings, instead of confining oneself to some narrations. If the universality of rights and social and ethical norms were employed as sources to be used while deducing a legal ruling, then sentencing the accused to death in absentia, thereby denying him the right of self-defence, would have been impossible. Do you notice the virtue of considering the totality of Islam and the wide disparity that exists between you and this approach?

The fact that a native-born unbeliever has a right to live (without being subjected to persecution) is a good contextual indicator that an apostate should have the same right because the right to life has nothing to do with one's belief. Whether one's belief is right or wrong is irrelevant in terms of receiving any privilege or punishment in this world. The outcome of this will be manifest on the Day of Judgement. A temporal punishment can be applied only to proven criminals. Therefore, no sin can be said to have a temporal punishment.

My contention is focused exactly on this point: apostasy, regardless of the person's underlying intention, warrants no temporal punishment let alone death, just as is the case with a native-born unbeliever who continues in his or her original belief. No competent court can convict and then punish a person for not converting to Islam or for abandoning it. My claim is based on reliable proofs from the Qur'an and Sunna, as well as the faculty of reason, all of which I have expounded upon so far. More will follow.

b. You pose the question, "According to the tenor of the Qur'an, is an apostate not worse than an unbeliever?" The answer is "No, he is not," for what is crucial is the end result of one's life, as opposed to just what has transpired. Rejecting truth is deviance, whether it is done at the beginning or at the present. These kinds of conjectural *istiḥsān* are unacceptable in the school of thought of the Qur'an and the *Ahl al-Bayt*.

Again, you ask, "'Why has Islam not prescribed the punishment of execution for a native-born unbeliever who continues in his unbelief?' The reason for this is that a Muslim who declares his apostasy is declaring war against Islam. It is, therefore, natural to deal harshly with such a person, in contrast to a native unbeliever."

## Response

First, these are conjectural *istiḥsān*.

Second, how is leaving Islam a declaration of war against it, something for which the person in question must be confronted so severely? It is possible that during the early days of Islam and in the Arab tribal culture that existed at that time, parts of the Hejaz were as such. But this has clearly not been the case for many centuries.

Third, a "declaration of war" falls under the category of "customs and conventions", not the categories of "religious (*sharʿī*) or absolute submission (*taʿabbudī*)". Based on custom, this category of "declaration of war" has a general and a specific relationship with apostasy. If you believe that the rationale and philosophy of the ruling on apostasy or the actual contextual situation (*mawḍūʿ*) is connected with punishment for declaring war against Islam, then why do you not apply the maxim of relationality? That is to say, connect the judgement on the *mawḍūʿ* with the declaration of war instead of apostasy, and identify the former as being the impetus for the death penalty instead of the latter.

## *Notes*

1. Kadivar, *Ḥaqq al-nās*, 85–166.
2. See Glossary.
3. Montazeri, *Pāsokh*, 35.
4. Ibid., 102, 103.
5. Read this excellent work, ʿAbd al-Hādī Ḥāʾirī, *Nokhostīn rūyārūyī-hā-ye andishehgarān-i Iran bā dow rūeyye-ye tamaddon-i bourjūvāzi-ye gharb* (Tehran: Amīr kabīr, 1993).
6. Sharīf al-Raḍī, *Nahj al-balāgha*, Aphorism 79.
7. Ibid., Aphorism 80.

## *Section IX: Alteration of the Subject (*mawḍūʿ*) of Apostasy and Objecting to the Perpetual Applicability of the Death Penalty for Blasphemy and Apostasy*

In this section, four issues will be analysed.

### The Method of Retaining the Permanent Nature of a Legal Ruling

You have repeatedly claimed that "condemning an apostate is a definitive and indisputable divine ruling" and, moreover, that

> . . . these hadith reports were not exclusively related during the time of Imam Ali's caliphate or during the Medinan state period of the Prophet in order to pre-empt one from speculating that such a ruling is political or governmental and thus only valid for a particular period. Rather, they are related by the infallible Imams, such as Imam Bāqir, Imam Ṣādiq, Imam Kāẓim, and Imam Riḍā, and thus demonstrate with glaring clarity that this ruling is timeless and perpetual, [and therefore] valid until the Day of Resurrection. These hadiths are instances of actual events and present a general rule on apostasy.

#### Response

(a) The ruling on the mandatory nature of condemning an apostate to death is an "apparent legal divine ruling" deduced by some respectable jurists; however, other eminent jurists have derived a different opinion. Thus, on this point of dispute, your claim that it is an "actual divine ruling" is exorbitant, unreasonable and contrary to the evidence.

(b) A temporary legal ruling is not confined to the political sphere dealing with government, for there is no evidence to substantiate that abrogated and temporary rulings pertain exclusively to such matters. Do slavery and other matters that flow from it pertain to politics and government?

(c) Proving a ruling to be permanent and immutable is no easy task. The following channels can be postulated to reach such a conclusion:

*First Method*: the general and absolute nature of the evidence, in the sense that it is not confined by time.

Although this is a necessary condition, it most certainly is not sufficient in and of itself because it cannot be confirmed or established that in every situation the Legislator intended to make a permanent and absolute pronouncement. Consequently, without this information the wisdom behind its absolute nature cannot be established.

*Second Method*: the inclusion of all capable human beings with those addressed in the legal ruling.

This maxim is secondary and can be invoked only after establishing the permanence and continuity of the injunction. In other words, if the injunction is of a permanent nature, then what is stated to those present is also valid for those who are absent. However, here the discussion is about what makes an injunction permanent.

*Third Method*: the finality of prophethood and the prophetic ministry in the person of Muhammad applies to the whole world.

Given that his reach, which is global and for all times, is the foundation and thus an integral part of Islam, it is a necessary corollary that everything he pronounced as permanent must be accepted as such. However, this is not equivalent to ascribing every conjectural ruling to him as permanent. In other words, while accepting the finality of his prophethood, one must also establish the continuity and permanence of each and every prophetic injunction. The finality of his prophethood is not evidence in favour of the permanence of all of his injunctions. Moreover, there is no lack of changeable rulings under the rubric of the Prophet's injunctions.

*Fourth Method*: the eternal miraculousness of the Qur'an.

At most, this may be relevant only for those rulings present in the Qur'an. One cannot conclude that all of the prophetic injunctions are permanent and continuous by relying upon the verse "And whatsoever the Messenger gives you, take it. And whatsoever he forbids you, abstain (from it)" (Q. 59:7), because the outcome depends upon the particularities of the two situations. The restrictions present in the Third Method above would also apply.

Although the Qur'an's miraculous nature is beyond dispute, there is a dispute as to the nature of this miracle. For example, Sayyid Murtaḍā does not look at this issue from the perspective of the Qur'an's content, but rather opines that the source of this miraculousness is the fact that God has prevented people from being able to replicate it. Most scholars view it as miraculous from a literary perspective, let alone being able to produce the same calibre of content. Whether each verse in and of itself or the Qur'an in its totality is a miracle, as well as whether it is a proof for the Prophet's contemporaries or for all time, requires diligent and meticulous scholarly discussion. In any event, its miraculousness has no bearing on the permanence and continuity of the explicit legal rulings therein. Moreover, the Qur'an prescribes no temporal punishment for blasphemy and apostasy.

*Fifth Method*: On the authority of Zurāra: "I asked the Prophet about the lawful and the unlawful. He replied, 'Acts assessed to be lawful by Muhammad will remain so forever until Judgement Day, and his prohibitions will remain so forever until Judgment Day. It will not be other than this, and none will come after him.'"[1]

The continuity and permanence of the injunctions are outcomes derived from theological, creedal and jurisprudential bases. As matters related to creed and theology require certainty, conjecture as well as an even greater likelihood are insufficient. Although a *thiqa* "isolated report" (*khabar al-wāḥid*) can be invoked to gain a probable opinion, it cannot be presented as a proof in matters of creed.

Preserving the continuity of the prophetic injunctions is vital. The criterion for an "isolated report" (*khabar al-wāḥid*) constituting a valid proof depends upon rational beings' customs and norms. In their estimation, such a report cannot establish important matters of such great magnitude.

If one were to accept this hadith as valid, it would still be confined to those prophetic legal rulings that lack any indicant as to whether it was meant to be temporary in nature. In other words, this hadith establishes that the prophetic injunctions are permanent unless proven otherwise. It does not extend to the injunctions issued by the infallible Imams that are invoked in Shi'i *fiqh* for most of the detailed and particular aspects of the *shari'a*.

If the subject matter changes, then as a corollary the ruling also changes. Therefore, this hadith would not apply to it because a change in the ruling is induced by a change in the subject matter. This is not equivalent to changing something lawful into something unlawful or vice versa. I will elaborate upon this later on.

## A Comparison between the Permanence of Killing an Apostate with the Ruling on Theft and some Rulings on Jihad

All rulings on slavery and concubines, which are plentiful in the Qur'an, Hadith literature and legal manuals, are now considered to have undergone a change in the subject matter or, rather, have been abrogated to such an extent that even if Muslims were to become the superpower, prisoners of war would not be enslaved and the women of conquered territories would not be reduced to concubines. Details of the many rulings on jihad are contained in numerous verses and hadiths, as well as robust chapters in legal manuals devoted to such matters. This was the situation up until the middle of the twentieth century, when they became void of subject matter due to the changed nature brought about by modern weaponry, international relations and conditions necessary to initiate a war. This is also true as regards slavery and concubinage.

Why, then, should we be so worried and agitated over the change of subject matter on a very minor issue like the ruling on executing an apostate or a blasphemer? Is it not true that the rulings on slavery and concubines were established by using verses and reliable hadiths? Is it not true that the consensus attained was to such an extent that some considered that it had been elevated to an essential component of religion? Did the change of the subject matter harm the Qur'an, the Hadith corpus or jurisprudence?

Rulings on slavery, freeing a slave, purchasing one's freedom from slavery, concubines and children born of concubines satisfied some of the special needs of that time. Due to the passage of time and the non-existence of the subject matter, they have been consigned to the archives. No one protested, when such changes occurred, that the principle "Acts assessed to be lawful by Muhammad will remain so forever until Judgement Day" was violated, that the Qur'an's miraculousness was called into question, and that the consensus of the community was ruptured.

The ruling of executing an apostate, which is devoid of any reliable Qur'anic evidence and replete with difficulties associated with the hadiths upon which a consensus was built, along with the non-existence of the subject matter have been discussed at great length elsewhere. When rational beings ascertain that the circumstances of a particular time and place have changed, the gradual non-existence of the subject matter or abrogation of slavery is far easier to accept. Likewise, given that enjoying freedom is an integral part of the essence of dignity, slavery negates that essence.

Thus, under no circumstances can anyone validate slavery and replace the freedom of religion with force and coercion, for that particular freedom cannot be separated from human dignity and nobility. Therefore, one cannot be punished or taken to task in this world for choosing a deficient religion or a false belief system because these are not crimes subject to temporal punishment. Such a choice would, however, prevent one from reaching the heights of excellence by embracing the true creed, and on the Day of Judgement this person will also be punished by the just God if he or she had rejected Islam due to animosity or rebelliousness. As this world is a place for actions, as opposed to punishments, neither unbelief nor hypocrisy can be punished here. This is also true for one who abandons Islam.

The firm resolve of rational beings on the inalienable nature of human dignity and religious freedom has now reached a stage such that if religion or any other ideology were to defend the validity of slavery and condemn an apostate to death, it would diminish its stature. In addition, it would be accused of not understanding humanity. In the final analysis, such a defence would lead to people accusing God of not being wise. As a result, other rulings would quite likely be viewed in a biased and prejudicial manner. Condemning an apostate to death cannot be compared with such a small matter like determining the ritual purity or not of boiled grapes that have been transformed into wine, as such things would have no impact upon the religion, regardless of the judgement. But given that the ruling on killing an apostate would call into question the credibility of religion's very foundation, the jurist has only two options: protect religion's foundation or choose this minor ruling (on apostasy) and weaken and impair the basis of religion.

Given that the eternal permission to rob (unbelievers) has been proven on the basis of Qur'anic verses, reliable hadiths and consensus, why has no such *fatwa* been issued? The problem is not with the proofs, but rather that these proofs were adduced for a time when this practice was accepted. As such, that ruling is defensible for that particular period. However, in this day and age, one in which rational beings have embraced the universality of human rights, a jurist cannot advance the same proofs and issue a similar *fatwa*. If a jurist is unable to realise that the definition of *ijtihād* is to appreciate the new circumstances of different times, all he can do is blindly follow existing precedents. Such an approach does not protect, but rather weakens, Islam. Assume that the ruling on executing an apostate was acceptable in the past and that using force and erecting strict limits for religious people was considered beneficial at that time. But today, rational beings view corporal punishment as unacceptable and freedom as the basis of progress for religious people. Thus, executing an apostate cannot be sanctioned.

## Change of the Subject Matter of Apostasy from the Time of the Imams to Now

In the estimation of rational beings, is the subject matter of apostasy in the Qur'an, the hadith corpus, and past rulings identical to its understanding in our times? In all likelihood the answer is "No", because the subject matter in the former is broader than changing one's religion or leaving Islam. In fact, it extends to both aligning oneself with the enemies (i.e., unbelievers and polytheists) of and propagandising against Muslims, which would constitute a form of political, military and cultural rebellion against the state's authority. But today, changing one's faith is understood to be merely a conversion without any ulterior motives. In other words, contemporary rational beings consider the subject matter of apostasy to be connected with religious and cultural freedom, whereas Islamic jurisprudence considers it to be a political crime: belligerency against the state. These two viewpoints are poles apart.

The Qur'an uses "apostasy" to indicate those hostile unbelievers who sought to disillusion the Muslims and cause them to abandon Islam by spreading negative propaganda, scheming and exploiting ex-Muslims to strike at Islam's stature. For example, "They ask you concerning fighting in the sacred month. Say, 'Fighting therein is a grave (transgression), but graver is, in the sight of God, to prevent access to the path of God, to deny Him, to prevent access to the sacred mosque, and drive out its members. Persecution and sedition (*fitna*) are worse than slaying . . .'" (Q. 2:217), and "And a party of the People of the Book say, 'Believe in that which has been revealed to those who believe at the opening of the day, and disbelieve at the end thereof, in order that they [too] may revert'" (Q. 3:72).

The Qur'an explicitly and absolutely prescribes temporal punishment for those guilty of belligerency (i.e., causing disorder and disturbing societal peace and security by using weapons, Q. 5:33), whereas in the case of apostasy – with all its potential political ramifications – it has contented itself with mentioning only the punishments of effacing good deeds in this life and eternal damnation in the Hereafter.

The first "apostates" killed in Islam's history were those Muslims who refused to remit their *zakāt* to the Prophet's first political successor.[2] Their number was so significant that the general populace inquired on the textual basis for this killing. As neither this issue nor the legitimacy of the first caliph could be justified by resorting to the Qur'an, the response was the coining of the novel term "consensus" (*ijmāʿ*) and attributing a statement to the Prophet: "My community will not unite upon an error." The response to the former consisted of ascribing this hadith to the Prophet: "Whosoever changes his religion, kill him." Ali, who was the door of knowledge to the Prophet, has narrated neither of these two hadiths and, moreover, they are absent from the collection of the Shiʿi reliable hadith sources. The latter hadith[3] has been related by the author of *Mustadrak*[4] from *Daʿāʾim*[5] with no chain of transmission.

The two succeeding caliphs followed the mode established by the first one in dealing with the so-called *ahl al-ridda* (apostates). At that time, apostasy consisted of leaving Islam and actively working with those who opposed the government. Imam Ali complained, very eloquently and with great anguish, of being surrounded by overflowing violence as a result of the errors made by the previous two caliphs: "He (Abū Bakr) put (the caliphate) in a tough enclosure (and reached a person [ʿUmar b. al-Khaṭṭāb]) whose utterance was haughty and whose touch was rough. Mistakes were plenty, and so were the excuses for them."[6]

During that period, the criteria for blasphemy and apostasy were based upon violence, which could be singled out as blameworthy. There is no credible evidence that Imam Ali played any role in the violence and killing of the *ahl al-ridda* or of any apostate. He never viewed his armed opponents in the battles comprising the *Nākithūn* (those who broke their covenants) in the Battle of the Camel; the *Māriqūn* (seceders; those who missed the truth of religion) in the Battle of Nahrawān; and the *Qāsiṭūn* (deviated from divine guidance) in the Battle of Siffin as apostates.

Musʿada b. Ziyād relates an authentic report on the authority of Imam Jaʿfar Ṣādiq, who relates it from his father, Imam Muḥammad Bāqir: "[During his caliphate,] Imam Ali never accused those who fought against him of polytheism or hypocrisy. Rather, he would say, 'They are our brothers who have wronged us and caused oppression.'"[7] Political killings under the guise of "apostasy" were rampant under the Umayyad and ʿAbbasid dynasties.

However, there is no reliable evidence that the infallible Imams played any role in the political sphere or in the issuance of *fatwa*s to execute an apostate.

This ruling on executing an apostate entered Shi'i jurisprudence from Sunni sources. Some of the earlier jurisprudential works, such as Shaykh Ṣadūq's *al-Hidāya*, Sayyid Murtaḍā's *Intiṣār*, and Sallār Daylamī's *al-Marāsim*, regarded this issue as of no significance and unworthy of being treated as an independent jurisprudential issue. Others have dealt with it in the *Book of Jihad*, which supports the contextual indicant referred to above (i.e., the subject of "apostasy" comprised both leaving Islam and actively working with the Muslims' enemies). This approach can be found in the works of Abū al-Ṣalāḥ al-Ḥalabī,[8] Quṭb al-Dīn Bayhaqī (d. 1066),[9] 'Alā' al-Dīn Ḥalabī,[10] Yaḥyā b. Sa'īd[11] and Shaykh Ṭūsī.[12] In some of the Shi'i jurisprudential works that condemn the apostate to death, most of the supporting evidence, such as Shaykh Ṭūsī's *al-Mabsūṭ*[13] and Shahīd I,[14] consists of prophetic statements from Sunni sources. For example, take note of the wordings and expressions advanced by Shaykh Ṭūsī at the start of his book on apostasy:

> (1) The Prophet has reported that, "It is unlawful to shed the blood of a Muslim except in one of these three instances: unbelief after belief, adultery after chastity, and murder"; (2) 'Abdallah b. 'Abbās relates from the Prophet that he said, "Whosoever changes his religion, kill him"; (3) [The Prophet] was told that a Jew had embraced Islam only to apostatise after two months. He said: "I will not sit [or, in some accounts: I will not rest] until he is killed." God's Messenger issued this judgement and [the apostate] was killed, and there is consensus on this fact. (4) It is narrated that people said to Ali, "You are God", so he prepared a fire and incinerated them in it. Ibn 'Abbās said, "Were it up to me, I would have killed them by the sword because I have heard the Prophet say, 'Do not punish people with the same punishment that God is going to inflict. Whosoever changes his religion, kill him'"; (5) On this matter, Ali said, "When I observed an evil act, I lit a fire and called Qanbar"; (6) It is narrated that an old man had become a Christian, so Ali asked him: "You have become an apostate?" He replied, "Yes." Ali followed up, "Perhaps in order to collect your share of the inheritance after which you will revert [to Islam]?" He said, "No." Ali asked, "Perhaps you proposed to a girl but she declined, so you want to marry her and then will revert?" He

said, "No." Ali demanded, "Return back [to the fold of Islam]," to which he responded, "No, not until I meet the Messiah." And so Ali killed him.[15]

Four of these six hadith reports have been related by transmitters in Sunni works. The caliphs related "Whosoever changes his religion, kill him" on the Prophet's authority. The infallible Imams, however, have related no such hadith from the Prophet.

Gradually, the ruling on killing an apostate was delinked from the initial political circumstances, which included joining the Muslims' enemies. From the tenth century onward, we come across hadith reports on this issue attributed to the Imams (without specifying any qualification); however, most of them either have no chain of transmission or the narrators are unknown or of deficient character. A large number of such hadith reports pertain to the Exaggerators (*Ghulāt*) and how Ali dealt with them. But all such reports must be treated with great caution, because under the Umayyads the fabrication of hadith reports was rampant.

Montazeri envisioned the change in the subject matter of apostasy as follows:

> In those days, apostasy was not confined to changing one's religion or belief system, for anyone who left Islam or killed a Muslim was immediately regarded as a belligerent for he would immediately offer his support to the Muslims' enemies. According to ancient Arab tribal custom, every person and tribe had to affiliate and bond with other tribes for self-preservation. As such, anyone who left Islam was viewed as a belligerent.[16]
>
> The subject of apostasy during the time of the Prophet and even that of the Imams was broader than changing one's religion or announcing this decision.[17]
>
> The benefits of discretionary punishments (*ta'zīr*) and *ḥudūd* are neither hidden nor incomprehensible, for they can be derived from the contextual indicants and many explanations found in the relevant narrations. As mentioned earlier, the Prophet's primary objective is to warn and admonish criminals and help them reform themselves. It is unlikely that there are other hidden benefits that are incomprehensible to us. On the other hand, progress in criminology, psychology, and methods

> of reforming and rehabilitating criminals has shown that the previous methods may not produce the effect intended by the Legislator.
>
> Moreover, these new methods may be better and more able to attain the Legislator's primary goal than the punishments that were then in vogue. If a jurist is able to deduce this from the proofs (i.e., from the perspective of promoting human welfare and averting corruption that some of the aforementioned rulings that were part of a subject matter have changed), then the rulings would also change. However, this process must be totally reliant upon the Qur'an, the Hadith corpus, and the norms of *ijtihād*, as opposed to under the pressure or influence of the environment and special circumstances.[18]

If this fails to establish for you that the subject matter (of apostasy) has changed (which, in my estimation, has been well established), then at a minimum the situation gives rise to a preponderance of doubt and ambiguity. As such, the principle of *dar'* (the lapse of the *ḥudūd* punishments in the presence of any doubt or ambiguity) would negate the "presumption of continuance" (*istiṣḥāb*) of the subject matter. This, in turn, would result in a change of ruling in accordance with the Prophet's instruction that the *ḥudūd* punishments lapse if any doubt is present. And, what doubt is stronger than a change of the subject matter?

Sentencing a blasphemer to death, as found in the works of Sayyid Murtaḍā,[19] is a rare occurrence in Shiʿism. In actuality, from the tenth century onward a type of Exaggerators who were less extreme than the *ghulāt* came of age,[20] and fabricated hadith reports to support the position that those who blasphemed the Imams were to be executed as well. It would be impossible to enact this punishment if the same penalty were not prescribed for blaspheming the Prophet. As a result, Shiʿi jurists are more vociferous, consistent and united than the Sunnis in arguing for the punishment's validity in the Prophet's case.

## Apostasy and Freedom of Thought

You write:

> Why do you view apostasy as a type of reflection and thought and present it as a type of fully-fledged competition of thought? Apostasy is a type of denial of reality that is impossible to deny.

It is taken for granted that one should enter the field of thought with logic, the best disputation, and solid proofs. However, how should one react to a person who rejects this method? If one denies the obvious and conspicuous truths and poses a danger for the rest, then what does human reason dictate? An apostate is an abominable person whose "abomination" (emanating from his whims, caprices, and love for the material world) is contagious and could spread in the society and religion. As such, he must be punished.

## Response

The language of jurisprudence defines conversion or leaving Islam as apostasy, even though the conventional understanding of 'rights' would categorise it as part of the freedom of belief and religion. In our view Islam is clearly the religion of Truth; however, followers of other religions have the same belief about their own respective religions. The ultimate arbiter will be God, Who will reveal the truth of everything upon the day we return to Him. Why do you mix the essence of Truth with the rights bestowed upon the people of this world? The discussion is about an apostate's temporal rights, not the veracity or truthfulness of his/her beliefs. Those who depart from Islam for whatever reason ought to be presented with convincing evidence to demonstrate the baselessness of their claims. The whole discussion revolves around the fact that neither punishment nor execution can cure this particular ailment and have no reliable religious justification. In fact, punishment has the exact opposite outcome: It ends up damaging Islam's status.

a. You have asked what I would do if others reject my proofs, cogent argumentation and logic? My clear and categorical response is that I will continue my scholarly work with the goal of cultivating a culture in which those who reject logic, proofs and cogent argumentation lose their credibility and will be unable to find an audience. I will devote myself to building a culture of critical thinking and diminishing the number of obstinate and illogical persons. I say unequivocally that executing a dissenter, an apostate or one who is obstinate is wrong. In the spheres of politics and culture, one ought to use methods that are appropriate for the environment. Killing, punishing and stigmatising people only intensify the existing political and cultural problems.

b. In your opinion, "whims, caprices, and love for the material world" are punishable. But from the perspective of rights, how could you possibly establish this? And upon what supporting evidence could such a temporal punishment be based?
c. If an apostate is viewed as suffering from an ailment then efforts ought to be made to find a cure, for it is not customary for such people to be punished. The remedy for such an ailment is increasing religious literacy and education. An in-depth understanding of the anthropology of human beings requires insightful and discerning *ijtihād*. In the present world, wherein social media and satellites provide a means to spread news instantaneously, no society can remain insulated as in the past. Open your eyes and issue *fatwa*s that are in accordance with the time in which you are living.
d. Montazeri argued:

> Accordingly, every person has a right to practise his religion, regardless of whether it is true or not. However, while doing so he has no right to insult and ridicule the religion and viewpoints of others and what they hold sacred, or to distort and defame their religion(s). Mere reversion or change of religion and viewpoint due to animosity and spite are not grounds, in and of themselves, for subjecting one to any penal punishment, provided that no criminal punishment is prescribed for such an act. Everyone has the right to espouse an opinion and a belief system, make changes to it, disclose it openly, and solicit information on different viewpoints and ideas. None of these can be used to implicate him and thereby punish him for "apostasy", "causing mischief and corruption" (*fasād*), "insulting", "defamation" and similar offences.[21]

By the way, your assertion that in the past Jews and Christians would condemn an apostate, based upon their holy scriptures, is true. However, have not their religious scholars revised their opinions during the modern era? As the Qur'an indicates no temporal punishment for an apostate, why should Muslim jurists retain the same mode of thinking as the Jews and the Christians of the Middle Ages? At a minimum, try to live in accordance with the times of the present-day Pope and rabbis.[22]

## *Notes*

1. al-Kulaynī, *al-Kāfī*, 1:58, hadith No. 19.
2. Shaykh Ṭūsi, *al-Mabsūṭ*, 7:267.
3. Muḥammad b. Ismā'īl Bukhārī, *al-Ṣaḥīḥ* (Beirut: Dār al-Fikr, 1980), 4:75, 9:138.
4. al-Ṭabrisī, *Mustadrak*, "Ḥadd Murtadd", Bāb 1, 18:163, hadith No. 2.
5. al-Qāḍī al-Nu'mān b. Muḥammad al-Tamīmī, *D'ā'im al-Islām wa dhikr al-ḥalāl wa-l-ḥarām*, ed. Āṣif b. 'Alī Aṣghar Fayḍī (Cairo: Dār al-Ma'ārif, 1964), 2:480, hadith No. 1717.
6. Sharīf al-Raḍī, *Nahj al-balāgha*, Sermon 3.
7. 'Abdulla b. Ja'far al-Ḥimyarī, *Qurb al-isnād* (Qom: Mu'assasa Āl al-Bayt li Iḥyā' al-Turāth, 1993), 45; Ḥurr al-'Āmilī, *Wasā'il*, Bāb 26, 15:83, hadith No. 10.
8. Abū al-Ṣalāḥ al-Ḥalabī, *Al-Kāfī fī al-fiqh*, 250.
9. al-Kaydarī, *Iṣbāḥ al-Shī'a bi miṣbāḥ al-Sharī'a*, 191.
10. 'Alī b. al-Ḥasan b. Abī al-Majd al-Ḥalabī, *Ishārat al-sabq*, ed. Ibrāhīm al-Bahādurī (Qom: Mu'assasat al-Nashr al-Islāmī, 1994), 144.
11. Yaḥyā b. Sa'īd al-Ḥillī, *Al-Jāmi' li-l-sharā'i'*, 240.
12. Abū Ja'far Muḥammad b. al-Ḥasan al-Ṭūsī (Shaykh Ṭūsī), *al-Khilāf* (Qom: al-Nashr al-Islāmī, 1986/7), 5:501–505; Shaykh Ṭūsī, *al-Mabsūṭ*, 8:71–74.
13. Shaykh Ṭūsī, *al-Mabsūṭ*, 7:281, 8:71; Shaykh Ṭūsī, *al-Khilāf*, 5:351.
14. Shahīd I, *al-Durūs*, 2:52.
15. Shaykh Ṭūsī, *al-Mabsūṭ*, 7:281.
16. Montazeri, *Ḥukūmat-i dīnī*, 91.
17. Ibid., 132.
18. Montazeri, *Mojāzāt-i shar'ī*, 86, 87.
19. Sharīf al-Murtaḍā, *al-Intiṣār*, 481.
20. A revised reading of history shows that the title *'ulamā'-ye abrār'* (pious, upright and virtuous learned men) was applied to the Imams at the dawn of Islam. See Kadivar, "Qarā'at farāmūsh shode", *Madrase*, 1(3) (23 May 2006): 92–102.
21. Montazeri, *Resāle-ye ḥuqūq*, 52.
22. For example, Pope Paul VI, "Declaration on Religious Freedom", 7 December 1965.

## *Section X: The Incompatibility of Executing a Blasphemer or an Apostate with Explicit Qur'anic Verses*

Two issues will be discussed in this most detailed and comprehensive section:

### The Absence of any Supporting Qur'anic Evidence that Favours a Temporal Punishment for a Blasphemer and an Apostate

The Qur'an is silent upon the issue of applying any temporal punishment (i.e., execution) and the non-inviolability of the blood of a blasphemer of the Prophet or an apostate. Your citation of these statements reveals either your lack of total diligence in interpreting the verses or your incomplete or deficient knowledge. You have documented in detail seven verses advanced by Sunni exegetes and scholars, such as imam Fakhr al-Rāzī, Ālūsī and Sarakhsī, to justify the continuity of their previous rulings as a basis to draw your conclusion:

> In any event, one should not categorically and dogmatically reject the absence of a Qur'anic proof for killing an apostate, even though it is fraught with difficulty. In other words, when the hadiths provide clear proofs in favor of killing an apostate then, at a minimum, the verses can be used as corroboration.

Your reliance upon the Qur'an for support is so weak that there is no need for a rebuttal. My claim was not that the exegetes or jurists have refrained from invoking the Qur'an to support the death penalty for an apostate and a blasphemer; rather, it was – and is – that a Qur'anic justification is indefensible. You also acknowledge, after having conducted a thorough research, that the seven verses collectively do not provide any degree of confidence to support such an injunction. Concluding that an apostate's blood has become legal due to the nullification of his or her good deeds in this world constitutes a form of *istiḥsān* that is diametrically opposed to the principles of theology, jurisprudence and exegesis found in the school of the *Ahl al-Bayt*.

Shaykh Ṭūsī starts his discussion in the section on apostasy by citing three verses to prove his case:

> "Whosoever denies the faith, his work is in vain and he will be among the losers in the Hereafter" (Q. 5:5); "As for those who believe [and] then reject the faith, then believe again [and] then reject the faith again, and then increase in disbelief, God will not forgive them, nor will He guide them to any path" (Q. 4:137); "And whosoever turns back from their faith and dies in unbelief, their works will bear no fruit in this life and in the Hereafter. Such are the inmates of the Fire, and therein [they] shall abide" (Q. 2:217). All of these verses collectively point to the gravity of apostasy. Thus, if apostasy is established to be unlawful, then the one who leaves Islam will face one of the following edicts. Either they are a man or a woman, and if a man, he should be killed on the basis of consensus. It is reported . . .[1]

Shaykh Ṭūsī could glean no more from the Qur'an than apostasy is a source of danger and prohibited. Thus, his proofs for executing an apostate rest on the hadiths and consensus.

Likewise, there is no Qur'anic basis for killing one who blasphemes the noble Prophet. Although the Qur'an clearly prohibits one from insulting, disrespecting and being rude towards him, it does not call for those who insult him to be punished. Denigrating and vexing God and the Prophet deprive the culprit of divine grace in this world and the Hereafter, and also invites severe punishment and humiliation in the Hereafter. However, barring one from God's grace and mercy does not warrant the most severe temporal punishment. Every person who is cursed or deprived of divine grace is not automatically condemned to death. An unbeliever, polytheist, oppressor, apostate, hypocrite, violator of divine covenant, Banū Isrā'īl, one who falsely accuses a chaste woman of sexual impropriety, and a premeditated murderer are among those referred to as "accursed" or "bereft of divine grace and mercy". But only one, the premeditated murderer, is condemned to death. A person convicted of falsely accusing a chaste woman is subject to flogging. Those who subscribe to a false belief system, although they are accursed, face no temporal punishment other than being deprived of God's mercy and grace.

## Do the Hadith Reports on Apostasy Conform to the Qur'an?

This section is devoted to demonstrating that the hadith reports on blasphemy and apostasy lack probative force and are non-authoritative because they do not conform to the Qur'an. The sequence of argumentation will be as follows:

Premise 1: The primary justifications that support executing an apostate or a blasphemer are "isolated reports" (*khabar al-wāḥid*).
Premise 2: These hadith reports do not conform to the explicit Qur'anic verses.
Premise 3: Every hadith report that does not conform to the Qur'an must be rejected.
Conclusion: Hadith reports on killing an apostate or a blasphemer are rejected because they do not conform to the Qur'an.

The validity of the first premise has been well-established in the earlier discourse. The fundamental basis of those who assert the death penalty for an apostate and a blasphemer are the hadith reports, which is the first premise. As for the other two premises, they will be established below in this section. The ruling on apostasy and blasphemy (1) lacks any support from the Qur'an; (2) if there is no rational argument against it, there is also none to support it; (3) it is an *ijmāʿ madrakī*, which relies exclusively upon hadith reports; and (4) is primarily based upon "isolated hadith reports" (*khabar al-wāḥid*) with some that contain sound chains of transmission or are *thiqa*.

## A Hadith must Conform to the Qur'an to be Probative

The Qur'an is the primary source, followed by the hadith reports of the Prophet and (for the Shiʿis) the subsequent hadith reports of the Imams. The essential condition here is that these must be in conformity with the Qur'an. This principle relies upon three definitive proofs:

1. Dependent rational proof: Premise 1: internal consistency is a rational condition that is justifiable in all religions; Premise 2: the Qur'an is the foundational and pre-eminent source. Conclusion: everything other than the Qur'an, inclusive of the hadith reports of the Prophet and the Imams, Companions and consensus, should not conflict with explicit Qur'anic verses. The first premise, that two contradictory things cannot be united, is a self-evident rational truth confirmed by the Qur'an and the hadith reports. Premise 2 comprises *a priori* aspects of Islam and is based upon

recurrent hadith reports (*mutawātir*). The conclusion of this reasoning is decisive and definitive. This independent argumentation is different from those based on the hadith reports to follow.

2. The Prophet conveyed this narrative principle in front of a large assembly at Mina, one that numbered in the thousands: "Present every hadith report that you hear [is] ascribed to me to the Book of God. If it conforms to it, then act upon it. If not, then it is not from me but has been falsely ascribed to me."[2] Both Sunnis and Shi'is have related this invaluable principle on the basis of recurring hadith reports. Its attribution to the Prophet is decisive and beyond any doubt.

   In *uṣūl al-fiqh*, any discussion on the necessity of conforming (or the lack thereof) to the Qur'an appears in three areas: preferring one of the contradictory reports; circumstances under which the condition incorporated into a binding contract is valid; and conditions for the hadith to have probative force. Although the first two issues have been adequately discussed under the section of *ta'ādul wa tarājiḥ* (balancing of evidence and preferring one over another), however, and most regrettably, sufficient discussion on the third issue is absent. At a minimum, the criterion of conforming to the Qur'an means that a hadith that is in absolute conflict with it has no validity. What is meant by being in "absolute conflict with the Qur'an" refers to the text's explicit verses.

3. The Imams, following the pattern established by the Prophet, have made the validity of their hadith reports conditional upon being in conformity with the Qur'an and the definitive prophetic traditions. They have commanded that a tradition ascribed to them must first be presented to the Qur'an and, if found to be in conflict with it, rejected as false and absurd because it does not originate from them. I will cite here three such traditions. Imam Ali said, "Whatever conforms to the Book of God, seize it and abandon whatever conflicts with the Book of God."[3] Imam Ṣādiq said, "Anything that does not agree with the Book of God and the Sunna is to be rejected, and any hadith that does not agree with the Book of God is absurd and nonsense."[4] Imam Ṣādiq said, "Anything that has been ascribed to us and comes to you, but is not testified to by the Book of God, is false and void."[5] Collectively, these traditions, if not *mutawātir* in meaning, are certainly *mutawātir ijmālī*.

## The Non-Conformity of the Hadiths with Explicit Qur'anic Verses on Killing an Apostate or a Blasphemer

In this section, I will attempt to prove two issues: the non-conformity of the hadith reports demanding a blasphemer's execution with the Qur'an and *mutawātir* hadith reports, followed by the same exercise but now dealing with apostasy.

### The Non-Conformity of the Hadith Reports on Killing a Blasphemer with the Qur'anic Method in Dealing with Those who Harassed and Persecuted the Prophet

Do the hadith reports on executing a blasphemer conform to the Qur'anic verses? One can divide the verses that do not conform to this ruling into two:[6]

#### Type 1 Verses: Qur'anic Verses on Harassing and Annoying the Prophet

1. In one of the crucial verses dealing with the Prophet's ministry, God emphasises that he should ignore his enemies' (i.e., the unbelievers and hypocrites) harassment, persecution and harm and put his trust in God, the best of all defenders, "O Prophet, We have sent you as a witness, a bearer of glad tidings, a warner, [as] one who invites to God by His permission, and as an illuminating lamp. Then announce to the believers the glad tidings that they will have great bounty from God. And incline not to the disbelievers and the hypocrites. Disregard their annoyances and put your trust in God. And sufficient is God as a Defender and a Protector" (Q. 33:45–48).

   The Prophet is not granted permission to retaliate against such people as long as they remain peaceful and do not take up arms against the Muslims. Clearly, these actions are not a subject matter for any religious punishment. God will assist the Prophet and His religion by depriving such people of His mercy in this life and the Hereafter. Without doubt, all such persecution and harm are incorporated in this verse because blasphemy is a verbal insult or a denigration.
2. "You shall certainly be tested in your property and in your persons, and you will hear much annoying talk from those who have been given the

Book before you and from those who are polytheists. But if you persevere patiently and guard against evil, then that will be a determining factor in all affairs" (Q. 3:186).

Persecution and harassment from the polytheists and adherents of earlier religions is part of a divine test and a trial. The persecution referenced here is verbal in nature, and the Muslims are told that they will have to endure a great deal of such abuse. Denigrating the Prophet and mocking a religion's sacred entities are part and parcel of such persecution. God commands Muslims to be patient, hopeful and God-conscious instead of retaliating in kind or worse. If the previous verse was addressed to the Prophet, then this verse informs all believers how to respond to such persecution. Any excessive act, be it physical or verbal, is equivalent to transgressing the limits set by God.

3. "Those who malign God and His Messenger will be cursed by God in this world and the next – He has prepared a humiliating punishment for them" (Q. 33:57).

   Those who persecute the Prophet will be accursed and barred from God's mercy in this world and in the Hereafter. In addition, they will be subjected to abject punishment. Thus, there is no mandate to punish such persecutors in this world, regardless of how prevalent this verbal persecution may be.

4. "And of them are those who annoy and irritate the Prophet and say, 'He is all ears'. Say, 'His listening [and accepting at face value] to what you say is best for you; he believes in God, has faith in the believers, and [is] a mercy to those who believe.' Those who hurt God's Messenger will have a grievous punishment" (Q. 9:61).

   This verse addresses the Prophet exclusively. Some were asserting that he could easily be duped. However, God informs them that it is better for Muhammad to take their words at face value instead of exposing their lies. At the end of the verse, the persecutors are assured that they have earned a painful punishment in the Hereafter only. Jalāl al-Dīn al-Suyūṭī (d. 1505) writes that the main persecutor was the hypocrite Nabtal b. al-Ḥārith.[7] According to 'Alī b. Ibrāhīm Qommī the hypocrite was by the name of 'Abdallah b. Nabtal who would tell the hypocrites what had transpired at the Prophet's assembly. Gabriel informed the Prophet that this man had become an instrument of transmitting Satan's words. But he denied it when the Prophet confronted him. The Prophet did not press the issue, because he did not want to humiliate this person. 'Abdallah b. Nabtal returned to his group and mocked the Prophet, stating that he had readily believed his lie.[8] This verse, which was revealed at that time, contains no mention of any punishment.

5. "Of them is he who says, 'Grant me exemption and draw me not into trial.' Surely into trial have they already fallen. And surely, Hell shall surround the unbelievers" (Q. 9:49).

This verse describes another form of disrespect and contempt. In response to the Prophet's call for jihad, some of the hypocrites petitioned him to excuse them on the ground that it might lead to them commit a sin. As this statement constitutes both an act of sacrilege and an insult directed towards God and His Messenger, God therefore informs them that they are already deeply anchored in sin and surrounded by Hellfire. This incident is comparable and closer to blasphemy, and yet the only punishment mentioned is the one waiting for them in the Hereafter and their descent into this world's trials and tribulations.

## The Outcome of Type 1 Verses

1. The Prophet's persecutors will receive a painful and abject chastisement in the Hereafter, as well as be surrounded by Hellfire and deprived of God's mercy.
2. Their immoral and contemptuous activities will nullify their good deeds. But this fact has nothing to do with inflicting a temporal punishment or making it lawful to shed their blood.
3. They are accursed in this world, bereft of God's mercy, and deeply sunk in this world's tribulations and sedition.
4. None of the five verses prescribe any temporal punishment for those who harass and annoy the Prophet.
5. The persecution mentioned in verses 2, 4 and 5 is verbal in nature.
6. Blaspheming the Prophet is certainly applicable in all five verses.
7. The first verse advises the Prophet to ignore the persecution meted out by the unbelievers and the polytheists, and the second verse asks the believers to be patient and God-conscious in the face of verbal persecution.
8. These verses are explicit, as opposed to allegorical or symbolic.
9. These verses were revealed in Medina. Some were revealed towards the end of the Prophet's ministry, when he was at the peak of his power.

Therefore, any speculation that he treated his persecutors mildly due to political weakness and the lack of military strength is untenable.

10. Hadith reports on killing the blasphemer are incompatible with these verses that talk about verbal persecution because:
    a. The subject matter of those verses that deal with persecuting the Prophet is connected with the hadith reports on denigrating and insulting him. In particular, verses 2, 4 and 5 categorically deal with verbal persecution. Blaspheming the Prophet and verbal persecution are related in the sense that every denigration constitutes an act of persecution. Likewise, verbal persecution cannot be described as something other than blasphemy.
    b. According to Q. 33:48, ignoring persecution and relying upon God provides evidentiary proof against the hadith reports, because the latter either mandate or permit the killing of a blasphemer. This shows that the directive of "ignoring" was not followed. The purport of this verse is confirmed in two other verses, "And the servants of the Beneficent are those who walk on the Earth in humility, and when the ignorant address them, they answer, 'Peace'" (Q. 25:63), and "And when they pass by what is vain, they pass by with dignity" (Q. 25:72).

       It should be clear that condemning a blasphemer to death contradicts these two verses. The Qur'an's ethical approach to dealing with those who insult and denigrate is to ignore them, extend a greeting of peace, be magnanimous and gracefully move away from them.

       Clearly, executing a blasphemer contradicts the explicit and weighty standard laid down in the Qur'an.
    c. The directive in the second verse, Q. 3:186, calls upon Muslims to remain steadfast and God-conscious when they face persecution, harm and harassment from the People of the Book and polytheists. It also lays out their obligations when confronted with such things. Although it was extremely painful for the Companions to witness the Prophet endure such hostility, they were nevertheless commanded to remain patient and God-conscious. Patience can only mean being magnanimous, entrusting the affair to God and assuaging one's anger. The Qur'an describes the God-conscious as: "Those who spend in ease and in adversity, those who control their anger and pardon people. God loves those who do good" (Q. 3:134). Acting upon *taqwā* (God-consciousness) means to assuage one's anger and overlook

another person's offences. Undoubtedly, killing the guilty blasphemer is contrary to exercising patience and conducting oneself with *taqwā*.

d. In Q. 33:48, the Prophet is commanded to disregard their annoyances. The imperative form, *wada' adhā-hum* (i.e., disregard the hurt that comes from them) appears to be an obligatory command and the other aforementioned contextual evidence confirms this. In all the three Qur'anic verses (Q. 3:186, 31:17[9], and 42:43) where the phrase *'azm al-umūr* (matters [worthy] of great resolve) appears, the attribute of patience (*ṣabr*) is mentioned, with the first instance being Q. 3:186 It is open to contestation whether one can infer from this verse that patience (*ṣabr*) and God-consciousness (*taqwā*) are commendable or obligatory. In the second instance, Q. 31:17, establishing prayers and enjoining the good and forbidding the evil are mandatory. The imperative form of the verb for patience along with the contextual orientation appear to suggest that patience is obligatory. In the third instance where *'azm al-umūr* appears, Q. 42:43, as well as in Q. 3:186, the attributes of patience, forgiveness, and God-consciousness are grouped under *'azm al-umūr*. Even though one could conceivably infer that patience is obligatory in these two verses, however, what is more apparent is that God-consciousness and forgiveness are commendable. As such, this conclusion does not contradict those hadith reports that condemn a blasphemer to death, which would have been the case if patience were obligatory.

e. Hadith reports that oblige one to execute a blasphemer conflict with Q. 33:48. First, even though this verse deals with the persecution and harassment originating from the hypocrites and the unbelievers, it is inclusive of everyone. Second, even though the Prophet is the addressee, the verse's content clearly includes all believers. The upshot is that the hadith reports on blasphemy contradict this verse.

## Type 2 Verses: The Prophet is an Exemplar

1. "And surely, you are an exalted exemplar" (Q. 68:4).

   The Prophet's ethical conduct is undoubtedly of the highest calibre. Perfecting his people's moral conduct is one of the goals of his prophetic ministry. The height of this excellence and grandeur is evident in these types of verses.

2. "We sent you only as a mercy to the worlds" (Q. 21:107).

The Prophet is a mercy to the cosmos, and this attribute is an integral part of his unequalled character.

3. "It is part of the mercy of God that you are lenient with them, for if you had been stern and hard-hearted, they would have dispersed from you. So pardon them, ask for forgiveness for them, and consult with them about matters. And when you are resolved in a decision then put your trust in God, for God loves those who put their trust (in Him)" (Q. 3:159).

   People gravitated to the Prophet because God's mercy softened his heart. Soft-heartedness is the second attribute of his impeccable ethical character, for harshness and hard-heartedness alienate people. Seeking forgiveness from God for the sinners, consulting people on various matters, and relying upon God are other aspects of his character. The Prophet did not behave like a king, a pharaoh or a dictator, many of whom sought to destroy and execute those who dared to cast aspersions or insults at them. Such behaviour is the norm for one who is hard-hearted, ignorant and rude. The Prophet's magnanimity was evident when he conquered Mecca, for he forgave almost all of its inhabitants.

4. "A Messenger has come to you from among yourselves. Your suffering distresses him; he is deeply concerned for you and full of kindness and mercy toward the believers" (Q. 9:128).

   The Prophet empathised with his followers' afflictions, suffering and grief. His sole concern was to guide all people, not to take revenge, and therefore he was merciful and kind-hearted with the believers. Here, three more attributes are added to his unequalled character.

## The Outcome of Type 2 Verses

The Prophet's traits contained the following elements: expansive mercy unto the cosmos, soft-heartedness, forgiveness of people's faults and petitions to God to forgive them, consultation with others, reliance upon God, empathy with and eagerness to guide the people, and kindness and compassion towards the believers. Executing an immoral person who casts aspersions and insults upon him accords with none of these traits.

Even if this verse were restricted to the Prophet, it follows that such a noble and peerless character would not issue a death warrant against someone who has insulted him. In other words, all such hadith reports attributed to him are invalid. According to the Shi'is, Ali was the soul of the Prophet and, as such, could not have a character that diverged from that of his master. If the Prophet could not issue such a sentence because of his noble character, then how could Ali do so? This reality is extremely relevant for jurisprudence, for it renders all of the pro-execution hadith reports non-probative because they contradict the Qur'an's clear-cut and explicit verses.

Finally, we can respond to the fundamental question pertinent for this section: hadiths on executing one who blasphemes the Prophet or considering it lawful to shed his blood with impunity contradicts the Type Two verses mentioned above. Response to persecution and mockery and insulting sacred entities results in nothing other than erasure of good deeds and bestowal of God's curse in this life. The duty of the believers and the Prophet in the face of persecution is to ignore the matter and exercise patience and God-consciousness; when present in a session where God's verses are mocked is to withdraw until a time that there is a change of subject. No permission is granted to reciprocate in kind and in no place has any temporal punishment been mentioned for these violations. On the contrary, given that the Prophet is an exemplar and pinnacle of excellence, he is to seek forgiveness for people's lapses and sins, exhibit soft-heartedness, plead for mercy for humanity and grace for the believers. Hadiths mandating killing of a blasphemer are incompatible with explicit and univocal Qur'anic verses.

The discussion revolves around the religious validity of the death penalty, not around rescinding or forgiving it after it has been religiously established.

## Imam Ali Forgives a Blasphemer

The Prophet's character was so unlike that of kings or tyrants that he never sought to revenge himself against all the evil and insults directed at him. On the contrary, he overlooked them and forgave their perpetrators in accord with: "Those who have been graced with bounty and plenty should not swear that they will [no longer] give to kinsmen, the poor, those who emigrated in God's way: let them pardon and forgive. Do you not wish that God should forgive you? God is most forgiving and merciful" (Q. 24:22).

Is not killing someone who insults or defames another the habit of a despot, a tyrant? How can one who possesses the most perfect noble character and who is a mercy unto the cosmos possibly engage in such an act? Here, we must recount an incident reported in the *Nahj al-balāgha* that reflects Imam Ali's wisdom and nobility. During the Battle of Siffin, he heard his followers cursing and insulting their opponents and forcefully told them to stop: "I dislike your [verbal] abuse of them. Describing their deeds and recounting their situations would be a better mode of speaking and a more convincing way of arguing. Instead of abusing them, you should say, 'O God! Save our blood and their blood, produce reconciliation between us and them, and lead them out of their misguidance so that he who is ignorant of the Truth may know it, and he who inclines toward rebellion and revolt may turn away from it.'"[10]

In another incident reported by Sayyid Raḍī, a Khārijī once said, "'May God kill this heretic (Imam Ali)!' People rose up and leapt toward him, fully intending to kill him. Imam (Ali) replied, 'Be calm. You should return an insult with an insult or by pardoning the sin.'"[11]

As Imam Ali was nurtured and raised by the Prophet, his reaction to blasphemy is a good way to discover the punishment for one who blasphemes the Prophet. This is especially true because the verse on mutual imprecation (*mubāhala*) refers to him as the Prophet's soul (Q. 3:61). This Khārijī unequivocally defamed this saint of God, the current caliph and the Prophet's political and spiritual successor, with two vicious insults: calling him an unbeliever and asking God to kill him. The Imam's companions wanted to kill the Khārijī, but the Imam restrained them with a response that remains a source of eternal pride for all Muslims: "[The proper] response to an insult is not death. Rather, it is to reciprocate in kind or forgive." Although in this case reciprocating in kind is allowed, based upon "So if anyone commits aggression against you, attack him as he attacked you" (Q. 2:194), it should not exceed the initial crime. This verse articulates the essence of justice, namely, proportional punishment, a practice to which all Muslims are to adhere. Thus, any hadith reports that allow the execution of a blasphemer contradict the Qur'an. Imam Ali chose forgiveness. If the Prophet had been confronted with a similar situation, without any doubt he would have acted in accord with the Qur'an.

If one were to object that this hadith has no chain of transmission, then note the following: first, it is employed here as confirmation, not as evidence; and, second, its content is both a rational ruling and endorsed by the Imam, whose actions are in perfect accord with the Qur'an and personifies the Prophet's Sunna. This incident clearly shows that death is not the appropriate punishment for such a deed. Ali was adhering to the directive contained within the Prophet's last will and testament: "O Ali, the three attributes at the peak of ethical conduct in this life and the afterlife are to forgive one who wrongs you, to resume relations with one who has cut them, and to show magnanimity to one who is ignorant."[12] Such conduct is very beneficial and is endorsed by rational beings as an act of virtue. Was the Prophet merely an admonisher who failed to act upon his own advice?

## The Qur'an, the Freedom of Religion and Apostasy

Those hadith reports that sanction death for an apostate must be in harmony with the Qur'an, or at least not conflict with explicit Qur'anic verses, in order to be considered evidentiary proofs. In order to respond, one must deliberate upon religious freedom under the rubric of the Qur'an in four parts. The relevant hadith reports will be juxtaposed to the verses contained in each part to see whether they conform or not. In the final analysis, we will prove that they do not conform to those explicit verses.[13]

### Type 1 Verses: The Negation of Force and Coercion in the Matter of Religion and Belief

1. "There is no compulsion in religion. True guidance has become distinct from error, so whoever rejects false deities and believes in God has grasped the firmest handhold, one that will never break. God is all-hearing and all-knowing" (Q. 2:256).

The above verse contains a negation (i.e., God has not established the basis of religion upon compulsion) and a prohibition (i.e., forced belief has no validity). Rejecting force is equivalent to accepting the freedom of religion in two respects: the freedom to both enter and leave a religion. Providing a choice between following a particular religion and death is equivalent to compulsion. If a person is free to enter but not to leave, then his or her staying is possible only through compulsion and the fear of punishment. At the same time, God has clearly distinguished between Truth and Falsehood in the Qur'an instead of using force.

> The derivation of religious freedom and prohibition of force from the verse (on "no compulsion"), based on absolute evidentiary proofs, is inclusive of all religions. This rule also applies in cases where one drops an aspect of the faith or creed. This is in harmony with the human being's natural and essential quiddity and so requires no legislation, either for or against.[14]

> The ruling of non-compulsion is present in all the shari'as, even the oldest one that was practiced by Noah, and up until today. It has not been abrogated, and therefore still has the same strength and relevance.[15]

The occasion of this verse's revelation has to do with apostasy.[16] Contrary to the opinion of some Sunni exegetes, it was not abrogated by the "sword verse" (Q. 9:5),[17] and will remain forever an emblem of Islam's allowance of the freedom of religion. Punishments ranging from permanent exile to death for an apostate or ordering an unbeliever to choose between Islam and death are examples of blatant coercion and therefore negate and contradict the verse under consideration.

2. "Had your Lord willed, all the people on Earth would have believed. So can you [O Prophet] compel people to believe?" (Q. 10:99).

Even though believing in God and the Hereafter is affirming the Truth, God does not invoke His unlimited cosmic authority (*takwīnī*) over humanity because if He did so the individual's freedom of choice would cease to exist and, subsequently, reward and punishment would become pointless. Belief has value only when it is chosen freely. When the Prophet became anxious about some people's non-conversion and thus pursued them persistently, God proclaimed: "How can you desire something else when your God is not pleased with using compulsion in the matter of faith?" If forced conversion is unlawful, then how could one use coercion to make people remain Muslim? Islam is the Truth (from the perspective of the Qur'an). But even so, God allows free choice in this matter. Thus, how can a person be ordered to choose between remaining Muslim or death? Remaining a believer in such a state has no value.

3. "He [Noah] said, 'My people, think: If I have a clear evidence from my Lord, which was blessed to me by His Mercy but obscured from your sight, could we force you to accept it despite your aversion to it?'" (Q. 11:28).

Prophet Noah presented the divine message to his people, but they rejected it, calling it a "lie". He continued to invite them to reflect upon the evidence that he had been sent by God, for perhaps this fact had been concealed from them. If a prophet cannot force his people to believe, then how could one imagine that it would be lawful for his followers to compel people to remain Muslim via pressure tactics, intimidation and the fear of harsh punishment?

## Outcome of Type 1 Verses

One can derive an impervious conclusion from the Qur'an: no one can compel anyone to embrace Islam, for doing so negates the principle of the freedom of religion. Hadith reports that sanction killing an apostate do nothing but force him or her to stay in the faith, something that contradicts those verses that mandate no compulsion.

## Type 2 Verses: The Freedom to Choose Guidance or to go Astray

1. "Say, 'Now the Truth has come from your Lord: let those who wish to believe in it do so, and let those who wish to reject it do so.' We have prepared a Fire for the wrongdoers that will envelop them from all sides" (Q. 18:29).

Even though Islam's truthfulness is beyond doubt, the Qur'an categorically states that people are free to voluntarily embrace either Islam or unbelief. God, however, has forewarned the unbelievers of what they can expect in the Hereafter. But is it mandated that in this temporal world of trial, the person be punished because of his or her belief system? If this were the case, then belief or unbelief would be meaningless and without merit. God reminds us of the consequence of making the wrong choice. In other words, believers have no right to exchange the refined divine logic for the logic of violence, force, and intimidation.

2. "Say, 'People, the Truth has come to you from your Lord. Whoever follows the right path follows it for his own good, and whoever strays does so to his own loss. I am not a guardian over you'" (Q. 10:108).

As the Qur'an does not consider the paths of Islam and of unbelief to have equal merit, the ability to freely choose the right path is a skill that deserves a reward. Forcing people to believe out of fear negates the need for trial in this world and divine reward and punishment in the Hereafter. The foundation of the Day of Judgement is based upon the freedom of religion. Punishing one for leaving Islam or embracing a false belief is incompatible with this verse.

3. "We have sent the Scripture down to you [O Prophet] with the Truth for people. Whoever follows the guidance does so for his own benefit, whoever strays away from it does so at his own peril. You are not a guardian over them" (Q. 39:41).

The Qur'an has shown people the path of Truth, and people have the option to follow or reject it, given that reward and punishment are reserved for the Hereafter. We do not have a licence to act upon something that displeases God. God and the Prophet both grant all of us this freedom and simultaneously remind us of the path of Truth. The Hereafter is the abode of peace, contentment and prosperity for those who voluntarily chose that path. Punishing an apostate and forcing one to remain a believer, as well as providing a choice only between leaving Islam and death, contradicts this verse's clear content.

4. "Say [O Prophet], 'I am commanded to serve the Lord of this town [Mecca], which He has made inviolable, and to whom everything belongs. I am commanded to be one of those devoted to Him. I am commanded to recite the Qur'an.' Whoever chooses to follow the right path does so for his own good. Say to whoever deviates from it, 'I am only here to warn.' Say, 'Praise belongs to God. He will show you His signs so that you will recognize them.' Your Lord is never unmindful of what you do" (Q. 27:91–93).

The Prophet warns people of the consequences of choosing the wrong path and recites the Qur'an to them to publicise the true religion and creed. Whoever accepts it will prosper, and whoever rejects it will suffer a loss and observe the consequences. God is the over-looker and aware of all peoples' choices. Punishing a person for leaving Islam conflicts with the message of admonishing those who have gone astray. If the Qur'an ordained the crucifixion of every such person, then the Prophet would have been the first one to implement it. But God gave him, let alone others, no such permission. Once again, killing an apostate is opposed to this clear-cut verse.

## Outcome of Type 2 Verses

These types of verses corroborate that the basis of religious freedom and belief is the freedom to choose between guidance and misguidance. Imposing any form of temporal punishment for leaving Islam contradicts the Qur'an, which proclaims "let those who wish to reject it do so", "whoever strays does so to his own loss", "I am not your guardian" and "I am only here to warn". If the negation of any temporal punishment were not interconnected with an unbeliever going astray, then this verse would be redundant, regardless of whether it was meant for native or non-native unbelievers. If people are given a choice between death or permanent exile in servitude, then how can the Qur'an proclaim "let those who wish to reject it do so". If no temporal punishment is to be instituted for an apostate, then it would be possible to say "and whoever strays does so to his own loss. I am not your guardian". Admonition would have meaning and purpose if there were no punishment in this world but only a painful chastisement awaiting them in the Hereafter. If such people were executed, then the Prophet's admonition and lack of guardianship over the believers would make no sense.

## Type 3 Verses: The Prophet's Mandate – To Convey the Truth, but Not to Force People to Accept It

The Qur'an lays out with precision the parameters of the Prophet's mandate: bring and convey the Message, provide guidance, and do not impose the Truth by force.

1. "So [O Prophet] warn them. Your only task is to give warning, [for] you are not there to control them" (Q. 88:21–22).

The Prophet's only obligations are to convey the Message and remind the people of the Truth. Those who voluntarily accept it will reap their respective rewards, and those who reject it will endure great loss. The full manifestation of each choice will become evident on the Day of Judgement, for this world is no more than the abode of trial and test. The Prophet was not the people's manager and thus had no authority either to force them to become or to remain a believer. Given this, how could his followers acquire such a wide scope of authority?

2. "We know best what the disbelievers say. You [O Prophet] are not there to force them, so remind, with this Qur'an, those who fear My warning" (Q. 50:45).
3. "We sent you only to give good news and warning. Say, 'I am not asking for any reward for it, but anyone who wishes should take a path to his Lord.' Put your trust in the Living [God] who never dies, and celebrate His praise. He knows the sins of His servants well enough" (Q. 25:56–58).
4. "Whether We let you [O Prophet] see part of what We threaten them with or cause you to die [before that], your duty is only to deliver the message. The Reckoning is Ours" (Q. 13:40).
5. "The Messenger's duty is only to deliver the message. God knows what you reveal and what you conceal" (Q. 5:99).

## Outcome of Type 3 Verses

Given that the content of both the Meccan and the Medinese chapters, even the last revealed one, makes it clear that the Prophet was sent only to guide and admonish, how can others have a greater mandate? If only God can evaluate and take account of people's faith, and the Prophet is entrusted only with conveying the Message via specific methods, then negating religious freedom and implementing the punishments and rewards in this temporal life would be, in a sense, arrogating God's mantle to oneself.

In order to preserve the Prophet's mission and to take account of God's prerogative, people must have the choice of freely entering and leaving Islam. If only execution awaits those who leave, then his mandate of being only a reminder, admonisher and conveyer of glad tidings would be meaningless.

My response to the claim that "if we were to accept the validity of the proofs from these verses, then it would follow that the Prophet would be unable to implement any of the punishments, even though we know that this is not the case", is as follows: punishments for theft, acts of immorality and debauchery, disturbing the society's security, and so on are necessary to preserve the social order. But this in no way conflicts with the Prophet's mission to disseminate God's message. However, punishments for changing one's religion do conflict with the standards established above and, moreover, render all verses of this type null and void. Any temporal punishment for apostasy is completely different from the other punishments and is in direct opposition to the general understanding of the key verses.

## Type 4 Verses: No Temporal Punishment for Apostasy

Although the Qur'an regards exchanging Islam for unbelief as something heinous, based upon its own refined logic it informs the person of punishment in the Hereafter only.

Verse 1: "They will not stop fighting you [believers] until they make you abandon your faith, if they can. If any of you abandon your faith and die as disbelievers, [then] your deeds will come to nothing in this world and the Hereafter, and you will be inhabitants of the Fire, there to remain" (Q. 2:217).

This verse has two parts: (1) fighting during the prohibited months, desecrating the Grand Mosque, and expelling the city's residents; and (2) apostasy. The points to note are given below:

a. The intention of the Meccan and Medinan unbelievers and polytheists was to convince the Muslims to abandon Islam. As such, the subject of apostasy here is tightly linked with their fighting the Muslims. The use of the plural pronoun confirms that this refers to apostasy at the group level.
b. The verse points to an apostate's natural death, as opposed to his or her execution or killing. If this individual were meant to be condemned to death, then the verse would have used verbs like "to kill" or "to crucify" instead. The phrase "die as disbelievers" shows that the apostate may feel penitent, return to Islam and die as a believer. Thus, apostasy in and of itself is not reason enough to prescribe the mentioned punishment; rather, he must stay in this state until death. In any other case, the verse indicates that an apostate's repentance would be accepted. As a result, not only will he not be punished or forfeit his or her good deeds, but, he or she also will not be punished in the Hereafter. This is, of course, contingent upon his or her capacity to seek repentance.
c. The first punishment contained in the verse is the forfeiture of one's good deeds in both worlds, for he or she has decided to replace a blessed life and the luminous light of faith with a wretched and constricted life. In addition, his or her good deeds will not help him or her attain prosperity.
d. The second punishment, eternal damnation in the Hellfire, is the punishment for those unbelievers and apostates who preferred unbelief.

Verse 2: "Why would God guide people who deny the Truth, after they have believed and acknowledged that the Messenger is true, and after they have been shown clear proof? God does not guide evildoers. They are those whose recompense is that upon them shall be the curse of God, the angels, and the people combined, and so they will remain, with no relief or respite for their suffering. Except those who afterward repent and mend their ways – God is most forgiving and merciful – [although] the repentance of those who, having believed [but] then increase in their disbelief, will not be accepted. They are the ones who have gone [far] astray" (Q. 3:86–90).

In this verse, an apostate will be subjected to three possible scenarios:

a. If he fails to repent and reform himself, then he will be categorised as an oppressor and deprived of divine guidance; receive the eternal curse of God, His angels and the people; and receive no relief or delay as regards the punishment waiting for him in the Hereafter.
b. If he repents and reforms himself, then God is most forgiving and compassionate. Thus, he will not be subject to any of the three punishments mentioned above.
c. If he further entrenches himself in disbelief, then he will be unable to seek repentance. Such a person is truly misguided.

## Outcomes of Verse 2

1. If apostasy were punished with death, then the possibility of repentance, reform and strengthening one's disbelief would be impossible.
2. An apostate engulfed in disbelief will still not be condemned to death.
3. The subject of apostasy in this verse concerns leaving Islam after its truthfulness has become clear with valid proofs (i.e., apostasy is exemplified in action and obstinate defiance and hostility, as opposed to being merely a change of religion prompted by scholarship and research).
4. Repentance, as long as it is not forced or occurs at the last moments of one's life, is to be accepted if the person has the capacity to repent. Strengthening one's unbelief removes this capacity.
5. This verse prescribes no temporal punishment for apostasy, whether for one who has just apostatised or one who remains an apostate.

6. The effects in this world of apostasy are the loss of divine guidance; curses descending from God, the angels and the people; and the inability to repent (if one's apostasy is repeated).
7. In these verses, just like in Q. 2:217, the discussion concerns a group of apostates. As a result, the plural form is used in all of them.

Verse 3: "As for those who believe [and] then reject the faith, then believe again [and] then reject the faith again, and then increase in disbelief, God will not forgive them, nor will He guide them to any path" (Q. 4:137).

This verse further explains and elaborates upon Q. 3:90, in which the person apostatises twice and thus becomes immersed in unbelief. Such a person will face two types of punishment: the loss of divine forgiveness and the loss of divine guidance. Here, once again, the plural form refers to the apostates. If an apostate were to be executed immediately, then apostatising for the second time and increasing in unbelief would be impossible. Once again, the verse mentions no temporal punishment.

Verse 4: "The deeds of anyone who rejects faith will come to nothing, and in the Hereafter he will be one of the losers" (Q. 5:5).

Two results of becoming a disbeliever are the forfeiture of one's good deeds and enduring loss in the Hereafter. However, this verse's last part could be used as an indicant to justify the forfeiture of good deeds in this world and the Hereafter, as in the case of Q. 2:217. Once again, no mention is made of condemning the apostate to death.

Verse 5: "[O] you who believe, if any of you go back on your faith, God will soon replace you with people He loves and who love Him, people who are humble toward the believers, hard on the disbelievers, and who strive in God's way without fearing anyone's reproach. Such is God's favour. He grants it to whoever He will. God has endless bounty and knowledge" (Q. 5:54).

Here, the verse points out God's desire to replace the apostates with courageous believers but mentions no form of punishment. The most grievous punishment for them is their ineligibility to become God's beloved (if they are able to appreciate this reality).

Verse 6: "They swear by God that they did not, but they certainly did speak words of disbelief and become disbelievers after having submitted; they tried to do something, though they did not achieve it; and being spiteful was their only response to God and His Messenger enriching them out of His bounty. They would be better off turning back [to God, for] if they turn away, [then] God will punish them in this world and the Hereafter and there will be no one on Earth to protect or help them" (Q. 9:74).

This particular verse contains a situational premise (*qaḍāya khārijiyya*): the reference is to those hypocrites who had manifested their unbelief prior to the Tabuk expedition and were planning to assassinate the Prophet. Despite the gravity of this sin, the door of repentance was left open. Regardless of whether this plot was a mischievous act to mock, based on their confession, or to assassinate the Prophet – the fact is that none of them were accused of apostasy and condemned to death. In the event of non-repentance, the effects of all of their infractions, including apostasy and bad intentions towards the Prophet, will result in a grievous chastisement in both worlds and their being deprived of God's guardianship and assistance in this world. In any event, this verse's content does not pertain exclusively to apostasy because: (1) the verse does not relate to an absolute premise (*qaḍāya ḥaqīqiyya*), but rather to a situational premise (*qaḍāya khārijiyya*) that occurred after Tabuk, based on the contextual evidence; and (2) it deals with people who, in addition to becoming apostates, intended to harm the Prophet, both of which are captured at the end of this verse. That is, it is not exclusively for apostasy. By the way, no historical evidence supports the view that the Prophet either fought or killed them.

Verse 7: "With the exception of those who are forced to say they do not believe, although their hearts remain firm in faith, those who reject God after believing in Him and open their hearts to disbelief will have the wrath of God upon them and a grievous punishment awaiting them" (Q. 16:106).

This verse points out two things: (1) proclaiming that one has become an unbeliever while under duress – here, the criterion is conviction of the heart and, as such, such a declaration has no value; and (2) pronouncing one's disbelief voluntarily and becoming an apostate actualises God's anger and His stern punishment in the Hereafter. The contextual evidence in Q. 16:109

shows that the loss incurred has to do with the Hereafter, which explains why no temporal punishment is mentioned.

Verse 8: "Those who turn on their heels after being shown guidance are duped and tempted by Satan. They say to those who hate what God has sent down, 'We will obey you in some matter' – God knows their secret schemes. How will they feel when the angels take them in death and beat their faces and their backs because they practiced things that incurred God's wrath and disdained to please Him? He makes their deeds go to waste" (Q. 47:25–28).

Based on the contextual evidence, the verse is a situational premise. The use of the plural form suggests that it concerns a group of apostates who were hostile to Islam, a form of apostasy linked with action and rebellion, not just a change of faith due to one's research and analysis: "Those who turn on their heels after being shown guidance." This type of apostasy has been characterised as the work of Satan through trickery and deceit. Despite this, there is no mention of any temporal punishment.

## Tying up Loose Ends on the Apostasy Verses

1. Effects in this world: the nullification of deeds;[18] receipt of the eternal curse from God, the angels and the people;[19] deprivation of divine guidance;[20] receipt of God's anger;[21] exclusion from being among His beloved;[22] and subjection to Satan's machinations and trickery.[23]
2. Effects in the Hereafter: nullification of deeds;[24] grievous punishment;[25] eternal punishment in the Hellfire;[26] deprivation of any concessions in the punishment or delay of its implementation;[27] deprivation of God's forgiveness;[28] and loss in the Hereafter.[29]
3. In most verses, apostasy refers to a group and thus the plural pronoun is employed.[30] This is true for all but two of the verses.[31]
4. The apostasy discussed in these verses is due to apostates' animosity and hostility after the Truth was made clear to them.[32]
5. The repentance of an apostate should be accepted.[33] If his or her disbelief grows stronger, then he or she will lose the capacity to repent.[34]

No temporal punishments (e.g., imprisonment, flogging, execution, exile or banning from participating in socio-political affairs) are mentioned. All the temporal punishments cited above for an apostate are of a non-physical nature and completely unrelated to the *ḥudūd* punishments. An apostate who dies in a state of disbelief will, just like an unbeliever, find his or her good deeds nullified and unable to help him attain prosperity. Just as a native unbeliever is not subjected to any temporal punishment, so, too, is an apostate not punished. The Qur'an mentions six groups of people who will experience these realities: polytheists; unbelievers; hypocrites; murderers of "prophets and inviters to justice", someone who talks in a loud voice with the Prophet or in his presence; and apostates.

Three groups will find their deeds nullified and of no benefit in both worlds: the unbelieving murderers of the "prophets and inviters to justice",[35] hypocrites[36] and apostates.[37] Only the first group will receive a temporal punishment for killing someone. This nullification has no correlation with being sentenced to death, or else all of the unbelievers, polytheists, hypocrites and those who raised their voices in the Prophet's presence would have been executed.

Reflecting upon all of the verses dealing with apostasy produces the following conclusions:

1. Replacing Islam with unbelief is a repugnant, repulsive and despicable act. This change can take two forms: (1) "deliberative and knowledge-based apostasy" (*irtidād naẓarī wa 'ilmī*) through study and research, even if it leads one to deny the existence of God and the Hereafter or to doubt Islam's veracity; and (2) one may renounce faith and reject the Truth, despite knowing them to be true, in order to gain worldly benefits and pleasures, or for political and other satanic temptations, as opposed to the doubts that grew out of one's own research and study. This may be called "political and action-based apostasy" (*irtidād siyāsī wa 'amalī*).
2. The Qur'an prescribes no punishment for *irtidād naẓarī wa 'ilmī* in either world. However, such a person will clearly be deprived of the blessings connected with having attained an understanding of the Truth and implementing its values.
3. As for *irtidād siyāsī wa 'amalī* (i.e., "Those who turn on their heels after being shown guidance"), their prescribed punishment in the afterlife takes the form of eternal punishment in the Hellfire. This is the type of apostasy with which the Qur'an is concerned.
4. The Qur'an neither categorically mentions nor prescribes any temporal punishment for apostasy.

It is now an opportune time to respond to a fundamental question on this issue: do the hadith reports on executing an apostate harmonise or conflict with the Qur'anic verses? The verses speak of a punishment waiting in the Hereafter and a non-physical punishment in this world, namely, stripping him or her of divine guidance and forgiveness, as well as nullifying all his or her good deeds. Clearly, these hadith reports are not in accord with the verses. Then, are they contradictory? If we were to consider the verses as not specifying an upper limit of punishment for an apostate, then there would be no contradiction for, at most, we could say that these verses are talking about punishments in the Hereafter and that the hadith reports are talking about punishments in this world. But if the punishments pointed out in the Qur'an are the maximum limits set specifically for apostates, then the verses and hadith reports would contradict each other, for the verses negate temporal punishment, whereas the hadith reports confirm it.

Do the verses on apostasy specify these maximum limits of punishment for an apostate? The verses apparently do and can be supported on the basis of the following core contextual evidences:

> First, God, being the Legislator, specifies the punishments that one would incur for many of the sins in order to indicate their maximum limits and scope. If He intended to add something to them later on, then a notice would have been given in the form of an expression like "possibly God will effect a [new] command" (Q. 65:1). (This conclusion would be uncontested if one were to assume that the Qur'an is a book of laws.)
>
> Second, the fact that other types of verses mention the freedom of religion confirms that there are no temporal punishments for apostasy. This is a good pointer in favour of the limits placed on such punishments.
>
> Conclusion: those hadith reports that condemn an apostate to death contradict the Qur'anic verses.

## Conclusions Derived from the Qur'anic Evidence

The following conclusions are derived after reflecting upon a sample of the most important Qur'anic verses on the freedoms of religion and expression. They can be grouped into four types that deal with the freedom of religion:

1. Islam, the true religion, has introduced its creed and belief system to the people in the clearest and most unambiguous way, along with a reminder of the perversion and adverse effects caused by leaning towards falsehood.
2. Islam proclaims that human beings can attain true prosperity by following it and severely denounces any digression from it.
3. From Islam's perspective, people are free to choose their religion.
4. Islam gives other religions an official status after inviting their adherents to choose it, in the sense that some will accept it and others will not.
5. According to Islam, anyone who rejects it knowingly and, out of obstinacy and stubbornness, opts to follow the wrong path will be punished in the Hereafter.
6. Islam prescribes no temporal punishment for following a wrong belief system.
7. The logic of Islam, when it comes to inviting others to the faith, is to use a rational approach that is peaceful, compassionate and non-dogmatic.
8. One cannot be forced to re-convert. Apostasy carries no temporal punishment; however, if accompanied by hostility and stubbornness, then the person will be severely chastised in the Hereafter.

Bearing all of these points in mind, it becomes clear that Islam has enshrined the freedom of religion and, as such, all hadith reports on killing an apostate or considering his blood lawful to shed conflict directly with the Qur'anic verses.

## *Notes*

1. Shaykh Ṭūsī, *al-Mabsūṭ*, 7:281.
2. Aḥmad b. Muḥammad b. Khālid Barqī, *al-Maḥāsin*, ed. Jalāl al-Dīn al-Ḥusaynī (Tehran: Dār al-Kutub al-Islāmiyya, 1951), 1:221, hadith No. 130.
3. Ibid., 1:226, hadith No. 150; Muḥammad b. ʿAlī b. al-Ḥusayn b. Mūsā b. Bābawayh (Shaykh Ṣadūq), *al-Amālī* (Qom: Mu'assasat al-Biʿtha, 1996), 449, hadith No. 608.
4. Barqī, *al-Maḥāsin*, 1:221, hadith No. 128.
5. Ibid., 1:221, hadith No. 129.
6. Two types of verses connected with the issue of blasphemy are worthy of study, although the exorbitant claims made by those who advocate execution based upon them cannot be sustained.

   *Type 1 verses*: How to Talk with the Prophet

   At the beginning of Chapter 49, God educates the Muslims by informing them that they should not raise their voices in the Prophet's presence or talk loudly with him, as they do with others, and that if they continue to do so He will cancel their virtuous deeds. One's *taqwā* (God-consciousness) is reflected in how one converses with the Prophet: with humility, in a mild manner, and with the proper etiquette. Those who shouted out to him from behind a barrier, instead of waiting their turn to talk with him, were unaware of such ethical norms. If they were to wait until he came outside and then present their requests, it would be better for them. In any event, God is all-forgiving and all-compassionate, "O you who believe! Raise not your voices above the voice of the Prophet, nor speak aloud to him in talk as you speak aloud to one another, lest your deeds be rendered vain while you perceive not" (Q. 49:2–3).

Denigrating and insulting the Prophet is far more severe than shouting in his presence or talking with him in a loud voice. If the outcome of the latter is the nullification of one's deeds, then it follows that denigrating and insulting him will also, at a minimum, mean that their deeds will have no effect in this world and will not produce the intended benefits in the Hereafter. One cannot attain more than this from these verses. Moreover, there is no conflict between this and the hadith reports on executing a blasphemer because these verses both erase and nullify the deeds' effects in such a case, whereas the hadith reports on killing a blasphemer pertain to a different subject matter, which necessitates the invocation of different Qur'anic verses as evidence. Thus, there is no overlap in the subject matter that would lead one to anticipate any conflict in the legal rulings.

*Type 2 verses*: What should be done with those who ridicule the signs of God and abuse and defile sacred entities?

*Verse 1*: "He has already revealed to you in the Scripture that, when you hear the revelations of God rejected and derided, you are not to sit with them until they turn to a different theme. If you did, you would be like them. Surely, God will gather the hypocrites and the unbelievers in Hell" (Q. 4:140).

A believer should walk away from those who refute and mock God's signs in order to encourage them to change the subject and also to avoid gradually coming under their influence. The abode of the hypocrites and the unbelievers is Hellfire. This verse only advises the believers to remove themselves from such groups. Undoubtedly, denigrating the Prophet is an evidentiary proof of mocking and refuting God's signs.

*Verse 2*: "And when you see those who engage in vain discourse about Our Signs, then turn away from them until they enter into some other discourse. If Satan causes you to forget, then after [your] recollection [of it], do not sit in the company of those who are unjust" (Q. 6:68).

Once again, the Prophet instructs his followers only to disassociate themselves from those who mock God's signs so that they will talk about something else. Based upon this mandatory directive, even if one forgets to do so he or she must instantly depart as soon as he or she remembers it. Those who mock are described as oppressors. Even so, the Prophet is not commanded to do anything in excess (like punishment) after he leaves such people.

*Verse 3*: "Revile not those whom they call upon besides God, lest they wrongfully revile God in their ignorance. Thus We have made alluring to each people its own doings. Ultimately they will return to their Lord, and We shall then tell them the truth of all that they did" (Q. 6:108).

Muslims do not have the right to ridicule and cast aspersions upon the sacred entities of other religions, for this will cause non-Muslims to respond in kind. This verse makes no mention of executing those who mock God, which is certainly a far greater abomination than denigrating the Prophet. God will adjudicate and pass His verdict on religions in the Hereafter. That this ruling was earmarked for a particular time when the Muslims were weak is not tenable, because it is not an issue that can be particularised; rather, it is a ruling with an efficacious cause, and the ruling is sustained so long as the efficacious cause is present. The claim of particularising the circumstances is void of any evidence and is therefore no more than a baseless assertion.

*Outcome of Type 2 Verses*: Muslims must leave any immoral assembly wherein God's signs are being mocked until the people talk about something else. In addition, they are forbidden to respond in kind by insulting and ridiculing the sacred entities of other religions. What relationship do those hadith reports that specify killing a blasphemer have with this verse? If these types of verses are used as evidence to limit their application to walking away from such a group, then the hadith reports on killing a blasphemer would be in conflict with them. However, if they are not considered restricted, then there is no conflict between such verses and the hadith reports. A case in point is the Qur'an's prohibition of wine and the hadith reports that prescribe punishment for its consumption, which are totally consistent and in harmony with each other. Do type 2 verses convey that they are restricted? Although there are indications of restriction, these indicants do not meet the threshold of making the restriction manifest. Thus, one cannot say that those hadith reports that mandate killing a blasphemer conflict with these second type of verses.

7. al-Suyūṭī, *al-Durr al-manthūr*, 1:169.
8. 'Alī b. Ibrāhīm Qommī, *Tafsīr al-Qummī* (Qom: Mu'assasat al-Imām al-Mahdī, 2013), 2:428.
9. "O my dear son, establish worship, enjoin kindness and forbid iniquity, and bear patiently whatever befalls you. Surely, these acts require resolve" (Q. 31:17).
10. Sharīf al-Raḍī, *Nahj al-balāgha*, Sermon 206.
11. Ibid., Aphorism 420.
12. Shaykh Ṣadūq, *Man lā yaḥḍuruh al-faqīh*, 4:357.
13. Three other types of verses are in apparent conflict with the hadith reports on blasphemy; however, it is difficult to establish this with any degree of certainty.

    *Type 1 Verses*: God's attitude towards the deities of other religions and differences in religion and creed.

    Verse 1: "If your Lord had wished, He would have made all people a single community, but they continue to have their differences – except those on whom your Lord has mercy – for He created them to be this way, and the word of your Lord is final: 'I shall definitely fill Hell with both jinn and men'" (Q. 11:118–119).

    God neither decreed nor desired that everyone must think the same way and believe in the same thing. He has officially recognised humanity's various belief systems and religions and, at the same time, has promised that those who go astray will be punished in the Hellfire. The uniformity of all religions and belief systems directly contravenes the Qur'anic worldview, which is based upon an open rivalry among them.

Verse 2: "The Jews say, 'The Christians have no ground whatsoever to stand on', and the Christians say, 'The Jews have no ground whatsoever to stand on', though they both read the Scripture. And those who have no knowledge say the same. God will judge between them on the Day of Resurrection concerning their differences" (Q. 2:113).

The Qur'an denounces any attempt to trivialise another person's religion. The truth of such matters will be made clear in the afterlife. Here, people are free to choose any religion or belief system. Although prophets and messengers are sent to remind them of the truth, humanity is allowed to realise it through trial and error.

Verse 3: "Say [O Prophet], 'Disbelievers: I do not worship what you worship, you do not worship what I worship. I will never worship what you worship, [and] you will never worship what I worship. You have your religion, and I have mine'" (Q. 109:1–6).

This chapter is one of the most important and well-founded proof-texts in favour of the freedom of religion. Given this, how can Muslims behave otherwise when confronted with other religions and belief systems?

*Outcome of Type 1 Verses*: God's desire for diverse belief systems and religions is a clear realty. This temporal world is a place for trial and tribulation, rivalry and voluntary selection. These verses appear to conflict with the hadith reports on blasphemy; however, they do not reach the threshold of making it manifestly clear.

*Type 2 Verses*: How to invite others to the faith and freedom of thought.

Verse 1: "[O Prophet], Invite to the way of your Lord with wisdom and goodly exhortation, and dispute with them in the most dignified manner for your Lord knows best who has strayed from His way and who is rightly guided" (Q. 16:125). The Qur'an applies logic (e.g., reason, intelligence, reminders of the Hereafter and civil argumentation), an approach that is both rational and peaceful, when inviting others to Islam. Inspiring fear through blackmail, coercion or killing has no place here. Given that Islam is a religion of mercy, any invitation to embrace it must likewise be compassionate. Executing those who leave Islam is one of the worst forms of disfiguring its visage. A logic-based religion that wins people over by rational argumentation does not need to employ violent and anti-rational methods to gain more followers.

Verse 2: "There is good news for those who avoid the worship of false deities and turn to God, so [O Prophet] give good news to My servants who listen to what is said and follow what is best. These are the ones God has guided; these are the people of understanding" (Q. 39:17–18).

The statement is generic: in order to follow and act upon the best advice, one has to listen to all of the good choices and then select the best one. The Qur'an recommends that its followers pursue this wise and reasonable method.

Divine guidance is provided in a non-coercive environment, and the outcome is nurtured by those who reflect and think. Anyone who selects another option should not be condemned to death, even if he or she has made that choice due to stubbornness and animosity. On the Day of Judgement, God will deal with His obstinate foes and punish them appropriately.

*Outcome of Type 2 Verses*: The Qur'an's approach to inviting others to the faith is the most progressive one, for it is firmly grounded in wisdom, goodly exhortation, sound argumentation and selecting the best option after having considered all of them. Death is not the consequence of making a wrong choice, and executing an apostate does not accord with these types of verses.

*Type 3 Verses*: Objection to punishing one who changes one's religion.

Invoking force in matters of religion and inflicting harsh punishments has a very long history. The Qur'an censures the application of any punishment for changing one's religion in three historical situations:

Verse 1: "His people's arrogant leaders said, 'Shu'ayb, we will expel you and your fellow believers from our town unless you return to our religion.' He said, 'What! Even if we detest it?'" (Q. 7:88).

After giving Prophet Shu'ayb and his followers two options, namely, exile or return to unbelief, he responds, "Do you expect us to return to our [former] religion even if we detest it?" Is it possible to [sincerely] change one's religion due to force? His logic conforms to the Qur'an: one cannot argue that converting from a "true" religion to a "false one" is not mandated by force, however, converting from a "false" religion to a "true" one is mandated by force. An analysis of "There is no compulsion in religion" (Q. 2:256) shows that the prohibition of any coercion in matters of religion is absolute and unconditional. To punish an apostate in any way, let alone by execution, would both engender revulsion towards that religion and conflict with the verse.

Verse 2: "They said, 'We believe in the Lord of the Worlds, the Lord of Moses and Aaron!' but Pharaoh said, 'How dare you believe in Him before I have given you permission? This is a plot you have hatched to drive the people out of this city! Soon you will see: I will cut off your hands and feet on opposite sides and then crucify you all!'" (Q. 7:121–124).

Upon seeing Moses' miracles, the Pharaoh's magicians proclaim their belief in God and thus apostatise. The Pharaoh, confounded that they have dared to do so without his permission, construes this as a conspiracy to both confuse and lead his people astray. He immediately circulates the news and carries out his threat. For him apostasy entails death; however, the Qur'an rejects this logic and censures him, for its logic is the freedom of religion and non-compulsion. The Pharaoh's approach clearly conflicts with the Qur'an, the prophetic practice, and the Imams' conduct.

Verse 3: "And Pharaoh said, 'Leave me to kill Moses – let him call upon his Lord! – for I fear he may cause you to change your religion or spread disorder in the land'" (Q. 40:26).

Given that Pharaoh considers death to be the appropriate punishment for this deed, he threatens Moses with it on the grounds that Moses wants to change the Egyptians' religion. In the Pharaoh's opinion, this would lead to mischief and corruption. The Qur'an rejects this approach because people are free to change their religion and cannot be forced to leave the right path, which has been clearly distinguished from the wrong path. In other words, if the Prophet and the Imams were to adopt Pharaoh's punishment for apostasy, they would be violating the Qur'an itself.

*Outcome of Type 2 Verses*: We gather from these verses, along with others that resemble them, that the Qur'an censures the approach adopted by haughty and arrogant people like the Pharaoh and instead adopts freedom in matters of religion.

Changing one's religion is an inalienable right under the freedom of religion, and inflicting any form of punishment for doing so is censured and contrary to the Qur'an. However, one can object that these types of verses are talking about exchanging falsehood for truth, but are silent about exchanging truth for falsehood.

14. Mahdī Ḥā'irī Yazdī, "*Islām wa i'lāmiyye-ye ḥuqūq-i bashar*", *Sālnāme-ye maktab-i tashayyu'*, 4 (1962): 76–77.
15. Muḥammad Ḥusayn al-Ṭabāṭabā'ī, *al-Mīzān fī tafsīr al-Qur'ān*, trans. Mohammad Bāqir Mūsawī Hamdānī (Qom: Daftar-i Intishārāt-i Islāmī, 1984), 10:207.
16. Ṭabrisī, *Majma' al-bayān*, 3:363, 364.
17. Abū al-Qāsim al-Khū'ī, *al-Bayān fī tafsīr al-Qur'ān* (Beirut: Dār al-Zahrā', 1975), 307–309.
18. Q. 2:217.
19. Q. 3:87.
20. Q. 3:86, 4:137.
21. Q. 16:106.
22. Q. 5:54
23. Q. 47:25.
24. Q. 2:217.
25. Q. 16:106.
26. Q. 2:217.
27. Q. 3:88
28. Q. 4:137
29. Q. 5:5
30. Q. 2:217, 3:86, 4:137, 9:74, 16:106, 47:25
31. Q. 5:5, 54
32. Q. 3:86, 9:74, 47:25
33. Q. 3:89, 9:74
34. Q. 3:90
35. Q. 3:22.
36. Q. 9:69.
37. Q. 2:217.

## *Conclusion*

1. You have stated:

> Some who have misgivings about the ruling on apostasy object to the method of *ijtihād* that is prevalent in the seminaries and argue that a new method of *ijtihād* should be formulated on the basis of anthropology, cosmology, and new Qur'anic hermeneutics. Whether this claim is true or not requires an independent study and falls outside the scope of this work. What I have penned here is in conformity with the *ijtihād* method that scholars have used for a thousand years. Therefore, there should be no doubt about the necessity to execute an apostate. In addition, this necessity is neither time-bound nor limited to its sheer political ramifications, although the latter could be one instance of apostasy. The proposed new method of *ijtihād* would result in changing many legal rulings and thus lead to nothing but the destruction of Islam and taking shelter under the aegis of man-made laws. Over and beyond this, using such a new method will efface the heritage of the *Ahl al-Bayt* and its jurisprudence.

### Response

First, you have labelled your opponents' view as questionable and full of misgivings, while at the same time you present your views as the absolute truth. Those who regard their own opinion as such have donned the mantle of pride and arrogance and have claimed something that no human being can attain.

Second, I surmise that you mean traditional *ijtihād* by the phrase, "the *ijtihād* method that scholars have used for a thousand years". It has become quite clear in your long treatise, however, that you have failed to remain faithful to even the traditionalists' method. The following five are just a sample:

a. Abandoning caution in the matter of life and death.
b. Grasping on to only one type of hadith reports, namely, those that condemn an apostate to death.
c. Permitting the issuance of a legal judgement by someone other than a *ḥākim sharʿ*.

d. Being unaware that the subject matter of apostasy has changed.
e. Being inattentive to a very important principle: A hadith report that contradicts the Qur'an cannot be cited as evidentiary proof.

On what basis do you believe that the method of traditional *ijtihād* has attained a stage of excellence such that its further evolution and progress have become unnecessary? What evidence have you derived from the fundamentals and principles of jurisprudence that favours "closing the doors of *ijtihād*"? In this work, at a minimum there were two instances to which traditional *ijtihād* could not have responded:

a. The non-evidentiary nature of an "isolated hadith report" (*khabar al-wāḥid*) on matters of vital importance.
b. Invoking the Qur'an's spirit as a primary basis for deriving a legal judgement.

I ought to say this with clarity and forthrightness: as long as the basis of anthropology, cosmology and the science of exegesis are not incorporated into the method of *ijtihād*, the process will bring forth nothing but even more imitation of past jurists. By further solidifying the principles and stultifying Islamic legal theory, the door of *ijtihād* will remain closed and the *fiqh* of the past will become the norm for present-day believers.

The apparent rulings derived by jurists using the traditional model are based upon an understanding of humanity that is oblivious to the conventions and customary practices of their own time. Employing my proposed method, which is a corrective to the present-day model, would bring forth different rulings, ones that are based upon a different understanding of humanity from the Qur'an, Sunna and the jurist's intellect. This method has many merits and distinctions over the traditional model, which has elevated and sanctified the conventions of the Hejaz and Iraq from the seventh to the tenth centuries and neglected the standards set by the Qur'an, well-attested hadith reports, and reason.

2. You write:

> . . . I would like to use this opportunity to announce that the *Markaz-i Fiqhī-ye A'imme-ye Aṭhār*, an institution that specializes in jurisprudence, is ready and equipped to engage in a debate on this subject. Islamic scholars and jurisprudential experts who wish to participate, independent of

the political furor and tumult[1] and any predisposition toward the West, could engage the subject matter under this framework.

In response, I will submit to you that,

First, I am grateful to you for declaring your institution's readiness to engage in a scholarly discussion and debate. In accepting this offer, my first act is a response with the evidence and proofs contained in this treatise.

Second, I have placed your responses on this issue verbatim on my website[2] without providing any commentary, explanation or critique. Do you possess the same level of broad-mindedness to place my response on your website and other outlets that belong to your institution?

Third, in one sweep you reject the collective experience of humanity and the advancements occurring in the West today, which are the outcome of collective intelligence exercised by different groups and sects (even though at times they are contradictory). This attitude is a sign of rigidity, for it is fossilised, narcissistic and lacks awareness. Thus, benefit from others and invoke "We say", instead of "I say". In any event, I consider this discussion open and will entertain all scholarly critiques and suggestions.

3. Outcome:

a. The ruling on killing a person accused of being an apostate or a blasphemer lacks any reliable evidence from the Qur'an, Sunna, consensus and reason. Rather, it stands in opposition to the Qur'an and reason due to the many negative consequences accruing from this punishment, all of which would certainly weaken Islam and disfigure its image.
b. Only a competent court can issue a judicial ruling, and only judicial functionaries can implement it. A qualified jurist's *fatwa* cannot take the place of a competent court.
c. The ruling on killing an apostate or a blasphemer has absolutely no credible proof in the Qur'an.
d. Traditional *ijtihād*, which dictates this particular ruling, relies upon some *ṣaḥīḥ* and *thiqa* "isolated reports" (*khabar al-wāḥid*) as well as claims of consensus.
e. It is not possible to implement such a ruling for the following reasons:
   i. Executing an apostate or a blasphemer would weaken Islam and disfigure its image. Thus, based upon "secondary injunction" (e.g., inflict

no harm, promote the public welfare or implement a governmental decree), it would have to cease.

ii. Suspending all *ḥudūd* punishments or, at a minimum, those that lead to a person's death during the Imam's occultation.
iii. Negating the ruling because it is based upon only *thiqa* "isolated reports" (*khabar al-wāḥid*), which should not be implemented due to the necessity of exercising caution in the matter of death.
iv. Negating the ruling because a *thiqa* "isolated report" (*khabar al-wāḥid*) cannot be presented as evidence for a vital matter.
v. Negating the ruling due to a change in the subject matter.
vi. Negating the ruling on the basis that a hadith report cited as proof, but one that contradicts the Qur'an's explicit verses, cannot be presented as evidence.
vii. Reason dictates that it is abominable to terrify a person merely for leaving Islam or insulting religion's sanctities.

f. No temporal punishment is prescribed for leaving Islam.
g. Condemning a person to death for denigrating and insulting the Prophet, the Qur'an or other sacred entities is indefensible.

## *Notes*

1. If you want to see an instance of heartbreaking "political furor and tumult", then you ought to review your last proclamation to commemorate the so-called "epic of 30 December 2009" [when the government summoned its followers to come out in full force to show their support for the Islamic government against the protest movement that was sparked due to the contested election of Ahmadinejad] in which you raise objections at the start of your class. This is available on your website.
2. On my suggestion, the full text of your writing without the slightest alteration has been posted under "andisheh" on the Jaras website at: http://www.rahesabz.net/story/46249.

# Appendix 1
## *Further Clarification of Mohammad Javād Fāzel Lankarānī's (Lankarānī Jr) Position*

Lankarānī Jr did not respond to the critique contained in my second treatise: "A Treatise on Refuting the Punishment for Blasphemy and Apostasy". However, I came across three items on his website that relate to this subject matter and present them here in their exact form.

1. His speech at Qom University, dated 18 September 2012, to inaugurate the start of the academic year.
2. His response to three questions on criminal law received from Ḥusayn Ja'farī, dated 3 February 2013.
3. His response to questions that are on the periphery of the subject of apostasy, dated 4 April 2013.

### *Speech to Inaugurate the New Academic Year at Qom University*[1]

. . . the second point I would like to mention in this assembly is a pertinent contemporary issue: denigrating and insulting the Prophet.

At one time, books were written to weaken and destroy Islam. But nowadays, it is clear and confirmed that movies are being produced with the same goal. Although, if we examine the past, we observe that other methods have also been employed, among them gaining influence by infiltrating the seminaries and universities. The primary objective of such acts is to destroy Islam by downgrading its sacredness – that is to say, to question things that the Qur'an and other sources have laid out for us as sacred matters.

The Prophet is a grand and holy personality. So high is his stature that no one has the right even to raise their voice in his presence. Moreover, whatever he utters is nothing but a revelation, "He does not speak of (his own) desire, it is nothing other than revelation revealed" (Q. 53:3–4). These are things that have become essential parts of a Muslim's personhood and identity. Our enemies have spent years studying how to rupture this bond.

Before the [Iranian] revolution, they would say that "religion is the opiate of the people" and that it is harmful for them. They portrayed it as something detrimental, destructive and the reason for humanity's continued backwardness. This strategy had an apparent effect, but only for a short time. When they saw that Islam had found a presence in Iranian society and that the Iranians pulled off a revolution and asserted that "We have prescriptions for every aspect of human life," they asked themselves, "What should we do?" Thus, they pursued these religious prescriptions one by one and searched for faults that would induce doubt.

Just note that the hijab has gradually become a centre of controversy in order to induce doubt and ambiguity, although it is an extremely clear and imperative issue in religion, one that is evidenced in the Qur'an as a permanent feature that will remain valid until the Day of Judgement. They claim that the Qur'an categorically does not discuss the issue of hijab and *chādor*![2] During the time of the Prophet a group of depraved youngsters picked on women, and so he advised the latter to cover their heads so they would not be recognised.

Or take the Qur'an, which they claim is not the Word of God! This and similar statements have become common in the West. A group of so-called "enlightened" scholars has been receptive to their message and argue that the Qur'an is the personal acquisition of a virtuous and chaste person. Unable to discredit its text, they target its recipient from three angles: the Qur'an, the Prophet and the Qur'an's directives.

At one time, these "enlightened" scholars intimated that religion should be in accord with the existing social conventions and customary practices of one's society. When asked, "What does this mean?" they replied that it should be in tune with the times, as well as with that time's circumstances and conditions. We asked them to elaborate further and understood that "to be in tune with the times, as well as with that time's circumstances and conditions" means that new circumstances dictate that non-related men and women can shake hands. In other words, they seek to permit what God has forbidden and vice versa. However, if we had told them from the outset that their goal of making religion "in tune with the times, as well as with that time's circumstances and conditions" means this, they would not have accepted it.

Religion has a precise meaning and, in our estimation, the merit of *fiqh* and *ijtihād* is found in their ability to respond to every new occurrence, regardless of the particular period. Our jurists have written such solid and astute papers on using the principles of deriving legal rulings and simulating situations such that they are able to provide a satisfactory response to any new issue with sound proofs. The Sunnis cannot make this claim, whereas the Christian and Jewish scholars have done no more than just analyse the issue.

Our religion is able to respond to new contingencies. If this is what is meant by being "in tune with the times, as well as with that time's circumstances and conditions", then we accept it. However, if this means to abandon any aspect of religion due to the passage of time, then we say "No".

On the matter of apostasy, Islam says that if someone converts and then leaves Islam in a public manner, then the judgement is death. If he had kept quiet about it, then doing so would have been fine. Some have raised a hue and cry, demanding to know "what sort of religion prescribes the death penalty [for this]?" We ask them to read the Hebrew Bible and the New Testament. For example, when Moses returned from his retreat on Mount Sinai, he found that seventy-five persons had apostatised and were worshipping the statue of a golden calf. Moreover, these apostates were selected from a batch of 750 persons. When they asked Moses to tell them how to repent, he replied that they should kill themselves (Q. 2:54). The detractors' desire to make the issue of apostasy problematic and questionable in order to induce thereby doubt and ambiguity. Nowadays, they are advancing their goals through the movie industry.

It would be a regressive and simplistic posture for the seminaries, universities, scholars and Muslims in general to keep their eyes closed and dismiss these efforts nonchalantly, claiming that only an insignificant movie-maker is tarnishing Islam's image in one small corner.

Take note of how firmly the imam [Khomeini] confronted Salman Rushdie by issuing a *fatwa* [in 1989] that he should be killed. Simultaneously, some who objected to this ruling asked, "What is the point of such a harsh response when it is just an author who wrote a novel [*The Satanic Verses*]?" Despite this, he stood firm and proclaimed, "No, this is a political machination against the Muslims and thus the judgment is death."

After his [Khomeini's] death, unfortunately, diplomatic efforts were made to rescind his *fatwa*, an undertaking of which I am fully aware, and a step was taken in this direction. My late father [Lankarānī Sr] had issued a circular that even if the imam himself were still alive, he would have no right to rescind his ruling because it was a divine ruling. He [Lankarānī Sr] remained steadfast until the end of his life, so much so that he wrote in his last will and testament that he takes pride in two of his declarations, one of which was that the ruling against Rushdie could not be revoked.

Today, the movie industry in America produces many films and has formulated a plan to denigrate all of the prophets. I read a report that a movie had been made about Moses, in which he bows down in front of Pharaoh and kisses his hand. Moreover, Moses is attracted to one of Pharaoh's nieces who was present. Is this the same Moses that the Qur'an portrays? They have done a similar thing regarding Jesus.

The strategy of the film-makers abroad is to desecrate the sacred by presenting the prophets as regular people who had the same kinds of whims and desires as we do. As such, their aim is wider than just tarnishing the Prophet's image; they want to inject these ideas into the minds of the present and future generations. In such a situation, who should respond? The first layer must be the experts who have the necessary discretion and power to frame cultural and religious issues.

Indeed, I wish that we were a bit more steadfast and vigorous in upholding the Islamic legal rulings, although I am not suggesting that we stop discussing or analysing them! In this very university, scholarly discussion on the hijab, apostasy and other issues must remain ongoing. On the matter of the prophets' infallibility, which is an established fact in the Qur'an, again I have heard that a movie has been produced about Prophet Adam. How shameful it is. If these issues are not talked about, we will quickly lose our capital.

We should not allow those personages whom the Qur'an presents as infallible and holy to be dismissed or subjected to doubt. Instead, we should oppose this campaign to desecrate sacredness, for these film-makers do not seek merely to insult just the Prophet or make one movie; rather, the plan is far broader. I have information that they are turning some of Salman Rushdie's novels into movies.

I must also say that our media outlets do not respond adequately to such doubts and apprehensions. For example, when the issue of apostasy was in the international spotlight a few months ago, the BBC and CNN poked fun at it and attacked the relevant Islamic ruling for a few days, perhaps a week. Our national media mounted no defence and did not respond to them.

After the imam's [Khomeini] death in 1989, unfortunately, our national media did not approach this subject and analyse it from a historical, religious and jurisprudential point of view. If they did so, it was only to a limited extent. However, if it had been extensive and broad, then we would not find ourselves in the present predicament.

Government officials and the aware people of Iran, who are the centre of the Muslim reawakening in the region, are expected to be more vocal than those Islamic countries that are objecting to the denigration so that our voices will reach the ears of the arrogant powers . . .

## *Response to Legal Questions on Apostasy*[3]

In the autumn of 2011, a written deliberation and debate was posted on your website between Lankarānī Jr and Mohsen Kadivar as well as other scholars. The catalysts were the killing of the Azerbaijani journalist Rāfiq Taqī, an action based upon the ruling issued by the late Lankarānī Sr, and the subsequent communique issued by his son Javād expressing delight and pleasure at this person's death.

The issue of killing a person [an apostate] was debated only from the perspective of Islamic jurisprudence, while another important dimension was left out, namely, that of conventional rights, especially the legal procedures and conditions that have to be fulfilled after a charge of apostasy has been levelled.

Due to my interest in the subject of apostasy and its mode of implementation, I posed a number of questions to Lankarānī Jr, who graciously responded to them despite his busy schedule.

I will defer to another time the issue of to what extent my questions were addressed, as well as my analysis and critique of the responses.

Below is the text of my questions and his answers.

3 February 2013
Dear Mohammad Javād Fāzel Lankarānī (Lankarānī Jr),
With apologies for imposing this inconvenience, I have three questions:

## Question 1

I have reviewed and studied your article on apostasy and your father's ruling concerning the journalist [Rāfiq Taqī], as well as the communique in which you expressed your delight and pleasure at his death. My question is not jurisprudential. Rather, it pertains to the merit and ramifications of an eminent jurist issuing a ruling that is subsequently implemented and ends in a person's death (irrespective of his followers' conviction that Taqī had forfeited the right to life and thus it was lawful to kill him, and, moreover, that a religious ruling had been issued against him).

There is no provision in the penal code (based on the fundamental principle that the law for crime and punishment becomes actualised and effectual only after reviewing the indigenous factors pertinent to the country and other aspects of international law) that a senior jurist's ruling can be construed as evidence of the law of the land (not one based on religious law), for this ruling can neither replace the mandate held by the overseer of criminal law, nor be the cause and the one to implement the punishment.

You are, of course, fully aware that even in Islamic Iran if someone kills someone else on the basis that he had forfeited his life and, as such, was lawful to kill, but is unable to establish this in a competent court (even if, in reality, the person in question should have been condemned to death), then the law of retribution (*qiṣāṣ*) is to be invoked on the one who undertook the killing (Penal Code, Article 295 under *Qiṣāṣ*). This principle is even more crucial when it involves other countries. Although the ruling issued by the religious authority may suffice in the religious domain, it has no effect and/or value when presented to the country's judicial system.

According to your pronouncement, implementing the ruling was linked to the legal ruling issued [by your father]. But even if this were not the case – and the linkage is difficult to establish – at a minimum the ruling motivated and encouraged this act. And if we take into consideration the fact that a reward was offered, then whether the person was enticed by it to commit the crime is worthy of investigation.

With this preface, my fundamental question is (assuming that your father was still alive): if tomorrow you, as his son, were summoned to the criminal justice bureau (for the above-mentioned linkage, your public communique of delight and pleasure, and the killer's admission that he acted upon his legal ruling) and informed that its members would like to put your father on trial, an eminent jurist, as an accessory to the Azerbaijani journalist's killing, what would be your response? Would you deny the relationship between the ruling and the killing? Would you accept him being an accessory to the killing?

## Question 2

My expertise is in the area of civil and criminal law. As such, I do not have the knowledge to enter the realm of Islamic jurisprudence and express an opinion on the validity of the jurists' various views (as each of you esteemed jurists regard yourself as being in the right and others as having erred, although the followers [*muqallids*] of each jurist are to emulate their respective jurist in order to acquit themselves before God). I do so only as an observer and a witness to the social consequences. My second question is based upon the observation that each follower is required to emulate the rulings of his or her respective jurist for his act to be valid. In addition, you know that each jurist has solid confidence in his own *fatwas* and considers them a proof between God and himself.

Imagine that in Iran, a Muslim or a non-Muslim Iranian kills an Iranian Muslim on the grounds that his eminent jurist had issued a death sentence for him (e.g., on the basis of a *fatwa* issued by a Sunni jurist). Would you consider the killer immune to the consequences by the state's criminal court system? Does the criminal justice department have the right to investigate the case and issue a fair ruling?

If you accept the court's jurisdiction in adjudicating this case, then does it have the right to summon the jurist who issued the death sentence? (It is irrelevant here whether the jurist was mistaken or unqualified and thus had no right to issue a legal ruling, because the killer regards him as a qualified jurist. The general public does not have the expertise to judge. When he is apprehended, the fact that jurists hold different opinions is of no importance, for the killer was relying upon his own jurist's ruling.)

## Question 3

In your opinion, does apostasy deal with the rights of God? Do you, like other jurists, consider it permissible to issue a ruling on such matters when the accused is not present? Was the ruling issued against the Azerbaijani journalist in absentia or after having heard his defence?

Ḥusayn Ja'farī

## Response

1. The cause of my joy and pleasure arises from the implementation of the divine ruling because killing another human being, in and of itself, cannot be the source of joy and delight.
2. My communique was issued after the act (i.e., the killing of Rāfiq Taqī) and thus cannot be construed as the motivating or influencing factor, unless you contend that the ruling (on killing) was itself the motivating factor.
3. With regard to your first question, bear in mind that the ruling on killing an apostate is not limited to Shiʿism or even to Islam, for all heavenly religions have reached a consensus on this. As such, if a state's law brings about the result that you point out, then certainly that law is flawed and efforts must be made to correct it. In other words, those who are in charge of and acquainted with the criminal law code ought to rectify this. When all [heavenly revealed] religions are united on an issue, is it possible for the state to issue a law whose implementation would result in a conflict with the religious ruling? Imagine that in a Muslim country women wear the hijab, even though the state law forbids this. What should be done in such a situation? Should the essential ruling on hijab be suspended, or should we raise our voices to express our dissent with that particular state law? Many other examples can be cited. I mentioned the hijab to point out that the issue is not confined to apostasy.
4. With regard to your second question, the discourse on the necessity of killing an apostate is an essential component of religion and a primary matter in *fiqh* and thus cannot be compared to those fatwas on which jurists have differing opinions. Certainly in the latter situation, one cannot act upon the basis of a legal ruling issued by the jurist that he emulates. This is the case even in the domain of human interrelations (*muʿāmalāt*) wherein, for instance, the seller's jurist regards a transaction as valid whereas the buyer's jurist considers it void. In such a situation, the transaction would be considered void. Accordingly, comparing the killing of an apostate, on which there has never been any dissent, to other situations in which there have been differences of opinion is an incorrect analogy.
5. Apostasy is a violation of God's rights and, as such, the qualified jurist can issue a ruling upon the basis of a person's open declarations, whether

in his writings or his speech. Moreover, because the apostate publicised his pronouncement, the matter of issuing a ruling in absentia does not arise. In other words, the issue of absentia would be relevant only if there were a probability that the accused would mount a defence. However, if he publicly declares his apostasy, he deserves death. There are no other options to consider. This ruling is akin to one whose depravity and debauchery are exposed to the public, which makes gossiping about him permissible. Or, if someone introduces an innovation in religion, then it is permissible to accuse him of doing so, even if his intention is not to denigrate the totality of religion. Just like the issue of ruling in absentia does not arise pertaining to these issues, the same is the case with apostasy.

Mohammad Javād Fāzel Lankarānī (Lankarānī Jr)

## *Response to a Question on the Periphery of Apostasy*[4]

Greetings,

I read on your website a question posed by a lawyer regarding the judgement on Rāfiq Taqī and your response to it. My question pertains to your response: "Moreover, because the apostate publicised his pronouncement, the matter of issuing a ruling in absentia does not arise." In *fiqh* and state law, ruling in absentia has been clearly defined, and this ruling constitutes one in absentia.

However, in the matter of God's rights, one cannot issue a ruling in absentia. You continue, "This ruling is akin to one whose depravity and debauchery are exposed to the public, which makes gossiping about him permissible. Or, if someone introduces an innovation in religion, then it is permissible to accuse him of doing so, even if his intention is not to denigrate the totality of religion. Just like the issue of ruling in absentia does not arise pertaining to these issues, the same is the case with apostasy." Are you referring to information that is widespread and in the public domain? In your estimation, could a judge issue a ruling based upon the proof that the report is pervasive and in wide circulation? For instance, if a person gains a widespread reputation as a drinker of wine, can the judge issue a ruling and implement the punishment?

## Response

In the domain of God's rights, issuing a ruling in absentia would be incorrect because the allegations might only be probable (as opposed to certain). For instance, a person accused of drinking wine may respond that he did so under duress or for medicinal purposes. Likewise, in the case of apostasy, there is a possibility that it was forced upon him or is merely an utterance. In such situations, the punishment would not be implemented. The primary reason for prohibiting the issuance of a ruling in absentia for God's rights is based upon the maxim of *dar'*.[5]

However, in situations where a person openly declares his apostasy and this is known to the public to such an extent that the apostate reaffirms it, then the jurist is permitted to issue a ruling against him.

Mohammad Javād Fāzel Lankarānī (Lankarānī Jr)
4 April 2013

### *Notes*

1. On the website of Mohammad Javād Fāzel Lankarānī (Lankarānī Jr) as of 18 September 2012 (the first part of the speech deals with paying tribute to knowledge).
2. See Glossary.
3. Ādam Beheshtī on the weblog of Ḥusayn Ja'farī (expert in law). It is also present on the website of Lankarānī Jr, with the exception of the introduction.
4. On the website of Lankarānī Jr, without any mention of the questioner's name.
5. Preventing harm has priority over procuring benefit.

# Appendix 2
## *Rāfiq Taqī in his Own Words and in the Words of his Defenders*

To gain greater familiarity with the thoughts of Rāfiq Taqī, we present here his words and those of his defenders. A full translation of his "Europe and Us" article was published in *San'at Qaz'atī* (October 2016), which was the catalyst for issuing the ruling and, ultimately, his death. Also included here are two open letters under a fictitious name of Ghonā-ye Tabrīzī, who knows the Azerbaijani language, in which he raises objections to Lankarānī Jr's first and second declarations. In his second declaration, Lankarānī Jr responds to a point raised by Tabrīzī but without mentioning him by name. The last part of the appendix consists of three interviews with Rāfiq Taqī before his killing, all of which were chosen and translated by Ghonā-ye Tabrīzī.

## *Europe and US*[1]

Europe, not only because of its geographical location but also from the perspective of spirituality, induces human beings to reflect. Thus, in essence, its people' achievements are actually success stories for all of humanity. This should not become a source of arrogance. Unfortunately, however, at times it did rear its head in the form of fascism or overt militarism and aggression.

Although fascism was an unforgivable blunder, the concepts of freedom and humanism that had originated there were actualised and put into practice in the same land. Christianity gained ascendance there because of its spiritual affinity with these concepts and ideas and, as such, no other religion could spread in Europe. It therefore rejected the false and pseudo-values of other religions like Islam.

Islam, presenting itself as a religion grounded in ethics and humanism, is a deception and a fraud. The standard of humanism found in Islam, which we have memorised and to which we pay lip service, cannot defend itself from the criticisms levelled against it by materialists and dialecticians. Islam is an ideology of imperialism with an Eastern flavour and can be placed in such a category. It can never overpower and prevail over Europe from the perspective of spirituality. Even though their religion had become impotent, Muslims tried to revive it by placing its coffin on the shoulders of the Ottoman Empire; however, they were not successful and thus were forced to return it to the East and bury it facing the direction of the Ka'bah. One who has attained faith in Jesus would never pay any heed to Muhammad, who was eminently in favour of declaring war and was only an object of dread and fear. At most, Islam can only have a small contingent of followers in Europe who are capable of making progress. Perhaps a country could be found in which one or two individuals prone to violence and dogmatism become representatives of Islam in that region.

Europe is outside the orbit of the East, as the latter could not or did not wish to embrace the value of human freedom. In the East, this value is viewed as having no significance and is therefore positioned at the lowermost tier of importance. Those from whom freedom has been snatched are distracted with offers of imaginary prosperity and glad tidings (in the Hereafter). The feeble path to paradise, one that is filled with adversities, is presented as a saviour capable of pulling oneself out of the social morass.

Islam is the chief motivator of creating a culture of duplicity in the East. The primitive system of the Bedouins has brought the East to its knees, and no ray of enlightened thoughts and ideas can be sustained in such an atmosphere. In Islam, the clerical class' mandate is to expand the domain of the prohibited, promote backwardness and work in earnest to drive this process toward completion.

The West is an exponent of dialectics and the East is an exponent of metaphysics. The latter's progress in the domain of metaphysics is quite evident. In the rivalry between these two approaches, it appears that the West is progressing and the East is regressing.

The Azebaijanis' efforts to secure a secular system can be traced to Europe's influence. Their diligence and hard work showed that they are a better fit with Europe. Our country's relation with other Muslim countries is burdensome, forced and only for the sake of propriety. Azerbaijan's enlightened thinkers appreciate that Islam and the East are forever intertwined with the remnants of violence brought about by the former. Throughout our history, even that of recent times, the (Azerbaijani) leaders' outwardly "sincere" respect for and honouring of Islam were only for the sake of gaining power. Muslims are merely the hordes that they call upon when their votes are needed. In brief, [Islam] is an impediment that must be removed.

The wide gulf between myself and the Pope is similar in size to the distance between the Azerbaijani government officials and their belief in Islam.

The Turkish Azerbaijanis were able to preserve their Europeanness despite the dominance of the extremist Shi'i Iranian regime. All of the pressure tactics and persistent efforts employed by the chauvinist Persians to make us unite with the Iranians as one community proved to be futile. Note that our comrades in the south generally migrate to Europe. This spiritual affinity and identity is already established and spares us the need for any elaboration or proofs. We should make maximum use of this tendency. We can say that every Azerbaijani carries the essence of Europeanness to such an extent that if he has a trait of the East inside himself, then the latter will appear as a defect. Any such trait has added nothing of value to his or her personality.

Russia did not desire to separate itself from the West even in the midst of military confrontation. Peter the Great (d. 1725) did not mince words and articulated his position categorically and courageously: he was in full agreement with remaining attached to Europe. Accordingly, Russian culture and literature has been profoundly influenced by Europe.

All countries are working to secure their freedom via different methods and approaches. In this enterprise, they look towards Europe as a role model in terms of establishing human rights, for these rights guarantee progress and prevent regression. Europe discovered them, and only its specific model is worthy of emulation.

European culture was able to remove the attribute of savagery from humans and reduce crime to its lowest level, so much so in fact that there was minimal need to engage in these acts of barbarity for survival.

Human beings achieved mastery over themselves for the first time in Europe to such an extent that they became distant from evil and near to goodness. Europe went through a bloody phase, after which it learned its lesson and became the first to say "No" to war.

The West has a better record in preventing outbursts of political and social revolutions because its members have a developed civil society.

It is good to remind ourselves here that the spark and inducement for knowledge and technology in America and Southeast Asia came from Europe. If it were not present, then perhaps today humanity would still believe that the Sun revolves around Earth. Perhaps the East would still believe that the world revolves on a cow's horn.

Europe is now bringing to completion weighty research on matters of spirituality, ethnicity, history and philosophy. Moreover, it managed to preserve those aspects that are beneficial and necessary. And now its inhabitants are enjoying the fruits of their predecessors' labour. They succeeded because their research was, more than anyone else's, more pragmatic and logical. The core of a human being comes to the fore only via logical acts. "Illogical" means that the act is separated from the intellect and thus of no benefit.

We see that an Easterner's intellectual reflections do not benefit contemporary life and his objective is not even comprehensible. A Western philosopher does not play around like an Eastern Sufi by resorting to stupor and insanity. Yes, an Eastern philosopher is a total pretender and full of lies. He talks only to talk, not for any other purpose. Either the destination is unknown or completely imperceptible. In any event, the final goal is to link it to the Hereafter. Their philosophical system is restricted to Islam, and this reality cannot be counted as a virtue for a philosopher.

[Friedrich] Nietzsche's (d. 1900) intelligence and creativity have to be attributed solely to his keeping a distance from religion. Even though Fyodor Dostoyevsky (d. 1881) was attracted to religion, it was not an integral part of his identity. His works were far more interesting and profound when he distanced himself from Christianity.

Generally, any comparative analysis between the East and the West is prejudicial because it is hastily undertaken with a spirit of envy and jealousy and, at times, leads to fierce confrontations. I have written this piece abruptly while being fully aware of all the pressure, reactions, and attacks that I will encounter as a consequence. But despite all of that, I say that "there is still more to say".

Rāfiq Taqī

## *An Open Letter from Ghonā-ye Tabrīzī to Lankarānī Jr*[2]

You are precisely what I had expected. The vast amount of discretionary authority you have arrogated to yourself by virtue of being a jurist, along with the silence and complicity of the governments of Azerbaijan and Iran, has intoxicated you to such an extent that you are blinded from appreciating the gravity of the crime committed by a gullible person (most likely on the basis of your deceased father's *fatwa*): "It is said that if the caliph does not possess such religious authority, then what to say of the judge, jurist, or Shaykh al-Islam? I [Muhammad Abduh] say that Islam has endowed none of them with a mandate and authority over the belief system or legal rulings. Whatever authority they possess is enshrined in civil law, and the Islamic Shari'a has endorsed it. No one can claim to have a right to force a belief system on anyone or prevent one from creative reflection and interrogation."[3]

Had I not seen your congratulatory and confirmatory pronouncement[4] in favour of killing the Azerbaijani journalist Rāfiq Taqī, there would have been no reason or motivation to write this letter, for: (1) if your late father was the cause of this killing, he is now deceased and I cannot say anything about his fate because I have no access to the unknown. However, I am confident that he will not leave behind a positive legacy in Azerbaijan's history; (2) if Iran's ruling elites were the cause, I have no opportunity to dialogue with them even though I am a citizen of that country, for they aspire to create a flock that is submissive and docile (whereas I am not); and finally; (3) if the cause is to be attributed to Azerbaijan then, at a minimum, I have written two articles in my native language, with which you are not familiar and, moreover, even if you were, you would not fathom the significance of the subject matter. Your latest pronouncement has dispelled all doubts that the grandiose titles you have concocted for yourself are void of any basis in knowledge, reason or spirituality. Perhaps your only justification could be familial affinity and following in your father's footsteps. However, your pronouncement has made you complicit in this crime. In any event, neither you nor your late father have proved that Rāfiq Taqī deserved death; in fact, numerous proofs can be advanced to establish that his blood was inviolable. A sample of these proofs is given below.

My method in dealing with this issue may transgress the limits of religious etiquette, for my interlocutor, Lankarānī Jr, has arrogated to himself such grand entitlements in religion that he believes he can decide a person's fate, whether that person should be allowed to live or not. As such, my method will be appropriate in his case. Hopefully, others will not misread it.

The Qur'an is the first foundational source invoked by every researcher. However, the handful of verses that deal with apostasy and related matters pertain to issues that are inapplicable to the situation under consideration, given that the Qur'an issues no judgement for an apostate and, as such, those jurists who have issued a ruling have had to resort to the hadiths to make their case.

For instance, Q. 2:217, 5:21, 16:106 and 9:74 were occasioned by circumstances that are unrelated to our discussion here, and other verses only speak of the consequences in the Hereafter and the erasure of good deeds. However, human exoteric (*tafsīr*) and esoteric (*ta'wīl*) interpretations have given a different twist to the verses. For instance, that part of the verse invoked by the jurists to justify dissolving the marriage of Naṣr Ḥāmid Abū Zayd (d. 2010), an Egyptian scholar and alleged apostate: ". . . and do not yourselves hold on to marriage ties with disbelieving women" (Q. 60:10) as a proof text. Note that this verse is addressed only to men. One is perplexed at the extent of human manipulation required to make it applicable to a spouse who espouses dissenting views and, even that, without the couple's consent. On another point, several verses state that only God can accept or deny a person's repentance. For instance, Q. 2:217 explains the subject matter,[5] and Q. 3:90 says explicitly that "The repentance of those who, having believed, then increase in their disbelief, will not be accepted." Similarly, Q. 9:74 makes an allowance for accepting one's repentance, and Q. 4:137 denies this possibility for those who are deeply anchored in apostasy. Moreover, as no verse prescribes any temporal punishment, those who clamour for the apostate's execution do so on the basis of hadiths. I will deal with this later on.

Aḥmad Ṣubḥī Manṣūr writes:

> Only two hadiths report on the prescribed punishment for an apostate. One is related by Awzā'ī without a chain of transmission and thus cannot be considered a proof-text. In addition, he was patronized first by the Umayyad and then by the 'Abbasid rulers, all of whom used such fabricated traditions to legitimize the killing of their opponents under the guise of apostasy. To be sure, after two centuries jurists attempted to rehabilitate the hadith reports by appending a chain of

transmission and incorporating them into the authoritative hadith works. The second hadith was cited by 'Ikrimā in *Saḥīḥ Bukhārī,* even though he was a deviant and unreliable in his transmission.[6]

Such deficiencies led Ṣubḥī Ṣāliḥ to conclude:

> On matters of life and death, one cannot rely upon "isolated hadith reports" (*khabar al-wāḥid*). Thus the justification for executing a person cannot be established by a proof text that is less than *mutawātir*, because the explicit Qur'anic verses and hadith reports underline the necessity of preserving human life. This principle can be set aside only if the Muslims have reached a consensus to do so; however, no such consensus exists that one who changes his religion deserves death.[7]

I ought to add that those jurists who have filled their works with the judgement of killing the apostate have combined four to five hadith reports to compensate for the weakness of their position and have collectively labelled them as *saḥīḥ* or *muwaththaq* in the hope of silencing their critics. But only those jurists who were (and still are) linked to oppressive rulers issue such judgements on the basis of such hadiths. However, it is a source of joy that the number of their critics continues to rise and that they are forced to defend their position with weak and flimsy arguments.

I contend that in the light of the global progress made in terms of knowledge and science, researchers and specialists have a right to express their dissenting opinions and that doing so should not be construed as apostasy. Instead, the scholars and specialists in their respective fields should attempt to respond to the critiques.[8] In another place, Jannātī writes: "The dissenting opinions expressed or doubts raised by the intellectuals in any field cannot be considered blasphemous, debilitating religion, or apostasy."[9] Just as Rūmī has stated: "Unbelief is ignorance, and the judgment against it is knowledge."[10] Instead of wasting money budgeted for religion by promoting superstitions, myths and intolerance, it should be channelled towards research and scholarly enterprises.

The contemporary *marja'* 'Abd al-Karīm Mūsawī Ardabīlī opines:

> No Qur'anic verse specifies the judgment for apostasy; only the warning of punishment in the Hereafter is mentioned . . . During the

> Prophet's time, apostasy was not determined on the basis of differing views and opinions, but on the basis of destabilizing the Muslim umma by the use of political, economic, and tribal power . . . There is no instance in the early history of Islam in which a person was executed for apostasy because of his belief system.[11]

In another place he says: "The religious scholars differ over what constitutes the 'essentials of religion' and whether negating the same is equivalent to apostasy . . . As such, the pre-modern jurists reached no consensus on this issue."[12] In the absence of consensus, how is it possible to pronounce one who denigrates, mocks or repudiates a legal ruling an apostate? It is so difficult and problematic to defend the ruling on apostasy that Nāṣer Makārem Shīrāzī was forced to consider it a political transgression: "Apostasy is the crime of rebelling against an Islamic government. Its punishment is execution, just as it is so in many laws of other countries around the world . . . This ruling pertains to a political crime [that is punished in order] to preserve the society and the Islamic government, and to struggle against hostile forces."[13]

First, no political ruling is inherently unchangeable. Second, and contrary to his opinion, many countries (except for a few regressive ones) have dropped the execution of such dissenters from their legal manuals. In the contemporary world they are not deprived of their social and political rights, let alone executed. In any event, acknowledging that apostasy is a political crime is a step in the right direction, one that would change the nature of the debate, although neither Shīrāzī nor the others have yet mustered the courage to pursue this line of argument.

In another place, Shīrāzī writes: "The ruling on apostasy does not apply to one who espouses a particular view in private; rather, it applies to one who publicizes and disseminates his view and, in reality, incites a rebellion against the government."[14] It is apparently clear to all that these words are uttered for political expediency, for he wants to support and defend Iran's suppression of public protests in the social and political domains. In the case of Rāfiq Taqī, against which political system had he rebelled that made him deserving of death?

It is interesting to observe that on 18 June 2000, the Iranian judiciary distributed circular No. 7/1948 to all courts: "Judges . . . have the discretion to implement the punishment prescribed in the Shari'a for those crimes, such as apostasy, when the civil statutes have not provided for any punishment."

This means that if a person were convicted of apostasy in a court where a jurist who shares your father's views was serving as a judge, then that person would be executed. However, if the court were presided over by a judge like Mūsawī Ardabīlī, then that same person would be acquitted. This is the standard of justice in Iran! Such a situation would provide opportunities for abuse, as was blatant when Khomeini invoked apostasy against his opponents in at least two situations: (1) the famous decree against Salman Rushdie; and (2) against the National Front of Iran (Jebhe-ye Mellī).

After the Iranian Revolution in 1979, *shari'a*-compliant laws were enacted under the supervision of the seminary jurists serving in the Parliament. One of these was the law of retribution (*qiṣāṣ*). The National Front of Iran was opposed to such enactments and considered them to be inhumane. Here, I do not intend to pass any judgement, but only to point out that a political group opposed, whether correctly or not, a jurist-supported measure presented in the Parliament. Khomeini made use of the jurisprudential ruling on apostasy, or rather desired to manipulate it, by not only enacting it, but also by using it as an instrument to remove that group from the political landscape. He clearly showed that he was acting in God's place by demanding that its members seek his repentance in his presence: "I feel sorry for them, for they dug their graves with their own hands. I did not want it to come to this, but I am prepared to accept their repentance . . ."[15]

Without delay, on 15 June 1981 he condemned the Front for merely opposing the enactment of *qiṣāṣ*: "As of today, the National Front of Iran is condemned to apostasy. It is possible that they may deny this. If so, this afternoon they should proclaim on the radio that this essential and indispensable ruling, which is applicable on Muslims, all of them, [and which they are] alleged to have labeled as 'inhumane', was not from them. If they do this, then we will accept it . . . Until the last moment of life, the doors of repentance are open."[16] But when foreign journalists asked him seven years after his decree against Salman Rushdie whether it could be rescinded if the author were to repent, the same Khomeini replied: "This is absolutely impossible. Even if Salman Rushdie were to become an ascetic of the time, still it would be imperative upon all Muslims to use their life, property, and whatever else is at their disposal to consign him to Hell."[17]

Just like the other legal rulings, not only is the ruling on apostasy deeply associated and linked with the situation and political climate at the time, but its determination also depends upon the worldview and depth of knowledge of the person assigned to do the research. In all of this, there is a distinct possibility of error creeping in. Given the gravity of the punishment and inability to correct the error in the case of apostasy, a greater amount of caution ought to be exercised. Being humans, we can discover new ideas and methods by using our intellect and learning from past experiences. Montazeri asserted: "The primary bases for jurisprudential rulings, even in the case of human interrelations, politics, and punishments that are generally enshrined and uncontested, are derived from the Qur'an and the Sunna. However, in the final analysis, their validity as sources is determined by the rational faculty."[18]

The other point is to consider whether one can regard a supposed "unbeliever" in the terminology of *fiqh* as an actual "unbeliever"? Can one assume that a person who was once considered an "unbeliever" by a jurist will always be considered an "unbeliever" despite the advancement in our understanding of Islam? Such a person could be a "believer" in the opinion of a mystic, and a person labelled an "unbeliever" by a mystic could be a "believer" in the estimation of a philosopher. Moreover, an "unbeliever" in the sight of a philosopher could be considered a "believer" by both a jurist and a mystic: "Your blasphemy is (the true) religion, and your religion is the light of the spirit: you are saved, and through you a (whole) world is in salvation."[19]

The insistence by some jurists on the validity of execution for apostasy has taken the form of antagonism and hostility (even though I and others have provided arguments against it). Rest assured that an ulterior motive lies behind the veil of this jurisprudential ruling, and that political and conventional benefits are accruing to its exponents. With the passage of time, it is becoming harder and harder to insist upon this punishment. In fact, this reality has led some jurists to acknowledge that implementing it is impractical. Sobhani writes: "If apostasy is to be carried out in a collective form, then it could not be implemented because, due to the likely wide circulation of this news, it would generate revulsion toward Islam and engender deviation from the creed. In such a culture and ambience, such an eventuality could not be hindered. As such, the judgment of apostasy cannot be implemented."[20]

Rāfiq Taqī, an educated man, a physician and master of literature, was not guilty of any crime that called for the death sentence. His short stories had an impact, and he experienced the pain felt by his society. He wrote comparative articles as regards the East and the West. He was neither subservient to anyone nor a mercenary. He also criticised the Azerbaijani government and those who circulated myths and superstitions. Were these attributes not enough to draw harsh enemies to him? He could have petitioned for asylum in either Europe or America after your father's 2006 decree, and most likely they would have welcomed him with a red carpet.

However, he resisted this possible avenue of escape and remained where he was. If the basis of the *fatwa* against him was his article "Europe and Us", then, even though it was harsh and abrasive, how did he denigrate or deny the essentials of religion? Did your father truly read this article? Have you read it? Is it at all coincidental that this man was murdered only nine days after he had written a very critical article about Iran? I am almost certain that the person I am addressing here is well aware of the issues raised, but that he is surrendering his religion to benefit the current powerbrokers.

I have explained the issues with brevity. If the honourable Lankarānī Jr would permit me to elaborate further, after he descends somewhat from the high pedestal upon which he has placed himself, then I would be glad to accommodate him.

Ghonā-ye Tabrīzī
30 November 2011

## *A Refutation of Apostasy: Second Letter from Ghonā-ye Tabrīzī to Lankarānī Jr*[21]

Perhaps the vocation of jurisprudence has endowed most of its practitioners with the ability to identify, announce and follow up on the commands and prohibitions. With the exception of a few who are prepared to engage in dialogue, most of them are cynical, impatient and incompetent. In order to prove the validity of their own position and elevate their own stature and besmirch their rivals, they will do whatever is necessary to achieve their goals. In the event that they cannot do so, they will remove themselves from the dialogue sessions and entertain devious plans against their opponents. These are the very same attributes that Abū Ḥāmid al-Ghazālī forewarned and prohibited his readers: "Do not get entangled in these issues and keep aloof from them, just as you would from the poison of an assassin. This pain is incurable, for all of the jurists are embroiled in self-pride and self-glorification."[22] As such, many of the debate sessions with them are fruitless and in vain.

I still remember the correspondence between the jurist Ja'far Sobhani and Dr Abdolkarem Soroush. I do not know why the former took offence at the explanation of the difference between a parrot and a bee, an explanation that led to what transpired in the third letter, as we know. And, at present, Lankarānī Jr chose the following title to respond to the objections levelled by his one-time classmate after Rāfiq Taqī's assassination: "The Response of Ḥājj Shaykh Mohammad Javād Fāzel Lankarānī (may His Blessings continue on him) to Doubts Surrounding the Jurisprudential Subject of Apostasy." Being one of the writers who had raised objections, I also received a response from his office. Perhaps you did not notice that your treatise is not really a response, but rather a series of importune assertions and perhaps an expression of animosity. I, and most likely the rest of those who wrote letters [of objection] to you, are familiar with the Qur'anic verses and hadiths that you cite. The proofs advanced by those who defend the execution of those classified as "apostates" are so similar that there was no need to repeat them. Actually, in the midst of the verses you cite for elaboration, you have failed to incorporate many of the other ones that I have seen in the books of earlier defenders.

Towards the end of my first letter, I had promised you that I would be more categorical and forthright if you were to respond. Let me say that in the place of the few verses that you took the trouble to cite as proof texts, even if tens of categorical verses on the obligation to kill an apostate were advanced, and that if in the place of two or twenty "isolated reports" (*khabar al-wāḥid*) you were to bring forth a thousand hadith reports that according to you are "authentic" on this subject, or if all the jurists – pre-modern, modern and contemporary – were united in their opinion that the punishment for apostasy is death, still I would say to you that, as a Muslim, this judgement is unacceptable because the God of my Islam would never have given such a permission. In your estimation, our opinion is "doubtful" and "misguided", and thus we are "adversaries". You do not even restrain yourself from taunting and reprimanding your critics in such a toxic atmosphere. This is not a sign of boldness and fearlessness in thinking; rather, these are the very attributes to which I referred in the beginning – and I distance myself from them. I will try to state briefly what I had not said in my first letter and expose the falsity of your objections.

I stated that the Qur'an contains no categorical evidence that favours any temporal punishment for apostasy, whereas you wish to establish otherwise on the basis of your personal inferences derived from the exoteric and esoteric exegeses of certain verses. However, you are looking at the evidence from a biased perspective in order to corroborate your pre-set opinion, and the converse could be established just as easily. You assume that there is no flaw or blemish in your argument, and thus produce no solid proof for it. You allege that we have failed to observe the imperativeness of this punishment due to "either a lack of (1) rigour and diligence in studying the Qur'an's verses or (2) information and/or deficient knowledge". So, let's see what you claim to be solid proofs from the Qu'ran. You write:

> One can invoke Q. 2:54, among other proofs, to establish that an apostate deserves to be killed: "Moses said to his people, 'O my people! You have wronged yourselves by taking up the calf [as your god]. So repent to your Maker and kill yourselves. That is better for you in the sight of your Maker.' Then He accepted your repentance. He is the Ever Relenting and Most Merciful." A large number of Israelites, after being delivered from the pharaohs of the time and prevailing over them, succumbed to worshipping the "speaking" calf and grew distant from monotheism after Moses had gone to Mount Sinai to receive the Tablets. Upon his return, he proclaimed, "You have wronged yourselves by this deviance and must seek repentance and

kill (*qatl*) yourselves." What is meant by *qatl* here is not to combat the lower self and lustful desires, but the literal killing and annihilation of the self.

The first verse that you adduce and explicate specifically pertains to Moses and his followers, who he rebuked for choosing idolatry. You infer that "and kill yourselves" refers to the literal killing of the self, as opposed to the metaphorical sense of overpowering the lower self. In all likelihood, you expect us to set aside all of the past historical and exegetical literature regarding this verse – none of which mentions a categorical judgement. And this is your very first solid proof! Regardless, we accept it for the sake of argument. In order to magnify your proof, you then present a hadith from Ali at the end of the verse, as follows: "He is held to have remarked that the Israelites had asked Moses about the nature and modality of this repentance and that the latter had stated, 'Those who are guilty of worshipping the calf should kill each other.' This led to the killing of blood brothers, parents, and children; God interjected and commanded that they stop it."[23] Are you aware that you are forcing us to accept your baseless proof as a judgement of God? Can the killing of a human being in 2011 be sustained on the basis of your inference from the Qur'an, in which reference is made to a historical incident or a fable of Moses? Should this suffice for us? Do you know how this story is related in the Hebrew Bible?

And when the people saw that Moses delayed to come down from the mount, the people gathered themselves together unto Aaron, and said unto him: "Up, make us a god who shall go before us; for as for this Moses, the man that brought us up out of the land of Egypt, we know not what is become of him." And Aaron said unto them: "Break off the golden rings, which are in the ears of your wives, of your sons, and of your daughters, and bring them unto me." And all the people broke off the golden rings which were in their ears, and brought them unto Aaron. And he received it at their hand, and fashioned it with a graving tool, and made it a molten calf; and they said: "This is thy god, O Israel, which brought thee up out of the land of Egypt" . . . And the LORD spoke unto Moses: "Go, get thee down; for thy people, that thou broughtest up out of the land of Egypt, have dealt corruptly; they have turned aside quickly out of the way which I commanded them; they have made them a molten calf, and have worshipped it, and have sacrificed unto it, and said: 'This is thy god, O Israel, which brought thee up out of the land of Egypt.'" And the LORD said unto Moses: "I have seen this people, and, behold, it is a stiff-necked people. Now therefore let Me alone, that My wrath may wax hot against them, and that I may consume them; and I will make of thee a great nation" . . . And when Moses saw that the people were broken loose – for Aaron had let them loose for a derision among their enemies – then Moses stood in the gate of the camp, and said: "Whoso is on the LORD's side, let him come unto me." And all the sons of Levi gathered themselves together unto him. And he said unto them: "Thus saith the LORD, the God of Israel: Put ye every man his sword upon his thigh, and go to and from gate to gate throughout the camp, and slay every man his brother, and every man his companion, and every man his neighbour." And the sons of Levi did according to the word of Moses; and that day about three thousand of the people fell dead (Exodus 32: 1–10, 25–28).

You write: "Fakhr al-Dīn al-Rāzī (d. 1209) writes in his exegesis that, 'Whosoever among you renounces his religion and dies as a disbeliever, their deeds will come to nothing (*ḥabaṭat a'māl*) in this world and the Hereafter, and they are the inhabitants of Hellfire, where they remain (Q. 2:217)' and 'Effacing or the perishing of the deeds (*ḥubūṭ al-a'māl*) in this world' means that he must be overpowered and killed. In the event that this is not possible, then he must be engaged in combat and killed."[24] You assert that "effacing of the deeds" applies to the punishment in the temporal world. In this verse the person "dies" while in the state of unbelief; there is no mention of "killing". However, you insist that this refers to killing an apostate, in accordance with your desire. You have, therefore, assumed the mantle of speaking for God. Surprisingly, you do not cite the occasion of Revelation, namely, that this verse was specifically revealed to alleviate the difficulties encountered by Sariyya 'Abdallah b. Jaḥsh, who was accused of having engaged in war during a forbidden month. In other words, it has no connection with the imperative to kill an apostate.[25]

You say that 'Shams al-Dīn Sarakhsī (d. 1090) writes under the section of apostasy that "the basis for the mandate to kill is His Word, 'submit', in the verse on apostasy (Q. 48:16)." No such judgement can be inferred from its text, especially apostasy. The proofs presented by Sarakhsī and yourself are incomprehensible to us.

(a) And the proof advanced by Shahīd II from the same verse.
(b) Again Q. 2:217.

(c) Q. 5:33 does not provide an explicit proof. You advance conjectural exegesis along with deficient proofs and arguments.

(d) Q. 4:137. As no temporal punishment can be inferred from this verse, you advance a hadith from Imam Ṣādiq in which he relates that Imam Ali had invoked this verse as proof of one's obligation to kill an apostate. Because all of these proofs are deficient and lacking, you add: "Although it is possible that we may be unable to fathom the argument and proofs, it is clear that the necessity of killing an apostate is derived from this verse." You know very well that the proofs you bring forth are so flawed that they satisfy no one, not even yourself. In the final analysis, you say: "Even if one were to accept that the Qur'an mentions no worldly punishment for the apostate, it does not puncture the validity of the legal ruling because there are many detailed legal rulings derived for such issues as pilgrimage, prayers and *zakāt* that are also not mentioned in the Qur'an." You then shrewdly exit from the main discourse and pivot to defaming your critics: "Do those who clamour that the Qur'an has prescribed no worldly punishment for the apostate also reject the explicit Qur'anic punishments for the *ḥudūd* crimes, such as adultery, theft, belligerency (*muḥārib*), and spreading mischief and corruption on Earth?" You will receive a response to this question if you continue to study the rest of this letter.

"More than twenty hadiths deal with apostasy." According to you, you are relating some of the authentic hadith reports as if we were totally unaware of their existence. Since I specifically referred to and elaborated upon them in my first letter, I do not wish to be repetitive. In your discourse you bring out a sentence from the *Nahj al-balāgha*, which you then translate according to your liking and desire to achieve your purpose. In fact, you relate it twice. I will therefore bring sentences from the same book, especially hadith reports that you yourself accept as authentic. We should also keep in mind that most of the hadith reports cited were written after Ali's death. If he had a negative opinion of a handful of hadiths that were in circulation during his lifetime, what, then, should be our stand regarding the many hadith reports related by narrators and jurists affiliated with the governments and loyal to different ideological currents?

Ali puts them into four categories: hypocrites and those who are mistaken, unaware of the rules of hadith, and memorise faithfully: "Certainly, what is current among the people is both right and wrong, true and false, repealing and repealed, general and particular, definite and indefinite, exact and surmised."[26] This perspective of abrogating and the abrogated, explicit and metaphorical, and so on to which Ali refers regarding the hadith reports of his own time have also been popularised by jurists with regard to the Qur'anic verses. Muhammad Arkoun writes: "When the legislators (jurists) quarrel with each other to identify which verses are abrogating and abrogated, then their opportunistic tendency becomes evident. They designate verses as abrogated when the rulings derived from them are not in their interest and view verses as abrogating that are in conformity with their wishes and desires."[27]

He has provided an interesting example of abrogation: Q. 2:180–182 and 2:240 were abrogated by Q. 4:11 and 4:12, respectively, for the sole purpose of restricting the inheritance. This is just the tip of the iceberg, for there are many similar instances. How is it that these laws are tampered with when, in the estimation of yourself and the jurists, they are restricted to God? He continues:

> The jurists have granted themselves permission to manipulate Qur'anic verses in order to conclude that knowledge is of an inherited form in accordance with the social and economic conditions and circumstances of the period in which the earliest jurists lived. Or, to say it with greater clarity, the conditions and circumstances that were beneficial within that particular social grouping and conventions present at that time.[28]

When the scope of authority in translating and interpreting religious texts is so dependent upon human understanding (taking into account the principles of hermeneutics), why are jurists so adamant that their inferences from religious texts are from God and then do their best to impose them upon others? "Ṭabarī, when he desires to provide his own commentary on a Qur'anic word or phrase, starts off by saying, 'God says', and then proceeds to provide his own interpretation. He does not pause and ask himself to what extent his interpretation is right and in conformity with the words of God."[29]

One cannot deny the historical fact and reality that what humans pronounce as God's judgements is nothing other than their own understanding and appreciation of the historical texts. Could this not be the reason why people interpret texts to their liking and promote their own interests, albeit in the name of God, and forbid anyone to raise objections? "Contemporary Islamic thought makes every effort to deny its past history and views its foundational texts and prominent Islamic personalities as non-historical."[30]

I was not surprised to read this in your response: "No person or group has any authority or competence to issue laws for the people, for only God [has the right to] do so." And, indeed, only you and your clique have the capacity to pronounce and implement these rulings. Moreover, no one has a right to critique them.

You say: "Is it proper for us to encourage the implementation of divine laws or the Universal Declaration of Human Rights? Can the latter, which bestows freedom upon homosexuals, guarantee success and prosperity for humanity?! The protesters should either accept Islam or this charter, because combining both is impossible." From what perspective and stance are you saying this? Is it not true that the jurist's role is confined to jurisprudence (which is associated with temporal knowledge of the world and humans and linked with their demands and rationality)?[31] However, now you are rejecting laws that humans have enshrined after numerous sacrifices and a long struggle to preserve the fundamental rights, despite their being in conformity with human reason. You seem to be elevating yourself above other humans, as if whatever you utter is God's verbatim speech and that this charter is contrary to the divine will. If the charter is man-made, then so are your inferences.

In 1870, Mīrzā Yūsuf Khān Mustashār al-Dawla Tabrīzī wrote the book *One Word* and presented a copy of it to Mīrzā Fatḥ ʿAlī Ākhunzāde. This book compares the charter's articles with Qur'anic verses and hadith reports, comments upon them, and shows that there is no clash or discrepancy between them. Ākhundzade replied that most of his [Mīrzā Yūsuf Khān] inferences from the verses and hadiths are something else and, in actuality, that there is a large gap with "mainstream" positions. By this statement, he is both expressing his gratitude to Mustashār al-Dawla and informing him that such a commentary does not stand a chance or deserve to be promulgated in the midst of jurists who can label someone an "unbeliever" on the basis of the most trivial excuse. Do you think that Ākhundzāde is in the right?

"O apostate! If the legislation conforms with Islam, then it cannot endow equality [with followers of other religions]. If it is contrary to Islam, then it cannot reach the threshold to be legislated. O unprincipled one and wimp, the ones responsible for preserving the Shariʿa (i.e., the jurists) have endowed you with honor and granted you distinction. But you are tarnishing this with your own hands by saying that 'I should be of the same status and in brotherhood with the Zoroastrians, [Christian] Armenians, and Jews.'"[32]

The jurists have extracted and deduced their fallible legal ruling that accords a special kind of honour and status to Muslims, one that is superior to that of the Zoroastrians, [Christian] Armenians and Jews. Moreover, the Shi'is enjoy a higher status than the Sunnis (*mukhālif*), such that the latter are not afforded "dignity and honour, and also their lives are not sacrosanct".

How much has been written to promote the so-called virtue of gossiping and mocking the Sunnis? The five goals of religion (viz., protecting life, religion, intellect, lineage and property) are easily altered by providing jurisprudential explanations. How unprincipled and timid we must be, according to Faḍlullāh Nūrī, for giving up such a distinction and accepting the charter, for then we would not be able to humiliate, exploit and even kill those who differ from us. However, thank God that not all jurists think like you and Faḍlullāh Nūrī, that at least some of them claim that their inferences are their own, accept the universality of human rights, and resist subjecting Muslims to a false choice: Islam or human rights! Mohammad Mojtahed Shabestarī says: "Adopting and choosing the universality of human rights as the basis of social and political life in our times is, for the Muslims, not only worthy of acceptance, but rather is auspicious and a blessing and is in accord with the divine tenets for our times."[33]

Amazingly, I agree with you on the suspension of the *ḥudūd* punishments. Your classmate has elaborated on this and provided the opinion of jurists who espouse this view. Let's set aside the meaning of *'isma* (infallibility) and *ghayba* (occultation), as well as the deliberations done in the past and the present about them. It appears that those who elaborate on *ḥudūd* and *ghayba* in our times do so because the critics have lost all hope of reforming or revising the juridical decree on *ḥudūd*.

In my estimation, instead of focusing upon the validity of their implementation during the [Twelfth] Imam's *ghayba*, we ought to deliberate upon *ḥudūd* and *qiṣāṣ* under the rubric of penal punishments because such an essential element, one necessary for a society to function, cannot be suspended upon the basis of such shallow excuses. Those who advocated suspension aroused the fury of al-Ghazālī, who wrote so harshly against the Shi'is, who espouse this view (it seems that conditioning the implementation of certain judgements upon the infallible Imam's presence was very common, unlike the position adopted by Lankarānī Sr): "What is startling is that the Rāfiḍis[34] have added another condition to it: that as long as the true Imam does not emerge [from his occultation], it is not permissible to 'enjoin the good and forbid the evil'. They are so contemptible to even engage. The response to them is that when they seek recourse to the judiciary to demand their rights for loss of life or property, they should be told that 'the time for forbidding oppression and demanding one's rights has not arrived because the true Imam has not yet emerged [from his occultation].'"[35]

I do not insist that killing an apostate constitutes one of the *ḥudūd* punishments. However, it appears that you do, because in your response you proclaim that you disagree with suspending this *ḥadd* (singular of *ḥudūd*) punishment. As such, one jurisprudential method that would allow this *ḥadd* to be suspended or reduced is the principle of *dar'*, which both Shi'ism and the four Sunni schools of thought accept: "Suspend the *ḥudūd* in doubtful situations."[36] Thus, your insistence upon executing an apostate, as well as the zeal with which you defend this position, is diametrically opposed to the principle of *dar'*. In other words, you ward off and repulse doubt with *ḥudūd*!

You consider executing an apostate part of the "essentials of religion" and add further that "jurists acknowledge that there is no *ijtihād* on such matters". First, there is no specific agreed-upon definition as to what constitutes these "essentials". It appears that your weak proofs prompted you to invoke this argument so that you would not have to respond to your critics. Second, all jurisprudential decrees, of which apostasy is one, have their own history, and *ijtihād* and rational inferences at every moment can propose a change in the judgement based upon the proofs:

> Those who are deeply rooted in knowledge know that the *shari'a*, in matters of marriage, divorce, human interrelations, ornaments, clothing, judgement and *ḥudūd*, and war booty, brought forth nothing new that the Arabs were unaware of or hesitated to accept. In 'Abdul Muṭṭalib's time, the *diya* for murder was 10 camels. Seeing that this is not a strong deterrent for committing murder, it was raised to 100 camels. The Prophet did not change this number . . . The Israelites used to stone adulterers to death, cut off the hand of a thief, and condemn a murderer to death. The Qur'an retained these punishments. Instances of such a nature are plentiful and not hidden for an incisive scholar.[37]

We can pause and reflect upon historical cases, especially those that led to the excommunication of critics and intellectuals, and try to verify your claim as to whether or not it expands opportunities for thinking and reflection. Or do the inferences of those who issue such decrees, which depends upon their breadth of scholarship and the extent to which they have preserved their self-interest, create a climate of dread and fear? Some of the jurists who are intertwined with the affairs of this world prohibit people from seeking knowledge and expertise in various secular fields under the pretence that those fields are worldly sciences. These sciences are necessary for a society's progress and ought to be mandatory instead of belittled: ". . . studying medicine, mathematics, astrology, astronomy, poetry, and music and such disciplines will not produce any delight and prosperity in the afterlife and, as such, it is not mandatory to pursue them."[38] Such a mindset became an impediment for any kind of innovation or progress, examples of which in history are plentiful.

Pay attention to Nāṣir al-Dīn Shāh's telegram to the sultan: "Why do the religious scholars and people engage in such senseless and foolish talk? For instance, they view banks as evil. What kind of a stance is this?"[39] In such an environment, anyone who expresses even a slightly dissenting opinion or strives for the society's intellectual progress would be in danger of being declared an "unbeliever". For example, Mīrzā Ḥasan Rashdiye aroused the jurists' fury when he established a new teaching method and made changes to his seminary's curriculum. And yet, despite being a virtuous person and deeply anchored in his religion, he was condemned as an "unbeliever" and persecuted.

Faḍlallāh Nūrī, when conversing with Nāẓim al-Islām Kermānī, said: "I take an oath on the reality of Islam. Do not the new seminaries contravene the *sharī'a*? Is entry into such a seminary not equivalent to destroying Islam? Will learning a foreign language, chemistry, and physics not taint and weaken the students' belief system?"[40] Eventually they shut down the seminaries in Tabriz, and Mīrzā Ḥasan was forced to flee to Mashhad. His pursuit of innovative and creative options there led to his excommunication: "The most effectual outcome was caused by their excommunication of me. I was barred from entering the shrine [of Imam Reza], and thus contented myself with saluting him from the outskirts of his mausoleum. They banned me from entering the public baths, so I showered at home. While walking on the street, they would spew profanities at me . . ."[41]

This was the ambience of the seminaries wherein "religious scholars and students in Mashhad were, for the most part, treated as sacred. Books on rational sciences were regarded to be devious, and if a volume of the *Masnavī* was seen in the living quarters, others would boycott the person and sever relations with him because he had become an unbeliever . . ."[42]

The small number of jurists who also dabbled in philosophy were persecuted severely. An example of this is Mohammad Bāqir Iṣṭahbānātī's complaint to Najafī Kūchānī: "I acquired notoriety, as a result of the rational sciences, as 'a wise person who has attained mastery of being irresponsible, irreligious, and is lacking in knowledge'. As a result, I spent a life in seclusion, poverty, adversity, and indebtedness."[43]

During the same period of constitutionalism, the jurists were furious at the activities of Ḥasan Taqī Zāde and, as a result, 'Abdullah Māzandarānī and Mohammad Kāẓim Khorasānī issued a decree: "The ideology of Taqī Zāde is against Islam and its tenets in the sacred *shari'a* . . . He is dismissed from the sacred national Parliament on the basis of civil law and the *shari'a* . . . and it is imperative that he be exiled from Iran immediately. Any dereliction and slackness [in implementing this ruling] are prohibited and constitute warring against the Imam of the Age."[44] Taqī Zāde was forced to move first to Tabriz and then to Istanbul for refuge. For one year he lived in secrecy in a room with Mohammad Amīn Rasūl Zāde.

The atmosphere, which had been poisoned with acute dread and fear, is evident in an anonymous letter from an open-minded Tabrīzī to Taqī Zāde: ". . . I request that only you read this amulet and do not show it to any Muslim, otherwise my house will be pillaged, I will be captured, and my head cut off like a sheep in the same week. Be aware that all the merchants and their sons in Istanbul possess the lineage of Muslims, Satan, and unprincipled ones . . . God-forbid that they find out about us – at that time their true nature will be exposed – savages who consider shedding our blood as lawful."[45]

I end these examples with the conclusion drawn by Majd al-Islām Kermānī, who was the chair of Isfahan's seminary. Regarding the incidents that unfolded during the constitutionalist movement, he wrote: "Constitutionalism, which was totally outside of matters pertaining to religion, was made to enter into the sphere of religion . . . One reason for Parliament's degeneration was the entrance of the religious preachers. If a similar situation as constitutionalism and Parliament comes to the fore in this country in the future, then definitely do not allow the turban wearers to enter Parliament, even if they try to do so under the guise of temporary proxy. Peace."[46]

It is so painfully regrettable that even though your former classmate is ashamed of the killing of Rāfiq Taqī, he agrees with you that the individual blasphemed the Prophet. I invite you, him, and all of those who make such a claim to present reliable evidence as proofs. I have in my possession his articles and interviews (presented below), in which he attests that he has neither slandered nor defamed the Prophet. I invite all of those who claim otherwise to a debate.

You state that "this discourse is open." I used to receive a short story every month from Rāfiq Taqī, which no longer happens . . . He is no longer in this world and, for him, what difference does it make whether the doors of deliberation on this issue are open or not?

# *Rāfiq Taqī in his Own Words and in the Words of his Defenders*

## *Three Interviews with Rāfiq Taqī*[47]

### Interview 1: "I Did Not Blaspheme the Prophet"[48]

*Question:* Can you share your thoughts and experience about your imprisonment?

*Rāfiq Taqī*: The imprisonment was like a story . . . Every person ought to experience this once in a lifetime, as it was a unique experience for me. I used to tell the other inmates that anyone confined to prison for six to seven months would discover that it is a huge university of learning. Overall, imprisonment helps a person become realistic and broadens his vision. Up until now, I used to live a romanticised life. When I reflect upon the path that I have traversed, I notice that there are also other actualities worthy of experiencing. If I restrain myself from saying that imprisonment was a calamitous tragedy, it is because of this. Nonetheless, I had to traverse this path. Every person can do so and, in my case, it passed.

*Question*: Let's move to the cause of your imprisonment. At that time, you were accused of blaspheming the Prophet. What do you think of this verdict?

*Rāfiq Taqī*: I had no intention whatsoever and had not even thought of defaming the Prophet in my article. "Europe and Us" was merely about Azerbaijan's future. In this philosophical piece, I was striving to provide ways by which the country could make progress. It provided a different perspective held by a thinker. And this is not a crime, because every person has the right to express his thoughts. In the system of democracy that we have created, barring the freedom of expression is abnormal. I expressed my thoughts on the basis of this freedom that I enjoy.

*Question*: Don't you think that "Europe and Us" mocks and ridicules the Muslims?

*Rāfiq Taqī*: In that article, I only ridicule ludicrous and superstitious things. Ākhundzāde Mīrzā Jalīl Mohammad Gholīzāde and Ṣābir have written on such matters as well. If one were to compare Kamāl al-Dawla Ākhunzāde's harsh tone in his writings with what I wrote, mine would appear extremely mild. Criticising and exposing superstitious things is beneficial for Islam, because doing so allows the original Islam to come to light. In order for the jewel of Islam to be revealed, all acts of superstition must be criticised. The merit of original and authentic Islam is worthy of the whole world and would help it to progress and advance. I have lived in accordance with Azerbaijan's cultural value system and am a Muslim. I strive to implement some of the virtuous deeds prescribed by Islam, like helping and siding with the poor.

*Question*: During the court proceedings, you mentioned that you felt your life was in danger. Some of the attendees made threatening statements against you. Do you still fear that they might implement their threats?

*Rāfiq Taqī*: I think that whatever happened then is now in the past. Certainly, my writing offended the people's sensibilities, because they got incited and irritated. Some of them exploited the situation for their own benefit and made a mountain out a mole hill. In brief, my remarks had offended some people and thus I apologised to them in court. Doing so is not a repugnant act. I had no intention of ridiculing anyone in my writings; however, some were deliberately scoping the article to unearth items that they could put forth as making a mockery of Islam. This has happened to me several times in the past. Likewise, some scrutinised my article to find things that they could misconstrue as insults. They magnified parts of the article, even though "Europe and Us" is not about religion but about Europe's merits.

*Question*: How were you treated in prison?

*Rāfiq Taqī*: No special restrictions were imposed upon me. I received newspaper articles. Some of those dealing with my imprisonment had a negative impact on me. One newspaper (whose name I do not wish to reveal) placed my photo on the front page with the title: "Rāfiq Taqī Ultimately Locked Up". I said to myself, "How sad that another journalist writes like this with pride when his colleague is locked up." Such things had an extremely adverse impact upon me.

*Question*: Did you receive adequate help from your guild?

*Rāfiq Taqī*: Overall, yes. Azādlīq, Voice of America and BBC Radio supported me and gave details of the situation. I also sensed the support of international organisations, especially that of Journalists without Borders, the European Council, Human Rights Watch, the International Association of Journalists, as well as foreign embassies and their staffs. I also received help, which I am unable to repay, from local attorneys, among them Leyla Younes, Arazu 'Abdallah Ya'ū, Sa'ide Ghojamanli, Nawawlila Ja'far Ughulu and Ra'na Sa'ādat Dīn Ūrā. In reality, female attorneys made great sacrifices and continue to do so in pursuit of full freedom for journalists.

*Question*: The president [Ilham Aliyev] decreed that five journalists were to be freed, but four of them are still in prison. What do you think about this?

*Rāfiq Taqī*: I was very upset, because the pardon should have applied to all. That is, to all of the journalists and political prisoners. I very much desire that Mīrzā Sākit, 'Aynullah Fatḥallah Ya'ū, Ghanīmat Zāhid and Mushfiq Ḥusaynaf be freed. But due to some issues pertaining to them, this has not happened yet. As such, my joy is half-hearted and lacklustre. I earnestly hope that my colleagues will soon be freed. I think that they will be released in the next presidential pardon. We have competent people in Azerbaijan, but we are unaware of their value. We cannot rely merely on the profits from selling oil . . .

*Question*: In the estimation of some, Rāfiq Taqī has followed in the footsteps of Salman Rushdie. Your opinion on this matter is important for us.

*Rāfiq Taqī*: I have never thought of following his path and will never do so. I would like to continue writing about my country in the newspapers. In essence, critical inquiry has an important place in my treatment of literature. Moreover, no one can dictate to Dostoyevsky what and how to write.

## Interview 2: "Tehran 'Ālishān Ūghlū' with Rāfiq Taqī"[49]

*Tehran 'Ālishān Ūghlū' (TAG)*: Rāfiq Taqī's contribution to literature: at the beginning of 1980 he wrote his first story in a newspaper, which attracted the attention of the general public. In 1987, his book *Neighbourly Stars* became so popular that short stories excerpted from it continue to be printed in the newspapers. His *For my Enemy* (1991) and *Positive and Negative* (1996) elevated his status to that of a major short story writer and gave him a foothold in the field. From 1990 onward, he dabbled in writing political pieces in newspapers, and the public became more familiar with him. In 2005, he published two volumes containing poetry and radical stories, which signalled the beginning of his discourse with the world.

Rāfiq Taqī, this path seems a normal one from a distance; however, it seems that the reality is contrary to this appearance. What do you think?

*Rāfiq Taqī*: What the late Bakhtiyār Wahhāb said about me is true: "I am happy knowing that I am not happy with myself." In the past I did little, but felt that time was plentiful. Now I sense that there is a lot to do, but that time is limited. This is what happens. In the past not much work was done, and in all likelihood the same will apply in the future. We are so entangled with the realities of this world that even if you were Alexander Pushkin [1799–1837], you would not have enough time left to be creative in literature.

I am not crying and sobbing, and thus this should not be interpreted as a complaint. My point is the following: imagine that within the blink of an eye, three-fourths of my life has passed by. The three-fourths is a reality, and the remaining one-fourth is still unknown [whether it will transpire or not]. Death is fast approaching, and it is not known whether one will be alive tomorrow. In a nutshell, time has betrayed me. It elapses and does not care if one is diligent, and easily shoves everyone into the void. Only enlightened thinkers reign supreme over time, and such people are few in number.

On the other hand, a group of inexperienced politicians rob us of our life. Up until today, I have not seen the government backing people, but only repeatedly harassing and persecuting them. How should I say it? The government killed the dead ones, and God preserved the still-living ones. Like animals, humans are interdependent when it comes to satisfying their life's needs. Parents do their best to feed their children, and the stringent social conditions make them oblivious of what is right and wrong. When their stomachs were full, they were joyful; when empty, they cried. They never paid any attention to how a just government ought to run, and instead focused on their past conduct that had produced those results.

As such, I felt myself pushed towards becoming radical, occupied with fighting against the unknown. At the outset I wished that the time allotted to me would become longer. I am reflecting on how to recover the lost time. I am trying to limit time spent in recovering from illness [by taking care of my health]. I need to sift through my friends and reduce my time with them by four-fifths. This is not due to any animosity. I, like others, can play with and gauge the merits of the historical experiences housed within me. In essence, there are many ways to recover time, and it is not too late for one to do this. However, I do not aspire for the long life of a crow, for I am content with whatever God has decreed as my limit. These strivings are, in reality, connected with God's wishes. The purpose of these remarks is to resolve the intricacies of life with reflection and analysis . . . At this hour, the only sign that I have aged is having opted for the path of radicalism.

*TAG*: Every writer introduces new concepts and methods. Mahdī Biyāzīd, who is familiar with literature and reviewed *Positive and Negative*, said that after Ja'far Jabārlī no one has enriched the story characters in literature as much as Rāfiq Taqī has. What is your assessment of this comment? Your own contribution should be evident to you, no matter how humble you would like to be in acknowledging this fact.

*Rāfiq Taqī*: If you don't take it as a joke, I have created so many characters that I have lost track of them. In fact, I have added a few to the numerical population of Azerbaijan. For now, let the population increase [if the government does not kill dissenters], and then we can think about other things later. Let me state clearly that the characters I have created are far removed from realism, unlike the characters of Don Quixote. However, all of the events surrounding them fall within two poles – good and evil – without which life would be at either one polar end or the other. We possess freedom to that extent.

From the perspective of their composition, my characters are humanists who lead people towards ethics. Because God exists, ethics must also be present. I am always amazed that humans, in the midst of so much evil and corruption, can still cultivate ethics. However, no matter how much they value ethics, the majority are unaware of ethics. When one is occupied with the challenges of personal life, then there is no opportunity to reflect upon human rights and, as such, ethics does not enter their minds. In such a situation, God is invoked merely as a habit.

The writer's mission ought to be to strengthen those public ethics that are universal, not those that are particularistic. Ethics, in the estimation of Mother Teresa, is already empowered and universal. In her understanding of humanism, there can be no restriction or discrimination based upon one's nationality, religion or ethnicity. In contrast to our system, in theirs there is no place for apostates, *zindiq*s or unbelievers. Beheading and execution are therefore meaningless. In totality, there is no evil human being. One's society compensates for the individual's deficiencies. An atheist needs love just as much as a believer does. In my view, anyone who dismisses such views as outdated is mistaken, because humanism and ethics never become stale. Humanity ought to override the rules enshrined by the oppressors.

My Azerbaijani characters are balanced and not on the extremes. Each one of them is moulded according to a particular plan, and each story has its own unique beauty. I could comment upon the ingredients that went into crafting the short story. Naturally, each commentary would be different. In any event, there is a lot to say on this.

*TAG*: The extent to which an author has fulfilled his or her social obligation is gauged by his or her writings' relationality and accuracy with unfolding events. You pointed out in one of your interviews the path that contemporary Azerbaijan ought to follow and added that its future is linked with Europe. Many people prefer Europe because of its embrace of democracy. What specific properties do you find worthy of emulation?

*Rāfiq Taqī*: I have always said – and do so again – that Europe's achievements are actually success stories for all of humanity and that we have a right to benefit from them. Europe has been the impetus for worldly progress. The East no longer dominates Europe. Earth is inhabited by humanity in a one-room site. Any type of geographical bias would be a source of adversity and ruin. In order to end such artificial adversity, I support globalism. Let's agree to live together on this small planet. In such a scenario, no one would be harmed and all of our efforts would be directed towards healing and reform. Wars are the worst thing for humanity. We should forget about history's bullies and tyrants, whom we have labelled "conquerors" with a positive connotation. Our assessment of their historical work is wrong. I cannot believe and am totally amazed that people who are so eager to go to war can possibly create a wholesome civilisation.

I did some research on the issues you mentioned about my article. I insist upon Europe because the matter is not taken seriously in Azerbaijan. Our leaders' claims of reconciling with the West are mere slogans uttered out of habit and thus totally insincere. In essence, they are terrified of its merits and strive to keep Azerbaijan apart. A nation that is accustomed to corruption and bribery would be harmed by this reconciliation. I have advocated vociferously for Europe's merits so that we could move in that direction. At a minimum, we are part of humanity and thus have a right to do so.

In my opinion, we are at the most primitive stage of accepting human rights. We need to recognise and understand that the era of monarchs who combat humanism has ended. But the weight of our Eastern baggage still hangs over us. I consider myself duty-bound to say these things, regardless of the outward and inward pain and suffering that I have to endure. What else can we do? We have to tolerate others. Adversity for a few, if it is endured for the welfare of the majority, is commendable. Searching for an ideal paradigm is meaningless and a waste of time, for no such model currently exists.

*TAG*: Every author goes through a process of evolution and growth. One time I wrote that you had passed through the phase of realism and appreciate modernism. Now it appears that you are in the phase of post-modernism. To what extent does your literary output conform to this, and is the ongoing process evolutionary?

*Rāfiq Taqī*: Evolution is a permanent process that starts at a young age. Lately, during an interview with Qāntorālī, I talked about the change of thought evident in his articles "The Tyranny of Ataturk" and "Mullā Naṣr al-Dīn III and Ākhunduf II". I also sense a change in the quality of my work approximately every three months. When I fail to observe it, I become uneasy and upset. If this were not so and I wrote 100 short stories with the same style, I would not enjoy it and would consider myself the most wretched person on Earth. Only writers who continually evolve benefit society, for they are akin to those who rejuvenate nature. Writers who boast only about the number of their works are oblivious of their need to evolve.

*TAG*: How do your readers view you, and how do you view them? How do you come to know this? Even if your stories are read numerous times online, criticism and objections regarding them are few. Does receiving rave reviews influence you? Who is your primary audience? Are you in contact with your readers and, if so, what type of people are they?

*Rāfiq Taqī*: While I was in prison, Akram Aghlīslī wrote: "Rāfiq Taqī's only error as a writer is that he does not take into account his readers' profile."

An interesting point. If a writer considers his audience to be independent of time and his own thoughts are also not tied to any period, then there would be no need for censorship. As you know, censorship has been one of my greatest anxieties. Likewise, today's audience changes rapidly, and so how would one deal with the new one? Does a writer become outdated in ten, fifteen or fifty years? The writer's audience is not only his fellow citizens and contemporaries, but rather humanity as a whole or even the ideal person and an imagined one. Such a person would be at ease living in any era. We can say that the contemporary audience is the least of all concerns for a writer.

Undoubtedly there is some resemblance with a future audience, and this approach makes conversing with them easy and comfortable. A writer should not consider today's audience, for even without focusing upon them they become part of the audience by gravitating towards the writer's path. The status of a writer is lofty.

## Interview 3: Rāfiq Taqī: "Europe and Us" will Block Azerbaijan from Becoming Iran[50]

*Rāfiq Taqī*: . . . The tumult that resulted from publishing this article became a good fortune provided by God to discuss this issue. Even if he [Lankarānī Sr] does not like me, God loves me. Even if he dislikes some of my statements, I am happy with my actions. In his case it is the opposite: the Ayatollahs' words are pleasing, but their actions are distasteful. They portray God in many ways and present knowledge from the sources to their liking, which they then use to create fear and terror. Their actions mostly lead to the suppression of humanity.

Situated on the other side of the border, they issue a decree of death. They desire to destroy things which they had no role in making. They have deviated from the path and consider killing a person as a virtue . . . I do not regret writing "Europe and Us", and it should be reread whenever Azerbaijan is turning towards the uninformed and irrational aspects of the so-called religion.

Nowadays, people are searching for and circulating this article. I have apologised to my Muslim brothers and sisters in the past and at the court for the slip that I made in one sentence, even though it was connected with the previous sentences and did not carry any meaning in and of itself . . . In any event, I accepted my error and am grateful to them for accepting my apology, given that I had offended their religious sensibilities. I think that "Europe and Us" will remain a shield against superstitions. May it deliver Azerbaijan from Iran.

### *Notes*

1. This was taken from the publication *San'at Qaz'ati* (October 2006), translated into Persian by an Internet group known as Mubīn, and uploaded to the website Terībūn (3 December 2011) under the title of "Rāfiq Taqī: Europe and Us, Translation to Persian, Article for which the Author Lost His Life" (with an introduction by Morteza Neghāhī, titled "From Sayyid Ahmed Kasravi to Rāfiq Taqī").

On 15 November 2006, *San'at Qaz'atī* extended an apology to its readers: "Dear Readers, the article by Rāfiq Taqī, entitled 'Europe and Us', was published in our newspaper as one of the articles submitted in a series that came out from 1 to 14 November 2006. We would like to remind the readers that Rāfiq Taqī is not employed by *San'at Qaz'atī* and is just one of hundreds of authors whose articles appear in this publication. His article 'Europe and Us' is one of them. He is the sole owner of the work.

It is befitting to point out that during the period in which we published his article, Editor-in-Chief Samīr Sedāqat Ūghlū was absent due to a medical emergency in the family. In the past, this paper has printed short stories by Rāfiq Taqī, who enjoys a reputation in our country as a writer. While preparing the newspaper, the person in charge of the logistics had reserved space, as is done routinely, for him based upon his submission of short stories via the Internet. Due to this logistical error, the article 'Europe and Us' was printed. We announce on behalf of this newspaper that even though state law provides freedom of the press and of belief system, we extend our apology for its publication and do not associate ourselves with the views expressed therein. Indeed, we reject them.

Even though the editorial board is not responsible for the views and opinions expressed by the writers, once again we at *San'at Qaz'atī* would like to apologise to our practicing Muslim brethren, not only in our own country but also worldwide, in order to dispel the misunderstanding that arose due to the above-mentioned logistical error." Editorial Board (*Azerbaijan News*, 16 November 2006).

2. See at: http://www.rahesabz.net, 5 December 2011.
3. Muḥammad 'Abduh, *al-Islām wa-l-naṣrāniyya* (Cairo: Matbaa Muhammad Ali Subih, 1922), 59.
4. See the first section of the book. "Lankarānī Jr's Statement after the Implementation of the Legal Ruling on Apostasy Against Rāfiq Taqī's Legal Ruling on Apostasy".
5. Ṭabāṭabā'ī, *al-Mīzān*, 2:253.
6. Aḥmad Ṣubḥī Manṣūr, *Ḥadd al-ridda* (Beirut: Beta, n.d.), 61.
7. Ṣāliḥ, *al-Islam wa Mustaqbal al-Haḍārah* (Beirut: Bita, n.d.), 213.
8. Ibrāhīm Jannātī, *Ṣubḥ-i Emroz*, newspaper, 7 August 1999.
9. Ibrāhīm Jannātī, *Humbustagī*, newspaper, 31 October 2000.
10. Jalāl al-Dīn Rūmī, *Masnavī*, dafter 3, 1991.
11. 'Abd al-Karīm Mūsawī Ardabīlī, *Ḥukūmat-i Islāmī*, No. 13, 17–20.
12. Ibid., No. 14, 69–95.
13. Nāṣer Makārem Shīrāzī, *al-Amthāl fī tafsīr kitāb Allāh al-munzil* (Qom: Madrasa-ye al-Imām 'Alī b. Abī Ṭālib, 2000), 2:586–587.
14. Nāṣer Makārem Shīrāzī, *Tafsīr-i namūne* (Beirut: Dār al-Kutub al-Islāmiyya, 1997), 11:428.
15. Ruhollah Mousawī Khomeini, *Saḥīfe-ye nūr* (Tehran: Mu'assase-ye Tanẓīm wa Nashr-i Āsār, 1995), 14:461.
16. Ibid., 14:461–465.
17. Ibid., 21:268.
18. Hosein-Ali Montazeri, *Kiyān*, "Bāb-i ijtihād maftūḥ", No. 47, 1999, 12.

19. Jalāl al-Dīn Rūmī, *Masnavī*, dafter 2, No. 1785, see at: https://archive.org/stream/RUMITheMathnawiVol1Vol2/RUMI The-Mathnawi-Vol-1-Vol-2_djvu.txt.
20. Jaʿfar Sobhani, *Maʿālim al-ḥukūma* (Isfahan: Maktaba Amīr al-Mu'minīn, 1980), 451.
21. See at: http://www.rahesabz.net, 1 January 2012.
22. al-Ghazālī, *Iḥyā ʿulūm al-dīn* (Beirut: Dār Ibn Hazm, 2005), 1:41.
23. al-Suyūṭī, *Tafsīr al-Durr al-manthūr*, 1:169.
24. al-Rāzī, *al-Tafsīr al-kabīr*, 6:40 (Egypt, n.d.), 287.
25. Shīrāzī, *Tafsīr-i namūne*, 2:67.
26. Sharīf al-Raḍī, *Nahj al-balāgha*, Sermon 210.
27. Muhammad Arkoun, *Naqd-i ʿaql-i Islāmī*, trans. Muḥammad Mahdī Khalajī (Tehran: Ideh, 2000), 46.
28. Ibid., 58.
29. Ibid., 73.
30. Muhammad Arkoun, *Qaḍāyā fī naqd al-ʿaql al-dīn, kayf nafham al-Islām al-yawm*, trans. and annotated Hāshim Ṣāliḥ (Beirut: Dār al-Ṭalīʿah, 1998), 50.
31. Ghazālī, *Iḥyā'*, "Book on Knowledge" (Beirut, Dār Ibn Hazm, 2005), vol. 1, ch. 2, 22–38.
32. Faḍlullāh Nūrī, "*Resale-ye ḥurmat-i mashrūṭe*", in Gholamhosein Zergerī-Nejād (ed.), *Rasā'il-i mashrūṭiyyat* (Tehran: Kavīr, 1995), 161, 162.
33. Mohammed Mojtahed Shabestari, "*Bister-i maʿnavī va ʿuqalā'i-ye ʿilm-i fiqh*", *Kiyān*, monthly, No. 46, p. 13.
34. See Glossary.
35. Ghazālī, *Iḥyā'*, Book X [IX]: "Enjoining the Good and Forbidding the Evil" (Beirut, Dār Ibn Hazm, 2005), 781–836.
36. Ḥurr al-ʿĀmilī, *Wasā'il*, vol. 18, Bāb 24, hadith No. 4.
37. Shah Waliullah Dehlavi, *Ḥujjat al-bāligha* (Cairo: Dār al-Turāth. 1936), 1:105.
38. Mullā Aḥmad Narāqī, *Miʿraj al-saʿāda* (Tehran: Enteshārāt-i Ketābforūshī-ye Islāmiyya, n.d.), 47–48.
39. Ibrāhīm Ṣafā'ī, *Asnād-i siyāsī dowrān-i Qājāriyye* (Tehran: Bābek, 1976), 13.
40. Nāẓim al-Islām Kermānī, *Tārekh-i bīdāri-ye Irāniyān*, manuscript, 1970, 322.
41. Mīrzā Ḥasan Rushdiyye, *Khāterāt-i Rushdiyye*, manuscript (London: Ketābkhāne-ye Muṭāleʿāt-i Irāni), 1:111, 112.
42. Āghā Najafī Kūchānī, *Siyāḥat-i sharq*, ed. Shākirī (Tehran: Amīr Kabīr, 1983), 72.
43. Ibid., 347.
44. Eraj Afshār, *Awrāq-i tāze-yāb-i mashrūṭiyyat va naqsh-i Taqī Zāde* (Tehran: Intishārāt-i Jāvīd, 1980), 207, 208.
45. Edward Browne, *Nāme-hā-ye az Tabrīz*, 2nd edn (Tehran: n.p., 1982), 170.
46. Majd al-Islām Kermānī, *Tārekh-i inḥiṭāt-i majlis*, introduction Maḥmūd Khalīlpour (Isfahan: Intishārāt-i Daneshgāh-i Isfahān, 1977), 284–288.
47. Ghonā-ye Tabrīzī criticised the *fatwa*. He translated three Turkish-language interviews by Rāfiq Taqī recorded before his assassination into Persian and posted them on the website Jaras at: http://www.rahesabz.net. Rāfiq Taqī, who was greatly enchanted by the West, says in them: "I had no intention whatsoever and had not even thought of defaming the Prophet" and if my writings hurt the

Muslims' feelings, then "I sought their forgiveness in the court of law." The rest of the interview in Persian, along with the citation of the original interview in Turkish, will follow. Publishing this one is a step in the direction of illuminating people's minds and subjecting things to scrutiny for the intellectuals and scholars. This is all accessible at Jaras: http://www.rahesabz.net, 9 January 2012.

48. Interviewed on 29 December 2007.
49. Interviewed on 5 September 2010.
50. This excerpt is taken from a long interview from the site "Kūlīs", which is more focused on the state of literature in Azerbaijan. I have therefore included an excerpt that is related to "Europe and Us" and what happened after it was published (Ghonā-ye Tabrīzī).

# Part II

## *The Freedom of Expression and Hate Speech – by Mohsen Kadivar*

# Section 1
## *Islam: Between the Freedom of Expression and the Prohibition of Hate Speech*[I]

At the outset, one must distinguish the Islam of the Qur'an and definitive hadith reports of the Prophet and the *Ahl al-Bayt* from the Islam of the "*shari'a*" (i.e., the opinions of past jurists derived from the Qur'an and Sunna). The former enshrines the freedoms of religion and expression, whereas the latter places many restrictions upon these freedoms.

### *Restrictions on Freedom in the Shari'a*

The *shari'a* mandates the execution of apostates. Spewing insults and denigrating the sacred entities make it lawful to kill such a person. Some of the jurists endow the public with the discretion of assessing the crime and implementing the punishment. They consider it lawful to impose force and discretionary punishments upon one who transgresses by neglecting the obligatory acts or engaging in a forbidden act. Propagation of any religion and customs, to the extent that even other Islamic schools of thought as well as the philosophical or mystical thoughts of some Islamic thinkers, are viewed as harmful. Therefore, all such activities are prohibited, as are publishing books and propagating cultural material viewed as leading one towards "misguidance".

### *Standard for the Freedom of Expression in Islam*

In contrast, the Islam that relies upon the standard of the Qur'an and the definitive Sunna of the Prophet and the *Ahl al-Bayt* has the following foundational principles:

(a) Even though Islam presents itself as the true divine religion, the multiplicity of religions and customs, whether they are true or false, and even unbelief, polytheism and apostasy are accepted as realities in the world. Any judgement on their merits and truth has been deferred to the Day of Judgement.
(b) People are free to accept whatever religion and belief system they desire.
(c) No one can be punished in this temporal world for following a particular religion or belief system. As only actions can be punished, belief by itself cannot be a crime.
(d) One cannot be punished for abandoning Islam. Any temporal punishment is contrary to Islamic standards.
(e) One cannot force a person to perform a mandatory act or desist from a forbidden one.
(f) People are free to criticise aspects of Islam, and doing so does not trigger any punishment in this life or the Hereafter.
(g) Insulting, ridiculing and belittling the belief system of religious adherents violates those believers' dignity. The Qur'an also explicitly forbids insulting and denigrating the belief system of apostates

## *Insulting (Blaspheming) as a Standard for Hate Speech*

In accordance with Part II, Article 20 of the International Covenant on Civil and Political Rights, "Any advocacy of national, racial or religious hatred that constitutes incitement to discrimination, hostility or violence shall be prohibited by law." Denigrating and belittling one's religious beliefs is categorised as "hate speech", which constitutes a crime. The accused is to be summoned to a civil court in front of an impartial committee (a random selection of citizens) for adjudication. Undoubtedly, the punishment meted out would not be execution.

There is a global consensus that hate speech must be prohibited by law. Instead of negatively impacting the freedom of expression, this legal sanction would actually enhance it. The United States is the only advanced nation that regards hate speech laws as contrary to the freedom of expression.[2] For instance, the United Kingdom's laws contain various provisions that prohibit people from different forms of hate speech: hateful expressions, intimidation and insults hurled against a religious belief system. The punishment can be monetary, imprisonment or both.[3]

The failure to distinguish between criticism and insult, on the one hand, and belittling and ridiculing religion by aggressive unbelievers, on the other, has led to violence at the hands of extremist traditionalist believers and will continue to do so.

Mutual respect is an essential condition for a peaceful world. One should anticipate a harsh and extreme reaction from some Muslim traditionalists when their religious beliefs, scripture and Prophet are insulted and mocked. After all, Muslims comprise one-fourth of the world's population. On the other hand, a culture of peaceful rivalry between religion and atheism can be created, provided that a clear boundary separates critical analysis from insult. This boundary would be subject to time and place, along with the society's level of cultural maturity. In relatively closed societies many of the critiques could be construed as insults, whereas in very open societies one could perhaps categorise many of the insults as critiques. Establishing such ground rules requires serious research and investigation. In any event, only coupling respect for religious beliefs with religious freedom can bring about a peaceful and dignified world.

If religious people do not have the right to impose their religious beliefs on others, then atheists should not have the right to do so under the guise of universal conventions and customs.

Alongside the declaration of human rights, another declaration is needed: a declaration on the universal obligations and human responsibilities for those who subscribe to a religious or an atheistic worldview under a "covenant to stop all forms of violence, insults, and hate speech".

Just as believers must nullify all punishments for apostates, atheists should proclaim and officially recognise the fact that insulting and mocking religious beliefs are both criminal and unworthy acts. Both groups need to officially embrace the freedom to criticise, as this undertaking is mutually beneficial. A healthy competition is attainable through mutual respect and is the only pragmatic method to defend the adherents of all religions and ideas.

## *Outcome*

In my estimation, the three principles cited below are essential to accommodating the "respect of the believer, not the belief", on the one hand,

and, on the other, to protect belief in Islam and also the freedom of expression:

1. The freedom to criticise aspects of religious beliefs.
2. A prohibition on insulting and denigrating the belief system(s) of the believers and the apostates under "hate speech".
3. The nullification of all punishments related to apostasy (e.g., execution).

Mohsen Kadivar
January 2012

## *Notes*

1. Presentation made on 19 January 2012 as part of a research project of the Dahrendorf Programme for the Study of Freedom at St Antony's College, University of Oxford.
2. Adam Liptak, "Hate Speech or Free Speech? What Much of the West Bans is Protected in U.S.", *The New York Times*, 11 June 2008.
3. Public Order Act 1986, see at: www.legislation.gov.uk.(Endnotes)

# Section 2
## *Letter of Censure to the Jurists who Issued the Latest Judgement on Apostasy*

### *Instead of Targeting the Effect, Target the Cause*

Ayatollahs Ja'far Sobhānī Tabrīzī, Loṭfollah Ṣāfī Golpayegānī, Mohammad 'Alī 'Alavī Gorgānī, Nāṣer Makārem Shīrāzī, Muslim Malakūtī and Ḥusayn Nūrī Hamadānī,

As you are aware, after the release of a derogatory song by an Iranian singer [Shahin Najafi] residing in Germany, some [of Iran's] governmental organs sought and received your judgement that he is guilty of apostasy or blaspheming the Prophet and, as such, condemned to death. One institution announced a reward of $100,000 to the person who carries out this ruling.

The reason for our imposition here is to study the consequences and the aftermath of such rulings.

Religious toleration and moderation, and the freedom of expression and criticism are two pillars of contemporary civil society. The first pillar calls upon us to respect and therefore refrain from ridiculing and insulting the religious beliefs of the followers of every religion and ideology. This constitutes the first ethical principle of civility. The second pillar is that criticising any matter, even the sacred aspects of religion, is permissible and that intellectual religious critiques cannot, under any circumstances, be banned. However, and most regrettably, we are witnessing extremism on both fronts.

## *Two Strands of Extremism*

On the one hand, some people ridicule the religious beliefs of others on political or non-political grounds by spreading defamatory statements and abhorrent pictures. Doing so constitutes an abuse of the freedoms of expression and belief. As a result, such people offend the religious sensibilities of millions of believers. They opine that the era of religiosity has ended and that if believers wish to live in modern times, then they have to accept this situation. They mistakenly believe that the freedom to insult the believers' beliefs and the latter's endurance of these actions is a corollary of modernity. They view themselves as breakers of idols. From this perspective, the freedom of expression is limitless and without boundary.

On the other hand, some believers tolerate no criticisms levelled against their religion and belief system, and thus regard such statements as affronts and insults. They portray religion as being immune to any questioning and criticism. From this angle, the slightest criticism or dissent is treated as an act of apostasy or blaspheming and defaming the Prophet and the infallible Imams. As a consequence, the blood of such people can be shed with impunity, even by an ordinary person [male or female] who heard this supposed insult.

These people think that by making the price of criticism and dissent on sacred matters so severe, no one will have the audacity to fabricate a mixture of truth and fiction as regards such matters or to offer an opinion and criticise religious beliefs without having the necessary expertise in the field. Thus, they support killing, even by members of the general public, for this will infuse terror into the defamers' hearts and cause them to seal their mouths to prevent weakening the believers' conviction. The upshot of this view is that any person or group can hold their religious beliefs to be essential and integral and, as a result, no criticism can be tolerated, let alone ridiculing and mocking the sanctities. In other words, they have no conviction in the freedom of expression.

The first radical perspective will provide momentum and growth to the second one and, in turn, the second one will strengthen and reinforce the first one. This is why religious toleration and the freedom of expression remain unrealised. Even though the first form of radical perspective is more common in the West and the latter is mostly in the East, the silver lining in both parts of the world is the growing number of serious objections being levelled against both perspectives. Thus, there is some hope for devising a balanced and equitable perspective on the basis of religious toleration and the freedom of expression.

## *The Compassionate Islam*

The essential components of the third perspective can be elaborated as follows:

1. Even though Islam presents itself as the true religion, the multiplicity of religions and customs, regardless of whether they are true or false, as well as unbelief, polytheism and apostasy, are accepted as realities in the world. Humanity as a whole desires peaceful co-existence.
2. People are free to accept whatever religion and belief system they desire.
3. No one can be punished in this temporal world for following a particular religion or belief system. As only actions can be punished, belief by itself cannot be considered a crime because crime is defined as "acting upon or neglecting an act for which a prescribed punishment has been sanctioned in law".
4. One cannot be punished for leaving Islam for another religion. Any form of temporal punishment (e.g., execution) for doing so is contrary to Islamic standards.
5. People are free to criticise aspects of Islam, and doing so triggers no temporal punishment.
6. Insulting, ridiculing and belittling the belief system of religious adherents is an unmerited act and violates its believers' dignity. The Qur'an explicitly forbids believers from insulting and denigrating the apostate's belief system.

## *The Distinction between Critique and Insult*

Although it is an enormous task to distinguish clearly among critique, insult and ridicule, jurisprudential bases do provide liberal guidelines: if the insult is not explicit or the existing social conventions would not consider it to be so, then it should be ignored. Thus, critique cannot be equated to insult and ridicule on the basis of reason, convention and the *shari'a*. In accordance with Part II, Article 20 of International Covenant on Civil and Political

Rights, "Any advocacy of national, racial or religious hatred that constitutes incitement to discrimination, hostility or violence shall be prohibited by law." Denigrating and belittling religious beliefs is categorised as "hate speech", which is a crime. The accused is to be summoned to a civil court in front of an impartial committee (a random selection of citizens) for adjudication. Undoubtedly, and based on the principle of proportionality, the accused would not be executed.

As there is a global consensus that hate speech must be prohibited by law, this legal sanction would not blemish the principle of the freedom of expression. The United States is currently the only advanced country that regards hate speech laws as contrary to the freedom of expression. The legal system of the United Kingdom contains provisions that prohibit different forms of hate speech: hateful expressions, intimidation and insults hurled against a religious belief system. The punishment is monetary, imprisonment or both. In Germany, denigrating the sanctities is a punishable offence.

The lack of any legal distinction between criticism and insult, on the one hand, and between belittling and ridiculing religion by aggressive unbelievers, on the other, has led to extremist traditionalist believers of Islam carrying out acts of violence. Mutual respect is an essential condition for a peaceful world. Clearly, one cannot insult and ridicule the religious beliefs, sacred scripture and the Prophet of one-fourth of the world's population and not anticipate a harsh and extreme reaction from some Muslim traditionalists, despite such a reaction being contrary to that religion's stipulations.

A peaceful rivalry between religion and atheism can take place, provided that a clear boundary separates critical analysis from insult. This boundary has to be subject to time and place, along with the level of cultural maturity. In relatively closed societies many of the critiques could be construed as insults, whereas in very open societies one could perhaps categorise many of the insults as critiques. Establishing such ground rules requires serious research and investigation. In any event, only coupling respect for religious belief with religious freedom can give rise to a peaceful and dignified world.

If religious people have no right to impose their religious beliefs on others, then why should atheists have that right under the guise of universal conventions and customs? Alongside the declaration of human rights should be another declaration – one that clarifies the universal obligations and human responsibilities for those who subscribe to a religious or an atheistic worldview: a "covenant to stop all forms of violence, insults, and hate speech".

Although it is an enormous task to distinguish clearly among critique, insult and ridicule, we can generally say that just as believers should not execute and/or punish accused apostates, any insult and ridicule expressed by apostates or unbelievers should be officially recognised as a crime and as being against human decency. Both groups should formally accept the individual's freedom to critique. Peaceful rivalry based upon mutual respect is the only rational, just and practical solution to this negative and unpleasant reality.

The three principles cited below are two sides of these rights and responsibilities:

1. The freedom to criticise aspects of religious and non-religious beliefs.
2. Classifying any insult and denigration of the belief systems held by the believers and the apostates under "hate speech", and thereby prohibiting them.
3. The absolute nullification of all punishments related to apostasy, including such violent ones as executing anyone judged guilty of insulting and deriding the sanctities.

## *Rejection of the* Fatwa *on Executing an Apostate and Blasphemer*

With respect to Iran, we should state both categorically and openly that insulting the beliefs of Muslims in general and of Shiʿism in particular, in whatever form, is condemned. Likewise, insulting the beliefs of non-Muslims and of Sunni Muslims is also rejected. The Imams of the *Ahl al-Bayt* are respected by all Muslims, and for Shiʿis they hold a special place as a source of understanding religion. The believers of a particular faith are the best ones to determine if something is an insult. Art, satire, cartoons and other forms of expression do not give one licence to insult, mock and ridicule others. If doing so is a crime, then doing the same things to the religious beliefs of 300 million Shiʿis or 1.5 billion Sunnis should be considered as more deserving of being called a crime.

The gist of my position is that those who insult, ridicule and/or mock believers or religions cannot be executed. The legislature should ensure that the prescribed punishments, at a minimum, meet the global standards on human rights. At present, many scholars and Muslim researchers critique and reject the legal validity of such violent traditional religious punishments as stoning or executing apostates and blasphemers of the Prophet. A critical analytical discussion, one that contains proofs and an explanation for condemning an apostate or a blasphemer to death, was published by me as a separate treatise in February 2012. In brief, my opinion in this regard is as follows:

1. Condemning to death an accused apostate or blasphemer is void of any reliable religious evidence from the Qur'an, Sunna, consensus and reason. Rather, it is contrary to the Qur'an and reason. Moreover, due to the many perversions resulting from this decree, it would certainly be a cause of weakening and impairing Islam.
2. Only a competent court is entitled to issue such a judicial ruling, and its implementation is restricted to court functionaries alone. The decree of a qualified jurist alone does not suffice.
3. Killing an apostate or blasphemer of the Prophet is absolutely void of any reliable Qur'anic proof.
4. The ruling issued by the type of *ijtihād* practised under the rubric of traditional jurisprudence is that it is mandatory to kill an apostate and blasphemer. This is based on some reliable "isolated reports" (*khabar al-wāḥid*) and claims of having attained a consensus.
5. The ruling on killing such people cannot be implemented for the following seven reasons:
    a. *Wahn* (weakaning or impairing) Islam falls under the category of "secondary injunction" (viz., rejecting harm and promoting welfare or governmental ordinances).
    b. Any implementation of the *ḥadd* punishments, especially those that lead to death, must be suspended or halted during the Imam's occultation.
    c. As the jurist must exercise caution in matters of life and death, he cannot issue a judgement based on *muwatthaq* "isolated reports" (*khabar al-wāḥid*).
    d. *Thiqa* "isolated report" (*khabar al-wāḥid*) lacks probative force on vital matters.
    e. There has been a change in the subject matter.
    f. The evidence gathered from hadith reports is non-probative because it contradicts explicit Qur'anic verses.
    g. Reason dictates that it is abominable to terrify a person merely for leaving Islam or insulting the sanctities.
    h. Leaving Islam (apostasy) has no temporal punishment.
    i. Executing a person for insulting the Qur'an, the Prophet, the Imams, and sacred entities is an indefensible act.

## *Resorting to Qur'anic and Hadith Standards when Confronted with Nonsensical and Absurd Talk*

From the Qur'anic perspective, believers and the Compassionate's servants are called upon to disregard the absurd talk of enemies and abandon polemical discussion: ". . . And when they pass by what is vain, they pass with dignity" (Q. 25:72) and "shun idle talk" (Q. 23:3).

The Qur'an points out that believers who find themselves in such situations should be dignified, forgive the lapses of those who engage in it, and say: "To us our deeds, and to you yours; peace be with you! We seek not the ignorant" (Q. 28:55).

Under the Rightly Guided Caliphs, this practice was observed to some extent. But if we specifically look at the behaviour of the Imams of the *Ahl al-Bayt*, especially at the five years of Ali's caliphate, we will find that at the height of his governmental power his opponents were given such expansive safety and freedom that those who shouted slogans against him during the formal Friday congregational prayer service and accused him of polytheism and digressing from Islam were neither harmed nor had their social rights reduced.

Ali recounts in *Nahj al-balāgha* that a Khārijī once said, "May God kill this heretic (Imam Ali). How knowledgeable he claims to be!" People leapt towards him and arrested him for insulting the Imam. They fully intended to kill him. Ali interjected, "Be calm. You should return an insult with an insult or by pardoning the sin."[1]

If at the peak of his power he disregarded such verbal insults, then how, after the passage of fourteen centuries of progress in freedom and human rights, can one who composed an unconventional and obscene song against one of the Imams be judged an apostate worthy of execution?!

## *Unwholesome Fallout from the Judgement to Assassinate*

In addition to the many objections that can be levelled against such a judgement, issuing such a decree embroils us in multiple hardships. Some of them are referenced below:

1. The jurists who issued the ruling to kill the singer [Shahin Najafi] for denigrating Imam al-ʿAskarī are exponents of the comprehensive authority of the guardian-jurist (*wilāya ʿāmma*) and repeatedly invoke this notion

as a proof for their mandate to issue such a judgement. Your accepted guardian-jurist (*walī al-faqīh*) has explicitly stated that implementing the *ḥudūd* is restricted to *walī al-amr al-Muslimīn*.[2] The group that magnified and fomented this issue belongs to the country's military wing and the state-run media, both of which are close to the *walī al-faqīh*. They are the ones who sought a *fatwa*. Have you been assigned part of the guardian-jurist's mandate, or was this judgement issued without his consent, even though you are advocates of the concept of *wilāyat al-faqīh*.

2. How was this judgement issued without any provision for the accused to defend himself in person or via his attorney? Allowing just anyone to carry out this judgement would result in disturbance and perversion. How could this be permissible on the basis of *sharīʿa* and reason?
3. The accused resides outside an Islamic state's sphere of authority. Most jurists do not consider it lawful to implement the *ḥudūd* punishments outside their territorial boundary. The proof for this stand can be found within the hadith reports connected with individuals who fled and joined the non-Muslims. How can the jurists and judges be oblivious of this fact?
4. Undoubtedly, this particular *ḥadd* punishment for apostasy or blasphemy cannot be officially implemented in the West at present. Thus, the only possible option is assassination. In other words, the *fatwa* is a judgement in favour of engaging in terrorism to kill the person accused of insulting the sanctities. This position has a number of serious objections, among them:
   (a) It would impair and weaken Islam. Today, the wave of fear of Islam generated by terroristic groups like al-Qa'ida dominates most Western media outlets. Is your issuance of such a careless and half-baked *fatwa* designed to corroborate that Islam is terroristic?!
   (b) Implementing such a *fatwa* would require a group of followers (to carry it out beyond Islamic state's borders). It is far-fetched that you would accept this method and the destructive consequences ensuing from it for Islam, Shiʿism, and/or your own country.
5. This *fatwa* has made the singer wealthy and popular. Some of these unknown and unheard-of individuals become popular overnight at lightening-speed due to such *fatwa*s, which only encourage others to copy them. Extremist media outlets exaggerate the situation to such an extent that the formerly unknown person becomes a sensation and thus

sells countless copies of his or her work. Did the ruling against Salman Rushdie reduce in any way the insults and defamation against Islam or did it only help this disgraceful person become popular and wealthy? Did the savage killing of Rāfiq Taqī in Azerbaijan, justified by an Iranian jurist's *fatwa*, bring honour and blessings to Islam and Shi'ism?

6. Such simple-minded and absurd actions (of issuing *fatwas*) reflect a lack of reasoning and uncontrolled zeal. Moreover, it is unethical to abuse the instruments of religion to solidify one's power and then justify the resulting perversion and inhumane acts, carried out with the deceptive and fraudulent government's help, under the veneer of religion. When religion is instrumentalised in the service of state power to justify violence, interference in people's lives and impose unnecessary restrictions, it is not far-fetched that a sudden radical reaction will occur, namely, mocking religion's teachings as a way to oppose religious authoritarianism. Tying Islam's fate with the government's indefensible actions is equivalent to tying the knot with perversion. Jurists ought to pay attention to the cause instead of the effect. Demonstrate to disillusioned youth and jaded people who are weary of the oppression committed in the name of "religion" by the Islamic Republic of Iran that it does not tally with Islam. By issuing these kinds of *fatwas*, you are leading the people towards destruction. Not only does this not help attract disillusioned youth towards religious authoritarianism, but it rather repels them from the compassionate Islam as well.

   Qom houses three kinds of jurists: traditionalists who are quiet and distant from politics; jurists who are critical; and those who support the government. The first two groups ignore all requests for a *fatwa* from the government's military organs, whereas the third one, by partnering with the government, now inspires terror and a fear of Islam, thereby impairing the faith.
7. The writers of this letter can observe the negative consequences emanating from the *fatwas* on killing non-Muslims, non-Iranian Muslims and Iranian Muslims, inclusive of those who are religious and the disillusioned. We see this with our eyes and are deeply regretful and aggrieved.

We have fulfilled the obligation to deliver our message and are hopeful that you will pay heed to our counsel, which comes from the bottom of our heart.

"I only want to put things right as far as I can. I cannot succeed without God's help. I trust in Him and always turn to Him" (Q. 11:88).

Abdolali Bazargan
Mohsen Kadivar
Sedigheh Vasmaghi
Ḥasan Yousefī Eshkavarī
26 May 2012

## *Notes*

1. Sharīf al-Raḍī, *Nahj al-balāgha*, Aphorism 420.
2. 'Alī Khāmenā'ī, *Istiftā'āt* (Tehran, on his website), section on *taqlīd*, question 66.

# Section 3
## *Insulting the Prophet is a Form of Hate Speech*[I]

Disseminating the film *Innocence of Muslims* via the Internet with Arabic subtitles resulted in blood-letting and discourse around the right to insult versus the freedom of expression. The following dialogue with Mohsen Kadivar, a university professor and expert in Islamic studies, focuses on two issues: "Insulting the Prophet of Islam" and "Violent Tendencies in Islam". According to him, when confronted with criticism against their Prophet and the Qur'an, Muslims should show tolerance and pursue those who spew insults and derogatory remarks (which he considers an instance of "hate speech") by peaceful measures to make their case under the rubric of rights, ethics and protests, while abstaining from all forms of violence and by producing appropriate cultural material to refute the other side's disdainful material.

*Question*: In your opinion, do those who deliberately compose films, songs or cartoons intend to incite Muslims?

*Kadivar*: I have no information about that as regards this derogatory and low-quality film. Of late, the production of cultural items has brought forth certain problems that can be categorised as follows: the first group consists of items that may or may not be derogatory. The second group comprises items that both Muslims and non-Muslims view as derogatory. It is important to determine whether the production of such material that millions of people find derogatory – whether it is about the Prophet, Jesus or some other subject – was accidental or deliberate. Only a competent judicial system can answer this question. The contextual evidence from the latest episode seems to indicate that it was deliberate.

*Question*: Why is it that Christians exhibit forbearance when their prophets are insulted, but Muslims do not?

*Kadivar*: This phenomenon did not begin during the past few decades, but rather has existed for centuries. If someone were to make a fair, equitable and informed analysis of this issue, he would discover that Catholic Christians, before secularism asserted its dominance over the Vatican during the Middle Ages, were neither tolerant nor non-violent.

For several centuries now, the Vatican has not had the power that it did in the Middle Ages. The tolerance it exhibits today is, strictly speaking, not out of conviction but rather due to its lack of political power and choice. We should not be oblivious of this fact, although it is indisputable that there are Christian groups who philosophically see no problem with blaspheming their prophets.

An example will make this clearer. What is the Vatican's opinion on same-sex marriage? The clerical hierarchy opposes it and regards it as invalid and inappropriate, but grudgingly accepts it because its leaders have no other choice. However, in recent centuries many believing Christians have begun to peacefully express their objection to the insults and ridicule levelled at Jesus Christ by producing artistic programmes in order to defend their convictions.

The situation of today's Muslims is to some extent analogous with that of the beginning of the Christian era. Looking at the history on this issue is useful. Violence is not the solution, for what is needed is peaceful and lawful means, along with great forbearance, when dealing with their opponents, critics and defamers.

We should note that Islam has come to the forefront in the past four decades, more so than ever before in the West. The "clash of civilisations" theory articulated by Samuel Huntington, Francis Fukuyama and Bernard Lewis, in particular between the West and Islam, is similar to the Crusades. Some followers of this theory advocate destroying the competitor by any means.

Insulting the religious beliefs and destroying, ridiculing, belittling and distorting the Prophet's personality is part of this strategy. However, fortunately, the Christians and the West strongly protest these calumnies. Those that are fair treat the Prophet with reverence and respect. For example Hans

Küng,[2] a contemporary Swiss Christian priest and theologian, believes that Christians should officially recognise Muhammad as the Prophet.

*Question*: What effect does the mayhem perpetrated by Muslims and displayed worldwide have on other Muslims residing in Muslim countries?

*Kadivar*: Hundreds of millions of people participated in the protests against this obscene and dubious film. One result was the deaths of the American ambassador to Libya and several of the American diplomats assigned there. The burning and ransacking of several Western embassies and other violent acts filled the world's newspapers. Innocent people were killed. The claim that America or its diplomatic staff somehow played a role in making this insulting film has not been established in any competent court, and no proof to that effect has so far been presented. Police killing demonstrators in the Middle East is repugnant, indefensible, and against the *shari'a* and ethics. An ugly and indecent act cannot be reciprocated in kind or by inflaming and aggravating the situation.

It is better to rephrase your specific question and say that a group of Muslims, when faced with an obscene and unethical act by a group that happen to be Christian, reacted in a virulent manner. It is unfair to interpret an egregious act by one side as the act of a lone person, whereas the act of the other side is seen as the work of the world's Muslims and, moreover, identify that particular act as being stipulated in their religion. Many Western media outlets are guilty of such a reading.

When an unwise pastor who heads a small American parish organises a Qur'an-burning event, no one says that Christians as a whole are displaying a lack of civility, ethics and tolerance. Or, if a few Coptic Christians or Jews residing in America produce an obscene film against the Prophet that offends the religious sensibilities of the world's 1.6 billion Muslims, no one says that the Christians, Jews, America or the West are the culprits. Rather, one hears that a few people were involved in this particular act and thus the blame cannot be attributed to all Christians and/or Jews, or to America and/or the West, as a whole.

Following the same logic and standard of this assessment, if a number of Muslims commit a violent and unethical act that is against the *shari'a*, the outrage should not be directed towards the world of Islam or its essence, because the perpetrators alone are responsible. No one made them the global Muslim community's representatives in this regard.

If we desire a peaceful world, then we should stop spreading hate speech and abandon our double standards. Otherwise, the only expected outcome is violence. Hate speech against gender, nationality, ethnicity, language, religion, and other belief systems is blameworthy and immoral.

Moreover, such actions are now considered crimes and can be pursued through the courts. If no appropriate laws and proportional punishments are enshrined as deterrents, then lone individuals who are emotionally impacted by such actions will take the matter into their own hands and resort to violence. The law is supposed to protect each citizen's life and dignity from insults and hate speech, as well as from violence and killing. Those subject to such abuses must file a complaint with the court, which determines the culprit's guilt or innocence via the defence presented to a fair jury by his or her lawyer, and then either sentences or frees the accused. If the crime is committed abroad, the country's representatives can file and pursue a complaint at the International Court of Justice for an appropriate punishment. This method will deter violence and also eradicate the roots of insult and derision.

In accordance with Part II, Article 20 of the International Covenant on Civil and Political Rights, by which all signatory countries must abide: "Any advocacy of national, racial or religious hatred that constitutes incitement to discrimination, hostility or violence shall be prohibited by law." Undoubtedly, prohibiting hate speech directed at a world religion's prophets actually preserves the freedom of expression. The critical analysis of religion is an integral part of the freedom of expression, the observance of which would help the progress of religion itself. However, the freedom to insult is nothing more than the freedom to engage in violence. Distinguishing between insult and critique is the mandate of a just council of the court system. America is the only advanced county that provides for the freedom of religion but does not consider insulting religion a violation of that right – only a blameworthy and immoral act. Some European countries have stipulated a financial penalty or short prison term for those judged guilty of hate speech.

The problem is that this obscene film was produced and circulated in a country that treats insulting religion not as violation of rights, but only a mere violation of ethical standards. This flaw opens up a path for some unanticipated violent actions.

*Question*: Was the ensuing violence due to the insult or, as some people claim, because the essence of Islam promotes violence?

*Kadivar*: One cannot label as "violence" every act made in response to the insult. A peaceful demonstration or filing a complaint with the court is the right of any person who feels that his or her religious beliefs have been ridiculed. However, in the absence of any law to support this right – Muslim countries offer only a timid and weak response and do not search for any peaceful avenues to restore the rights – then a person or a group will inevitably feel that the only option left is violence. In any event, violence and aggression are blameworthy and therefore rejected.

I consider mockery and insult to be the root causes of this violence, and not that violence is an inherent part of Islam. As for your statement that many assert the presence of violence in Islam's teachings, I ought to say that most of those people are Orientalists who have written a lot and unfairly targeted Islam by generalising certain rulings meant to be applied under particular conditions, places and contexts. This approach enabled them to present Islam as inherently violent. In addition, the conduct of some dogmatic groups has played no small role in disseminating this particular message. For example, Salafis and literalists, whose understanding is both superficial and one-dimensional, envision Islam as physical jihad joined with political and financial power and the forcible implementation of judgements. These movements scarcely reach one per cent of all Muslims, and generalising their ideas to the world's Muslims is akin to generalising fascism and racism to the entire West or Christian Zionism to all Christians.

From another angle, violence is accomplished by power or a regressive culture. In general, it is more prevalent in countries that have fallen behind due to their own actions or forced by an external power to remain so. Backward cultures perceive religion through their own lens and provide a suitable meaning to it. For instance, Afghanis or Pakistanis might conduct themselves differently from their European or Turkish counterparts due to the degree of their discernment and insight, as well as their level of cultural advancement. If violence and aggression were inherent to Islam, then the conduct of Muslims would be similar throughout the world, which is not the case. Thus, some aspects of the culture give birth to violence.

Another point worth mentioning is that some of these incidents are connected with people's fury at the presence of American and NATO forces in the region. To interpret their reactions to these incidents as constituting the essence of Islam is a very shallow assessment indeed.

*Question*: Do the Qur'an and hadiths contain any admonition on using violence against the defamers?

*Kadivar*: I have published a detailed treatise on this subject that refers to blaspheming the Prophet. In accordance with both Sunni and Shi'i *fatwas* and hadith reports, insulting or blaspheming the Prophet would result in a severe punishment, one that can be carried out by anyone [male or female] who witnesses the insult. In that treatise, I first established that fundamentally apostasy, that is, conversion or changing one's religion is not a crime to warrant any punishment, let alone execution. Blaspheming and insulting the Prophet must be prosecuted in a competent court in which the accused is allowed to defend himself or herself in the presence of fair jurors. No individual has the right to carry out the punishment based on whatever he or she fancies as an insult. Only the court can sentence a person and carry out the punishment which will, of course, not be as severe like execution or permanent exile. The punishment should seek to make the person realise that he or she erred and committed an immoral act. The Prophet was magnanimous and forgave those who insulted him.

*Question*: Even though the number of people who meet an insult with violence are very few, governments still prefer to make no distinction between them and the rest of the Muslims. Why do you think they do so?

*Kadivar*: As I intimated earlier, until America can separate defamers from others and make the former responsible for their actions, Muslim countries can deceptively claim that even though they regret the violence, they cannot restrain their citizens' emotions.

And, as I pointed out earlier, we must not apply a double standard. If there were appropriate laws against hate speech and the West would factor in the negative outcome of circulating such films on the Internet while supporting the freedom of expression, and consider categorical insults directed at the Muslims' prophets a crime, then Muslim countries would prohibit violent acts and urge their citizens to use legal channels to address their grievances peacefully. Those who continue to oppose peaceful avenues would then be punished.

We all aspire for a peaceful world. Tolerance and forbearance in terms of belief and thought is the first condition for attaining such a world. However, understanding the limits of this tolerance requires some elaboration: tolerance for (1) other worldviews and religions; (2) when faced with criticisms of your particular religion's belief system; and (3) when insulted. What I mean here is clear-cut insults directed at the Prophet and the Qur'an, as opposed to how Iran interprets any scrutiny and critique of the concept of *wilāyat al-faqīh* as an instance of insulting the sanctities.

The first two types are perfectly acceptable on the basis of ethics and the *shari'a*. But as for the third, why would one be ethically, legally and religiously obliged to exercise tolerance? Although I am an exponent of the first two types of tolerance, but not in the case of insulting (not criticising) the bases and foundation of religion, nevertheless I, as a Muslim, consider it impermissible to resort to violence – killing, harming and reciprocating in kind – when confronted with insults levelled against the Qur'an and the Prophet, for they violate ethics and the divine law.

If there is a law against hate speech, then a person could pursue his or her case in court by filing a complaint. In terms of rights, one is prohibited from insulting or slandering a person on the basis of his or her race, gender and so on. Why should insulting (not criticising) a particular religion not be prohibited, for implementing an appropriate punishment in this regard would uproot violence. If a country such as America lacks such a law, then we should caution its government and point out the necessity of formulating one and then applying it.

I invite others to exercise tolerance in all such cases in the sense that instead of engaging in killing and violent demonstrations, Muslims should impose an economic boycott against those countries that do not conduct themselves ethically in such matters. We should give them some time so that they can feel the adverse impact of insulting our religious sensibilities. In any event, we should all know that criticising the Qur'an or the Prophet is an integral part of the freedom of expression, but that insulting them constitutes hate speech and is a blemish on that same freedom. Most importantly, the best way to oppose derogatory and obscene acts is to strengthen our cultural heritage and knowledge base under the Prophet's shadow of mercy and ethics.

## *Notes*

1. Interview with 'Abdol-Reza Aḥmadī, 5 October 2012.
2. Hans Küng, *Christianity and World Religions: Paths of Dialogue with Islam, Hinduism, and Buddhism*, trans. Peter Heinegg (Maryknoll, NY: Orbis Books, 1993); Hans Küng, *Islam: Past, Present, and Future*, trans. John Bowden (London: Oneworld, 2007).

# Section 4
## *Request for Clarification from the Jurists who Defend "Suffocating the Religionists"*

I adhere to the school of the *Ahl al-Bayt* of the merciful Prophet and, having studied at the seminary in Qom, respectfully request clarification from the eminent jurists who defend "suffocating the religionists" and intolerance in matters of religion, as well as justify religious authoritarianism by issuing *fatwas*.

Makārem Shīrāzī's opinions and *fatwas* represent the vanguard of an inquisition in Shiʿism, especially the horrific *fatwas* he issued against Dr ʿAlī Aṣghar Gharavī, author of the article "Imam [Ali]: Political Leader or Exemplary Role Model?" These are briefly and critically analysed below. It has seven sections and a conclusion: (1) the inability to tolerate a dissenting article; (2) the stance of a *marjaʿ al-taqlīd* of Qom on matters that differ from "mainstream" opinion; (3) Makārem Shīrāzī's previous opinions on the freedom of expression; (4) the jurisprudential basis of imposing limits on circulating a dissenting opinion; (5) issuing new *fatwas* to narrow the limits of expression of those who think differently; (6) other examples of restrictive *fatwas*; and (7) the difference in status between a *marjaʿ* and ordinary citizens. Finally, I tie up loose ends and provide a conclusion.

### *The Inability to Tolerate a Dissenting Article*

Shīrāzī, a *marjaʿ al-taqlīd* in Qom, has the largest number of students attending his seminary class on jurisprudence. In his capacity as the general editor of the twenty-seven-volume *Tafsīr-i namūne*, he has rendered an important service. He has expressed an opinion on the minutest issue on different subject matters, and thus it can be said that his views have dominated the Shi'i seminaries. I was born in Fars state and, during my youth, listened to the lectures he delivered from the pulpit of Shiraz's Valī-ye 'Asr mosque on religious commemorative events and read his books and magazine, *Najāt-i nasl-i javān*. Even though I am aware of his opinions on the subject of jurisprudence and its theory, exegesis, and politics, my views have never converged with his.

The position he adopted after the publication of Dr 'Alī Aṣghar Gharavī's "Imam [Ali]: Political Leader or Exemplary Role Model?" compelled me to write this brief note. The essence of the article in his own words is as follows:

> In the words of the Prophet, one obligation of the divine messengers is to appoint his successor (caliph), an undertaking that is technically referred to as *naṣb*. However, I contend that this was not done to set up a government and manage the people's temporal affairs. Prophets, and in particular the last prophet, were commissioned to remove the yoke that induced all kinds of limitations, as well as the chains of ignorance, slavery, and bondage. Designation or appointment itself has a negative connotation vis-à-vis freedom and is a type of slavery and bondage. From this perspective, it would be contrary to his mission, as mentioned in Q. 7:157.
>
> Obviously, the Prophet would not infringe upon the message that he himself had brought. This is why the Shi'is are intensely opposed to Abū Bakr's designation of 'Umar and 'Umar's designation of 'Uthmān, and consider such a practice to be in conflict with the teachings of the Qur'an and the Sunna and antithetical to the freedom that the Prophet advocated. When God has proclaimed in the Qur'an that a person can choose to accept or reject faith and even to recant after embracing it, then how could He permit the rulers to be chosen – such an important matter – without any input from the people? Thus, the message of Ghadīr from the Messenger who brought freedom, liberty, and justice was to introduce the *walī* and Imam of the people until the Day of Judgement, not to select and appoint a political leader for a short period of time.[1]

This article provides a different reading from the perspective of an educated Shi'i who has examined the Sunni–Shi'i dispute over the succession and the meaning of *Imāma*. By splitting the political mandate from the religious role model, the author concludes that no designation was made on the political front. In contrast, the "orthodox" Shi'i position is that these two domains (political and role model) cannot be separated and that they are an integral part of the Prophet's designation.

## *The Stance of a* marja' al-taqlīd *of Qom on Matters that Differ from "Mainstream" Opinion*

a. Before proceeding further, let me quote verbatim the reaction of five eminent jurists to the mentioned article:

i. The first one to express an opinion was Makārem Shīrāzī, who said during his advanced jurisprudence class session on 30 October 2013: "There was a major assault on Shi'i beliefs in one of the newspapers, with very few precedents or perhaps even unprecedented. A heinous and ugly discourse is found about the *wilāya* of Amīr al-Mu'minīn [Ali]. Even though this paper has been shut down, we should not be satisfied with just that."
ii. At the same time, Ḥusayn Nūrī Hamadānī said in his advanced jurisprudence class session: "The Qur'an contains numerous verses on *wilāya* and, as such, we should explain this matter with such clarity that no one would have the audacity to question its validity . . . Logic dictates that those who lack in expertise in this field should not intrude . . ."

Ultimately, in keeping with the counsel provided by the eminent jurists, the author (Dr Gharavī) was arrested on 10 November 2013 because the *marja*'s would not be content with just the closure of the Bahār newspaper.

b. The second phase began with the Friday prayer leader of Nā'īn, who announced during a demonstration that Dr Gharavī was "a hired foreign illiterate Wahhabi". On 21 December 2013, he, along with a group sympathetic to his views, went to the offices of the *marāji'* to seek their counsel.

i. Naṣer Makārem Shīrāzī referred to the report that he received from this Friday prayer leader and of the steps they had taken to express their objection to the insulting article published in the *Bahār* newspaper: "I was one of those who forcefully and emphatically injected myself into this subject to an extent that some complained that I was too harsh in my comments. However, I acted in accordance with my obligation. In this insulting article not only is Imam Ali denigrated, but also all Shi'is, religious scholars, jurists, and eminent Shi'i scholars of the past." He emphasised that authors who incite chaos and tumult must be blocked from writing: "The pen is an instrument that can render the best service or the worse form of treason . . . Preparing petitions by various groups to convict this person is commendable. If this action is accompanied with media publicity and propagation, then it will have the intended effect."

ii. Loṭfollah Ṣāfī Golpayegānī, after expressing his appreciation to the zealous *wilāya* supporters of Nā'īn: "Your actions merit spiritual reward and serve as an example of jihad in the path of God. For others, it is a test . . . Know that the *wilāya* of the impeccable Imams and the Amīr al-Mu'minīn [Ali] is not an issue on which people can fall short and to which they can be oblivious. Everyone must help out and not allow these people to rupture the subject of *wilāya*."

iii. Ja'far Sobhānī: "Undoubtedly, the commission of sin starts with matters dealing with minor issues. If it is aggressively confronted, then it will stop there. But if the attitude is one of indulgence and carelessness, then the issue will grow and expand. Undoubtedly, the family (of Gharavī), his father, and now his children were not religious people and so were unable to discern the reality and truth about Shi'ism. If you see them teaching the *Nahj al-balāgha*, then it is [no more than] a form of cover that they use to express their own thoughts and beliefs. Otherwise, they have not accepted it. They claim that they are with Ali in order to misguide people."

iv. Mohammad 'Alī 'Alavī Ghorgānī: "In our times, the Wahhabis and those under their tutelage and groups in the region are all against you. Their goal and policy is to work against religion. We must not fall short in defending the religion of truth."

c. A summary of the eminent jurists' remarks:

i. It is an aggressive assault against Shi'i beliefs with very few precedents; an ugly insult against the Amīr al-Mu'minīn [Ali]. Not only is it an insult against Imam Ali, but also against all the Shi'is, religious scholars and jurists.

ii. One should not be content with just shutting down the newspaper. To pre-empt chaos and disarray, such authors must be blocked from writing such material.
iii. The author (Dr Gharavī) has no expertise in religion and the history of Islam.
iv. The author and his father were not religious people and thus were unable to discern the truth about Shiʿism. The pretence for teaching the *Nahj al-balāgha* is to use it as a cover to spread their own views; otherwise, they do not accept it. They claim that they are in solidarity with Ali in order to misguide people.
v. The author and his ilk are Wahhabi mercenaries who oppose religion.
vi. One cannot fall short on or be oblivious of the Imams' *wilāya*. We should not allow such misguided people to breach this subject.
vii. Demonstrations and other actions taken by the Friday prayer leader and his sympathisers are signs of jihad in the path of God and thus entitle them to spiritual reward in the Hereafter. The media should help the people compile petitions to convict the author and then disseminate them widely to obtain the intended outcome.

d. Analysis: what can be gathered from the jurists' collective views is the following:

- One cannot circulate an opinion to the public that differs from the official view of the eminent Shiʿi jurists, for doing so would constitute insulting the sanctities, disseminating Wahhabism, and be a sign of ignorance about Islam and its history. The main impetus for doing this is that the person is misguided and should therefore be unable to find any way to circulate his or her writings. In addition, the person should be punished so that no one else would dare enter this arena. Presenting any reading that differs from official Shiʿism is the red line that the eminent jurists will not, under any circumstances, tolerate.
- Fairness demands that the following be said: not only is there no sign of any insult against anyone in the article, but the Amīr al-Muʾminīn [Ali] is consistently referred to in honourable and dignified terms. Inferring the author's intention and that of his father is ethically blameworthy and contrary to the method of verifying a Muslim's sayings and actions.

- Apparently, any opinion that dissents from the official view of the eminent jurists is perceived as insulting them and the infallible Imams. Is not the basis of such a principle a clear instance of "suffocating the religionists"?

## *Makārem Shīrāzī's Previous Opinions on the Freedom of Expression*

From January 1979 (i.e., at least two months before the [Islamic] Revolution's success) onward, each week Makārem Shīrāzī expressed his views on political issues from the perspective of religion in the *Kayhan* newspaper. He stated his opinion with clarity and forthrightness on the freedoms of expression and writing. Revisiting these opinions will be fruitful.

a. "We must scrutinise and critique ourselves before others do. Despite all of the luminous and praiseworthy things brought forth as a result of the people's revolution, it is possible that an issue worthy of criticism exists at the fringes. We should state our objections with courage and candidness and bravely rectify them, thereby depriving our enemies of the chance to say that we have brought 'another form of censorship'."[2]
b. "In this system [the Islamic Republic], all of the freedoms enjoyed under a democratic system have been anticipated, among them the freedom to express [oneself], write, and think. The only condition is that this freedom should not harm society and contradict Islam's laws. Under no circumstances will followers of other worldviews and schools of thought be pressured to change their beliefs. I say so categorically that those who pressure writers, such as (Shapour Bakhtiar) who, according to you has formed a religious wing of SAVAK, is certainly against our platform. SAVAK's actions conform with authoritarian regimes, not democratic ones like Islam . . . Likewise, those who wish to use violence, fear, terror, and intimidation to have their own say are not part of us. We know very well that the majority of people decisively desire an Islamic democracy. With such a noticeable majority, violence would not only be illogical but also harmful. Those who enjoy a resounding majority support are generally accused of being dictatorial. For this reason, we should refrain from any act that could be used as an excuse by our enemies."[3]
c. "We should be in favour of the press to the same extent that we desire freedom, justice and independence for ourselves, because the press is the bulwark of the revolution and a fundamental pillar of its continuance. Any

shackles placed upon it are equivalent to putting those on our hands and feet. We only recently escaped from these confines and, as such, striking the body of the press is the same as striking our own oppressed people! . . . I think the most clear-cut and logical definition I can compose of freedom is 'setting up and making available all opportunities and removing all obstacles that inhibit the growth of the individual and the society' . . . Freedom of the press is one of the most basic necessities for a progressive society, and every law prepared on this subject must provide for, protect, and guarantee the maximum amount of freedom. There is no need for any proof or justification, because these are inherent within the subject . . ."[4]

d. "I do not know of any place in the world where the accused's fate is determined on the streets by shouting harsh slogans and using machine guns. Or do people pursue their case in court? If it was intended that demonstrations should determine a person's innocence or guilt and issue a judgement accordingly, then what was the point of setting up the courts? Let's abolish them and, instead of deliberations, put our trust in demonstrations, which are both fun and a spectacle!"[5]

## Analysis

1. Makārem Shīrāzī was prompted to express the above opinion in response to an incident related to Mohammad Rezā Sa'ādatī, who the protestors accused of committing an act that violated the judicial system. His opponents and supporters would shout on the streets, "He must be killed" and "He must be freed", respectively. Based on the ayatollah's own logic expressed in his opinion piece above, how can he explain his encouragement of petitions against Dr Gharavī in order to pressure the court system?
2. How could he align his flowery language in 1978 and 1979 regarding the freedoms of expression and the press with his prohibitions designed to silence the religionists and pressure the news media in light of his actions during the past few decades?
3. Thinkers and scholars can change their opinions and beliefs, but only on the condition that they clarify their new stance to the public or the reader with sincerity. Otherwise, such changes are morally blameworthy. But if his above statements on democracy were motivated by dissimulation (*taqiyya*) or the intent to misinform, then it would be ethically objectionable and compounded on many grounds.

## *The Jurisprudential Basis of Imposing Limits on Circulating a Dissenting Opinion*

Shīrāzī details his opinion on "misguiding books" in his works on demonstrative jurisprudence, *Anwār al-faqāha* and *Kitāb al-tijāra*, which I will abbreviate here:

Deliberation on guarding the books of misguidance is divided into four groups: (1) the intention is to misguide people; (2) there is certainty or a high probability that it will lead people astray, even if the intention is not such; (3) there is a likelihood that it will lead people astray; (4) none of the previous three properties. The first two groups are by necessity prohibited even though the intention of the second group is not to mislead, because the possible harm ensuing is inevitable. Prohibiting the third group is not far-fetched, based on reason. No proof supports prohibiting of the fourth, however, buying and selling of such items is not permitted except in rare cases.

First, "preservation" is not the exclusive subject of the ruling. Writing, publishing, editing, distributing and other activities pertaining to the books of misguidance all fall under the same ruling. Second, the ruling is not restricted to "books", as it applies to all types of cultural products. Third, "misguidance" (*ḍalāl*) has no subject matter and brings forth nothing but immorality, depravity, the weakening of beliefs and similar issues. In any event, the most important criterion of misguidance is misleading one in the belief system. Some philosophical and mystical books were once prohibited because they were apparently viewed as misleading, and as a cause of deviation and misguidance. This was regardless of how useful and beneficial their content may have been, even though the potential harm is unintended. The Hebrew Bible and the New Testament contain distortions, and from this perspective they are counted among the misleading books.

The books of the Sunnis can be divided into two: (1) scholarly books to which only scholars can have access, provided that they do not result in harm and misguidance, as mentioned above; and (2) books distributed among the laity that cause harm and weaken one's faith. The prohibition on preserving, buying and selling such books can be lifted in exceptional instances in order to enhance knowledge about the beliefs of those who are misguided, to guide them to the right path, to defend the people against their clever and deceptive arguments, and to exercise dissimulation with them. These exceptions are only for those who deal with such issues. In any event, only as many books as are needed can be produced, and they must not be circulated among those who are not in the field. In addition to the prohibitions cited, it is not far-fetched to eliminate and destroy such books, excluding their precious covers and other such valuable things.

## Analysis

1. Who will determine exactly what constitutes misguidance? Although this question has not been explicitly answered, in the later section he says that, according to him, the conventions of the believers and every jurist can make this determination.
2. In determining whether a book is one of misguidance, the author's "intention" is irrelevant in cases where it is certain, probable or likely to cause misguidance.
3. Anything that can cause deviation or weaken one's belief is a yardstick for determining the books of misguidance. Even if the book is famous for promoting misguidance but the content is otherwise, it remains prohibited. Books on other religions and other Islamic schools of thought are to be kept away from the laity because they could weaken their belief in the right religion.
4. The many generalisations he makes on this subject are not based on clear-cut proofs from the Qur'an or the reliable hadiths. In fact, there is only one basis for this claim, namely, his peculiar perspective of human beings. In this paradigm, the laity are weak souls and, as such, can easily fall under the influence (of misguidance) the very moment they hear about other religions, schools of thought and different opinions. Thus, the only way to preserve their belief system is to deny them information and keep them uninformed. Only the jurists can study these books.
5. Recognising the truth is self-evident, and thus not accepting it is a sign of ignorance and misguidance. One can present his doubts, ambiguities, and criticisms to the religious scholars and receive a response from them. However, under absolutely no circumstances can an individual air his doubts and misgivings (i.e., a different reading or understanding) in public and thereby become a cause of misguidance.

## *Issuing New* Fatwas *to Narrow the Limits of Expression of Those who Think Differently*

Shīrāzī's website has published those of his *fatwa*s that eloquently depict his peculiar understanding of human beings, as represented in his constricted *fatwa*s on the issue of the freedom of expression. Several of these responses are reproduced here verbatim:

1. Disseminating dissenting views

*Question*: Some people have thoughts and opinions that are inconsistent with the majority of Shiʿi jurists and the jurisprudence of the person occupying the seat of the guardian-jurist (*walī al-faqīh*) of the Islamic Republic. Are they allowed to circulate their views and opinions in public so that people can listen to different opinions and then select the best one? If your response is in the negative, then how would you interpret: ". . . who listen to what is said and follow what is best" (Q. 39:18)?

*Response*: This act is good, provided that it does not constitute an adverse teaching. This potential problem can be pre-empted primarily by employing an appropriate method of presenting the opponents' opinions. In other words, their views should be presented fairly and not in an insidious and destructive manner, co-joined with lies and slander, and imputing an ulterior motive. However, you must note that the nature of the issues would make a difference – some of them can be talked about at the level of ordinary people, whereas others must be brought up in the seminary, university and learned circles because they require expertise. Certainly, the error in distinguishing between these two can cause many problems in society.

2. Critique and analysis of dissenters' views

*Question*: Some people are close-minded and prefer to follow their established worldview, for they have no desire to hear fresh things. Others like to shed more light on society by presenting the views of others (even of atheists and of those against the present system of governance). They then critique these views and pit them against each other. Keeping in mind the practice of our Imams (such as Imam Ṣādiq and Imam Bāqir) and their followers, who used to discuss with the *zindiq*s and other such groups, which method is suitable for an Islamic society?

*Answer*: As long as presenting and subjecting them to critique and analysis promotes the Muslims' intellectual and cultural progress, this method must be invoked. But when doing so creates a front for causing destruction, one must abandon it.

3. Definition of causing *ikhlāl* in the principles of Islam

*Question*: Please respond to the following questions, keeping in mind Article 24 of the Constitution, which repeatedly states: "Publications and the press are free to present all matters, except those that are detrimental (*ikhlāl*) to Islam's fundamental principles or the public's rights." (1) What is meant by *ikhlāl* and "Islam's principles"? Does the latter mean the integral legal rulings, the essentials of religion, *fiqh* or something else? (2) Is the style of the question or the new understanding with respect to Islamic issues held to engender *ikhlāl*? (3) Is there a difference between presenting the questions and new understandings in scholarly and specialised journals versus public journals?

*Answer*: The "principles of Islam" are the necessities and essentials of religion, be they in matters of belief like monotheism, the Hereafter, the infallibility of the Prophets and the Imams, and so on; or on the secondary principles and legal rulings of Islam or of ethics or society. *Ikhlāl* refers to any act that weakens the above-mentioned principles or creates scepticism, doubt and ambiguity regarding them, be it through the publication of an article, a short story, pictures, cartoons and so on.

If the intention of posing the question is to seek an answer, then it is not *ikhlāl*. But if the goal is to create doubt and suspicion in the public's mind, then it is considered *ikhlāl*. If it is a highly probable scholarly opinion reached through research, then it would not be *ikhlāl*; however, wherever the author claims certainty (instead of probability) or if the idea spread is against the essentials of religion then it would constitute *ikhlāl* on the principles.

Undoubtedly there is a stark difference between the two (outlets for publication). It is possible for a subject matter to be construed as *ikhlāl* in an ordinary newspaper but not in a specialised publication.

4. Definition of sanctities of Islam in law

*Question*: In some of Iran's Articles of Constitution, the phrase "sanctities of Islam" has been used and legal rulings have been established on it. In order to gain clarity on these articles with a clear-cut frame of reference as to applying them to the political and cultural spheres to prevent the extremes of "excess and neglect" (i.e., seek moderation), please answer the following questions:

i. What is the definition of the "sanctities of Islam"? Is it possible to define a criterion that can be used to resolve differing opinions?
ii. Is the criterion of defining the "sanctities of Islam" based on customs and conventions, or on the opinion of experts and specialists? If it is the former, then clearly the jury, as the representative of the public's thinking, can decide on the newspaper's alleged crime by defining "sanctities of Islam". In the case of the latter, reference must be made to the experts and specialists. However, a complication would arise here if the specialists hold differing opinions. In such a case, whom should they follow?
iii. Would being critical of the legal rulings or understanding of the Qur'an or the *Ahl al-Bayt* and their conduct constitute an insult? Does invoking a method of critical analysis via-à-vis the verses, hadiths, biographical literature and legal rulings that differ from the one prevailing among the religious scholars (at any given time) constitute a type of insult? In principle, how does one determine if an insult has occurred in these kinds of research? In any event, does the critic's intention make any difference?

*Answer 1*: Defining what constitutes the "sanctities of Islam" in each case depends upon the speech's context, for it might have a specific interpretation. However, this phrase generally applies to a thing that all religionists view as worthy of reverence, such as God, the Prophet, the Imams, the Qur'an, a mosque, the Ka'bah, the undisputed legal rulings of Islam and so on. In some instances, this definition might be broader and more expansive.

*Answer 2*: The source of defining is the customs and conventions of the practising religious people who are familiar with Islamic issues. In certain intricate matters, people might need to secure an opinion from the intellectuals and religious scholars.

*Answer 3*: If the critical analysis pertains to the law or the Lawgiver, then it would definitely be an insult. However, if the objection is levelled at the person who issued such a ruling or his deduction process, as opposed to the divine ruling itself, then it would not constitute an insult against the "sanctities of Islam".

## Critical Analysis

The first and second responses are double-edged. With all of this talk about broad- mindedness, it is categorically clear that some of the issues (i.e., those on which the individual and the religious scholars differ) cannot be brought forth or discussed with the general public. According to these jurists, university scholars do not have the capacity to enter the discussion. An example of this view is Dr Gharavī, who holds a doctorate in Islamic philosophy from St Joseph University in Lebanon. Nūrī Hamadānī says explicitly that Gharavī lacks expertise in religion and Islamic history. An ambiguous adverb of "destruction" (which, like its source, is unknown) permits the jurists to ban whoever and whatever they dislike.

The "principles of Islam" are defined as the "essentials of religion", which is very expansive with many undefined connotations. This further expands the discretionary sphere of actions that the jurists can invoke. Whatever the jurist (not even a consensus of the jurists) regards as "essentials" would count as "principles" of Islam, and thus any discussion of them among the general public would be prohibited. *Ikhlāl* means "any act that weakens the principles or creates scepticism, doubt and ambiguity regarding them via the publication of an article, a short story, pictures, cartoons and so on". In addition, "if the goal (of asking the question) is to create doubt and suspicion in the public's mind, then it would be considered *ikhlāl*" and "wherever the author claims certainty (instead of probability) or if the idea spread is against the essentials of religion then it would constitute *ikhlāl* on the principles". With this broad interpretation, anything that the government's reliable jurist does not like would be considered *ikhlāl*. The red line for these types of jurists is publishing and circulating such things to which the general public can gain access, although no specialised publication would be prepared to publish a matter that differs from the seminary's official reading of anything related to the beliefs! Why? Because it would instantly be shut down.

Matters that all religionists hold in respect and that are undisputed Islamic legal rulings are part of the "sanctities of Islam". "The source of defining them is the mandate of those practising religionists who are familiar with Islamic issues." With such a definition, any matter that the Muslims view as "sanctities" would be treated as such, anyone who holds a dissenting opinion would be arrested, and the publication would be shut down.

## *Other Examples of Restrictive* Fatwas

Non-Muslims are ritually impure (*najis*)

a. Shīrāzī considers non-Muslims, even People of the Book, to be unbelievers (*kāfir*) and absolutely ritually impure based upon caution: "A *kāfir* is one who does not believe in God or the Prophet of Islam, or associates partners with God. On the basis of caution, they are ritually impure even if one of them has faith in another scriptural religion, such as Judaism or Christianity."[6]

Monists are ritually impure (*najis*)

b. He considers monists (*waḥdat al-wujūd*) to be ritually impure, based on obligatory caution: "One should avoid those who believe in *waḥdat al-wujūd* (i.e., God is the only existent in the cosmos, and everything is God itself) and those who believe that God resides in humans or another existent (having entered and united with that person), as well as those who say that God has a body, for they are ritually impure. Based on obligatory caution, one should avoid them."[7]

Reason for prohibiting joining of Facebook

c. He reasons that joining Facebook is prohibited for ordinary people because it could be a means "of spreading corruption and many other types of sins".[8]

Prohibition on buying, selling and installation of satellite antenna

d. He prohibits the buying and selling, as well as the installing, of satellite dishes: "Bringing such instruments into the home is, in most cases, the cause of inciting immorality and perversion and thus is not permissible. Buying and selling them are also prohibited."[9]

e. Prohibition on benefiting from useful satellite programmes:
*Question*: What is the ruling on using satellite dishes to benefit from the useful programmes that are aired?

*Answer*: Viewing such programmes is not permissible. Programmes may appear to be apparently good or harmless; however, (in reality) they are a means to propel one towards licentious programmes. Muslims should not be oblivious to the stratagems that their enemies have set up to spread immorality and perversion among them.[10]

Avoid reading websites that are against the government [of Iran]

f. "Given that the aim and goal of these anti-government radio stations and websites are designed to lead one towards misguidance, evil and inauspicious things, one must avoid listening to or studying them."[11]
g. Prohibition on the use of Facetime: "The harmful effects and corruption emanating from the Facetime phone option would make it a new source of spreading corruption in our society. Also, there is no pressing need to have this option. As such, public and private companies must refrain from it, and religious followers should avoid buying them."[12]
h. Spreading fabricated news:
   *Question*: To what extent is it allowed to spread fake news? Does it have a place in an Islamic government if one takes into account the best interest of the government, individual and other such things?
   *Answer*: For such type of matters, one should take into consideration the most important benefits in favour of the government and society.[13]
i. The religious centres of the dervish group led by Ne'matollāhī Ghonābādī were destroyed in 2005 in Qom, Boroujerd and Karaj on the basis of *fatwas* from some of the eminent jurists. The *fatwas* were implemented by government forces. Ghonābādī pointed the finger at Shīrāzī as the main actor in this regard.

## Analysis

On the basis of Shīrāzī's *fatwas*, non-Muslims and monists are, as an obligatory caution, absolutely ritually impure. All of the following are not permissible: joining Facebook; buying, selling and watching programms aired on satellite dishes; examining, reviewing and studying anti-government websites; and using Facetime. When circulating fake news, one must take into consideration the most important benefits in favour of the government and society. In other words, this is the understanding of a Muslim who only views his fellow believers as ritually pure; that social websites, satellite dishes and Facetime are absolutely corrupting; and that propagating fake reports is allowed only if they are in the best interests of the government and society. The fundamental problems with such *fatwa*s is their basis of ethics, anthropology, and cosmology, not to mention their mischaracterisation of the contextual subject matter (*mawḍūʿ*).

## *The Difference in Status between a* Marjaʿ *and Ordinary Citizens*

It is quite an eye opener to review Shīrāzī's reaction thirty-four years ago to the objections levelled by some against the law on freedom of the press, wherein he compares the station of the jurists, monarchs, ministers, and ordinary citizens:

> I think that those who quibble and chide are relying primarily on Articles 17, 18 and 19 of the Constitution, which state that the press should be held accountable for and prohibited from publishing any material that is against the fundamentals of Islam, the undisputed legal rulings, and the [Iranian] Revolution. Likewise, defaming the station of the eminent jurists and circulating material and pictures that are against moral decency. However, it seems that these quibble mongers have forgotten that only a few days ago, the majority and almost the unanimity of the nation voted in favor of the Islamic Republic.
>
> Is there any meaning to an Islamic Republic in the absence of Islam or of a revolution that is inattentive to and heedless of all the sacrifices made? How can one imagine a regime formed on Islamic principles to have a press that would publish perverted, unethical, unchaste, and immodest material that would destroy public decency? You cannot have your cake and eat it too. If so, it would have been better if you had not voted for the Islamic Republic. If you did not vote in favour, others did. Even then, you should have attempted to convince them not to vote for it. Now that Iran has selected its path, you must accept its worldview and reconcile yourself to it. Nothing would be taken away from the press, however, now is the time for them to help build a new path . . .
>
> [If we were to limit freedom of the press,] it could be said that nothing much has changed, because yesterday it was considered a

crime to insult the monarch's majestic family, and yet today the eminent jurists and the religious class enjoy this supposed right. What a peculiar and unintelligible comparison. That family was nether majestic nor lofty or royal; rather, its members were thieves who pillaged the country and sold it to foreigners. In contrast, the godly and virtuous religious scholars rose up from within the society after undergoing a rigorous test of their thoughts and knowledge. After passing it, they came to the fore and were recognised as the society's leader. In particular, I am certain that not one of them is aspiring for and will never seek to secure an official political position; rather, they are always beside their people in a supervisory role.

. . . What is so unique about the members of Parliament or the ministers that a specific law was formulated to prohibit anyone from insulting them so that no one would dare to do so? This same law would shackle the press from scrutinising and critiquing the actions of government officials. The latter are always open to critique – and they must be critiqued. They should not be differentiated from others and should be considered part of the same law, which states that insulting and slandering anyone is prohibited and can be prosecuted (by filing a grievance with a court). This law [earmarked for members of Parliament] must certainly be abrogated.[14]

## Analysis

1. Publishing material that is against the basis of Islam and undisputed legal rulings is construed as *ikhlāl* on the principles of Islam. This is then expanded to incorporate insults to the sanctities, eminent jurists and the supreme religious leader.
2. Shīrāzī's original deduction (on the jurists' role) in 1979 in the Assembly of Experts was identical to that of the late Shariatmadārī, namely, that the *marāji'* should be free of any political responsibilities: "I am certain that not one of them is aspiring to and will never seek to secure an official political position; rather, they are always beside their people in a supervisory role." But his opinion has changed – something that, incidentally, he fails to tell us. Today, he is one of the leading and zealous defenders of *wilāyat al-faqīh*, which is an appointed position.

3. This is how Shīrāzī depicted the *marāji'*: "The godly and virtuous religious scholars rose up from within the society after undergoing a rigorous test of their thoughts and knowledge. After passing it, they came to the fore and were recognised as society's leader." Now, thirty years after the establishment of the Islamic Republic and having undergone the test, the same public opinion would not give them a passing grade. Their score on instituting the principle of "enjoining the good and forbidding the evil", defending the oppressed nation from a tyrannical government, promoting compromise and tolerance, as well as protecting the freedoms of expression and of the pen, is regrettably unsatisfactory. And if they do not attend to this matter with all due speed, they will receive a failing grade. One of the tests is their reaction to an article published by a Shi'i thinker on the occasion of this year's Eid al-Ghadīr.
4. When some of the *marāji'* like Shīrāzī interfere and proffer opinions on every aspect, big or small, such as dealing with foreign affairs to environmental ethics, economic issues to media, and internal political issues, then what difference is there between them and a minister or a parliamentarian? By the way, why does the law contain a special provision for the supreme leader and the *marāji'* when it comes to insulting and challenging them? What is so unique about them (based on the same valid proof that he had advanced earlier regarding the ministers)?
5. Have they not heard from the pulpit the repeated virtue of Imam Ali regarding how he conducted himself before the judge against an ordinary plaintiff? Are they demanding a station and rights loftier than his?

## *Summary*

1. Shīrāzī is not alone in holding inflexible and dogmatic positions on religion. Most of the traditional jurists think like him, more or less.
2. These types of *marāji'* think that Islam and Shi'ism can be defended and protected by preventing the circulation of thoughts that differ from the jurists' official view. They claim to have no objection to the dissemination of dissenting points of view in specialised journals, at the university or seminary; however, this does not conform to the reality of what has occurred since the Islamic Republic's establishment thirty-four years ago.

3. I can testify to the claim of strict censorship by advancing strong proofs. Just relating the constraints and restrictions they imposed upon me would itself constitute an independent monograph. The latest example is their treatment of Dr Gharavī.
4. The *fatwa*s of Shīrāzī and of other *marāji*ʿ with the same outlook represent the most regressive, static, fossilised and despotic rulings. These are then projected as the face of Shiʿism. According to them, Shiʿism can survive only by sealing the mouths of its critics. Such a sickly jurisprudence, one that guards and protects the beliefs of the ordinary people, would be destroyed at the very instant they become aware of a new perspective. Thus, the only option to preserve faith is to limit the people's discernment and understanding of religion and incite their emotions by striking the preachers' thighs during the commemoration ceremony for Imam Ḥusayn.
5. This frail jurisprudence, which relies upon beliefs that cannot be critiqued, bears no resemblance to the method advocated by the Qur'an, the Prophet and the Imams. Our Imams were fond of discourse, logic and debate. Despotism, force and enforcing one's personal opinion is the conduct of the Umayyads, not of the Imams.
6. Unfortunately, the classes offered by such *marāji*ʿ have the largest enrolment of Iranian and non-Iranian students. Such classes focus on cultivating both narrow and closed minds and injecting into them fossilised and petrified views.
7. The *fatwa*s of Shīrāzī and other *marāji*ʿ on the freedom of expression are a source of humiliation and disgrace for the followers of the Amīr al-Mu'minīn (Ali). Never has a school of thought made progress by inaugurating an inquisition. The same will be true for Shiʿism.
8. Dr ʿAlī Aṣghar Gharavī and his views, which were largely unknown beyond Nā'īn and Isfahan, have now attained fame both inside and outside Iran due to the inquisition instituted by Shīrāzī, other traditionalist *marāji*ʿ and leaders of the Islamic Republic. Consequently, their fossilised opinions are now compared with those of Dr Gharavī.
9. Contemporary Shiʿism suffers from the Islamic Republic's "religious despotism" and from those *marāji*ʿ who advocate "suffocating the religionists" in the name of a desire to protect the religion of the *Ahl al-Bayt*. But in reality, both of these groups are weakening Islam.

10. At one time the institution of *marja'iyya* was portrayed as the vanguard of the opposition to the yoke of despotism in the persons of Ākhund Khorāsānī, Mullā 'Abdullah Māzandarānī, Mīrzā Mohammad Ḥusayn Ṭehrānī, Mīrzā Nā'īnī, Khomeini (during the Islamic movement) and Montazerī (after 1986). However, after the 1979 Iranian Revolution, this institution (represented by Shīrāzī and Nūrī Hamadānī) became the forerunner of those who silence the religionists, advocate religious intolerance and vindicate religious despotism.
11. In his *Tawḍīḥ al-masā'il* (the section on "enjoining good and forbidding evil"), Shīrāzī adheres to the same opinion as Khomeini: "Every time that an innovation in Islam is put forth (such as prohibited acts that non-righteous governments commit in the name of Islam), then everyone, especially the religious scholars, must set the record straight by propounding the truth and denying falsehood. If the religious scholars' policy of quietism leads people to tarnish the status of knowledge or entertain a negative opinion of the scholars of Islam, then they must circulate the truth by any means possible, even if they recognise the futility of doing so"[15] and "Whenever there is a likelihood that silence will become the cause of making a forbidden act appear moral and vice versa, everyone, especially the religious scholars, must make the truth evident. In such a situation, silence is not permissible."[16]

    I humbly say that sullying the luminous face of the *Ahl al-Bayt* school by silencing the religionists, as well as by supporting religious despotism and religious intolerance, are all innovations. To speak the truth, by which I mean being free to express an opinion and to circulate different religious views, is obligatory. Remaining silent in such a situation tarnishes the station of knowledge and inspires misgivings about bona fide religious scholars. As such, it is prohibited.
12. The President of the Republic is both legally and religiously responsible for securing the release of the innocent Dr Gharavī from prison.

I hope that this brief admonition to the *marāji'* who are in favour of silencing the religionists will suffice, and that they will correct past errors with wisdom and insight so that there will be no need to engage further with this unpleasant topic.

Mohsen Kadivar
26 December 2013

# *Notes*

1. *Bahār*, newspaper, 23 October 2013.
2. Nāṣir Makārem Shīrāzī, "*10 aṣl berāy-i pīrozī-ye Enkelāb*", *Kayhān*, 10621 (24 January 1979): 3.
3. Nāṣir Makārem Shīrāzī, "*Uṣūl-i asāsi-ye ḥukūmat-i Eslāmī*", *Kayhān*, 10626 (31 January 1979): 8.
4. Nāṣir Makārem Shīrāzī, "*Sanad-i āzādī yā zanjīr-i esārat*", *Kayhān*, 10728 (10 June 1979): 6.
5. Nāṣir Makārem Shīrāzī, "*Man az dādsetān-i kull-i enkelāb shekāyat dāram*", *Kayhān*, 10760 (18 July 1979): 8.
6. Nāṣir Makārem Shīrāzī, *Tawḍīḥ al-masā'il*, section on *najāsāt*, issue 113.
7. Ibid., issue 121.
8. Nāṣer Makārem Shīrāzī, *Esteftā'āt*, see at: http://www.makarem.ir/index.aspx.
9. Ibid.
10. Ibid.
11. Ibid.
12. Ibid.
13. Ibid.
14. Nāṣer Makārem Shīrāzī, "*Sanad-e āzādī ya zanjīr-e esārat*", *Kayhān*, 10728 (10 June 1979): 6.
15. Ibid., issue 2415.
16. Ibid., issue 2416.

# Appendix 3
## *Imam [Ali]: Political Leader or Exemplary Role Model*

by ʿAlī Aṣghar Gharavī[1]

Since we believe that the Prophet of Islam was the last and therefore the seal of the divinely sent prophets, his death carries a special meaning – one that is beyond grief, distress and emotional bereavement – because his last breath inaugurated the last call from Heaven for humanity's guidance. And yet God remains connected to His servants in order to guide them to the Straight Path. However, the revelation of the realities of the cosmos and an explanation of the secrets of human prosperity came to an end. With this preface, it should be clear that the Prophet's last words merit enormous importance. As such, we should deeply probe the injunctions he proclaimed at Ghadīr, which was one of his last speeches. It is no accident that this event has engendered numerous discussions. Likewise, what I am presenting here is only one opinion among many.

One of the most important issues that the Qur'an has emphasised and sought from all of the prophets and their followers is the implementation of *Imāma*, namely, leadership from one side and setting up a community from another in order to reach a station at which the people's thoughts about life are united and they follow one Imam. According to our Qur'an, Abraham was the first prophet to call people towards monotheism and then form a community by bringing together those who shared a similar belief and thinking in terms of ethics, disposition, temperament, deeds and inclination – a community that was bonded, homogeneous, cooperative, accommodating, synchronous and contractually bounded: "When Abraham's Lord tested him with certain commandments, which he fulfilled, He said, 'I will make you a leader (Imam) of men'" (Q. 2:124).

We can gather from this verse that Abraham, given the knowledge of the words bestowed upon him, had all that was necessary to guide his society towards God and serve as its leader. Does *Imāma* only signify political leadership? For a response to that question, the above verse should be read in conjunction with Q. 5:3, which has been invoked to prove Ali's political succession: "Today, I have perfected your religion for you, completed My blessing upon you, and chosen as your religion *islam*: total devotion to God" (Q. 5:3).

Is it acceptable to derive the aforementioned meaning from this specific verse? By exploring it from different perspectives, we will search for a response.

1. The verses preceeding and following Q. 5:3 attest that God had commissioned the Prophet to convey everything that is revealed to him without adding or subtracting anything; to ignore the danger and potential harm directed towards him for carrying out the prophetic function; and to feel no dejection when confronted by the unbelievers' revolt, opposition and insubordination. Thus, given the verse's context, it appears that the blessing that was ended refers to the revelation from God (the Qur'an) and the fulfilment of Islam. In other words, now that the pure revelation, one without any deficiency or blemish, has been proclaimed to the people, the blessing upon them has ended.
2. If the subject matter of "O Messenger, proclaim everything that has been sent down to you" (Q. 5:67) was to introduce Ali as the [political] successor, then without any interruption his name should have been mentioned there in the verse because God, Who is Wise, does not delay anything from its proper time, as doing so would be detestable.
3. Specifying a verse's occasion of revelation requires that it be accompanied by many clear-cut proofs, for otherwise there will be a lack of concordance between the verses. If we interpret the verse as a political appointment, then it contradicts the instruction given to the Prophet to consult people in the temporal matters of administration: "Consult with them about matters" (Q. 3:159) and ". . . who [i.e., believers] conduct their affairs by mutual consultation" (Q. 42:38).
4. At various places in the *Nahj al-balāgha*, Ali himself underscores that political governance takes form via the public's choice to pledge allegiance. For instance, in the sixth letter the Amīr al-Mu'minīn [Ali] says to Mu'āwiya:

> Verily, those who swore allegiance to Abū Bakr, 'Umar, and 'Uthmān have sworn allegiance to me on the same basis on which they swore allegiance to them. [On this basis] he who was present has no choice to consider, and he who was absent has no right to reject. Consultation is confined to the *Muhājirūn* and the *Anṣār*. If they agree on an individual and accept him as caliph, it will be deemed to mean God's pleasure.[2]

Ali's words here clearly testify that [political] succession is not a matter of appointment from God and that the Prophet's successor must be chosen by the people.

5. Ali never asserted that it was his right to be the political successor on the basis of God's decree, which the Prophet had proclaimed to the public. Even in places where he defends his right to political succession, he firmly posits his worthiness and qualification and alerts the people to the fact that they should not err when "choosing" [the leader]. In the *Nahj al-balāgha*, the interconnectedness of "alertness and choosing" is so conspicuous that there is no room for any ambivalence or hesitation on Ali's theory on government! In addition, observing his conduct and attitude throughout the twenty-five years [of the first three caliphs' rule] and the five years of his own caliphate confirms this point.
6. Ali's conduct towards the first three caliphs, especially Abū Bakr and 'Umar, which has been recorded in many historical books, clearly shows that he did not view them as having trampled upon the Prophet's instruction and, therefore, as usurpers! His cooperation with them is so startling that on many occasions they endorsed him and showed their appreciation of him. Their mutual relationship was so gentle and kind that there can be no doubt about it. In *al-Ghārat*, Thaqafī (Shi'i) relates a report on Ali's authority: "When the Prophet completed the responsibilities with which he was charged, God (Majestic and Exalted) took him up from this finite world to the infinite abode (may God's Mercy and Blessings be upon him), the Muslims appointed two worthy leaders as his successor. They followed the Book and the Sunna and the pattern of doing good. They did not transgress the Sunna and the Prophet's conduct. When God took their souls away, He considered them worthy of receiving His mercy."
7. If Ali considered his political appointment as a divine command, would his sense of courage, bravery, chivalry and justice not demand that he

unsheathe his sword in order to implement God's command and justice, even if he stood alone?! And would it not be far-fetched for the "gate of wisdom" and the "city of knowledge" to delay the proclamation of this right?!

8. Going over Ali's apprehensions at that time on the matter of "government", which is recorded in historical works and also in the *Nahj al-balāgha*, shows that all of his objections pertained to his concern about curtailing the people's participation in the process. That is, the caliph or someone else would narrow the scope of their choice by, for instance, appointing [on his own or under pressure from someone] his successor or paving the way for his candidate to be elected. Ali's objections pertain to the process. He raised no objection as to why he was not chosen at the Saqifa; rather, his reaction was in response to other people limiting the scope of choices and that he had been unable to offer himself as a candidate to those who had assembled there. This can be inferred quite easily from his statements.

The eight points enumerated above, despite being brief and summarised, nevertheless make it apparent that the phrase "completed My blessing upon you" in the above verse means neither government nor temporal leadership, but rather the completion of the prophetic mission, revelation and proclamation of the Qur'an's message without the slightest change or distortion. It is the same completed Qur'an that can become our community's Imam and leader. This is akin to what happened to Abraham, who achieved the station of leadership (*Imāma*) and became the role model for the community because the blessings bestowed upon him became completed. In the same way, by commissioning the Prophet to proclaim His message through revelation and compiling the complete Qur'an, the blessings ended. Therefore, Muslims are now obliged to act according to the Book of God and His Messenger so that their thoughts and actions can become models for others in the community.

Ali directed all his energy towards implementing this very verse through reflection and precision to such an extent that, according to Muhammad Abduh, his conduct transformed him into a personification of the Qur'an. However, regrettably, the Shi'is act "as if they're the leaders of the Book instead of accepting the Book as their leader".

And, contrary to his wishes, they have become ignorant of his character and continuously mourn the loss of his right to a temporal government of a few days – the same government that Ali had described as being less than the "sneezing of a goat". Is it possible for him to value it as a worthless thing if it had been assigned by God and, moreover, considered the completion of blessings and perfection of religion?! Ali conveyed the situation of his time in a very learned manner and with dexterity:

> Certainly, a time will come upon you after me when nothing will be more concealed than rightfulness, nothing more apparent than wrongfulness, and nothing more current than untruth against God and His Prophet. For the people of this period nothing will be more valueless than the Qur'an being recited as it ought to be recited, nor anything more valuable than the Qur'an being misplaced from its position. And in the towns nothing will be more hated than virtue, nor anything more acceptable than vice.
>
> The holders of the Book will throw it away and its memorisers would forget it. In these days the Qur'an and its people will be exiled and expelled. They will be companions keeping together on one path, but no one will offer them asylum. Consequently, at this time the Qur'an and its people will be among the people but not among them, will be with them but not with them, because misguidance cannot accord with guidance even though they may be together.
>
> The people will have united on division and will therefore have cut [themselves] away from the community, as though they were the leaders of the Qur'an and not the Qur'an their leader. Nothing of it will be left with them except its name, and they will know nothing save its writing and its words . . .[3]

Who would consider it believable and possible that the Shi'is of Ali, whose conduct and admonition was to grasp the "rope of God" and create Muslim unity, would abandon it? In the place of precision and reflection on the Qur'anic verses and acting upon that which God has prescribed in the Book, they invoke his name with a faulty and incorrect understanding by mixing together the Qur'an and fabricated traditions. They add fuel to the fire of sectarianism and magnify differences between the Muslims under the umbrella of love for the *wilāya* of the Amīr al-Mu'minīn [Ali]. They commit the greatest injustice against the divine lofty objectives and against the most noble person, a precious jewel of the world. Although they possess not even the minutest relationality with his vision, conduct and character, they nevertheless take pride that they are his Shiʿis and are waiting to receive his intercession in the Hereafter!

This state of affairs is nothing new, for even during Ali's caliphate the people did not like to adhere to his conduct and customs. His sermons and letters show that after he was chosen to lead the government and they had pledged their allegiance to him, he was fully aware that they would be unable to endure his justice. Thus, he always reproached his Shiʿis and was offended and hurt that they called out his name but did not follow his practices and conduct. How can one even imagine that his thinking was inclined towards acquiring and preserving power?! How can one even reconcile the report that he was hankering for power with the historical reality that he knew that Ibn Muljim Murādī was commissioned by the Kharijis, who, incidentally, had previously considered themselves his Shiʿis and disciples, intended to kill him and yet neither enlisted a guard to protect himself nor punished the criminal before he acted?!

Ali was an Imam, and this was his most important role. It is this very *Imāma* that will provide leadership for the community until the Day of Judgement. He was not a political ruler for a few years in this transient world. In other words, prior to being the Muslims' ruler he was an Imam and a role model for humanity. He is endowed with leadership until the Hereafter, which makes his political role of caliph so insignificant that he could easily discard it by letting himself be murdered in order to become a role model for future leaders and rulers for all time. He was, before anything and anyone else, an Imam of ethics, honour, nobility, freedom and tolerance, justice, and humaneness; an Imam devoted to teaching others about the clear path that God has elaborated in His Book and through His Messenger. His mind was never preoccupied with the caliphate or temporal government: "I will release the reins of the camel and let it go where it wants".[4] A complete embodiment of the revelation, he wished to be the Imam of the community so that the blessing of guidance could be completed with the Word of God.

Imam Ali acted in such an exemplary manner that Muslims and non-Muslims, Shiʿis and Sunnis, have written about and praised him extensively. Thus, he has wholly fulfilled the role of an Imam, namely, being a role model for the community and for humanity. The late ʿAllāma Gharavī said in his Friday sermon on 9 November 1979 that after studying the scope of Ali's uncontested and unique activities during his lifetime, as well as his exposition and understanding of Islam's foundation, that he considered Ali "part of one of the last causes to complete and perfect the religion of Islam":

> He [Ali] implemented and showed [himself] to be a role model for the values of equality, fairness, and the freedoms of expression and thought with such diligence and earnestness that he would relinquish his right out of respect for accommodating the public's views in order to ensure that this Islamic rule would remain perpetual, i.e., a government of the people [and] for the people, and that the fate of their future should lie in their own hands. This represents Islam's distinctive and special characteristic. These accounts and statements of Ali have all been recorded . . . In this sense, the subject matter has attained completion and fulfillment and, as such, he became a part of one of the last causes to complete and perfect the religion of Islam.

Such a perfect human being is naturally deserving of such a description by the Prophet: "Of whomsoever I am the guardian (*mawlā*), Ali is also their guardian (*mawlā*). O God, support those who support him and be hostile to those who are hostile to him."[5]

If we go back and examine the verse cited at the beginning regarding Abraham's *Imāma*, we will notice that he attained the status of "Imam" after he acquired a complete understanding of the "names of God". In other words, the rank of Imam becomes actualised when one personifies and fulfils in himself the message of divine guidance and, as a result, achieves the status of a representative of God. Ali, likewise, actualised the "words of God" in himself and revealed His attributes in himself, and thus was qualified to become the community's Imam. Not only was he an Imam throughout his lifetime and during the five years of his caliphate, but he is also an Imam until the Day of Judgement, for all times and for all peoples. This is the meaning of "vital and great leadership".

One whose Imam is the Qur'an and who follows it assiduously with zeal and passion can attain the rank of an Imam for the world: "God has called you Muslims – both in the past and in this [message] – so that the Messenger can bear witness about you and so that you can bear witness about other people" (Q. 22:78). Could this "vital and great leadership" that will last until the Day of Judgement be anything other than this? Is there any relationality or homogeneity between this "vital and great leadership", for which Ali is advanced to attest and affirm its completion, with the caliphate and political leadership? Or is it just a simple congruence of words that has caused such a strange and bizarre deviance?!

In the words of the Prophet, one obligation of the divine messengers is to appoint his successor (caliph), an undertaking that is technically referred to as *naṣb*. However, I contend that this was not done to set up a government and manage the people's temporal affairs. Prophets, and in particular the last prophet, were commissioned to remove the yoke that induced all kinds of limitations, as well as the chains of ignorance, slavery and bondage. Designation or appointment itself has a negative connotation vis-à-vis freedom and is a type of slavery and bondage. From this perspective, it would be contrary to his mission, as mentioned in Q. 7:157. Obviously, the Prophet would not infringe upon the message that he himself had brought. This is why the Shiʿis are intensely opposed to Abū Bakr's designation of ʿUmar and ʿUmar's designation of ʿUthmān, and consider such a practice to be in conflict with the teachings of the Qur'an and the Sunna, and antithetical to the freedom that the Prophet advocated. When God has proclaimed in the Qur'an that a person can choose to accept or reject faith and even to recant after embracing it, then how could He permit the rulers to be chosen – such an important matter – without any input from the people?

Thus, the message of Ghadīr from the Messenger who brought freedom, liberty and justice was to introduce the *walī* and Imam of the people until the Day of Judgement, not to select and appoint a political leader for a short period of time.

O God, from the beam and light of Your Book, deliver us from the darkness, bias, blight and ruin, and infuse in us the light of conviction and awareness so that Your promise can become actualised and, like Ali, we can become role models for all people. O God, send continuous blessings upon him who is an excellent Imam for us, and what a virtuous servant he is for You.

## *Notes*

1. *Bahār*, newspaper, 23 October 2013. This newspaper was shut down because it printed this article.
2. Sharīf al-Raḍī, *Nahj al-balāgha*, Letter 6, 464–465.
3. Ibid.
4. Ibid., Sermon 3, 106.
5. al-Kulaynī, *al-Kāfī*, 1:293.

# *Bibliography*

## *Arabic*


'Abdul Rasoul, Aiman. "*Min baqāya al-turāth al-siyasi fi al-Islām: hadd al-ridda*", *Adab wa Naqd*, monthly, Cairo, March 1998.

'Ābedinī, Ahmad, "*Auqūba al-Murtadd: Dirasa Jadiadh fi al-Mulabasāt wa al-Zurūf*, trans. Hassan al-Hāshimī, *Majjala al-Ijtihad wa al-Tajdid*, quarterly, Beirut, 3(9/10) (2008): 109–145.

al-Alwani, Taha Jabir, *Lā ikrāha fi aldīn: ishkāliyya al-raddah wa al-murtaddin min sadr al-Islām ilā al-yaum* (Morocco: al-Markaz al-Thiqāfi all-'Arabī, 2014).

'Ammarah, Muhammad (ed.), *al-Islam hal huwa al-Qur'an wahda?* (Cairo: Majjala al-Azhar, 2019).

al-'Āmilī, al-Ḥurr, *Wasā'il al-Shī'a* (Qom: Mu'assasat Āl al-Bayt li Iḥyā al-Turāth, 1993).

al-Anṣārī, Murtaḍā, *Farā'id al-uṣūl*, ed. Members of the Turāth al-Shaykh al-A'zam (Qom: Majma' al-Fikr al-Islāmī, 1998).

al-Ardabīlī, Aḥmad b. Muḥammad, *Majma' al-fā'ida wa al-burḥān fi sharḥ Irshād al-adhhān*, ed. Mujtabā al-'Irāqī, 'Alī Panāh al-Ishtihārdī and Ḥusayn al-Yazdī (Qom: Mu'assasat al-Nashr al-Islāmī, 1983).

al-'Ashmawi, Muhammad Sa'id, *Ma'ālim al-Islām* (Beirut: Intishār al-'Arabi, 2004).

al-'Ashmawi, Muhammad Sa'id, *Usūl al-Sharia* (Cairo: Maktaba Madbūli, 2003).

Ibn 'Āshūr, Muhammad al-Tāhir, *Usūl al-Nizām al-Ijtimā'i fi al-Islām* (Tunisia: al-Shika al-Tūnisiyya lil Tawzī', 1985).

al-Awa, Mohammad Salim, *Fī usūl al-Nizām al-Jinā'ī al-Islāmī* (Cairo: Nihda Misr, [1978] 2006).

al-Bayhaqī al-Kaydarī, Quṭb al-Dīn, *Iṣbāḥ al-Shī'a bi miṣbāḥ al-Sharī'a*. ed. Ibrāhīm al-Bahādurī (Qom: Mu'assasat al-Imām al-Ṣādiq, 1995/6).

al-Banna, Gamal/Jamal, *Ḥurrīyat al-I'tiqād Fī al-Islām* (Cairo: Dār al-Anṣār, [1977] 1981).

al-Banna, Gamal, *Kallā, Thumma Kallā ... Kallā li-fuqahā al-Taqlid wa Kallā li-Adyā' al-Tanwir: Muhākima al-Fikr al-Misri* (Cairo: Dār al-Fikr al-Islāmī, 1994).

al-Banna, Gamal, *al-Islām, wa al-Hurriyya wa al-'Almāniyya* (Cairo: Dār al-Fikr al-Islāmī, 1997).

al-Banna, Gamal, *Khamsa Ma'āyīr li-Misdāqiyya al-Hukm al-Islāmi*) Cairo: Dār al-Fikr al-Islāmī, 1997).

al-Banna, Gamal, *Ḥurrīyat al-Fikr wa al-I'tiqād fi al-Islām* (Cairo: Dār al-Fikr al-Islāmī, 1998).

al-Banna, Gamal, *al-Islam wa Ḥurrīyat al-Fikr* (Cairo: Dār al-Fikr al-Islāmī, 1999).

al-Banna, Gamal, *Tafnid da'wa Hadd al-Ridda* (Cairo: Dār al-Fikr al-Islāmī), 2006.

al-Banna, Gamal, *Lasta 'alaihim bi Musaitir [Q. 88:22]: Qadiyya al-hurriyya fi al-Islām* (Beirut: Mu'assasat al-Intishār al-'Arabī, 2011).

al-Barqī, Aḥmad b. Muḥammad b. Khālid, *al-Maḥāsin*, ed. Jalāl al-Dīn al-Ḥusaynī (Tehran: Dār al-Kutub al-Islāmiyya, 1951).

al-Bukhārī, Muḥammad b. Ismā'īl, *al-Ṣaḥīḥ* (Beirut: Dār al-Fikr, 198).

Charafi, Abdelmadjid, *al-Islām wa al-Hidātha* (Tunisia: al-Dār al-Tunisiyya fi al-Nashr, 1991).

Charafi, Abdelmadjid, *al-Islam bayn al-Risālah wa al-Tārikh* (Beirut: Dār-al-Talī'a, 2001).

Charfi, Mohamed, *al-Islam wa al-hurriyya: sū' tafāhum al-tārikhī* (Damascus: Dār Petra, 2002).

Dār al-Quṭnī, 'Alī b. 'Amr, *al-Sunan*, ed. Majdī b. Manṣūr b. Sayyid al-Shūrā (Beirut: Dār al-Kutub al-'Ilmiyya, 1996).

al-Daylamī, Sallār, al-Marāsim al-'alawiyya fi-l-aḥkām al-nabawiyya, ed. Mahmūd Bustānī (Qom: Haramayn, 1984).

Ennaifer, Hmida, "*Min al-Riddah ilā al-Imān ilā wa'i al-Tanāqud*", *Al-Hawār*, quarterly, Beirut, 2(7) (1987): 71–78 .

Fadlallah, Muhammad Hussein, *Qarā'ah Islāmiyya sari'ah li mafhumai al-hurriyya wa al-dimuqrātiyya fi jānib al-fikrī al-hidāri*, *al-Muntalq*, Islamic Union of Lebanese Students, No. 65, Beirut, 4–21, *Azadi va democracy: qarā'ti Eslāmi*, trans. to Persian Majid Moradi, *Majalleh Oloum Siyāsi* 1(3) (Qom, 1999).

Fathi 'Uthmān, Muhammad, *al-Fikr al-Islami wa al-Tatawwur*, 2nd edn (Kuwait: al-Dār al-Kuwaitiyya, 1969).

Fathi 'Uthmān, Muhammad, *Huqūq al-Insān bayn al-Sharia wa al-Qānūn al-Gharbī* (Cairo: Dār al-Shurūq, 1982).

Fāzel Lankarānī, Mohammad (Lankarānī Sr), *Tafṣīl al-sharī'a fī sharḥ Taḥrīr al-wasīla* (Qom: Markaz-i Fiqh al-A'immat al-Aṭhār, "Kitab al-amr bi-l-ma'rūf wa-l-nahī 'an al-munkar", 2009), "Kitab al-ḥudūd", 2006.

Ghannouchi, Rached, *al-Hurriyāt al-'Āmma fī al-Dawla al-Islāmiyya* (Beirut: Markaz Dirāsāt al-wahda al-Islāmiyya, 1993).

al-Ghazālī, Abū Ḥāmid Muḥammad, *Iḥyā 'ulūm al-dīn*, ed. 'Abd al-'Azīz 'Izz al-Dīn Sayrawān (Beirut: Dār Iḥyā al-'Ulūm, 1990; Beirut: Dār Ibn Hazm, 2005).

al-Ghazālī, Muḥammad, *Huqūq al-Insān bayn Ta'līm al-Islām and I'lān al-Umam al-Muttahidah* (Cairo: Nihda Misr, 1963).

Golpāyegāni, Mohammad Rezā Mousawī, *Taqrīrāt al-ḥudūd wa-l-ta'zīrāt*, transcribed Muḥammad Hādī al-Muqaddas al-Najafī (Qom: n.d.).

Golpāyegāni, Mohammad Rezā Mousawī, *al-Durr al-mandūd fī ahkām al-hudūd*, transcribed 'Ali Karīmī Jahromī (Qom: Dār al-Qur'an al-Karīm, 1996).

Gomaa, Ali, *al-Bayan limā yashghil al-Azhān* (Cairo: al-Maqtam, 2005).

Grami, Amel, *Qadiyya al-Ridda fī al-Fikr al-Islāmī al-Hadīth* (Tunisia: Dār al-junūb lil-Nashr, 1996).

al-Ḥalabī, Abū al-Ṣalāḥ, *Al-Kāfī fī al-fiqh*, ed. Riḍā Ustādī (Isfahan: Maktabat al-Imam Amīr al-Mu'minīn al-Āmma, 1982/3).

al-Ḥalabī, 'Alī b. al-Ḥasan b. Abī al-Majd, *Ishārat al-sabq*, ed. Ibrāhīm al-Bahādurī (Qom: Mu'assasat al-Nashr al-Islāmī, 1994).

al-Ḥalabī, Abū al-Makārim 'Izz al-Dīn Ḥamza b. 'Alī b. Zuhra, *Ghunyat al-nuzū'*, ed. Ibrāhīm al-Bahādurī (Qom: Mu'assasa Imām al-Ṣādiq, 1996).

Hassan, Hassan Ibrāhim, *Tārikh al-Islām al-siyāsī wa al-dīnī wa al-thiqāfī wa al-ijtimā'ī* (Cairo: Maktaba al-Nihda al-Misriyya, 1996).

al-Haythami, Ali b. Abi Bakr, Majma' al-zawa'id wa manba' al-fawā'id, ed. Muḥammad 'Abd al-Qādir Aḥmad 'Aṭā (Beirut: Dar al-Kutub al-'Ilmiyya, 2001), 6:261.

al-Ḥillī, Ḥasan b. Yūsuf b. al-Muṭahhar ('Allāma), *Mukhtalaf al-Shī'a* (Qom: Mu'assasat al-Nashr al-Islāmī, 1992).

al-Ḥillī, Ḥasan b. Yūsuf b. al-Muṭahhar, *Taḥrīr al-aḥkām al-shar'īyya*, ed. Ibrāhīm al-Bahādurī (Qom: Mu'assasa Imām al-Ṣādiq, 1999).

al-Ḥillī, Ḥasan b. Yūsuf b. al-Muṭahhar, *Muntahā al-maṭlab* (Mashhad: Majma' Buḥūth al-Islāmiyya, 2007).

al-Ḥillī, Ḥusayn, *Dalīl al-'urwat al-wuthqā*, ed. and annotated Ḥasan Sa'īd Tehrānī (Najaf: n.p., 1962).
al-Ḥillī, Ibn Fahd, *Muhadhdhab al-bāri' fī sharḥ al-Mukhtaṣar al-nāfi'*, ed. Mujtabā al-'Irāqī (Qom: Mu'assasat al-Nashr al-Islāmī, 1987).
al-Ḥillī, Ibn Idrīs, *al-Sarā'ir al-ḥāwī li-l-taḥrīr al-fatāwā* (Qom: Mu'assasat al-Nashr al-Islāmī, 1989).
al-Ḥillī, Ja'far b. Ḥasan (Muḥaqqiq), *Sharā'i' al-Islām*, ed. al-Sayyid Ṣādiq al-Shīrāzī (Tehran: Istiqlāl, 1989).
al-Ḥillī, Ja'far b. Ḥasan (Muḥaqqiq). *Al-Mukhtaṣar al-nāfi'* (Tehran: Mu'assasat al-Bi'tha, 1990).
al-Ḥillī, Yaḥyā b. Sa'īd, *al-Jāmi' li-l-sharā'i'*, ed. Ja'far Sobhani (Qom: Mu'assasa Sayyid al-Shuhadā', 1985).
al-Hindī, Fāḍil Muḥammad b. Ḥasan, *Kashf al-lithām fī sharḥ Qawā'id al-aḥkām* (Qom: Mu'assasat al-Nashr al- Islāmī, 1995).
al-Ḥimyarī, 'Abdulla b. Ja'far, *Qurb al-isnād* (Qom: Mu'assasa Āl al-Bayt li Iḥyā' al-Turāth, 1993).
Ibn al-Barrāj, Qāḍī 'Abd al-'Azīz, *al-Muhadhdhab* (Qom: Mu'assasat al-Nashr al-Islāmī, 1986).
al-'īlī, Abdul Hakīm Hassan, *al-Hurriyāt al-'Āmma fī al-Fikr wa al-Niżām al-Siyāsī fī al-Islām* (Cairo: Dār al-Fikr al-'Arabī, 1983).
al Jabri, Mohammed Abed, *Dimqrātiyya wa huqūq al- insān, Kitāb fī Jarida* (Beirut: UNESCO, 1994), No. 94.
Jāwīsh, 'Abdul'Azīz, *al-Islam dīn al-Fitrah wa al-Hurriyah* (Cairo, Dār al-Kitāb al-Misrī, 2011).
al-Khālisī, Muhammad, *al-Islām sabīl al-sa'ādah wa al-salām* (Beirut: al-Mu'assisa al-Islamiyya lil-Nashr, 1987).
al-Khashin, Hussain Ahmad, *al-Fiqh al-janā'i fī al-Islām, al-ridda numūzijan* (Beirut: Mu'assisa al-Intishār al-'Arabī, 2015).
al-Karakī, 'Alī b. Ḥusayn (Muḥaqqiq Karakī), *Rasā'il*, ed. Muḥammad al-Ḥasūn (Qom: Maktabat al-Mar'ashī al-Najafī, 1988).
Khāmena'ī, 'Alī, *Durar al-fawā'id fī ajwibat al-qā'id* (Beirut: Dār al-Wasīla, 1992).
Khāmena'ī, 'Alī, *Ajwibat al-istiftā'āt* (Beirut: Dār al-Ḥaqq, 1995).
Khomeini, Ruhollah Mousawī, *Taḥrīr al-wasīla* (Damascus: Iranian Embassy in Syria, 1998).
al-Khū'ī, Abū al-Qāsim, *al-Bayān fī tafsīr al-Qur'ān* (Beirut: Dār al-Zahrā', 1975).

al-Khū'ī, Abū al-Qāsim, *Mabānī takmilat al-minhāj* (Najaf: Mu'assasat al-Khū'ī al-Islāmiyya, 1976).
al-Khū'ī, Abū al-Qāsim, *al-Tanqīḥ fī sharḥ 'al-'Urwat al-wuthqā'*, transcribed al-Mīrzā 'Alī al-Gharawī al-Tabrīzī (Qom: Dār al-Ḥādī li-l-Maṭbū'āt, 1990).
al-Khū'ī, Abū al-Qāsim, *Mu'jam al-rijāl al-ḥadīth wa tafṣīl ṭabaqāt al-ruwāt* (Najaf: Mu'assasat al-Imām al-Khū'ī, 1993).
al-Khū'ī, Abū al-Qāsim, *Mustanad al-'Urwat al-wuthqā*, transcribed Murtazā Boroujerdi (Qom: Manshūrāt Madrasa Dār al-'Ilm, 1993).
al-Khurāsānī, Muḥammad Kāẓim, *Kifāyat al-'uṣūl* (Qom: Mu'assasa Āl al-Bayt li Iḥyā al-Turāth, 1989).
Khwānsārī, Aḥmad, *Jāmi'al-madārik fī sharh al-mukhtasar al-nāfi'*, ed. 'Alī Akbar al-Ghaffārī (Tehran: Maktabat al-Ṣadūq, 1976–81).
al-Kulaynī, Muḥammad b. Ya'qūb, *al-Kāfī*, ed. 'Alī Akbar al-Ghaffārī (Tehran: Dār al-Kutub al-Islāmiyya, 1968).
al-Mahdi, Sadiq, *Nahw-i Marja'iyya Islāmiyya Mutijaddida* (Cairo: Maktaba al-Shurūq al-Dawliyya, 2006).
al-Majlisī, Muḥammad Bāqir, *Mir'āt al-'uqūl fī sharḥ akhbār Āl al-Rasūl* (Tehran: Dār al-Kutub al-Islāmiyya, 1984).
al-Majlisī, Muḥammad Bāqir, *Malādh al-akhyār fī fahm tahdhīb al-akhbār*, ed. Mahdī al-Rajā'ī (Qom: Maktabat al-Mar'ashī al-'Āmma, 1986).
Makārim al-Shīrāzī, Nāṣer, *al-Amthāl fī tafsīr kitāb Allāh al-munzil* (Qom: Madrasa-ye al-Imām 'Alī b. Abī Ṭālib, 2000).
Mansour, Ahmad Subhi, *Hadd al-Ridda* (Beirut: Mu'ssisa al-Fikr al-'Arabi, 2008).
Manūn, 'Isā, "*Hukm al-Murtadd fī al-Sharī'a al-Islāmiyya*", *Majjala al-Azhar*, Cairo, March–April 1956.
al-Montazeri Najaf Ābādi, Hossein-Ali, *Dirāsāt fī wilāyat al-faqih wa fiqh al-dawlah al-Islāmiyya* (Qom: Markaz al-I'lām al-Islāmi, 1988).
Morvarīd, Ali Asghar (ed.), *Silsilah al-Yanābī' al-Fiqhiyya*, vol. 9 (Beirut: Mu'assisi Fiqh al-Shi'a, 1990).
al-Mufīd, Muḥammad b. Muḥammad b. Nu'mān, *al-Muqni'a* (Qom: Mu'assasat al-Nashr al-Islāmī, 1990).
Āl Mursī, Fārūq Ibn 'Abdul-'Aleem, *Fiqh al-Hudūd fī al-Sharī'a al-Islāmiyya: Jarimah al-Riddah: Dirāsa tafsīlīyyah lil-Jarimah wa al-'Uqubah wa Ahkām al-Qadā' al-Misrī al-Mu'āsir* (Egypt: Dār al-Falaḥ lil-Baḥth al-'Ilmī wa-Taḥqīq al-Turāth, 2008).

Murtaḍā, 'Alī b. al-Ḥusayn ('Alam al-Hudā), *al-Intiṣār* (Qom: Mu'assasat al-Nashr al-Islāmī, 1995).

Mutawalli, Abdul-Hamid, *Mabādi Nizām al-Hukm fi al-Islam ma'a al-Muqārana bil-Mubtada al-Dastūryya* (Alexandria: al-Ma'ārif, 1978).

Mousawi Ardebili, Abdul-Karim, *Fiqh al-ḥudūd wa al-ta'zīrāt* (Qom: Intishārāt Dāneshgā-e Mufid, 2005), vols 1–3 (vol. 4, 2009).

al-Najafī, Muḥammad Ḥasan, *Jawāhir al-kalām fi sharḥ Sharā'i' al-Islām*, ed. 'Abbās Qūchānī (Tehran: Dār al- Kutub al-Islāmiyya, 1988).

Nāṣif, Manṣūr 'Ali, Al-Tāj al-jāmi' li-l-uṣūl fī aḥādīth al-Rasūl (Beirut: Dār al-Jīl, n.d.).

al-Qaradāwī, Yūsuf, *Jarima al-Radda and 'Uqabah fi Daw' al-Qur'an wa al-Sunna* (the author's website, 1996).

al-Qaradāwī, Yūsuf, *Malāmih al-Mujtama' al-Muslim Alldhi Nanshuduhu* (Cairo: Maktaba Wahba, 2012)

al-Qaradāwī, Yūsuf, *Fiqh al-Jihād* (Cairo: Maktaba Wahba, 2014).

al-Rāwandī, Quṭb al-Dīn Sa'īd b. Hibatullah, *Fiqh al-Qur'ān*, ed. al-Sayyid Aḥmad al-Ḥusaynī al-Ishkawarī (Qom: Maktabat al-Mar'ashī al-Najafī, 1985).

al-Radi, Muhammad ibn al-Hassan al-Mūsawi, *Nahj al-Balagha*, ed. Subhi Sālih (Beirut: Dar al-Kitab al-Lubnani, 2004).

al-Rāzī, Fakhr al-Dīn, al-Tafsīr al-kabīr, first print (Egypt) (Beirut: Dār al-Fikr, 1981).

Rida, Muhammad Rashid (ed.), *Majalah al-Manār* (monthly), Cairo, 1906–1908.

Rida, Muhammad Rashid, *Tafsir al-Manār* (Cairo: Dār al-Manār, 1910–1934).

Ṣadr, Muḥammad Bāqir, *Buḥūth fi 'ilm al-uṣūl*, transcribed Sayyid Mahmūd Hāshimī (Najaf: n.p., 1976).

Ṣadūq, Muḥammad b. 'Alī b. Bābawayh (Shaykh Ṣadūq), *Man lā yaḥḍuruh al-faqīh*, ed. 'Alī Akbar al-Ghaffārī (Tehran: Maktabat al-Ṣadūq, 1972).

Ṣadūq, Muḥammad b. 'Alī b. Bābawayh, *al-Amālī* (Qom: Mu'assasat al-Bi'tha, 1996).

Ṣadūq, Muḥammad b. 'Alī b. Bābawayh, *al-Hidāya* (Qom: Mu'assasat al-Imām al-Hādī, 1997).

al-Ṣa'idi, 'Abd al-Mit'āl, *Al-Hurriyya al-Diniyya fil-Islam*, Introduction 'Ismat Nassār (Cairo: Dār al-Kitāb al-Misrī, 2012).

Sarakhsī, Shams al-Dīn, Mabsūṭ (Beirut: Dār al-Ma'rifa, n.d.).

al-Sālih, Subhi, *al-Islam wa al-Mujtami' al-'Asri: Hawār Thulāthi pawl al-din wa Qadāyā al-Sā'a* (Beirut: Dār al-Ādāb, 1977).
al-Sālih, Subhi, *al-Islam wa Mustaqbal al-Hidarah* (Beirut: Dār al-Shaurā, 1982).
Shaftī, Muḥammad Bāqir, *Risāla fi taḥqīq iqāmat al-ḥudūd fi hādhi-hi a'ṣār*, ed. Pazhūheshgā 'ulūm va farhang-i Islāmī (Qom: Daftar Tablīghāt-i Islāmī Hawze-ye 'Ilmiyye, 2006).
al-Shahīd al-Awwal (Shahīd I: Muḥammad b. Makkī), *al-Durūs al-shar'iyya* (Qom: Mu'assasat al-Nashr al-Islāmī, 1991).
al-Shahīd al-Thānī (Shahīd II: Zayn al-Dīn b. 'Alī), *al-Ri'āya fi 'ilm al-dirāya*, ed. 'Abd al-Ḥusayn Muḥammad 'Alī Baqqāl (Qom: Maktabat al-Mar'ashī al-Najafī, 1988).
al-Shahīd al-Thānī (Shahīd II: Zayn al-Dīn b. 'Alī), *Ḥāshiyat al-irshād*, contained in Muḥammad b. Makkī (Shahid I), *Ghāyat al-murād*, ed. Rezā Mukhtārī (Qom: Markaz al-Abḥāth wa al-Dirāsāt al-Islāmiyya, 1994).
al-Shahīd al-Thānī, Masālik *al-afhām ilā tanqih sharāyi' al-Islām* (Qom: Mu'assisa al-Ma'ārif al-Islmiyya, 2004).
al-Shāhrūdi, Mahmūd al-Hashimi (chief ed.), *Mawsú'a al-Fiqh al-Islāmi tibqan li Madhab Ahl al-Bayt* (Qom: Mu'assisa Mawsú'a al-Fiqh al-Islāmi, 2007).
Shahrour, Muhammad, *Tajfif Manābi' al-Irhāb* (Beirut: Mu'ssisa al-Dirāsāt al-Fikriyya al-M'aira, 2008).
Shaltut, Mahmoud, *Tafsīr al-ajzā' al-'shara al-ulā min al-Qur'an* (Cairo: Dār al-Shurūq, 2004).
Shaltut, Mahmoud, *al-Islām,'Aqida wa Shari'a* (Cairo: Dār al-Shurūq, 2015).
Shamseddine, Mohammad Mehdi, *al-Ijtihād wa al-Tajdīd tī al-Fiqh al-Islāmī* (Beirut: al-Mu'assisa al-Dawliyya, 1999).
al-Shirāzī, Muhammad al-Husseinī, *Al-Fiqh, vol. 88: Kitāb al-hudūd wa al-ta'zirāt* (Beirut: Dār al-'Ulūm, 1988).
Sidqī, Muhammad Tawfīq, Rashid Rida and Tāhā Bushrā, *Hawār hawl al-Islām huwa al-Qur'an wadah.* ed. 'Abdul 'Aziz, Hushām (Beirut: Jadāwil, 2011).
al-Suyūtī, Jalāl al-Dīn, al-Durr al-manthūr (Beirut: Dār al-Fikr, 2011).
al-Ṭabarī, Muḥammad b. Jarīr, *Ta'rikh al-umam wa al-mulūk* (Beirut: Mu'assa al-A'lamī, 1983).
al-Ṭabrisī, Faḍl b. al-Ḥasan, *Majma' al-bayān fi tafsīr al-Qur'ān* (Beirut: Mu'assasat al-A'lamī li-l-Maṭbū'āt, 1994).

al-Ṭabrisī, Ḥusayn al-Nūrī, *Mustadrak al-Wasā'il* (Qom: Mu'assasat Āl al-Bayt, 1988).

al-Ṭabāṭabā'ī, 'Alī b. Muḥammad, *Riyāḍ al-masā'il* (Qom: Mu'assasat al-Nashr al-Islāmī, 1992).

al-Ṭabāṭabā'ī, Muḥammad Ḥusayn, *al-Mīzān fī tafsīr al-Qur'ān* (Qom: Daftar-i Intishārāt-i Islāmī, 1984).

al-Tamīmī, al-Qāḍī al-Nu'mān, Abū Ḥanīfa b. Muḥammad al-Maghribī, *D'ā'im al-Islām wa dhikr al-ḥalāl wa-l-ḥarām*, ed. Āṣif b. 'Alī Aṣghar Fayḍī (Cairo: Dār al-Ma'ārif, 1964).

al-Taskhirī, Muhammad 'Ali, "*Hukm al-riddah wa madā Insijāmihi ma' huriyyah al-i'tiqād*", *Risalat Al-Taqrīb*, bimonthly, Tehran, 14(67) (2008): 137–156.

al-Ṭūsī, Abū Ja'far Muḥammad b. al-Ḥasan (Shaykh Ṭūṣī), *al-Istibṣār*, ed. Ḥasan al-Mūsawī al-Khirsān (Tehran: Dār al-Kutub al-Islāmiyya, 1970).

al-Ṭūsī, Abū Ja'far Muḥammad b. al-Ḥasan, *Tahdhīb al-aḥkām*, ed. Ḥasan al-Mūsawī al-Khirsān (Tehran: Dār al-Kutub al-Islāmiyya, 1970).

al-Ṭūsī, Abū Ja'far Muḥammad b. al-Ḥasan, *Ikhtiyār ma'rifat al-rijāl* (aka *Rijāl al-Kashshī*), ed. Mīr Dāmād al-Astarabādī and al-Sayyid Mahdī al-Rajā'ī (Qom: Mu'assasa Āl al-Bayt, 1984).

al-Tūsī, Muhammad ibn al-Hassan, al-Khilāf (Qom: Mu'assisa al-Nashr al-Islami, 1987).

al-Ṭūsī, Abū Ja'far Muḥammad b. al-Ḥasan, *al-Ṭibyān*, ed. Aḥmad Ḥabīb Quṣayr al-Āmilī (Beirut: Dār Iḥyā al-Turāth al-'Arabī, 1989).

al-Ṭūsī, Abū Ja'far Muḥammad b. al-Ḥasan, *al-Mabsūṭ*, ed. Sayyid Muḥammad Taqī al-Kashfī (Tehran: al-Maktabat al Murtaḍawiyya li iḥyā' al-Āthār al-Ja'fariyya, 1999).

al-Tustarī, Muḥammad Taqī, *Qāmūs al-rijāl* (Qom: Mu'assasat al-Nashr al-Islāmī, 1998).

'Uthman, 'Abdul-Karim, *Ma'ālim al-thaqāfa al-Islāmiyya* (Cairo: Mu'assisa al-Risāla, 1998).

al-Zuḥaylī, Wahba, *al-Fiqh al-Islāmī wa adillatuh* (Damascus: Dār al-Fikr, 1996).

## *Persian*

al-'Āmilī, Bahā' al-Dīn (and Niẓām al-Dīn Sāwujī), *Jāme'-e 'Abbāsī* (Tehran: Farāhānī, n.d.).

Ayāzī, Mohammad 'Ali, *Azādī dar Qur'ān*, 2nd edn (Tehran: Mu'assese-ye Nashr va Tahqiqāt-e Żekr, 2016).

Bazargan, Mehdi, "*Aya Eslam yek khatar-e jahāni ast?*" in *Ta'ābir-e khod-khasteh az Eslām: ghabāri bar chehreh-ye tabnak-e din*, *Kayhan Havāi*, weekly, Tehran, 7 September 1994.

Bazargan, Mehdi, "*Pasokh be Kayhan Havāi*", in *Ta'yyon-e hauzehāy-e tamaddoni va chārchoubhā-ye mashrou' barāye tabligh-e Eslām*, *Kayhan Havāi*, weekly, 21 December 1994.

Bazargan, Mehdi, "*Dovvomin pasokh be Kayhan Havāi*", in *Akharin mobahetheh ba Mehdi Bazargan: Nazdiki fi bāvarhāy-e Nezam-e solteh bā ddourī jostan az esālathā! Kayhan Havāi*, Tehran, Weekly, 22 February 1995.

Fanaei, Abolghasem, *Akhāq Deen-shenāsi: pejooheshi dar bāb-e mabāni-ye akhlāqi va ma'refat-shenāsāne-ye feqh* (Tehran: Negāh-e Mo'āser, 2010).

Fāzel Lankarāni, Mohammad (Lankarānī Sr), *Jāmi' al-masā'il, Istiftā'āt* (Qom: Amīr al-'Ilm, 2004).

Fāzel Lankarānī, Mohammad Javād (Lankarānī Jr), *Talqīḥ-i maṣnū'ī* (Qom: Markaz-i Fiqhi-ye A'imme-ye Aṭhār, 2006).

Fāzel Meybodi, Mohammad, "*Ensān, adyān wa irtidād*", *Aftāb*, monthly, Tehran, 23 (March 2004).

Fāzel Meybodi, Mohammad, *Shari'at, 'urf, wa 'aqlāniyyat* (Tehran: Hermes, 2015).

Golzādeh Ghafourī, Ali, "*Hame haqq dārand hame chīz rā bedānand: Āzādi-ye bayān, hoqouq aqalayyathā, ertedād, qesās, va lozoum-e baznegari-ye fiqh va ejthād*", interview, *Payām-e Hājar*, weekly, Tehran, 18(276) 26 July 1996.

Golzādeh Ghafourī, Ali, *Qazā dar Eslām* (Tehran: n.p., n.d.).

Golzādeh Ghafourī, Ali, *Zarourat baznegari feqhi* (Tehran: n.p., n.d.).

Ḥā'irī, 'Abd al-Hādī, *Nokhostīn rūyārūyī-hā-ye andishehgarān-i Iran bā dow rūeyye-ye tamaddon-i bourjūvāzi-ye gharb* (Tehran: Amīr kabīr, 1993).

Hā'irī Yazdī, Mahdī, "*Islām wa i'lāmiyye-ye ḥuqūq-i bashar*", *Sālnāme-ye maktab-i tashayyu'*. Qom, 4 (1962).

al-Halabī, Abū al-Salāh, al-Kāfī fi al-Fiqh, ed. Reza Ostādī (Esfahan: Maktaba al-Imam Amir al-Mu'minīn, 1983).

Kadivar, Mohsen, "*Marzhā-ye āzādī az manẓare-e dīn*", *'Aṣr-e mā*, biweekly, Tehran, 13 January 1999, 10 February 1999 and 23 August 1999.

Kadivar, Mohsen, *Dagdage-hā-ye ḥukūmat-i dīnī* (Tehran: Ney, 2000).

Kadivar, Mohsen, "*Āzādi-ye 'aqīde va madhhab dar Islam va asnād-i ḥuqūq-i bashar*", in *Majmū'e-ye maqālāt-i hamāyesh-i bayn al-melalī-ye ḥuqūq-i*

*bashar va goftegū-ye tamaddon-hā* (Qom: Intishārāt-i Dāneshgā-ye Mofīd, 2001); *Aftab*, monthly, Tehran, 23 (March 2003): 54–63.
Kadivar, Mohsen, "*Ḥuqūq-i bashar va roshanfekri-ye dīnī*", *Āftāb*, monthly, Tehran, 27 (August 2003).
Kadivar, Mohsen, "*Qarā'at-e farāmūsh shode*", *Madrase: bāzkhāni-e nazarie-ye 'ulāma-ye abrār, talaqqi-ye avvali-yye Eslām-e Shi'ea az asl-e emāmat*, quarterly, Tehran, 1(3) (23 May 2006).
Kadivar, Mohsen, *Siyāsatnāme-ye Khorāsānī* (Tehran: Kavīr, 2006).
Kadivar, Mohsen, *Ḥaqq al-nās: Islām va ḥuquq-i bashar* (Tehran: Kavīr, 2008).
Kadivar, Mohsen, "*Mujāzāt-i mokhālefān bā qavānīn-i falle'ī, murūrī ijmālī bar mohemtarīn qavānīn-i kayfarī-ye jumhūrī-ye Islāmī-ye Īrān*", Kadivar's website, www.kadivar.com, March 2010.
Kadivar, Mohsen, *Sūgnāme-ye faqīh-i pākbāz*, Kadivar web-book, 2013.
Kadivar, Mohsen, *Ibtizāl-i marja'iyyat-i Shī'e: istīzāḥ-i- marja'iyyat maqam-i rahbarī Hojjatoleslam va-l-Muslimīn Sayyid 'Alī Khāmena'ī*, Kadivar's web-book, 2014.
Kātūziyān, Nāṣer, Kulliyāt-i ḥuqūq (Tehran: Tehran University, 1968).
Kātūziyān, Nāṣer, *Qānūn-i madanī dar neaẓm-i ḥuqūqī konūnī* (Tehran: Nashr-i Mīzān, 2005).
Majlisī, Muḥammad Bāqir, *Resāle-ye ḥudūd va qiṣāṣ va diyāt*, ed. 'Alī Fāḍil (Qom: Nashr-i Āsār-i Islāmī, 1983).
Mar'ashī Shoushtarī, Mohammad Hassan, *Didgāhhāye nō dar huqūq kiifarī-ey Islām* (Tehran: Nashr-e Mizan, 1994).
Moḥaqqeq Dāmād, Moṣṭafā, "*Ḥudūd dar zamān-i mā ejrā yā ta'ṭīl?*" *Taḥqīqāt-i ḥuqūqī* (Dāneshgāh-i Shahīd Beheshtī), Tehran, Nos 25 and 26 (summer 1999).
Mojtahed Shabestari, Mohammad, *Naqdi bar qarā'at-e Rasmi az Dīn: bohranhā, Chaleshhā va vāh-e Halhā* (Tehran: Tarh-e Nō, 2000).
Montazeri Najaf Ābādi, Hossein-Ali, *Tawḍīḥ al-masā'il* (Qom: Nashr-e Tafakkor, 1996).
Montazeri Najaf Ābādi, Hossein-Ali, "*Dīn, mudārā va khushūnat*", *Kiyān*, monthly, Tehran, No. 45, 1999.
Montazeri Najaf Ābādi, Hossein-Ali, *Dīdgā-hā* (Qom: Office of Montazeri, 2002).
Montazeri Najaf Ābādi, Hossein-Ali, *Resāle-ye ḥuqūq* (Qom: Arghavān-i Dānesh, 2004).

Montazeri Najaf Ābādi, Hossein-Ali, *Islām: Dīn-i feṭrat* (Tehran: Sarā'i, 2006).
Montazeri Najaf Ābādi, Hossein-Ali, *Ḥukūmat-i dīnī va ḥuqūq-i insān* (Qom: Sarā'i, 2008).
Montazeri Najaf Ābādi, Hossein-Ali, *Pāsokh be porsesh-hā-ye peyrāmūn mujāzāthā-ye Islāmī va ḥuqūq-i bashar* (Qom: Arghawān-i Dānish, 2008).
Motahhari, Morteza, *Yaddashthaye Ostad Motahhari*, vol. 2 (Tehran: Sadrā, 2000).
Mousavaian, Abolfazl, "*Keifar Mortadd Hokmi Siasi*", *Majalleh-ye Motale'āt-e Fiqh va Hoqouq-e Eslāmī*, quarterly, Semnan, 1(1) (2009): 145–171.
Mousawī Bojnourdī, Mohammad, *Fiqh-e Tatbiqī, bakh-e Jazā'ī* (Tehran: SAMT, 2008).
Mousawi Gheravi, Mohammad Javād, *Feqh-e estedlālī dar masā'e-el Khelāfi, be enzemām-e khums, rajm, ertedād*, trans. from Arabic Ali Asghar Gheravi (Tehran: Negāresh, 1998).
*Nihdaz-et Azadi-ye Iran, Defāiyye az Eslām: Aya Eslam yek khatar-e jahāni ast?* Tehran, online documents of *Nihdazt-e Azadi-ye Iran*, 5 May 1994.
Nowbahār, Raḥīm, *Aṣl-i qazā'ī būdan-i mujāzāt-hā: taḥlīl-i fiqhī-ye ḥaqq bar muḥākime-ye 'ādilāne* (Tehran: Mu'assase-ye muṭāle'āt va pazhūhesh-hā-ye ḥuqūqī shahr-e dānesh, 2010).
Qābel, Aḥmad, "*Aḥkām-i jazā'ī dar Sharī'at-i Muḥammadī*", in *Majmū'e-ye āsār-i Aḥmad-i Qābel*, ed. Mohsen Kadivar, 2013.
*Qānūn-e Asāsi-ye Jomūrī-ye Eslāmī-ye Iran*, Tehran, 1989.
*Qānūn-e Mojzāt-e āEslāmī*, Tehran, *Ruznāme-ye Rasmī*, 2013.
Qommī, 'Alī b. Ibrāhīm Mīrzā, Tafsīr al-Qummī (Qom: Mu'assasat al-Imām al-Mahdī, 2013).
Qommī, Mīrzā Abū al-Qāsim, *Jāmi' al-shitāt*, ed. Murtaḍā Raḍavī (Tehran: Kayhān, 1992).
al-Qummī, Muḥammad b. Muḥammad b. Riḍā, Kanz al-daqā'iq wa baḥr al-gharā'ib (Qom: Jāmi'e-ye Mudarassīn, n.d.).
Ra'īs-zāde, Mohammad, "Madkhal-i Jāme'-i 'Abbāsī", *Dāneshnāme-ye jahān-i Islām*, 9, Tehran, 2005.
Saanei, Yousef, *Majma' al-masā'il* (Qom: Mo'assese-ye Farhangi-ye Fiqh al-Thaqlain, 2008).
Sarrāmī, Sayfullāh, *Ahkām Murtadd az Didgāh Islām wa Huqūq Bashar* (Tehran: Markaz-e Tahqiqāt-e Esteratejik, 1997).
Soroush, Abdolkarem, *Fiqh dar tarāzū: Ṭarḥ-e chand porsesh az Ḥazrat-e Ayatollah Montazeri*, *Kiyān*, monthly, Tehran, 46 (May 1999): 14–21.

Soroush Mahallāti, Mohammad, "*Ayā ertedād keifar-e hadd dārad? Ta'ammoli bar māhiyyat-e keifar ertedād*", *Majjalah Hukūmat Islāmī*, quarterly, Qom, 6(1) (19) (2001): 15–61.

Soroush Mahallāti, Mohammad, *Andisheh wa Imān dar Āzādī* (Tehran: Rawzaneh, 2016).

Vara'ee, Mohammad Javād, "*Ertedad negāhi nobāreh: taqrīri az mabāheth Ramazan 1420 of Ayatollah Mousawi Ardebili*", *Majalleh Hokoumat Eslāmi*, quarterly, Qom, 4(3/4) (1999/2000); and 5(1) (2000).

Velā'ī, 'Isā, *Ertedād dar Eslām* (Tehran: Nashr-e Ney, 2001).

## *English*

Abdel Haleem, M. A. S., *The Qur'an: A New Translation* (Oxford: Oxford University Press, 2005.

An-Na'im, Abdullahi Ahmed, *Toward an Islamic Reformation: Civil Liberties, Human Rights and International Law* (New York: Syracuse University Press, 1990).

Algar, Hamid, Islam and Revolution (Berkeley, CA: Mizan Press, 1981).

Ayoub, Mahmoud, Redemptive Suffering in Islam: A Study of the Devotional Aspects of Ashura in Twelver Shi'ism (The Hague: Mouton, 1978)

Ayoub, Mahmoud The Qur'an and Its Interpreters, 2 vols (New York: SUNY Press, 1984 and 1992).

Ayoub, Mahmoud, "Religious Freedom and the Law of Apostasy in Islam", *Islamochristiana* 29 (1994): 75–90.

Ayoub, Mahmoud, The Crisis of Muslim History: Religion and Politics in Early Islam (Oxford: Oneworld, 2003).

Ayoub, Mahmoud, Islam: Faith and History (London: Oneworld, 2005).

*Dignitatis Humanae*, Pope Paul VI, "Declaration on Religious Freedom", 7 December 1965, available at: http://www.vatican.va/archive.

Ghamidi, Javed Ahmad, *The Penal Shari'a of Islam*, trans. Shehzad Salaam (Lahore: Mawrid, 2004).

Kadivar, Mohsen, "Freedom of Religion and Belief in Islam", in Mehran Kamrava (ed.), *The New Voices of Islam: Reforming Politics and Modernity – A Reader* (London: I. B. Tauris, 2006), 119–142.

Kadivar, Mohsen, "Human Rights and Intellectual Islam", trans. Nilou Mobassser, in Kari Vogt, Lena Larsen and Christian Moe (eds), *New Directions in Islamic Thought: Exploring Reform and Muslim Tradition* (London, I. B. Tauris, 2009).

Mansour, Ahmad Subhi, *Penalty of Apostasy: A Historical and Fundamental Study*, trans. Mustafā Sābet (Toronto: International Publishing, 1998).

Matsunaga, Yasuyuki, "Mohsen Kadivar, an Advocate of Postrevivalist Islam in Iran", *British Journal of Middle Eastern Studies* 34(3) (2007): 317–329.

al-Raḍī, Muḥammad b. al-Ḥusayn al-Mūsawī, *Nahj al-balāgha: Selection from the Sermons, Letters and Sayings of Amīr al-Mu'minīn 'Alī b. Abī Ṭālib*, trans. S. A. Reza (Rome: European Islamic Cultural Centre, 1984).

Rahman, Shaykh Abdur, *Punishment of Apostasy in Islam* (Lahore: Institue of Islamic Culture, 1972).

Sachedina, Abdulaziz, *Islam and the Challenge of Human Rights* (Oxford: Oxford University Press, 2009).

Sachedina, Abdulaziz, David Little and John Kelsay, *Human Rights and the Conflict of Cultures: Western and Islamic Perspectives on Religious Liberty* (Columbia, SC: University of South Carolina Press, 1988).

Saeed, Abdullah and Hassan Saeed, *Freedom of Religion, Apostasy, and Islam* (Aldershot: Ashgate, 2004).

Soroush, Adbolkarim, Reason, Freedom, and Democracy in Islam: The Essential Writings of Adbolkarim Soroush, trans., ed. with Introduction M. Sadri and A. Sadri (Oxford: Oxford University Press, 2000).

Soroush, Adbolkarim, The Expansion of Prophetic Experience: Essays on Historicity, Contingency, and Plurality in Religion, trans. Nilou Mobassar, ed. with Introduction Forough Jahanbakhsh (Leiden: Brill, 2008).

Talbi, Mohamed, "Religious Liberty: A Muslim Perspective", *Islamochristiana* 11 (1985): 101.

## *Other Languages*

Bazargan, Mehdi, *Der Koran predigt weder Terrorismus noch Despotie: Glauben Privatsache*, *Die Zeit*, weekly, Germany, 23 September 1994.

Bazargan, Mehdi, "L'islam est-il un danger international?" *Le Monde*, Paris, 19 April 1994.

## *Websites*

Ahlolbait online Research and Publication Institution, available at: www.ahlolbait.ir/main.
Fāzel Lankarānī, available at: http://www.lankarani.com/far.
Jaras, available at: http://www.rahesabz.net.
Mohsen Kadivar, available at: www.kadivar.com.
Khamenei, available at: http://farsi.khamenei.ir/treatise-index.
Makarem Shirazi, available at: https://makarem.ir/index.aspx?lid=0.
Shiʿa online library, available at: www.shiaonlinelibrary.com.
Tanzil, available at: www.tanzil.net.

# *Glossary*

Prepared by Hamid Mavani

| | |
|---|---|
| *ʿāda* (pl. *ʿādāt*) | habitual practice; see *ʿurf* |
| *ʿādil* | a person with moral probity, good moral character, upright |
| *ʿadilla sharʿiyya* | textual indicators, i.e., Qur'an and Sunna; legal indicators |
| *ʿadl* | moral rectitude of a witness required in order for the testimony to be accepted |
| *āḥād* | "isolated hadith reports"; see *khabar al-wāḥid* |
| *aḥkām* | pl. of *ḥukm* |
| *aḥkām khamsa* | the scale of five religious–legal–moral values |
| *aḥkām al-lāh ẓahirī* | a deduced ruling that is subject to error |
| *aḥkām al-lāh wāqiʿī* | a ruling about which there is no doubt that it is from God |
| *Ahl al-Bayt* | People of the House; Prophet's family from the lineage of his daughter Fāṭima and her husband ʿAlī; some Sunni scholars apply this term to the wives of the Prophet, and still others say it includes all of Muhammad's blood relations |
| *ahl al-dhimma* | see *dhimmi* |
| *ahl al-ḥadīth* | stringent adherence to prophetic tradition, traditionist; literalist that de-emphasise the role of reason; compare with *ahl al-ra'y* |
| *ahl al-kitāb* | People of the Book or Scriptuaries; traditionally applied to Jews and Christians as recipients of the Hebrew Bible and the New Testament, respectively. As the Arabs began conquering their neighbours, it was extended to include Zoroastrians and other faith groups |

| | |
|---|---|
| *ahl al-ra'y* | strict followers of independent reasoning; compare with *ahl al-ḥadīth* |
| *ahl al-sunna wa-l-jamā'a* | lit. adherents of the Sunna of the Prophet and the collective body; Sunnis |
| *aḥwat* | more cautious |
| *'ālim* | sing. of *'ulamā'* |
| *'āmm* | general, generic; co-joined with its complement, *khāṣṣ* |
| *'aql* | intellect; human reasoning, rationality |
| *amr bi-l-ma'rūf* | commanding the good, commendable and wholesome |
| *'Āshūrā'* | lit. tenth; climax of ten days of mourning by the Shi'is to commemorate the massacre of the Prophet's grandson Ḥusayn along with some of his family members and companions in 680 in Karbala, Iraq |
| *aṣl* (pl. *uṣūl*) | the basis, which allows the analogy to be drawn in a derivative case; original case |
| *awlā* | preferable, superior |
| *'awwām* (sing. *'āmm*) | laymen, non-experts |
| *bāghī* (pl. *bughāt*) | rebel, transgressor |
| *bāligh* | of majority age to undertake religious responsibility; has attained mental and physical maturity |
| *barā'a* | exempted from the obligation |
| *bātil* | void, invalid |
| *bātin* | esoteric issues in Islam, hidden, inner |
| *bayān* | clear explanation, demonstration |
| *bayt al-māl* | public treasury |
| *bid'a* | innovation, deviation |
| *bid'a maḥmūda/ḥasana* | praiseworthy and desirable innovation |
| *bid'a sayyi'a/ḍalāla* | harmful and misguided innovation |
| *bughāt* | pl. of *bāghī* |
| *bulūgh* | physical maturity needed before religious obligations are imposed |
| *chador* | Persian word that refers to the one-piece large black cloak that falls from the top of the head to the ankles; commonly worn in Iran and by |

| | |
|---|---|
| | Lebanese Shi'i women, especially by those who subscribe to conservative values |
| *da'īf* | weak hadith with a flaw; unreliable |
| *dalāla* | signification, to signify |
| *dalīl al-'aql* | rational argument, proof based on reason; hermeneutic techniques derived from reason |
| *dalīl al-naql* | textual proof and argument from Qur'an or Sunna |
| *dalīl al-qaṭ'* | unequivocal evidence and proof that generates absolute certainty |
| *dalīl al-ẓann* | equivocal proof that is open to differing interpretations; presumptive proof that is not binding. |
| *ḍarar* | harm; damage |
| *ḍarūrā* | the principle of necessity (to entitle one to a dispensation) |
| *ḍarūriyyāt al-dīn* | essentials of religion; denying any one of them would constitute apostasy |
| *dhimmī* | protected recognised religious minority living in Muslim territory |
| *diya* | financial compensation for civil wrongs such as homicide and injuries |
| *faqīh* (pl. *fuqahā'*) | jurist, legal scholar qualified to deduce legal rulings from the Qur'an, Sunna and other sources. |
| *far'* | a derivative case, new case |
| *farḍ 'ayn* | individual duty |
| *farḍ kifāya* | collective duty, communal obligation |
| *fasād* | mischief and corruption |
| *fāsid* | defective and ineffective transaction |
| *faskh* | cancellation of contract, annulled |
| *fatwa* | non-binding legal opinion issued in response to a question, which could be hypothetical |
| *fiqh* | Islamic jurisprudence; substantive law, applied law, practical legal rulings |
| *fiqh al-istidlāl* | demonstrative jurisprudence |
| *fitna* | seduction or trial of faith; revolt, rebellion; civil strife |

| | |
|---|---|
| *fiṭra* | primordial human disposition; human nature; original normative state in which humans are created (Q. 30:30) |
| *fiṭrī* | in accordance with natural constitution or disposition |
| *furūʿ* | derivation of subsidiary rulings; applications and branches of jurisprudence; compare with *uṣūl* |
| *ghalabat al-ẓann* | preponderance of opinion; see *ẓann* |
| *ghayba* | occultation of the Twelfth Imam starting from the tenth century |
| *ghulāt* (sing. *ghālī*) | individuals guilty of exaggeration and extremism in religion and in attributing supernatural attributes to the Shiʿi infallible Imams or consider them incarnations of the Deity |
| *ghuluww* | exaggeration, extremism |
| *ḥadd* | prescribed penalty; sing. of *ḥudūd* |
| *ḥadīth* (pl. *aḥādīth*) | statements, practices and tacit approvals attributed to the Prophet, his Companions and the Shiʿi Imams (in Shiʿism) |
| *ḥāja* | need |
| *ḥākim sharʿ* | legitimate judicial authority |
| *ḥalāl* | permissible; synonymous with *mubāḥ* |
| *ḥaqīqī* | literal as opposed to metaphorical |
| *ḥaraj* | hardship; constraint |
| *ḥarām* | prohibited and sinful |
| *ḥasan* | in the Science of Hadith, a hadith that has been corroborated but not as extensively as a *ṣaḥīḥ* hadith |
| *Hijra* | Muhammad's emigration from Mecca to Medina in September 622, which is the starting point of the Muslim lunar calendar |
| *ḥīla* (pl. *ḥiyal*) | legal stratagem or evasion |
| *ḥirāba* | waging war against God and society; punishment is crucifixion, cross-amputation (right hand and left foot) or exile based on Q. 5:33 |
| *ḥiss* | sense-perception based knowledge |
| *ḥiyal* | pl. of *ḥīla* |

| | |
|---|---|
| *ḥawza ʿilmiyya* | centre of Shiʿi learning; Shiʿi religious seminaries, primarily in Iraq and Iran |
| *ḥubūṭ al-aʿmāl* | nullification of deeds; Q. 2:217 |
| *ḥudūd* (sing. *ḥadd*) | delimit, boundary, restriction; prescribed punishments for serious crimes which have been explicitly forbidden in the Qur'an and/or hadith such as adultery, fornication, theft, sedition and highway robbery; a right due to God for violating His decrees; evidentiary standards to prove the crime are very high |
| *ḥujja* | proof, evidence |
| *ḥujjiyya* | probative force |
| *ḥukm* (pl. *aḥkām*) | legal injunction or ruling; determination based on religious sources; assigned a moral/ethical/legal value by placing it in one of the five categories (*aḥkām khamsa*): *wajib* (obligatory); *mustaḥabb* or *mandūb* (recommended); *mubāḥ* (allowed); *makrūh* (reprehensible, discouraged); and *ḥarām* (prohibited) |
| *ḥukm awwalī* | primary injunction |
| *ḥukm taklīfī* | injunctive legal ruling on practical matters that is assessed one of the five legal values. See *al-aḥkām al-khamsa* |
| *ḥukm thānawī* | secondary injunctions; ruling's implementation would be suspended under extenuating circumstances, however, the original ruling would remain intact |
| *ḥukm waḍʿī* | declaratory legal ruling related to human actions that is not subject to a classification |
| *ḥusn* | good, beauty, praiseworthy in moral epistemology. |
| *ʿibadāt* | acts of worship and devotional observances (e.g., prayers and fasting) that are static and unchanging; compare with *muʿāmalāt* |
| *ibāḥa aṣliyya* | fundamental rule that all things are permissible unless proven otherwise |
| *ʿidda* | waiting period for a divorced or widowed woman during which she may not marry |

| | |
|---|---|
| *iḍṭirār* | necessity, emergency |
| *ifrāṭ wa tafrīṭ* | excessiveness and laxity; not in the centre (*wasaṭ*) |
| *iḥtiyāt* | caution |
| *iḥtiyāṭ istiḥbābī* | recommended caution |
| *iḥtiyāṭ wujūbī* | obligatory caution, i.e., the follower (*muqallid*) has the option of reverting to another senior jurist next in rank to resolve that particular issue concerned |
| *ijmāʿ* | jurists' consensus and unanimous agreement on a juridical matter or doctrine; like *qiyās*, it is procedural or derivative source of Islamic law rather than a formal source; it is accorded infallible legal value; contentious debate on its exact definition. In Shiʿism, it is an indirect way of discovering the will of the infallible Twelfth Imam |
| *ijmāʿ madrakī* | a type of *ijmāʿ* whose basis and origin is available for scholarly interrogation |
| *ijmāʿ manqūl* | an *ijmāʿ* reported by another scholar |
| *ijmāʿ muḥaṣṣal* | one's scholarly study of the past reveals that an *ijmāʿ* was acquired on a particular issue |
| *ijmāʿ murakkab* | a composite *ijmāʿ* of two such that the third is negated |
| *ijtihād* | strenuous effort, exertion to carry out a laborious task; utmost intellectual endeavor by a qualified person (*mujtahid*) to derive a juridical ruling on an issue by applying the textual sources, i.e., Qur'an and the Hadith, and other legal devices such as analogy and consensus; plays a more significant role in Shiʿism due to a larger scope assigned to *'aql* (reason) in derivation of legal rulings; opposite is *taqlīd* |
| *ijtihād fi al-furūʿ* | *ijtihād* at the level of secondary principles; traditional *ijtihād* (*ijtihād sunnatī*) |
| *ijtihād fi al-uṣūl* | structural *ijtihād*; foundational *ijtihād* |
| *ijtihād jamāʿī* | collective *ijtihād* |

| | |
|---|---|
| *ikhtilāf* | differences of opinion on a legal issue; contradistinct to *ijmā*ʿ |
| *ikrāh* | duress, coercion; defense for a crime committed |
| *ʿilla* | efficacious and operative cause; *ratio legis*; sometimes referred to as *manāṭ* |
| *ʿilm al-rijāl* | the science of critical engagement of the transmitters of hadith to investigate their reliability and credibility; consists of biographical dictionaries of hadith transmitters |
| *Imām* | (lit. leader) In Shiʿism, the title refers to the infallible successors of the Prophet, descending from Ali and Fāṭima, each one of whom possesses temporal and religious authority. The Twelver Shiʿis recognise a line of twelve, the last of whom went into occultation in the ninth century. Sunnis use this title for the male prayer leader as well as for the founders of the four Sunni schools of law and head of the Muslim community |
| *Imāmī* | Twlever Shiʿi |
| *insidād bāb al-ijtihād* | the so-called 'closure of the door of *ijtihād*' in Sunni Islam |
| *irtidād* | 'one who turns back'; apostasy; a person may become an apostate by denying an essential principle of belief or an essential act of worship, such as prayer, fasting, and *zakāt*; synonymous with *ridda* |
| *irtidād naẓarī wa ʿilmī* | knowledge-based apostasy |
| *irtidād siyāsī wa ʿamalī* | political and action-based apostasy |
| *isnād* | chain of transmitters of a hadith |
| *istidlāl* | inference; seeking evidence and proof |
| *istiḥsān* | juristic preference; one possible solution to a problem is given preference over another because it is more equitable; aiming for the best; occasionally in breach of *qiyās* |
| *istinbāṭ* | to extract, derive; inference or deduction |
| *istiṣḥāb* | presumption of continuance |
| *istiṣlāḥ* | see *maṣlaḥa* |

| | |
|---|---|
| *Ithnā Āsharī* | Twelver Shiʿis; synonymous with Jaʿfarī and Imāmī |
| *Jaʿfarī* | Twelver Shiʿis |
| *Jāhiliyya* | 'Age of Ignorance.' This refers to the pre-Islamic period, an era of moral bankruptcy, female infanticide, bloody and long-lasting tribal feuds, and tribalism; a society characterised by an elite steeped in economic exploitation and greed and the lack of belief in any type of afterlife |
| *jāʾiz* | allowed, permissible |
| *jarḥ wa taʿdīl* | disparaging or impugning and declaring trustworthy (individuals in the chain of transmission of hadith) |
| *Javāb* | answer; response to a question in the form of a *fatwā* |
| *jihād ibtidāʾī* | offensive jihad |
| *jihad difāʿī* | defensive jihad |
| *jizya* | a poll tax levied on non-Muslims in exchange for granting them protected status as minorities in a Muslim State; exempts them from military service and *zakāt* |
| *kaffāra* | atonement; expiation for breach of religious rules |
| *kāfir* (pl. *kuffār*) | (lit. conceal, cover, deny blessings of God); rejector, ungrateful; unbeliever, one who denies God or the prophethood of Muhammad |
| *kāfir aṣlī* | a child born of unbelieving parents who decides to be an unbeliever at the age of maturity |
| *kāfir harbī* | an unbeliever who is inimical and hostile to the Muslim State |
| *khabar* (pl. *akhbār*) | hadith, tradition, account |
| *khabar al-thiqa* | reliable hadith, tradition or account |
| *khabar al-wāḥid* | 'isolated hadith report;' not *mutawātir*; open to suspicion and misgiving about its authenticity because the multiplicity of narrations in each generation or at least one generation is inadequate to produce certainty; has no probative force on issues of vital and critical importance; |

| | |
|---|---|
| | does not give rise to *'ilm* (knowledge) except if it is connected with strong external evidence (*qarā'in*); epistemological distinction between *'ilm* and *ẓann* |
| *khabar al-wāḥid al-thiqa* | trustworthy *khabar al-wāḥid* hadith wherein all the narrators in all generations are trustworthy |
| *Khārijī* | (lit. those who went out); secessionist; initially supported Ali but subsequently revolted against him for having signed a truce with Muʿawiya and one of its members killed him |
| *khāṣṣ* | particular, specific; co-joined with *'āmm* |
| *khums* | (lit. one-fifth); Shiʿi tax levied primarily on net annual income, gold, and silver. Half of the *khums* is deemed *sahm al-Imām* which, during the Twelfth Imām's Greater Occultation, can be used to further human welfare and the other half (*sahm al-sādāt*) is reserved for the poor and indigent members from the Prophet's lineage; in Sunnism, *khums* applies to war booty only |
| *kufr* | unbelief; ungrateful; concealing the truth |
| *la ḍarar wa la ḍirār* | harm is neither inflicted nor reciprocated on a person |
| *liʿān* | a divorce in which a husband, under oath, accuses his wife of adultery |
| *madhhab* | the five schools of law comprising Hanafi, Maliki, Shafiʿi, Hanbali, and Jaʿfari; collective legal doctrine of a scholar; his orientation, opinion |
| *mafhūm al-laqab* | it particularises and limits the applicability of a ruling; e.g., the command 'honor the orphans' does not imply that one should not honour other than the orphans; least accepted form; a type of *mafhūm mukhālafa* |
| *mafsada* | corruption, evil; an act which usually results in harm or corruption; opposite of *maṣlaḥa* |
| *mahdūr al-dam* | lawful to shed his/her blood with impunity |
| *mahr* | bride dower; marital gift |

| | |
|---|---|
| *mahr al-mithl* | the average dower a bride would receive upon marriage of equal status, prestige, age, etc |
| *maḥram* | a person closely connected due to familial relationship and, as a result, falls within the forbidden degree of relationship with whom marriage is forbidden; opposite of *namaḥram* |
| *majāz* | figurative expression |
| *majhūl* | unknown; refers to hadith transmitter when no information is available about him |
| *makrūh* | reprehensible, disapproved, strongly discouraged |
| *mandūb* | recommended; synonymous with *mustaḥabb* |
| *mansūkh* | abrogated passage; see *naskh* |
| *maqbūla* | lit: accepted; a hadith that has attained the status of 'approved' through practice |
| *maqṣad* (pl. *maqāṣid*) | objective, intent, or goal |
| *maqāṣid al-sharīʿa* | objectives of the law |
| *marjaʿ al-taqlīd* (pl. *marājiʿ*) | in Shiʿism, point of reference; the highest religious authority whose rulings are followed by the laity |
| *maʿrūf* | in the Science of Hadith, a tradition that is well-known but lacks strong evidence for its authenticity; that which is known and accepted as a good common practice on the basis of social convention; in most cases, stands for kindness, goodness, wholesome, commendable, and benevolence |
| *mas'ala* | question posed, enquiry |
| *mashaqqa* | hardship |
| *mashhūr* | well-know, popular, widespread; a hadith initially transmitted by only a few at first, but later by many |
| *maṣlaḥa* | public benefit, interest, or welfare, social good; in conformity with the general objectives of the Law; used as a basis for legal decisions; opposite of *mafsada* |
| *maslaḥa mursala* | textually unattested rulings that takes into account universal public benefit and welfare |

| | |
|---|---|
| *maʿṣūm* | sinless, infallible, immune from committing error and sin; Shiʿis believe that all the prophets, messengers, the Prophet's daughter, and the Twelve Imams are infallible |
| *matn* | text of a hadith report, content |
| *mawḍūʿ* | fabricated and forged hadith |
| *mawḍūʿ al-ḥukm* | the specific subject matter of a ruling whose conditions and contingencies have been actualised |
| *muʿāmalāt* | personal and societal laws; the civil-criminal aspects of Islamic law that are subject to change for they are based on socio-historical context; compare with *ʿibādāt* |
| *mubāḥ* | permissible, allowed |
| *mufassir* | exegete |
| *muftī* | a specialist in Islamic law who is entitled to issue authoritative legal opinion |
| *muḥaddith* | hadith scholar; traditionist |
| *muḥārib* | a belligerent in a state of war against Muslims |
| *muḥkam* | explicit, clear-cut, univocal |
| *mujtahid* | (lit. one who strives); a person who is competent to perform *ijtihād* to deduce new legal rulings; opposite of *muqallid* |
| *mukallaf* | legally competent individual; a legally major person (*bāligh*) who is of sound mind (*ʿāqil*), possesses legal capacity to fulfill the religious duties and is liable for his actions |
| *mukhālif* | dissenter, i.e., Sunni |
| *munāfiq* | hypocrite |
| *munkar* | forbidden, wrong, detestable, condemnable; universally recognised and acknowledged moral vice and wrong; opposite of *maʿrūf* |
| *muqallid* | follower; the person doing *taqlīd* |
| *mursal* | in the Science of Hadith, a tradition whose chain of transmission (*isnād*) is interrupted and lacks continuity or has no chain at all |

| | |
|---|---|
| *murtadd* | apostate; a person who is either a native Muslim or embraces Islam and then renounces it by explicit words and conduct |
| *murtadd fiṭrī* | a person born to Muslim parents and subsequently renounces faith in Islam |
| *murtadd millī* | a person who converts to Islam and subsequently renounces faith in Islam |
| *mushrik* | polytheist; see *shirk* |
| *musnad* | hadiths gathered and published in collections arranged according to the name of the original narrator, beginning with the first four caliphs |
| *mustaftī* | petitioner requesting expert opinion |
| *mustaḥabb* | recommended, encouraged; synonymous with *mandūb* |
| *muta'akkhirūn* | the latter-day scholars/jurists; in Shiʿism, starting from 'Allāma Ḥillī (d. 1325) |
| *mutaqaddimūn* | Imāmī jurists from the earliest times until the end of 13th century |
| *mutashābih* | allegorical, figurative, symbolic, polyvalent |
| *mutawātir* | hadith related via multiple independent chains of transmission such that it would be inconceivable for them to have conspired; hadith treated as authentic and unquestionable and enjoys the highest level of authenticity; wide-scale transmission |
| *mutawātir ijmālī* | consensus that the hadith has been issued by one of the divine guides without knowing exactly which one |
| *mutawātir lafẓī* | *mutawātir* in wording or verbatim; hadiths that are recurrent in their exact wording by all narrators resulting in certainty |
| *mutawātir maʿnawī* | *mutawātir* in meaning; hadiths that are recurrent and capture the same meaning but not word for word; not verbatim but still obtain certainty |
| *muwaththaq* | reliable, trustworthy |

| | |
|---|---|
| *nahī ʿan al-munkar* | to dissuade others from that which is prohibited, wrong, and unwholesome |
| *nāʾib* | representative, deputy, designated person |
| *najis* | ritually impure; not synonymous with unclean or dirty |
| *nāṣibī* | lit. those who possess hatred; pejorative term to refer to those who hate and detest the *Ahl al-Bayt* |
| *naskh* | repeal, abrogation; one passage of the Qurʾan or Sunna can abrogate another based on Q. 2:106 |
| *nāsikh* | abrogating passage |
| *naṣṣ* (pl. *nuṣūṣ*) | in law, revealed text present in either the Qurʾan or Hadith which convey meanings that are self-explanatory and not polyvalent; in Shiʿism, it refers to explicit designation of each of the Twelve Imams from the Prophet or previous Imam |
| *nikāḥ* | marriage contract |
| *niyya* | intention; an act's moral worth is determined by the purity of one's intention |
| *qadāya ḥaqīqiyya* | situational premise |
| *qaḍāyā khārijiyya* | absolute premise |
| *qadhf* | one of the *ḥadd* offences in which an accusation is made of unlawful intercourse without being able to support it with adequate witnesses; slander |
| *qāḍī* | Islamic judge whose judgements are binding, unlike a *muftī* or *faqīh* whose judgments are only advisory |
| *qaḍiyya fī wāqiʿa* | applies to a particular and special case; not general |
| *qāʾida darʾ* | maxim that calls for suspension of *ḥadd* punishments in case of doubt |
| *qarīna* (pl. *qarāʾin*) | contextual evidence |
| *qatʿ* | definitive |
| *qawāʿid fiqhiyya* | legal maxims |
| *qiṣāṣ* | law of retribution in kind for murder, unintentional homicide, bodily injury or aggravated assault; talion law |

| | |
|---|---|
| *qiyās* | judicial reasoning by analogy; a source of Islamic Law; a methodology by which a ruling of a precedent is extended to a new case |
| *qiyās al-awlā* | analogy of the superior |
| *qubḥ* | ugliness, abominable, blameworthy in moral epistemology |
| *qur'ān nātiq* | in Shiʿism, the 'speaking Qur'an,' i.e., the infallible divine guides |
| *qur'ān ṣāmit* | in Shiʿism, the 'silent Qur'an,' i.e., the Qur'anic text |
| *rājiḥ* | preponderant opinion |
| *rajm* | stoning of the adulterer/adulteress |
| *ra'y* | sound opinion or considered opinion |
| *ridda* | apostasy; synonymous with *irtidād* |
| *riwāyāt* | see *hadith* |
| *rukhṣa* | legal dispensation and permission; exception made under special circumstances; exemption |
| *ṣabb* | insulting, reviling, vilifying |
| *ṣabb al-nabī* | insulting, defaming, and blaspheming the Prophet |
| *ṣaḥīḥ* | a sound and reliable tradition that is supported by an uninterrupted and strong chain of transmission (*isnād*) |
| *shakk* | epistemological category of doubt; doubtful |
| *sharʿan* | in accordance with the divine law |
| *al-Shāriʿ* | the Legislator (i.e., God) |
| *sharʿī* | pertains to divine law |
| *shariʿa* | (lit. path, way or road that leads to a source of water); comprises universal norms, values, and ideals, as well as moral and ethical principles |
| *shatm* | insult, revilement, vilification, and defamation; if done against the Prophet or other sacred personalities then it constitutes an act of blasphemy (*sabb*) |
| *shirk* | polytheism and idolatry; the attribution of partners with God; excessive adoration of anything other than God; the worst possible transgression |

| | |
|---|---|
| *shubha* | obscure, vague, uncertain |
| *sīra 'uqalā'iyya* | practice and conduct of rational beings or reasonable people |
| *Sunna* | paradigmatic practice of the Prophet, his Companions (in Sunnism) and the Shiʿi Imams (in Shiʿism) that are emulated by Muslims; a source of Islamic Law, which is second in importance only to the Qur'an |
| *taʿabbudī* | full and unquestioning compliance and obedience to God; devotional |
| *tafsīr* | exoteric Qur'anic exegesis |
| *tāhir* | ritually pure; not synonymous with clean and hygienic |
| *takālīf sharʿiyya* | religious obligations; see *mukallaf* |
| *takhṣiṣ* | particularisation, specification of the general expression |
| *takhṣīṣ al-'illa* | particularisation of the operative clause |
| *takhṣīṣ al-ḥukm al-'āmm* | particularisation of the general ruling |
| *takhyīr* | free to choose from different options |
| *taklīf* | imposition of religious obligations by God; religious accountability; obey ruling within his/her capacity (*qudra*); see *mukallaf* |
| *taklīf mā lā yuṭāq* | unbearable obligation |
| *taqiyya* | dissimulation of one's faith and dispensing with the religious ordinances when there is a possibility of great harm |
| *taqlīd* | emulation, following; in Shiʿism it refers to a layperson relying on and following uncritically a competent jurist for guidance on religious matters; in Sunnism, reference is to adherence to the doctrines of one of the four schools of thought with limited scope for *ijtihād*; see *ijtihād*; a person who does this is a *muqallid* |
| *taqyīd* | limitation, restriction, qualified |
| *tarjīḥ* | giving priority; preponderance |
| *tarjīḥ bi ghayr murajjiḥ* | to grant preponderance to one ruling over its contrary without grounds |

| | |
|---|---|
| *taṭbīq* | application of the universals to particular circumstances |
| *tawātur* | see *mutawātir* |
| *tawātur lafẓī* | see *mutawātir lafẓī* |
| *tawātur maʿnawī* | see *mutawātir maʿnawī* |
| *tawba* | repentance |
| *tawḍīḥ al-masāʾil* | in Shiʿism, legal manual containing rulings prepared by a jurist for his followers in the area of applied *fiqh*; also referred to as *risāla ʿamaliyya* |
| *taʾwīl* | esoteric or mystical Qurʾanic exegesis |
| *taʿzīr* | discretionary punishment assessed by the judge in some circumstances |
| *thiqa* | in the Science of Hadith, a transmitter who is reliable and trustworthy; also used in reference to hadith classification |
| *ʿudūl al-muʾminīn* | revert to the common believers to resolve an issue |
| *ʿulamāʾ* (sg. *ʿālim*) | religious scholars |
| *ʿuqalāʾ* | rational beings; reasonable people |
| *ʿurf* | custom, customary law or practice, source of law in Islamic legal methodology |
| *uṣūl* (sg., *aṣl*) | foundations, roots, normative basis |
| *uṣūl al-fiqh* | (lit. roots of jurisprudence); the science of the methodology of the law, which specifies hermeneutical rules for the derivation of legal rulings from the legitimate sources of the law, including, first and foremost, scriptural texts, such as the Qurʾan or the Sunna; legal theory |
| *wahn Islam* | weakening or 'impairing' Islam |
| *wājib* | obligatory |
| *wājib al-qatl* | obligatory to kill |
| *walī* | guardian |
| *wilāya* | guardianship; authority |
| *wilāyat al-faqīh* | 'guardianship of the jurist' espoused by Khomeini in connection with the clergy's role in governing a state |

| | |
|---|---|
| *wilāya muṭlaqa* | absolute and limitless authority endowed on the guardian jurist |
| *yaqīn* | epistemological category of certainty; certitude |
| *ẓāhir* | apparent meaning of the texts; univocal |
| *zandaqa* | heresy |
| *ẓann* | epistemological category of supposition; speculative; in contrast to *yaqīn* |
| *ẓannī* | speculative, conjectural |
| *zinā* | illicit sexual intercourse, fornication |
| *zindīq* (pl. *zanādiqa*) | an apostate pretending to be a Muslim; heretic |

# Index


'Abbāsid dynasty, 21, 22, 23, 25, 76
'Abdallah b. Abī Ya'fūr, 128
'Abdallah b. Nabtal, 243–4
'Abduh, Muhammad, 7–8, 9, 10, 14, 21
'Ābedinī, Ahmad, 54–6, 61, 82
Abraham, 363–4, 366, 369
Abū Bakr, 7, 9, 23, 76
Abū Ḥanīfa, 3
Abū Yūsuf, 3
al-Afghani, Jamal al-Din, 7
Afghanistan, 161
afterlife *see* Hereafter
Āghājarī, Hāshim, 158
Aghlīslī, Akram, 313
Ākhunzāde, Kamāl al-Dawla, 307
Ākhunzāde, Mīrzā Fatḥ 'Alī, 301–2
'Alī b. Ḥadīd, 170
'Alī b. Ja'far, 169–70
'Ali ibn Abī Tālib, Imam, 38, 54, 55, 76, 118, 128–30
  and apostasy, 231–3
  and assassination, 160
  and blasphemy, 248–50
  and divine covenant, 149
  and execution, 186–90, 191–2
  and Gharavī, 342, 343–4, 363–70
  and hadiths, 241, 299–300
Aliyev, Ilham, 309
Alteration of the Subject (*mawḍū'*), 225–36
al-Ālūsī, Shihāb al-Dīn, 118
al-Alwani, Taha Jabir, 95n86
Amman Message, xvi
'Ammār Sābāṭī, 128, 167–8
anarchy, 132–7
apostasy, ix–x, xi–xii, xiii–xviii
  and Alteration of the Subject (*mawḍū'*), 225–36
  and anarchy, 132–7
  and caliphate, 190–2
  and consensus, 182–4
  and criminal law, 89–90
  and death penalty, 166–81
  and doubts, 116–17
  and execution, 141–3
  and general public, 159–61
  and hadiths, 126–32, 239–41
  and ideas, 82–4
  and "isolated hadiths", 207–12
  and judiciary, 157–9
  and Kadivar, 70–5, 325–34
  and Lankarānī Jr, 85–6, 275–82
  and moderate Sunnis, 6–15
  and Montazeri, 158–9
  and progressive Sunnis, 15–25
  and the Prophet, 140–1, 186–90
  and Qur'an, 116–26, 238–9, 271–2
  and rejection of penalisation, 75–9
  and religious freedom, 250–63
  and Shi'i conservatives, 26–36
  and Shi'i reformists, 61–9

and Shi'i semi-reformists, 37–61
and Sunni Islam, 1–6
and Tabrīzī, 289–93, 295–306
*see also fatwas*; Taqī, Rafīq
Ardabīlī, Muḥaqqiq, 111
Ardebili, Abdul-Karim Mousawi, 44, 55, 58, 61, 167–8
and execution, 82
and *ḥudūd*, 201–2
and Tabrīzī, 290–1
al-'Ashmawi, Muhammad Sa'id, 16–17, 24
assassination, x, 4, 23, 160, 331–2
atheism, 2, 4, 15, 17–18, 79–80, 328
Ayāzī, Mohammad 'Ali, 61
*Azādī dar Qur'ān*, 49–51, 55
Ayoub, Mahmoud, 38–40, 58, 61
Azerbaijan, ix, xiv–xv, 285; *see also* Taqī, Rafīq

Bahā' al-Dīn Muḥammad 'Āmilī, 198–9
Bakhīt, 'Abd al-Ḥamīd, xii–xiii
Banī Fazl, Morteẓā, 105
al-Banna, Gamal, 15–16, 21, 24
Bāqir, Imam, 128, 131
Bazargan, Abdolali, 334
Bazargan, Mehdi, 61–3, 68, 73
belligerence, 14, 43, 53, 56, 65, 76
Biyāzīd, Mahdī, 311
blasphemy, ix–x, xi–xii, xiii–xviii
and Alteration of the Subject (*mawḍū'*), 225–36
and consensus, 182–4
and criminal law, 89–90
and death penalty, 166–81
and hadiths, 242–50, 265n13
and hate speech, 322–4
and "isolated hadiths", 207–12
and judiciary, 157–8
and Kadivar, 329–30
and Lankarānī Jr, 85–6
and legal rulings, 134–5
and Qur'an, 62, 238–9, 263n6, 271–2
and rejection of penalisation, 75–9
and Shi'i Islam, 28–9, 46–9, 83
and Taqī, 307–9
*see also fatwas*

caliphate, 21, 190–2; *see also* Abū Bakr; 'Ali ibn Abī Tālib
caution, 211–12
censorship, 80–1
chaos, 132–7
Charafi, Abdelmadjid, 22–4, 84
chastity, 211
Christianity, 2, 16, 39, 284, 336–7
and apostasy, 141
and conversion, 129–30
and Taqī, 106
coercion, 250–2
collective apostasy, 33–4, 38
colonialism, 2, 39
communism, 95n86
competence, 156–9
consensus (*ijmā'*), xvii–xviii, 3, 182–4
conversion, 5–6, 21
courts *see* judiciary
Criminal Code, ix, xv
criminal law, 89–90

al-Daylamī, Sallār, 139
death penalty *see* execution

denial of truth (*jahd*), 29, 42, 50, 52, 56, 60
despotism, 80–1
disbelief *see* apostasy; unbelief
dissenting opinions, 322–4, 349–50; *see also* freedom of expression
divine covenant (*'ahd maqṭū'*), 149–52, 162
Dostoyevsky, Fyodor, 287, 309
due process, xiv, xv–xvi

Egypt, xv–xvi, 10, 14, 24
Ennaifer, Hmida, 20–2, 23, 24, 68, 84
Europe, 284–7, 312
Exaggerators (*Ghulāt*), 186
execution, 3, 12, 15, 82
  and 'Ābedinī, 54–5
  and apostasy, 141–3
  and Ayāzī, 50–1
  and Bazargan, 62
  and consensus, 182–4
  and Fanaei, 67–8
  and Gheravī, 65
  and hadiths, 166–81, 186–90
  and Kadivar, 72–3, 329–30
  and the Prophet, 76
  and Qābel, 53
  and Qur'an, 77–8
  and Shi'i Islam, 58, 60, 61
exiting Islam (*al-khurūj 'ani-l-Islām*), 12
extremism, 326–7

Facebook, 355, 356–7
Fāḍil Miqdād, 139
Fadlallah, Muhammad Hussein, 42–3, 58
Fanaei, Abolghasem, 67–8, 82
fasting, xii–xiii
*fatwas*, 4, 17, 23, 88
  and apostasy, 132–7
  and Bazargan, 62
  and divine law, 162–3
  and freedom of expression, 351–4
  and impairing Islam, 137–9, 214–24
  and judiciary, 77–8
  and jurists, 155, 157
  and Kadivar, 329–30, 331–3
  and Khwānsārī, 34–5
  and restrictive, 355–7
  and Rushdie, 6, 275–6
  and Saanei, 97n123
  and Sarrāmī, 41–2
  and Shamseddine, 43
  and Makārem Shīrāzī, 70, 342
  and Taqī, 85, 105–8, 109–13
Fawda, Faraj, xv, 4, 6, 23, 88
*Fedāeyān-i Islām* (Devotees of Islam), 88
*fiqh*, 38–9, 41, 42, 73, 74–5, 90
*fiṭrī* apostates, 26, 27, 29–33, 36, 37, 42, 44, 50, 55, 58
forbidding (*taḥrīm*), 12
Forūher, Dariush and Parvāneh, 152n2
freedom of expression, 86, 234–6, 321–2, 347–8
  and *fatwas*, 351–4
  and Taqī, 284, 286
French Revolution, 2
Fuḍayl b. Yasār, 168
Fukuyama, Francis, 336

general public, 159–61
Germany, 328

Gharavī, 'Ali Aṣghar, 343–6, 354, 360
*Imam [Ali]: Political Leader or Exemplary Role Model*, 70, 87, 342, 363–70
al-Ghazālī, Abū Ḥāmid, 295
al-Ghazālī, Muḥammad, xv
*Freedom of Apostasy*, 4
Gheravī, Mohammad Javād Mousawi, 64–5, 68, 73
Ghojamanli, Sa'ide, 309
Gholīzāde, Ākhundzāde Mīrzā Jalīl Mohammad, 307
Ghonā-ye Tabrīzī (fictitious name), 86, 153n5, 283, 288–94, 295–306
Ghorgānī, Mohammad 'Alī 'Alavī, 345
God's covenant *see* divine covenant
Golpāyegāni, Mohammad Rezā Mousawi, 35, 57
Golzādeh Ghafourī, Ali, 63–4, 66, 68, 100n182
and execution, 82
and Kadivar, 73, 74
guidance, 252–4; *see also* misguidance

hadiths, 7, 8–9, 10, 76
and 'Ābedinī, 54–5
and Ali, 299–300
and apostasy, 126–32, 289–90
and 'Ashmawi, 17
and Ayoub, 39
and blasphemy, 242–50, 265n13
and execution, 186–92
and Gheravī, 64–5
and Kadivar, 72–3, 331
and Khwānsārī, 34–5
and *mursal*, 151–2
and Qur'an, 239–41
and Shi'i Islam, 35–6, 60–1
and Talbi, 19–20
and violence, 340
*see also* "isolated hadiths"
*ḥākim shar'*, 154–5
al-Halabī Taqī al-Dīn ibn Najm, Abū al-Salāh, 41–2, 51, 139
Ḥanafī school, 3
Ḥanbalī school, 3
Hassan, Hassan Ibrāhim, 9, 14
hate speech, 79–80, 86, 322–4, 328, 335–41
Hereafter, 71–2, 75, 78, 124–5
heresy (*zandaqa*), 22–3, 25, 57
Ḥillī, 'Allāma, 139, 169, 200–1, 202
al-Hindī, Muḥammad b. Ḥasan, 111, 169, 199
Hishām b. Sālim, 170
*ḥudūd* punishment, 15, 48, 77–8, 83, 89, 116–17
and divine covenant, 149, 151–2
and Imam's occultation, 195–205
and jurists, 35, 40, 154–6, 194–5
and Qur'an, 125–6
and Shaltūt, 10–12
and Tabrīzī, 302–4
and Twelfth Imam, 139–40
human rights, xiv, 16, 42, 133–4, 161–3; *see also* Universal Declaration of Human Rights (UDHR)
humanism, 284
Huntingdon, Samuel, 336
Ḥusayn, Imam, 151
Ḥusaynaf, Mushfiq, 309
hypocrisy, 60

Ibn 'Abbās, 11
Ibn Abi al-'Awjā', 55
Ibn al-Jawzī
  *al-Muntazam*, 22–3
Ibn al-Junayd al-Iskāfī Muhammad ibn Ahmad, 37
Ibn 'Āshūr, Muhammad al-Tāhir, 2, 4–5
Ibn Fahd, 139
Ibn Idrīs Ḥillī, 110, 139–40, 195–6
Ibn Muljim Murādī, 160
Ibn Sa'īd, 139
Ibn Zuhra, 139, 140
*ijtihād*, x, xii–xiii, 9, 63, 64, 66
  and apostasy, 142–3
  and consensus, 183–4
  and contemporary, 220–1
  and method, 269–72
  and types, 83
*ikhlāl* (in the principles of Islam), 352, 354, 358
"Imam [Ali]: Political Leader or Exemplary Role Model" *see* Gharavī, 'Ali Aṣghar
Imams, 39–40, 54, 55, 59; *see also* 'Ali ibn Abī Tālib; Ṣādiq, Imam; Twelfth Imam
impairing (*wahn*), 214–24
imprisonment, 3, 307, 308–9
Infallible Imam *see* Twelfth Imam
*Innocence of Muslims, The* (film), 86, 335–9
insults, 113–14
International Covenant on Civil and Political Rights (ICCPR), 73–4, 79, 158, 327–8, 338
Iran, 36, 58, 80–1, 84, 157–8
  and Civil Code, 163n5, 164n6
  and jurists, 357–8
  and media, 356
  and Tabrīzī, 291–2
  and Taqī, 107, 285, 288, 314
Iraq, 36, 58
Islam, 75, 89
  and compassion, 327
  and freedom of expression, 321–2
  and human rights, 161–3
  and impairing, 214–24
  and sanctities, 352–3, 354
  and Taqī, 284–5, 286
  *see also fatwas*; hadiths; jurists; Prophet; Qur'an; *shari'a*; Wahhabis; Shi'i Islam; Sunni Islam
"isolated hadiths" (*thiqa*), 11–13, 15, 24–5, 34–6, 57, 60, 78
  and apostasy, 131–2
  and death penalty, 166–81
  and execution, 82
  and non-probative, 207–13
  and Soroush, 66
  and Taqī, 110–11
Israelites, 118
Iṣṭahbānātī, Mohammad Bāqir, 305

Ja'fari, Ḥusayn, 277–9
Jamīl b. Darrāj, 128, 129, 178–9
*Jawāhir see* al-Najafī, Muḥammad Ḥasan
Jāwīsh, 'Abdul' Aziz, 9, 14
jihad, 72, 228–30
Judaism, 17, 25, 64–5, 141
judiciary, 77–8, 156–9

jurist (*faqih*), 133–7, 143, 150, 342–61
and denigration of Prophet, 171–3
and hadiths, 127
and *ḥudūd* punishment, 194–5
and jurisdictions, 154–6

Kadivar, Mohsen, ix–x, xi–xii, xiii, xiv–xv, xvi–xviii, 334
and apostasy, 70–5, 325–34
and *fatwa* objection, 109–14
and freedom of expression, 321–4
and "Treatise", 85–6
al-Karakī, Muḥaqqiq, 139, 194
al-Karkhī, Abu al-Hassan, 11–12
al-Kashshī, Muḥammad b. 'Umar, 170–1
Kasravi, Ahmad, 88
Kāẓim, Imam, 128, 129, 131, 169–70
Kermānī, Majd al-Islām, 305–6
al-Khālisī, Muhammad, 37, 58
Khāmena'ī, Ali, 156
al-Khashin, Hussain Ahmad, 61
*Al-fiqh al-janā'i fi al-Islām, al-ridda numūzijan*, 56–7, 58
Khomeini, Ruhollah Mousawī, 94n56, 109, 133, 275–6, 292
*Taḥrīr al-wasīla*, 26–7
Khorāsānī, Ākhund Mullā Mohammad Kāẓim, 163, 305
al-Khū'ī, Abū al-Qāsim, 119, 129, 140, 168, 178
Khwānsārī, Aḥmad, 34–5, 66, 73, 111, 196–8, 201
Kūchānī, Najafī, 305
al-Kulaynī, Shaykh Muḥammad b. Ya'qūb, 127, 167, 170
Küng, Hans, 336–7

Lankarānī Jr, Moḥammad Javād Fāżel, ix–xii, xiv–xv, xvii–xviii, 70, 84
and apostasy, 116–27, 277–82
and Qom University, 273–7
and "Response to Doubts Surrounding Apostasy", 85
and Tabrīzī, Ghonā-ye, 288–94, 295–306
and Taqī, 108
Lankarānī Sr, Moḥammad Fāżel, ix, xi, xiv, 51, 133, 141
and decree, 69–70
and *fatwa*, 105–7
and human rights, 163
and Taqī, 85
Lebanon, 58
legal rulings see *fatwas*
Lewis, Bernard, 336
loss of life (*dimā'*), 211–12; *see also* execution

*mafhūm laqab*, 179–80
al-Mahdi, Sadiq, 13–14
al-Majlisī, Muḥammad Bāqir, 168, 170, 176, 178, 180, 194–5
Makārim Shīrāzī, Nāṣir, 291, 342, 343–62
Mālikī school, 3
Manṣūr, Aḥmad Ṣubḥī, 23, 24, 65, 289–90
Manūn, 'Īsá, xii–xiii, xvii, 10, 83–4
Mar'ashī Shoushtarī, Muhammad Hassan, 40–1, 42, 53, 58, 61, 70
*Markaz-i Fiqhī-ye A'imme-ye Atḥār*, 270–2
marriage, 3, 26–7, 32
Matsunaga, Yasuyuki, x

Maududi, Abul A'la, 21, 90n4
*Mawsū'a al-fiqh al-Islāmi tibqan li madhab Ahl al-Bayt*, 27–34
Māzandarānī, Mullā Abdallāh, 163, 305
media, 276–7, 337, 355–7
*millī* apostates, 26–7, 29–33, 36, 37, 42, 55, 58
misguidance, 249, 321, 349–50
mockery, 113–14
Montazeri Najaf Ābādī, Hossein-Ali, x, 44–9, 50, 58, 61, 66
  and apostasy, 158–9, 233–4
  and execution, 82
  and human rights, 163
  and Kadivar, 73–5
  and legal rulings, 97n125–7
Moses, 118, 141, 276, 296–8
Mudarris, Ḥasan, 203–4
Mufīd, Shaykh, 139
Muḥammad b. Makkī *see* Shahīd I
Muḥammad b. Muslim, 128
al-Muhaqqiq al-Hillī, Ja'far Ibn al-Hassan, 34, 110
Mukhtārī, Mohammed, 152n2
murder, xv; *see also* assassination
Mustashār al-Dawla Tabrīzī, Mīrzā Yūsuf Khān
  *One World*, 301
Mutawalli, Abdul-Hamid, 12–13, 14

*Nahj al-balāgha*, 149, 299–300
Nā'īnī, Muḥaqqiq Mīrzā, 163, 211
al-Najafī, Muḥammad Ḥasan (author of *Jawāhir*), 140, 169, 180, 182, 184, 196, 204, 206
Nāṣif, Manṣūr, 128–9
Naṣr Ḥāmid Abū Zayd, xv–xvi, 6, 88, 289
National Front of Iran (Jebhe-ye Mellī), 292
negation of force, 250–2
Nietzsche, Friedrich, 287
nullification of one's deeds (*ḥubūṭ al-a'māl*), 120–2, 124–5
Nūrī, Faḍlullāh, 163, 302, 304
Nūrī Hamadānī, Ḥusayn, 344

Ottoman Empire, 2, 21, 284

Pakistan, xv
Peter the Great, 285–6
politics, 76, 77, 363–70
"preservation of life", 111
propaganda, 76
Prophet, 7, 10, 12–13, 44
  and apostasy, 123, 128, 140–1, 232–4
  and execution, 76, 186–90
  and harassing, 242–50
  and hate speech, 335–41
  and Lankarānī Jr, 273–4
  and Taqī, 106, 307–9
  and truth, 254–5
  *see also* hadiths
puberty (*bulūgh*), 13
punishment, 4–6, 10–15, 51–2, 56–7, 71–2
  and Qur'an, 238–9
  and Shi'i Islam, 59
  *see also* execution; *ḥudūd* punishment; temporal punishment
Puyandeh, Mohammad Ja'far, 152n2

Qābel, Ahmad, 52–3, 55
Qadhafi, Muammar, 160
al-Qaradāwī, Yūsuf, 4, 5–6, 160
Qom, ix–x, 58, 273–7
Qommī, Mīrzā, 202
Qur'an, 7, 8–9, 10, 11, 14–15, 238–72
  and apostasy, 116–26, 141
  and Ardebili, 44
  and Bazargan, 62
  and blasphemy, 263n6
  and execution, 77–8, 82
  and Gheravī, 65
  and hadiths, 239–41
  and *ijtihād*, 271–2
  and interpretation, 289–91
  and Kadivar, 71–3, 331
  and al-Khashin, 57
  and Lankarāni Jr, 274–5, 296–300
  and leadership (*Imāma*), 363–5, 366–7, 369–70
  and the Prophet, 242–50
  and Qābel, 52–3
  and religious freedom, 16–17, 19, 25, 250–63
  and Sarrāmī, 42
  and violence, 340–1
Qutb, Sayyid, 21

Ramadan, xii–xiii
Rashdiye, Mīrzā Ḥasan, 304
al-Rāzī, Fakhr al-Dīn, 119, 298
rebelling against Islam (*al-khurūj 'alā-l-Islām*), 12
religious expectations, 89
religious freedom, 6–8, 24–5, 69, 79–80
  and Qur'an, 16–17
  and recognition, 113–14
  and Shabestari, 66–7
  and Shi'i Islam, 61
  and Sunni Islam, 1–2
  and Talbi, 17–20
repentance (*istitāba*), 3–5, 7–10, 21, 26–7, 43, 50, 59
  and Gheravī, 65
"Response to Doubts Surrounding Apostasy" (Lankarānī Jr), 85
Riḍā, Imam, 131
Rida, Muhammad Rashid
  *Tafsīr al-Manār*, 7–8
*ridda* wars (wars of apostasy), 38, 76, 190
"right to life", 111
ritually impure (*najis*), 355, 356
Rushdie, Salman, 5, 6, 62, 88, 133
  and Lankarānī Jr, 275–6
  *The Satanic Verses*, 106, 109
  and Tabrīzī, 292
  and Taqī, 309
Russia, 285–6

Sa'ādatī, Mohammad Rezā, 347–8
Saanei, Yousef, 97n123
Sachedina, Abdulaziz, 95n104
al-Sa'dāwī, Nawāl, xvi
Ṣādiq, Imam, 119, 123, 128, 129–30, 131, 167
  and hadiths, 186, 205n13–14, 241
Ṣāfī Golpayegānī, Loṭfollah, 345
Sahl b. Ziyād, 166–7
al-Ṣa'īdī, 'Abd al-Mit'āl, xii–xiii, xvii, 10, 14, 83–4
Sākit, Mīrzā, 309
al-Sālih, Subhi, 91n22, 290

*San'at Qaz'atī* (newspaper), ix, 86, 106, 107, 284, 314n1
Sarakhsī, Shams al-Dīn, 121, 298–9
Sarrāmī, Sayfullāh, 58, 61, 70, 82
*Ahkām Murtadd az Didgāh Islām wa Huqūq Bashar*, 41–2
satellite antenna, 355–7
Saudi Arabia, 161
secularism, 285, 287
Shabestarī, Mohammad Mojtahed, 66–7, 68, 82, 101n187, 302
and Kadivar, 73, 74
Shāfi'ī school, 3
Shaftī, Muḥammad Bāqir, 139–40, 163, 204–5
Shahīd I, 139, 168, 216, 232
Shahīd II, 37, 122, 139, 169
Shaltūt, Mahmoud, 53
*Al-Islam, 'Aqida wa Shari'a*, 10–12, 14
Shamseddine, Mohammad Mehdi, 43, 58
*shari'a*, 8, 13–14, 90, 218–19, 321
and "isolated hadiths", 208, 209
"shedding of blood", 111–13
Shi'i Islam, 1, 25, 76, 302–3, 360
and Ali, 367–8
and apostasy, 76–7
and conservative approach, 26–36
and despotism, 80–1
and execution, 83
and inquisition, 86–7
and jurists, 344–6
and reformists, 61–9
and semi-reformists, 37–61
al-Shirāzī, Muhammad al-Husseinī, 38, 58, 86–7, 347–8, 357–61
and *fatwas*, 70, 355–7
Sidqī, Muhammad Tawfīq, 8–9, 14, 63
slavery, 228–9
Sobhānī, Ja'far, 295, 345
Soroush, Abdolkarim, 66, 68, 73, 74, 82, 295
Soroush Mahallāti, Mohammad, 51–2, 61
state theory, 16–17
Sudan, xv–xvi
Sunni Islam, 1–6, 76–7, 83, 128–30, 302
and moderate reformers, 6–15
and progressive reformers, 15–25

Taha, Mahmud Muhammad, xv–xvi, 6, 88
takfirism, xvi
Talbi, Mohamed, 21–2, 23, 24, 39, 51
"Religious Liberty: A Muslim Perspective", 17–20
and Shi'i reformists, 64, 65, 66
Taliban, 161
Taqī, Rafiq, ix, xv, 70, 85, 88
and apology, 152n2
and articles, 86
"Āshūrā", 107
"Europe and Us", 107, 284–7
and *fatwa*, 105–8
and Ghonā-ye Tabrīzī, 288–94, 295–306
and interviews, 307–14
and Lankarānī Sr, 133
Taqī Zāde, Ḥasan, 305
Tāsīr, Salmān, xv
*tawātur*, 175–8, 180–1

temporal punishment, 48–9, 52–3, 69–72, 74, 78, 114, 116, 120–1
and apostasy, 217, 219–20, 223, 227, 229–30, 235, 238–9, 256–62
and worldly, 78–9
terrorism, xvi, 152n2
theft, 228–30
tolerance, 336–41, 342–4
"Treatise on Refuting the Punishment for Blasphemy and Apostasy" (Kadivar), 85–6
Tunisia, 23–4
al-Ṭūsī, Abū Ja'far Muḥammad b. al-Ḥasan, 120, 123, 131, 139, 144, 190, 192–3, 195, 205
and consensus, 182
and *fatwa*, 167, 168–9
and Qur'an, 238–9
al-Tustarī, Muḥammad Taqī, 168
Twelfth Imam, 72, 139–40, 154, 156, 195–205

Ūghlū', Tehran 'Ālishān, 309–14
Ughulu, Nawawlila Ja'far, 309
'*ulamā*' (experts of Islamic law), 2, 9, 11–12
Umayyad dynasty, 21, 23, 25, 76, 81
unbelief (*kufr*), 2–3, 42, 52
uncertainty (*shubuhāt*), 50
United Kingdom (UK), 322, 328
United States of America (USA), 322, 328, 337, 340
Universal Declaration of Human Rights (UDHR), 66–7, 73–4, 80, 112, 149
and Iran, 158
and Tabrīzī, 301
Ūrā, Ra'na Sa'ādat Dīn, 309
'Uthmān, Muhammad Fathi, 13, 14

Vasmaghi, Sedigheh, 334
violence, 337, 338–40

Wahhabis, 161, 345, 346
women, 3, 27, 29–33

Ya'u, Arazu 'Abdullah, 309
Ya'ū, 'Aynullah Fatḥallah, 309
Younes, Leyla, 309
Yousefi Eshkavarī, Ḥasan, 158, 334

Zāhid, Ghanīmat, 309
*zakāt*, 7, 9, 76
Zayn al-Dīn b. 'Alī (Shahīd II), 37, 122, 139, 169
Ziyād b. 'Ubaydallā Ḥārithī, 169–70
al- Zuḥaylī, Wahba, 2–3

EU representative:
Easy Access System Europe
Mustamäe tee 50, 10621 Tallinn, Estonia
Gpsr.requests@easproject.com

www.ingramcontent.com/pod-product-compliance
Lightning Source LLC
Chambersburg PA
CBHW052054300426
44117CB00013B/2118
* 9 7 8 1 4 7 4 4 5 7 5 8 3 *